The Weimar Century

The Weimar Century

GERMAN ÉMIGRÉS AND THE IDEOLOGICAL
FOUNDATIONS OF THE COLD WAR

Udi Greenberg

PRINCETON UNIVERSITY PRESS

PRINCETON AND OXFORD

Library of Congress Cataloging-in-Publication Data

Greenberg, Udi, 1980–
    The Weimar century : German émigrés and the ideological foundations of the Cold War
/ Udi Greenberg.
        pages cm
    Includes bibliographical references and index.
    ISBN 978-0-691-15933-1 (hardback : alkaline paper)   1. Germany—History—1945–
1955.   2. Military government—Germany—History.   3. Nation-building.   4. Elite
(Social sciences)—Germany—Biography.   5. United States—Foreign relations—
Germany.   6. Germany—Foreign relations—United States.   7. United States—Foreign
relations—1945–   8. United States—Military policy.   9. Cold War.   10. Political
science—United States—History.   I. Title.
    DD257.2.G65 2014
    909'.04310825–dc23   2014013274

British Library Cataloging-in-Publication Data is available

This book has been composed in Sabon

Printed on acid-free paper. ∞

Printed in the United States of America

10 9 8 7 6 5 4 3 2 1

Contents

Acknowledgments

IT IS WITH GREAT JOY that I write these acknowledgments, for the debts I owe to others are both wide and deep. This book was written over many years and in many places—Jerusalem, Berlin, Leipzig, Madison, Berkeley, and Hanover—and at all stages, I was blessed with the support and generosity of friends, colleagues, and institutions. I am grateful for the chance to finally thank them all.

My first thanks go to the many scholars of European thought and politics who commented on my work and gave me invaluable encouragement and advice. They helped me develop my ideas, rescued me from countless embarrassing errors and misconceptions, and will recognize their insights in the best parts that follow. They will also recognize the places where my stubbornness led me to overlook their advice. Steven Aschheim, Moshe Zimmermann, and Dan Diner guided this book's very first stages during my graduate studies in Jerusalem. Malachi Hacohen offered thoughtful insights as I embarked on rewriting and rethinking this project. Samuel Moyn and Jan-Werner Mueller made the effort to read a full draft of this manuscript, traveled to Dartmouth, and spent an invaluable day discussing it with me. They encouraged me to reconsider many issues, and provided thoughtful suggestions. Peter Gordon's penetrating observations had a profound impact on this book's final form. He pushed me to make explicit my own judgments about ideology and its political consequences, and my observations owe a great deal to his critique.

Other scholars whose valuable advice benefited this book include Michael Brenner, Arie Dubnov, Martin Jay, Rudy Koshar, Michael Gordin, Adi Gordon, Jerry Muller, Anson Rabinbach, Jeremi Suri, and Noah Strote, all of whom commented on parts of this project in different stages and formats and helped me improve it considerably. Thanks are also due to James Chappel and Giuliana Chamedes, who read the messiest parts of the manuscript with much care and attention. They will recognize my indebtedness to their work in many parts of this book. Ofer Ashkenazi deserves special acknowledgment for his incredible patience, friendship, and generosity as he repeatedly commented on lengthy drafts. I am especially grateful to my editor at Princeton University Press, Brigitta van Rheinberg. Her enthusiasm and professionalism have made the completion of this book a privilege, and her advice made me a better historian. I cannot think of a scholarly community more exciting and generous. This book is my first attempt to contribute to it.

I also thank my colleagues at Dartmouth College who provided valuable advice, mentorship, and assistance. I am thankful to Chris Hardy Wohlforth of the Dickey Center, who organized a manuscript review, and to Leslie Butler, Bill Wohlforth, and Klaus Mladek, who took part in it. They kindly gave me much of their time and provided phenomenal feedback, which helped me to drastically revise and improve this work. I am especially grateful to Ed Miller and Bob Bonner, who carefully read drafts, provided insightful suggestions, and spent many lunches offering mentorship, advice, and good conversation. I am also blessed with having Cecilia Gaposchkin and George Trumbull as colleagues; their friendship and guidance were profound. Thanks are also due to Susannah Heschel, who discussed this book with me on multiple occasions, and whose own work has been a source of much inspiration to me. Nancy Marion, associate dean for the social sciences, went above and beyond in her support, providing me with the resources I needed for research and writing. Dartmouth students Caitlin O'Neil, Emily Tomlinson, Andrew Park, Rebecca Jacobson, and Ben Levander provided much-needed assistance. Becky Kohn, with her supernatural editing skills, made incomprehensible passages into readable prose and improved this text in more ways than she knows.

Thanks are due also to the many programs and institutions that have funded my research and hosted me over the years. These include the German Academic Exchange Program (DAAD); the Israeli Ministry of Education; the Simon Dubnow Institute in Leipzig; Studienstiftung des deutschen Volkes; the history departments at the University of California–Berkeley and the University of Wisconsin–Madison; the Walter and Constance Burke Research Initiation; and the Rockefeller Center at Dartmouth College. I am especially indebted to John Tortorice of the George Mosse Program at the University of Wisconsin-Madison. He provided me the first opportunity to come to the United States, and the two years I spent in Madison enriched my professional and personal lives in ways that I could never have imagined. John has supported me in countless ways ever since, and I cherish his generosity and friendship.

I am also pleased to thank the many archivists and librarians who helped me access countless forgotten documents and uncover dusty publications. They make the work of historians possible, and I would have missed many hidden treasures without them. In Europe, I received the help of archivists at the Bundesarchiv Koblenz; Hauptstaatsarchiv Düsseldorf; Kommission für Zeitgeschichte in Bonn; Universitätsarchiv der Ruprecht-Karls-Universität, Heidelberg; Universitätsarchiv der Freie Universität, Berlin; and the Institut für Zeitgeschichte, Munich; the British Library in London; and the London School of Economics. In the United States, I benefited from the assistance of the staff at the National Archives, College Park, Maryland; Leo Baeck Institute at New York; Harvard University; the Library of Congress,

Washington, D.C.; Seeley G. Mudd Manuscript Library at Princeton University; the Rockefeller Foundation Archives in Tarrytown, NY; the University of Notre Dame; Amherst College; the New York Public Library; the Hoover Institute, Stanford University; and the library at Dartmouth College.

I would also like to thank the friends whose companionship made the completion of this work possible. Stephen Russell, Daniela Blei, and Sarah Cramsey made my time at Berkeley a joy. In Madison, I enjoyed the company of Vanessa Walker Gordon and Robbie Gross, who also hosted me for a month of research. Yulia Frumer kindly saved me much effort by copying documents at Princeton. I am grateful to Maya Maxwell, for her friendship and for her company during my time in New York. And finally, my thanks go to my friends in Israel, Eitan Grossman, Nadav Lazar, Yossi Weiss, Yishai Kessler, Maya Asher, Noam Badrian, and Doron Djerassi.

But I owe more than anything—truly everything—to my family. My parents, Ofra and Avner, and my brother, Noam, created an environment that was as intellectually curious as it was loving. The Millers—Cathy, Bob, Chris, Lucas, and Rose, as well as Jenn Young—accepted me within their family and hosted me on countless visits and archival trips. Their support made me feel at home in a new country. But above all, it is to my wife, Jennie, that I owe my gratitude. She has been my intellectual companion for years and shaped my entire thinking about history, politics, and ideas. She read every word of every draft with a care and patience that never ceased to amaze me. The life that we built together with our daughter, Elizabeth, is the heart and center of our own century. It is to her that I dedicate this book.

The Weimar Century

Introduction

THERE WERE FEW REASONS FOR OPTIMISM in Germany in the summer of 1948. Three years after the most destructive war in history, German cities still lay in ruins, dislocated refugees and wounded ex-soldiers wandered the streets, and widespread hunger sparked unrest and protest. Although Marshall Plan aid had begun to arrive from across the Atlantic, most Germans expected long years of poverty and desolation. To make matters worse, it was becoming evident that the emerging Cold War would cast a dark shadow over Germany's future. As the world's new superpowers—the United States and the Soviet Union—transitioned from wartime alliance to postwar hostility, both were determined to fasten their grip on Germany, even at the price of the defeated nation's division. In June 1948 the world held its breath as Germany drew ever closer to military conflict. After Soviet troops placed Berlin's western sectors under military blockade, American and British planes dropped supplies into the besieged city, marking the end of superpower negotiations. The blockade would end nine months later, but it firmly demonstrated that the Americans and Soviets would be unable to overcome their mutual mistrust. The specter of Germany's division into two separate states loomed large. After the devastation and humiliating defeat of the Third Reich, the century-old dream of a united Germany now lay in tatters.

Yet Carl J. Friedrich (1901–1984), chief legal adviser to General Lucius Clay, the U.S. military governor of Germany, was strikingly cheerful. In August 1948, two months after the start of the Berlin blockade, Friedrich happily reported to Clay that his mission to restructure Germany's western occupation zones into a decentralized, democratic, and peaceful West German republic was coming to a successful conclusion. Having supervised countless meetings of German legal scholars, elected local politicians, and Allied occupation personnel on Clay's behalf, Friedrich had helped complete drafts of democratic constitutions at the regional and national level. The German parliaments that the U.S. and British authorities created in their occupation zones would soon ratify these constitutions, turning them into West Germany's foundational legal contracts for the remainder of the century. Friedrich was also energetically engaged in constructing new educational programs designed to train Germans in democratic thought. With the assistance of Rockefeller Foundation officials and U.S. diplomats, he helped found a new university in West Berlin, developed a new democratic research center in Heidelberg, and drafted new curricula that would soon be embraced by universities across Germany. For Friedrich, the impending tragedy of Germany's Cold War division was marginal compared to the exhilarating prospect of democratization. The creation of a democratic West German state out of the rubble of Nazism and war was a source of great promise and optimism.

Friedrich's faith in Germany's radical transformation was not merely the product of enormous personal ambitions. His confidence also stemmed from decades of intimate links to the United States. Although he was born in Germany, Friedrich spent the 1930s and 1940s as an émigré scholar in Harvard University's Department of Government, where he cultivated extensive connections to U.S. academic leaders, politicians, military leaders, and philanthropists. The graduate programs, research centers, and training institutions that he founded, such as Harvard's School of Overseas Administration, educated thousands of future policymakers and military personnel for postwar careers and, more broadly, American global hegemony. Friedrich's prominence increased further after the end of Germany's occupation in 1949, when he became a renowned anti-Communist intellectual in both the United States and West Germany. His flurry of writings, which warned against the evils of global communism and called for a firm German-American alliance, electrified the minds of many readers and inspired intellectuals and politicians such as David Riesman, Hannah Arendt, and Henry Kissinger. Alongside his role as an agent of German democratization, Friedrich was also a major figure of Cold War thought and international politics.

To many of Friedrich's contemporaries, these two campaigns—democratizing Germany and forging an anti-Communist international alliance—were a response to the miseries of World War II and the dreadful threat of Soviet power. For Friedrich, however, these efforts marked the resurrection of older ideas and networks formed as a young German political theorist during the Weimar period (1918–1933). Years before the National Socialists' rise to power, Friedrich developed an idiosyncratic theory of democracy and international cooperation. Democracy, Friedrich wrote, emerged not from the Enlightenment but from seventeenth-century German Protestant political thought. Democracy therefore had authentically German roots, which Germans had to embrace. Friedrich further maintained that Protestantism and democracy had spread from Germany to the United States with the Puritan migration. Germans and Americans thus shared natural religious and political foundations. These two nations had to form an international, Protestant, and democratic alliance, one that would help ensure the survival of democracy in Europe. Throughout the Weimar era, Friedrich sought to spearhead the creation of this alliance through the drafting of a pro-democratic curriculum and German-American educational and cultural exchange programs. Blazing a trail he would walk twenty years later, he convinced American philanthropists and policymakers to support these programs. For Friedrich, then, the post-Nazi world did not require new ideas. The democratic theories, networks, and institutions that he had first developed in the 1920s would serve as the recipe for German democracy and international stability after World War II.

In this blend of distinctive intellectual visions from the Weimar era, bold aspirations for democratic reform, and service with the U.S. political establishment, Friedrich was not alone. Countless German émigré thinkers drew on ideas first formed in Germany's interwar ferment to participate in both Germany's reconstruction and the formation of American Cold War hegemony. Among them were Ernst Fraenkel (1898–1975), a Socialist theoretician who served as a senior official in the U.S. occupation of Korea after World War II, participated in Korea's division, and became one of the most important writers on democracy and labor in West Germany; Waldemar Gurian (1902–1954), a Catholic journalist who worked for the Rockefeller Foundation's cultural outreach programs to Germans after World War II, coined the anti-Communist "theory of totalitarianism," and became one of the foremost specialists on the Soviet Union in the United States; Karl Loewenstein (1891–1973), a liberal lawyer who during the war worked at the U.S. Department of Justice, where he led a campaign of mass incarceration in Latin America, and then became one of the leading pro-democratic and anti-Communist thinkers in postwar Germany; and Hans Morgenthau (1904–1980), whose "realist" theory of international relations was highly influential among anti-Communist U.S. diplomats. These émigrés hailed from varied religious, political, and intellectual backgrounds. They all pursued a distinctive ideological mission. But in different ways and through diverse institutions, they were all crucial architects of both democratization and anti-Communist mobilization. Their ideas, policies, and institutional connections stood at the heart of the postwar Atlantic order.

The unlikely paths that led these émigrés from Weimar to the center of American power are far more than mere biographical curiosities. They illustrate three crucial intellectual and political trends that helped shape the world after World War II. First, these German émigrés, who spent the dark years of the Third Reich in exile, were vital yet often unrecognized players in Germany's postwar reconstruction. With support and funding from American authorities, they introduced comprehensive theories of democracy and anti-communism, took part in constitutional and cultural reforms, and founded pro-democratic academic curricula and institutions. By the end of the 1950s, their teachings about the legitimacy of democratic institutions and the need for anti-Communist mobilization had become cornerstones of the new Federal Republic of Germany (or West Germany, as it was colloquially called). Equally important, their conception of democracy, based on strong state institutions, spiritual consensus, and vigilant suppression of Communists, helped delegitimize and exclude alternative political visions. Their ideas marked the harsh limits and brutality of postwar imagination. The stories of German émigrés thus chart the ideological contours of Germany's postwar political order, both its vibrancy and its constraints. They uncover the forces that facilitated what historian Tony Judt called "the most dramatic instance of political stabilization in post-war Europe."[1]

Second, the long careers of these émigrés show that the intellectual roots of Germany's democratization lay not in the postwar era, nor was this dramatic change merely a response to the trauma of Nazism. Rather, these émigrés drew their thinking about politics from their experiences during Germany's short-lived first democracy, the Weimar Republic, which emerged from the destruction of World War I and ended with the Nazis' rise to power in 1933. Weimar was an era of great democratic promise but also of intense violence and instability. Its rocky years generated passionate intellectual debates about the nature of democratic politics. As young men, the future émigrés took part in these debates. They spawned a stream of innovative theories about the nature of democratic institutions, democracy's relationship to welfare and religion, and necessary responses to anti-democratic political forces. They ambitiously argued that democracy was the sole legitimate regime, one that had the right to violently crush its enemies. Decades later, as they participated in Germany's rebuilding, they reached back to these ideas and plans. They resurrected older thought patterns, educational institutions, and political rhetoric. Weimar was thus far more than a cautionary tale of democratic collapse. When Germans once again sought to build democracy after the trauma of World War II, Weimar provided powerful intellectual models for political reconstruction.

Third, and least recognized by scholars, the stories of Friedrich, Fraenkel, Gurian, Loewenstein, and Morgenthau shed light on the nature of U.S. power and policymaking during World War II and the early Cold War. Their careers exemplify how the rising American leviathan absorbed European political thought and helped disseminate it around the world. As the global conflicts with Nazism, Japanese militarism, and then communism evolved, German émigrés accompanied the U.S. military, State Department, and private American organizations to unexpected locations. They became political advisers in Korea, legal reformers in Latin America, officials in philanthropic foundations in the Rhineland, and consultants at the State Department in Washington, D.C. Equally important, their writings and theories provided some of the most influential intellectual frameworks that mobilized American democracy for a crusade against communism. In an avalanche of journals, books, and lectures, these five émigrés framed Communist regimes as evil, violent, and ever-expanding tyrannies and explained how democratic states could defeat and destroy them. Though these ideas ostensibly celebrated

---

[1] Tony Judt, *Postwar: A History of Europe since 1945* (New York: Penguin, 2005), 265.

democratic principles, they often led to ironic, tragic, and brutal consequences. As the following pages show, the emigrés' conceptions of democracy
often ironically led to repression. Yet for these individuals, the democratization of Germany and the defeat of global communism were inseparable campaigns that informed and fueled each other. By taking part in both, they
combined two major transformations of the postwar era—Germany's reconstruction and the emerging Cold War—into a single international structure.

The intellectual foundations laid in Weimar were thus fundamental to
the architecture of postwar politics in both West Germany and the United
States and to the Cold War alliance between them. The ideas originally
crafted to support the fragile Weimar Republic helped facilitate Germany's
turn to democracy as well as German and American mobilization to combat communism. Each chapter of this book focuses on an individual from a
particular background and the political theory he developed in Weimar
Germany; his integration into wartime American political, intellectual, and
diplomatic networks; and his participation in recruiting institutions and
populations to aid in the creation of a democratic Western alliance. Each
offers a window onto broad intellectual and political currents within West
Germany and the United States during the postwar era. Together, these stories uncover the ideas, ironies, organizations, and experiences that shaped
the early Cold War on both sides of the Atlantic. They explain the intellectual origins of titanic political projects.

The "Miracle" of Germany's Reconstruction

The rapid and colossal transformation of postwar Germany, from racist dictatorship to liberal democracy, was one of the most exceptional sagas of the
modern era. Having fought for the Nazi regime with ferocity throughout
the war, even in the face of impending defeat, Germans performed a volte-
face and, within just a few years, embraced democracy. With astonishing
speed, this previously polarized and violent society developed democratic
institutions, electoral organs, the rule of law, vibrant democratic norms, and
an active participatory public. This transformation was especially astound-
ing given the deep penetration of Nazism into German society. Hitler and
his followers had not merely controlled state institutions (as all dictatorships do) but had also aggressively Nazified and supervised Germany's
school curricula, cultural institutions, largest corporations, and voluntary
associations, from book clubs to hiking groups. Germany's shift to democracy has thus continued to stir the minds of political leaders, theorists, and
reformers. When the American authorities planned the occupation of Iraq
in 2003, for example, specialists studiously consulted the literature on the
occupations of Germany and Japan. In the eyes of many, Germany's politi-

cal reconstruction in the aftermath of 1945 remains one of the greatest "miracles" of the twentieth century.[2]

What explains this rapid change? What accounts for the speed with which Germans of diverse political and religious backgrounds came not only to tolerate democratic institutions but to embrace democratic norms of open debate and peaceful competition as the key legitimate political standard? The many historians who have sought to answer these questions generally embrace one of two perspectives. The most common interpretation focuses on the decisive role of the United States. First, during the occupation of Germany (1945–1949), and later as part of the Cold War, the new superpower heavily invested in the reconstruction of Germany's political institutions, economy, and educational system as part of a frenzied effort to secure Europe from the threat of Soviet dominance. From 1945 on, an army of American educators, labor unionists, businessmen, and philanthropists rushed to join the project of restructuring the ruined country. For over a decade, with massive financial, logistical, and political support from the U.S. government, this web of activists founded new educational programs, invested in political education, and flooded the country with pro-democratic, anti-Soviet magazines, books, and radio shows. Many historians maintain that this prolonged and multifaceted campaign profoundly influenced Germany's transformation into a stable and democratic culture. Its mistakes and setbacks notwithstanding, the United States successfully imposed its own ideas and norms that led Germans to abandon their extreme nationalism and violence and instead embrace peaceful political competition.[3]

In contrast, a second interpretation of Germany's transformation sees it primarily as the work of Germans. Despite the scale of their efforts, Americans quickly recognized that they could not single-handedly transform the cultural and intellectual terms by which Germans understood the postwar

---

[2] The term "miracle of democracy" is borrowed from Konrad H. Jarausch, Arnd Bauerkämper, and Marcus M. Payk (eds.), *Demokratiewunder: transatlantische Mittler und die kulturelle Öffnung Westdeutschlands* (Göttingen: Vandenhoeck & Ruprecht, 2005). On recalling the occupation of Germany and Japan during the planning of the invasion of Iraq, see James Dobbins et al., *America's Role in Nation-Building: From Germany to Iraq* (Santa Monica, CA: Rand Monograph, 2003).

[3] The scholarship on American influence on Germany is vast. For classic and helpful examples, see Volker R. Berghahn, *The Americanisation of West German Industry* (Cambridge: Cambridge University Press, 1986); Klaus Naumann (ed.), *Nachkrieg in Deutschland* (Hamburg: Hamburger Edition, 2001); Jeffry M. Diefendorf, Axel Frohn, and Hermann-Josef Rupieper (eds.), *American Policy and the Reconstruction of West Germany* (Cambridge: Cambridge University Press, 1993); Hermann-Josef Rupieper, *Die Wurzeln der westdeutschen Nachkriegsdemokratie: der amerikanische Beitrag 1945–1952* (Opladen: Westdeutscher Verlag, 1993). On the debates concerning the Marshall Plan, see the essays in Charles Maier and Günter Bischof (eds.), *The Marshall Plan and Germany* (Oxford: Berg, 1991).

world. As many frustrated observers have noted, West Germans might have consumed American culture, listened to American radio stations, and flocked to watch American movies, but they just as often condemned what they saw as "foreign" American culture and values. Indeed, both during and after the occupation, Germans frequently ignored American cultural diplomacy. They even interpreted its content as an affirmation of anti-American sentiments.[4] Many historians therefore argue that Germans embraced democracy primarily because of postwar domestic conditions and experiences. The defeated nation, they claim, came to value peaceful democratic competition owing to its shame over Nazi crimes, the economic prosperity it enjoyed in the 1950s, or the growth of a new generation after the war. According to this narrative, Germans found their own path to democratic ideas and norms.[5]

Both of these interpretations are helpful in understanding Germany's dramatic turn. Yet they overlook several crucial factors that played a decisive role in the making of a democratic Germany. First, democratization was not the product of the individual activities of American *or* German agents. It was the outcome of prolonged collaboration, in which both sides were crucial players. No group embodies this synergy better than the émigrés who returned to postwar Germany. In the decade after 1945, they worked for the U.S. military, diplomatic establishment, foreign aid programs, academic institutions, and philanthropic foundations. They established academic centers for the study of democracy in Heidelberg, Berlin, and Munich, conducted public outreach campaigns aimed at workers, and published a stream of democratic theories in books and journals. But despite their dependence on American wealth and might, they did not merely transmit American ideas or values. Rather, they utilized their positions in order to disseminate their own ideas. The complex project of building democracy was the product of symbiosis. It was a process in which consistent American pressure and the efforts of German actors were inseparable.

Second, scholars of Germany's reconstruction privilege economic and political measures, such as the Marshall Plan, the introduction of the West German currency (D-Mark) in 1948, or the writing of the West German Constitution in 1949. In doing so, they often ignore the role of ideas and democratic theories in shaping action. In fact, scholars have often claimed that Germany's democratization evolved without any intellectual infra-

---

[4] On the limits and failures of American cultural diplomacy in Germany, see, for example, Mary Nolan, *The Transatlantic Century: Europe and America 1890–2010* (Cambridge University Press, 2012), 154–266; Uta G. Poiger, *Jazz, Rock, and Rebels: Cold War Politics and American Culture in Divided Germany* (Berkeley: University of California Press, 2000).

[5] See, for example, Konrad H. Jarausch, *After Hitler: Recivilizing Germans* (Oxford: Oxford University Press, 2006); Axel Schildt, *Ankunft im Westen: ein Essay zur Erfolgsgeschichte der Bundesrepublik* (Frankfurt a.M.: Fischer, 1999); Axel Schildt, *Zwischen Abendland und Amerika: Studien Zur Westdeutschen Ideenlandschaft* (Oldenbourg: Wissenschaftsverlag, 1999).

structure. Mark Lilla echoed a widespread notion when he asserted that Germany's democratization was a "revolution without ideas," a strange rebirth of democracy without democratic thought.[6] But postwar Germany was shaped by vibrant intellectual debates and theories. As the following pages show, returning German émigrés provided new intellectual frameworks for democratic reform and offered a plethora of political languages and terminologies. They argued that democracy was rooted in older German religious traditions and called on Germans to strengthen democracy against the Communist enemy. These German thinkers took it upon themselves to convince their countrymen that democracy was not a foreign system imposed by the victorious Allies but rather the product of indigenous ideas. In a multifaceted campaign of lectures, publications, and teaching, they sought to demonstrate that German cultural traditions were naturally and organically democratic. In doing so, they helped reshape German political behavior. And as evidence shows, these émigrés' ideas resonated powerfully among many. The people who read their works, listened to their lectures, or passed through the institutions they helped build explicitly acknowledged their influence. In order to understand how people thought about and understood democracy, one must therefore examine the development and implementation of émigré ideas and theories. They provided a crucial intellectual arsenal for Germany's democratic transformation.[7]

Finally, historians of Germany's democratization generally begin their stories in 1945, obscuring longer continuities. They tend to agree that, in the words of one scholar, "it was catastrophe that rendered the Germans capable of democracy."[8] But the political ideas that shaped West Germany were not a product of the postwar world. Rather, this book contends that many of the intellectual foundations of Germany's democratization, its possibilities and limitations, lay in the intense discussions of the Weimar era. As

---

[6] Mark Lilla, "The Other Velvet Revolution: Continental Liberalism and Its Discontents," *Daedalus* 123:2 (1994): 129–157.

[7] Several excellent studies have begun to explore the intellectual reconstruction of Germany. Most, however, focus primarily on questions of national identity and historical memory rather than on democratic theory per se. See, for example, Dirk Moses, *German Intellectuals and the Nazi Past* (Cambridge: Cambridge University Press, 2007); Jens Hacke, *Philosophie der Bürgerlichkeit: Die Liberalkonservative Begründung der Bundesrepublik* (Göttingen: Vandenhoeck & Ruprecht, 2006); Jan-Werner Müller (ed.), *German Ideologies since 1945: Studies in the Political Thought and Culture of West Germany* (New York: Macmillan, 2003); and Clemens Albrecht et al. (eds.), *Die Intellektuelle Gründung der Bundesrepublik: eine Wirkungsgeschichte der Frankfurter Schule* (Frankfurt: Campus, 1999). For an exception, which explores the works of several liberal thinkers in postwar Heidelberg, see Sean Forner, *German Intellectuals and the Challenge of Democratic Renewal* (Cambridge: Cambridge University Press, forthcoming). See also the special forum edited by A. Dirk Moses, "The Intellectual History of the Federal Republic," *German History* 27:2 (2009): 244–258.

[8] Peter Graff von Kilemansegg, *Nach der Katastrophe* (Berlin: Siedler, 2000), 10.

historian Daniel Rodgers has noted, moments of crisis and upheaval rarely generate new ideas and new policies. When societies experience radical transformation and old hierarchies and institutions collapse, "men are much more prone to fall back on inherited and instinctive values in an effort to cope with a totally unprecedented situation."[9] Despite the cataclysmic effects of total war and devastating defeat, the democratic concepts that replaced Nazism were not simply a response to the trauma of war, although they gained a new appeal in the postwar era. When thinkers sought to democratize Germany, they dipped into an intellectual reservoir developed in the 1920s and the early 1930s, when the country had first experimented with a democratic system. While historians have devoted considerable energy to uncovering continuities between the Third Reich and the postwar Federal Republic, the earlier and more obscure forces that linked the two German republics were equally if not more significant for Germany's stabilization. Had it not been for the existing ideas and traditions of the Weimar era, Germans would not have quickly embraced democracy as their own project.[10]

It was no coincidence that German émigrés were among the principal conduits for Weimar's democratic language and theories. Prior to 1945, the Nazis had relentlessly suppressed or co-opted alternative cultural and intellectual traditions.[11] Some three hundred thousand Germans whom the Nazi regime defined as "un-German" or "Judaic" fled or were forced out of central Europe during the six years between the Nazi revolution in 1933 and the outbreak of war in 1939. The émigrés who fled Nazi oppression, however, carried with them a democratic language and institutional frameworks that the Third Reich could not reach. Of these exiles, a small fraction, fewer than fifteen thousand, returned to Europe after 1945 to take part in Germany's reconstruction. Though these numbers may seem vanishingly small, returning émigrés profoundly contributed to the development of intellectual alternatives to disgraced Nazi ideology by invoking earlier theories of German democracy as a source of national renewal. While scholars have produced innumerable studies of German émigrés' contributions to culture, music, journalism, medicine, and art during their exile, historians have only recently begun to explore the vital role that these individuals played in the postwar reconstruction of Europe. Through their agency,

[9] Daniel T. Rodgers, *Atlantic Crossings: Social Politics in a Progressive Age* (Cambridge, MA: Belknap Press of Harvard University Press, 1998), 413.

[10] For a representative and excellent example, see Norbert Frei, *Adenauer's Germany and the Nazi Past: The Politics of Amnesty and Integration* (New York: Columbia University Press, 2002).

[11] The scholarship on the Nazification of German thought and culture is enormous. For an overview of Nazism's relationship with different fields of thought, see the excellent essays in Wolfgang Bialas and Anson Rabinbach (eds.), *Nazi Germany and the Humanities* (Oxford: Oneworld, 2007).

Weimar-era ideas returned to Germany and provided crucial building blocks for political stabilization.[12]

In addition to drawing attention to the crucial continuities driving Germany's democratization, the stories of German émigrés demonstrate how different groups *inside* Germany came to think about democracy. Like all nations, Germany was never a homogeneous entity and comprised diverse communities—Protestants, Catholics, and Jews, conservatives, liberals, and Socialists—that developed autonomous cultural, religious, and political traditions. Friedrich, Fraenkel, Gurian, Loewenstein, and Morgenthau were rooted in different political and cultural milieus. Each crafted a democratic theory that borrowed heavily from ideas and concepts unique to his background, and devoted considerable effort—both before and after the war—to mobilizing his own community in support of democratic politics. Each of these men therefore serves as a window for tracing the broader shifts that led Protestants and Catholics, Socialists and liberals, to understand and embrace democracy. They reflect the intellectual efforts, glaring lacunae, and disturbing political neglectfulness that enabled these broad transformations. Taken together, these stories show that there was no single foundation for West Germany's postwar transformation. No one key idea, event, or group was the sole architect of postwar thought and politics. Rather, Germany's reconstruction is best understood as the amalgamation of varied individual and collective transformations. It is only by observing these changes as a whole that one can fully understand Germany's path to democratic norms and values.

German émigrés not only took part in Germany's domestic transformation; they also helped steer West Germany's broad international shift. In the years following the end of American occupation, West Germany unequivocally renounced its earlier quest for continental hegemony and instead became a staunch member of the "Western alliance." Under the banner of "Western integration," the West German government subordinated its military power to NATO, forged a firm alliance with the United States, and willingly compromised its sovereignty by hosting American military forces,

---

[12] Scholarship on returning German émigrés has begun to develop in recent years. For important sociological overviews, see for example Marita Krauss, *Heimkehr in ein fremdes Land: Geschichte der Remigration nach 1945* (Munich: Beck, 2001), and Irmela von der Lühe and Axel Schildt (eds.), *"Auch in Deutschland Waren Wir Nicht Wirklich Zu Hause": Jüdische Remigration nach 1945* (Göttingen: Wallstein, 2008). On German émigrés and political science in postwar Germany, see Alfons Söllner, "Normative Verwestlichung. Der Einfluss der Remigranten auf die politische Kultur der frühen Bundesrepublik," in Heinz Bude and Bernd Greiner (eds.), *Westbindungen: Amerika in der Bundesrepublik* (Hamburg: Hamburger Edition, 1999), 72–92; and Alfons Söllner, *Deutsche Politikwissenschaftler in der Emigration* (Opladen: Westdeutscher Verlag, 1996). For an excellent study on the intellectual role of German émigrés in the country's cultural reconstruction, see Noah Strote, *Emigration and the Foundation of West Germany 1933–1963* (Ph.D. diss., University of California, Berkeley, 2011).

abandoning the bellicose aspirations that had characterized German politics for decades. In the eyes of many Germans, including Konrad Adenauer, West Germany's chancellor from 1949 to 1963, this diplomatic reorientation transcended economic, security, or anti-Soviet considerations and was integral to the country's domestic democratization. By participating in a broad transnational alliance, many believed, Germans would gain a new sense of national mission and would associate democracy with international prestige and security.[13]

German émigrés were paramount in this postwar reformation. Having lived in exile in the United States and participated in its war effort, these individuals blended an awareness of German culture with intimate knowledge of the American establishment. They acted as mediators between these two worlds and presented the American reconstruction and anti-Communist efforts in Europe in familiar terms, compatible with domestic traditions. By claiming that its alliance with the West stemmed from "natural" similarities between Germany and other nations, they helped moderate Germany's intense nationalism and imperialism in favor of supranational commitments. Aware of the émigrés' unique position, both the American authorities and the West German government actively encouraged them to expand their work in Germany. Through state institutions and private programs, the émigrés were regularly brought to Germany and placed in key educational and cultural centers. Émigrés often served as a connecting tissue, key actors that linked domestic democratization with the forging of the Western alliance. They stood at the center of the German-American symbiosis.

The stories of the German émigrés that form the core of this book thus trace two major and interdependent forces that drove Germany's democratization: the convergence of German and American efforts and the resurrection of ideas and theories from the Weimar period. Their efforts do not provide a comprehensive or exhaustive account of Germany's democratization. But their trajectories show how intellectual and institutional models from Weimar survived in exile and, through the enormous investment and pressures of the United States, returned to shape German political values, practices, and traditions for years to come.

THE FOUNDATIONS OF POSTWAR THOUGHT: THE WEIMAR REPUBLIC AND ITS DISCONTENTS

The revolution that rocked Germany in November 1918, ending World War I and leading to the foundation of Germany's first democracy—the Weimar

[13] Ronald J. Granieri, *The Ambivalent Alliance: Konrad Adenauer, the CDU/CSU, and the West, 1949–1966* (New York: Berghahn Books, 2002).

Republic—meant different things to different people. For the workers and soldiers who stormed state buildings in Berlin, Munich, and across Germany, it was a moment of hope after four miserable years of senseless war. Impeaching the German kaiser and establishing a republic, they believed, would smash the authority of the dominant Prussian nobility, bring political equality, and end the war. For conservatives and nationalists, on the other hand, the revolution marked Germany's horrific downfall. The destruction of the monarchy, and Germany's subsequent surrender to the Allies, was a humiliating end to a decades-long quest for world power and glory. For German intellectuals, the Weimar Republic raised as many questions as it answered. It inspired intense debates about the fundamentals of democratic politics, such as sources of political legitimacy, the role of welfare and religion, and the content of education in a democratic polity. For Carl J. Friedrich, Ernst Fraenkel, Waldemar Gurian, Karl Loewenstein, and Hans J. Morgenthau, the Weimar revolution—which one observer called "one of the most memorable and dreadful [events] ... in German history"—and the political and intellectual debates it generated were the intellectual motors that drove their entire careers and ambitions.[14]

The creation of Germany's first democracy was unanticipated, to say the least. Although strikes and anti-war demonstrations had proliferated throughout the increasingly unpopular war, no one expected them to morph into a revolution. The abysmal failure of the kaiser, the Prussian nobility, and the military to lead Germany to victory ignited a widespread sentiment that more power should be transferred to the parliament and elected politicians. Yet few called for the total abolition of the monarchy. Thus on 9 November 1918, when Socialist politician Philipp Scheidemann stood on the balcony of the Reichstag and proclaimed Germany to be a republic, he did so without any planning or consulting with his party. His declaration was merely an attempt to quiet angry demonstrators who demanded the kaiser's resignation. But the revolution could not be stopped, as soldiers' and workers' riots swiftly spread across Germany. The kaiser and his family fled the country, and revolutionaries took over the state and declared an end to the war. Within a year, a coalition of Socialists, Catholics, and liberals had composed a new democratic constitution—the Weimar Constitution—in which authority stemmed from the people. During its fourteen years, the Weimar Republic opened up new democratic horizons by granting equal rights to women, establishing a comprehensive welfare state, and making all religions equal under the law. It undermined old ideas about the divine legitimacy and authority of the monarchy and aristocracy

---

[14] The quotation is from the diary of Count Harry Kessler, the German diplomat and writer, cited in Peter Fritzsche, *Germans into Nazis* (Cambridge, MA: Harvard University Press, 1998), 88.

and allowed new political actors, including Jews, Socialists, and Catholics, to hold positions of power for the first time. Even those who opposed the republic recognized that it fundamentally broke with the past, and that Germany would never again revert to monarchy. Essayist René Schickele mused that November 1918 "would remain unforgettable."[15]

At the same time, Weimar also inaugurated a decade of misery and anxiety that threatened to tear apart the German nation. In 1919 the victorious Allied Powers forced Germany to sign the humiliating Treaty of Versailles, which severed a massive amount of territory from Germany, obliged it to pay draconian reparations, and subjected its western regions to foreign allied occupation. Bedeviled by the treaty's toxic legacy, Weimar revealed the hollow promises of four years of wartime sacrifice. For millions of Germans who, in the words of Erich Maria Remarque, "even though they may have escaped its shells, were destroyed by the war," the republic never overcame these weaknesses.[16] In the following years, Germans also experienced devastating economic disasters, such as hyperinflation, that destroyed the savings of millions. They also observed recurring attempts at violent coups and waves of political assassinations. The republic was plagued by the rise of revolutionary forces that sought to violently restructure society. On the left, the new Communist Party envisioned a Bolshevik dictatorship, which would abolish private property and dismantle democratic institutions. On the right, a burgeoning hypernationalist ideology prophesied a new racial order and renewed imperialist expansion. Both openly challenged the republic's legitimacy and often resorted to violence in their attempt to overthrow it. The Germany of the Weimar era was more polarized, violent, and anxious than ever before. With its cocktail of utopian visions and deep anxieties, Weimar was the epitome of the "age of extremes."[17]

Although Weimar was Germany's first democracy, historians have long debated the depth of German democratic thought in this time period. Because Weimer generated such intense anger and frustration and collapsed in 1933 with little resistance, historians have often attributed Weimar's catastrophic demise in part to the lack of a developed intellectual framework. The traumatic defeat in World War I and Weimar's chronic instability, they claim, dealt a harsh blow to Germans' faith in progress, peaceful political

[15] Cited in Fritzsche, *Germans into Nazis*, 109.

[16] Erich Maria Remarque, *All Quiet on the Western Front* (New York: Ballantine Books, 1982), preface.

[17] The term is borrowed from Eric Hobsbawm's *The Age of Extremes: The Short Twentieth Century, 1914–1991* (New York: Vintage, 1994). The scholarship on Weimar is of course enormous and beyond the scope of this study. The best overviews of the period's inner tensions and conflicts are Eric D. Weitz, *Weimar Germany: Promise and Tragedy* (Princeton: Princeton University Press, 2007); and Detlev Peukert, *The Weimar Republic: The Crisis of Classical Modernity* (London: Penguin Press, 1991).

life, and liberal self-confidence. Liberal ideology and constitutional democracy seemed bankrupt and predicated on discredited convictions. According to this narrative, the intellectual energy generated by the disintegration of the monarchy and traditional authority contributed to innovations in aesthetics, literature, and philosophy but left German democracy intellectually crippled. As one scholar put it, German democracy's downfall in 1933 "was in part prepared by the demise of [liberalism's] . . . cultural and intellectual forms" after World War I.[18]

This interpretation of Weimar and its collapse, however, neglects the wide array of democratic theories, debates, and projects developed during the Weimar period. Despite what many scholars have argued, Weimar was not "a democracy without democrats."[19] Throughout the 1920s and 1930s, various intellectuals embarked on diverse campaigns to strengthen the fragile German republic's intellectual foundations. In a stream of publications, the figures that stand at the center of this book offered new democratic theories and terminologies. Unlike previous thinkers, they did not merely call for modest reforms that would increase electoral participation. Instead, they argued that a democracy based on elected officials was the *only* truly legitimate political system.[20] These thinkers also sought to put their ideas into action by establishing a variety of educational organizations. In Heidelberg, Berlin, Frankfurt, and Munich, they founded and joined new educational centers for students and adults and cultural exchange programs, all aimed at strengthening and stabilizing the Weimar state. These efforts did not enter mainstream German thought in the 1920s, and most intellectuals and political theorists did not embrace them. Nevertheless, they constituted an important feature of the era's intellectual landscape. No portrait of Weimar thought is complete without these attempts at democratization.[21]

[18] The quotation is from Benjamin Lazier, *God Interrupted: Heresy and the European Imagination between the World Wars* (Princeton: Princeton University Press, 2008), 5. See also Rüdiger Graf, *Die Zukunft der Weimarer Republik: Krisen und Zukunftsaneignungen in Deutschland, 1918–1933* (Munich: Oldenbourg, 2008); Rüdiger Graf and Mortiz Föllmer (eds.), *Die "Krise" der Weimarer Republik: zur Kritik eines Deutungsmusters* (Frankfurt a.M.: Campus, 2005); Bernd Widdig, *Culture and Inflation in Weimar Germany* (Berkeley: University of California Press, 2001).

[19] The famous quote appears in many scholars' writings. See, for example, Jan-Werner Müller, *Constitutional Patriotism* (Princeton: Princeton University Press, 2007), 18.

[20] As several scholars have shown, Germany developed many democratic institutions and practices throughout the imperial era, such as parliamentary elections, universal male suffrage, and political autonomy; however, German thinkers vested little effort in developing a comprehensive democratic theory. See Margaret Levinia Anderson, *Practicing Democracy: Elections and Political Culture in Imperial Germany* (Princeton: Princeton University Press, 2000).

[21] For an exceptional study of democratic thought in the Weimar era (which does not explore the thinkers covered in this book), see Kathrin Groh, *Demokratische Staatsrechtslehrer in der Weimarer Republik* (Tübingen: Mohr Siebeck, 2010).

These campaigns to bolster the republic were not abstract reflections, but responses to burning and concrete political questions. Each of these thinkers grappled as a young man with a key problem wrought by Germany's democratic transition. How, for example, could Weimar produce a democratic elite in a country where business, political, and academic leaders had long supported the monarchy? What was the relationship between economic conditions and political rights, and was democracy obliged to spread wealth equally? What was religion's role in the new democracy; was the separation of church and state strengthening or weakening Germany? How should Weimar treat those who called for its overthrow, such as Communists and extreme nationalists? And how should the young republic engage with the nations surrounding it, through cooperation or imperial competition? Each of these questions generated fierce debates among Germany's thinkers and politicians. By trying to provide concrete answers, prodemocratic thinkers touched raw nerves in German political culture.

Friedrich, Fraenkel, Gurian, Loewenstein, and Morgenthau each focused on a different dilemma of democratic politics; their questions about democracy drew from their diverse political, religious, and intellectual backgrounds. Ultimately, however, they shared a fundamental agreement. In contrast to the claims of German nationalists, they all believed that democracy was not a foreign imposition, nor a legacy of weakness and humiliation. They feverishly sought to show that a division of power, electoral politics, and group participation in peaceful political competition stemmed from domestic German thought and traditions. The republic's young defenders further argued that democracy did not divide the nation from within. The ultimate goal of politics was not national unity and homogeneity but vibrant competition between groups, parties, and associations. Democracy enabled a multitude of groups to live alongside one another and flourish in a pluralist environment. It allowed citizens to come together through mutual interests and joint political action and coalition building. While these ideas appear obvious to a twenty-first-century reader, they were profoundly innovative in Weimar's intellectual landscape. Such theories introduced new thinking about politics, offering an intellectual arsenal that was unfamiliar to German readers.

This support for free political competition, however, was deeply limited by virulent anti-communism. Long before the Cold War, anxieties over Communist domination permeated German life, cutting across class, region, and political affiliation. The shocking success of Russia's Bolshevik Revolution in 1917 and the subsequent emergence of militant Communist parties across Europe sparked widespread fears that Communists would soon take over the state, abolish private property, destroy traditional social hierarchies, and violently suppress religion. In the eyes of these five future émigrés, communism posed an overriding threat because it explicitly sought to destroy their visions of democracy. During the 1920s, German Communists openly opposed elections and the division of power, lambasting them as veils for capitalist exploitation. These five men therefore conceived of democracy as continually subject to domestic and foreign threats. Democratic institutions required constant mobilization and innovative defense mechanisms to combat potential Communist aggression and subversion. For this generation, anti-communism and democracy were thus deeply intertwined. Their hostility to communism underpinned a comprehensive democratic project.[22]

These ideas and experiences continued to guide the work of these five men decades after Weimar's collapse. And the central role that these émigrés and their ideas played in Germany's democratization after World War II thus necessitates a fresh assessment of the legacies of the Weimar Republic, both its liberating and its limiting effects. Scholars have frequently noted how Germany's first democracy served as a negative model for post–World War II attempts to revive German thought and democratic politics. Haunted by the memory of its collapse, German intellectuals, journalists, and politicians developed a "Weimar complex" or "Weimar syndrome," namely, an obsessive need to juxtapose and contrast current goals and actions with the 1920s. Indeed, throughout the 1950s, the catchphrase "Bonn is not Weimar" appeared not only in books and articles but also in political slogans and election campaigns.[23] Weimar, however, also offered *positive* models, theories, and terminology. Despite its weaknesses, many of the architects of postwar democracy regarded the republic as an unfinished yet admirable venture. Because of Weimar's tainted reputation, the intellectual architects of the postwar order rarely commented on the origins of their democratic thought. They often presented old ideas as new and fresh. But Weimar was not merely a cautionary tale. It generated long-lasting models for postwar thought and was an incubator of democratic theory.

[22] As recent scholarship has shown, anti-communism constituted a crucial intellectual and political force long before the Cold War in many societies and cultures. See, for example, Giuliana Chamedes's excellent "The Vatican and the Making of the Atlantic Order" (PhD diss., Columbia University, 2013); Alex Goodall, *Loyalty and Liberty: American Countersubversion from World War I to the McCarthy Era* (Urbana: University of Illinois Press, 2013); Markku Rutsila, *British and American Anticommunism before the Cold War* (London: Frank Cass, 2001).

[23] Sebastian Ullrich, *Der Weimar-Komplex: das Scheitern der ersten deutschen Demokratie und die politische Kultur der frühen Bundesrepublik* (Göttingen: Wallstein, 2009); Christoph Gusy (ed.), *Weimars lange Schatten: "Weimar" als Argument nach 1945* (Baden: Nomos, 2003); A. Dirk Moses, "The Weimar Syndrome in the Federal Republic of Germany," in Holgar Zaborowski and Stephan Loos (eds.), *Leben, Tod und Entscheidung: Studien zur Geistgeschichte der Weimarer Republik* (Berlin: Duncker & Humblot, 2003), 187–207. The origin of the slogan "Bonn is not Weimar" is the title of the book by journalist Fritz René Allemann, *Bonn ist nicht Weimar* (Cologne: Kiepenheuer & Witsch, 1956).

At the same time, these émigrés also carried close and long-standing ties between democracy and anti-communism with them when they returned to Germany. This connection explains not only the profound hopes invested in democratic possibilities but also the limits and ironies of Germany's postwar reconstruction. Against a Europe increasingly divided along ideological lines, this generation reintroduced to the postwar era a highly combative and dichotomous conception of democratic politics: one was either democracy's friend or its mortal enemy. As a result, the figures at the center of this book anxiously sought to delegitimize and suppress ideas that challenged their own. They deemed anyone who doubted whether the West German state should persecute Communists or bind itself to the Cold War Western alliance an anti-democratic agent, to be stripped of the right of legitimate democratic participation. This profound inflexibility meant that Weimar democratic ideas constrained the postwar political imagination just as much as they enabled it. Their liberating effect was profoundly diminished by their rigid nature.

Moreover, in a disturbing irony of postwar culture, these agents of democracy rarely recognized how their zeal for anti-communism perpetuated elements of Nazi thought. The hatred of communism was one of the Nazis' central ideological foundations, a profound source of their legitimacy and popularity. The fierce anti-Semitism of Hitler and his followers was partially fueled by the perverse conviction that Jews were the cunning vanguard of a global "Judeo-Bolshevik" revolution. The émigrés' anti-Communist phobias stemmed from radically different worldviews. They predated the Third Reich and were divorced from its racism. But in their attempts to harness Germany's anti-Communist fervor in the service of democracy, these émigrés helped preserve and perpetuate this Nazi obsession. Ideas from Weimar, then, not only enabled democratic revolutions but also constrained postwar democracy by their anti-communism. The democratic revolution that the émigrés helped unleash was a bittersweet one, simultaneously heroic and tragic.[24]

ÉMIGRÉS AND THE AMERICAN COLD WAR: KNOWLEDGE AND POWER

The stories of these German émigrés, however, have implications beyond German history. By tracing the influence of these individuals on American thought, diplomacy, and institutions, this book contends that Weimar traditions also helped shape the United States' ambitious efforts to construct

---

[24] On the links between Nazi and postwar anti-communism, see Maria D. Mitchell, *The Origins of Christian Democracy: Politics and Confession in Modern Germany* (Ann Arbor: University of Michigan Press, 2012), esp. 76–104; Frei, *Adenauer's Germany and the Nazi Past.*

global hegemony during the early Cold War. Their stories reveal the European origins of terminologies, ways of thinking, and institutional structures that undergirded American pursuit of the Cold War at home and overseas.

The Cold War unleashed the most ambitious diplomatic campaign in human history. Intent on preventing what they perceived to be an imminent Communist threat to an American "way of life," U.S. policymakers did not confine themselves to military means. They enlisted philanthropists, academics, businessmen, and artists as they sought to recruit entire nations to an anti-Communist alliance. Indeed, few spheres of human activity remained untouched by this recasting of international outreach and the broad employment of American resources. From psychology and the economy to education, entertainment, and sports, U.S. international campaigns altered norms and institutions as the United States engaged in what one scholar has accurately described as a "total Cold War."[25] Germany became a central site of this titanic campaign. For American policymakers, overcoming the hostilities of war and occupation by recruiting Germany's enormous industrial capacities and popular resources were the key to security and triumph in Europe and around the globe. Germany was among the countries that would determine whether the United States would ascend to world leadership and if the twentieth century, as Henry Luce famously mused, would become "the American Century."[26]

This monumental effort ignited a radical reconfiguration of the relationship between ideas and power, between intellectuals and policymaking. Many Americans believed that the Cold War was a clash of ideas and ideologies; to their minds, the most effective "free world" alliances drew from the ideological education and consent of entire populations. The United States therefore conducted an unprecedented "cultural offensive" in galleries, cinemas, publications, and universities. Authors, scholars, and artists founded international organizations and traveled the world, lending their ideas, works, and prestige to the service of "total diplomacy."[27] Equally impor-

[25] Kenneth Osgood, *Total Cold War: Eisenhower's Secret Propaganda Battle at Home and Abroad* (Lawrence: University Press of Kansas, 2006). See also Laura A. Belmonte, *Selling the American Way: U.S. Propaganda and the Cold War* (Philadelphia: University of Pennsylvania Press, 2008).

[26] Henry R. Luce, "The American Century," *Life* (17 February 1941): 61–65. On Germany in U.S. Cold War strategy, see John Lewis Gaddis, *Strategies of Containment* (New York: Oxford University Press, 2005 [1982]), esp. 24–86; James McAllister, *No Exit: America and the German Problem* (Ithaca: Cornell University Press, 2002).

[27] The term "total diplomacy" was coined in 1946 by Dean Acheson, then under secretary of state. See Robert L. Beisner, *Dean Acheson: A Life in the Cold War* (Oxford: Oxford University Press, 2006), 236–251. On cultural diplomacy and the Cold War, see, for example, Volker Berghahn, *America and the Intellectual Cold Wars in Europe* (Princeton: Princeton University Press, 2001); Penny M. von Eschen, *Satchmo Blows Up the World: Jazz Ambassadors Play the Cold War* (Cambridge, MA: Harvard University Press, 2004); David Caute, *The Dancer Defects: The*

tantly, the Cold War opened up new paths for thinkers to join the practice of international politics. American policymakers' urgent need for knowledge and analysis of foreign cultures led them to consult and rely on historians, literary scholars, and political theorists. Scholars, for their part, directed their research, teachings, and cultural production toward the needs of the American state. During the early years of the Cold War, the demarcation line between scholarship and state power was fundamentally blurred, as ideas and individuals flowed between the two worlds as never before. More so than in any previous or subsequent period, this was the era of intellectuals in power.[28]

German émigrés were among the most direct beneficiaries of this process, as the Cold War propelled them to the centers of American power. They were quick to recognize the opportunities presented by the occupation of Germany, the German-American alliance, and the broader Cold War, and both state institutions and private organizations were eager to secure their services. During the 1940s and 1950s, Friedrich, Fraenkel, Gurian, Loewenstein, and Morgenthau made the transition from penniless and uprooted refugees on the margins of society into members of the American diplomatic, educational, and cultural leadership. They served as chief legal advisers in the occupations of Germany and Korea; consultants to the State and Justice Departments; founders of area studies programs in American universities; and senior officers in the foremost American philanthropic organs, such as the Rockefeller Foundation. Their writings, memoranda, and reports circulated extensively among American diplomats and policymakers. While other American minorities and women continued to suffer from harsh discrimination, German émigrés enjoyed remarkable mobility and rapidly became part of the American elite. Some historians have noted this process, but they have focused on the work of émigrés at the Office of Strategic Services (OSS) during World War II, where their advice was largely ignored. It was the Cold War that opened up the most important spaces for German émigrés and endowed them with new influence.[29]

Struggle for Cultural Supremacy during the Cold War (Oxford: Oxford University Press, 2003); Michael Hochgeschwender, *Freiheit in der Offensive? der Kongress für Kulturelle Freiheit und die Deutschen* (Munich: Oldenbourg, 1998).

[28] I discuss this transformation (and the scholarship pertaining to it) in further detail in chapter I. For an overview, see Mark Solovey and Hamilton Cravens (eds.), *Cold War Social Science: Knowledge Production, Liberal Democracy, and Human Nature* (New York: Palgrave Macmillan, 2012); Jeremi Suri, *Henry Kissinger and the American Century* (Cambridge, MA: Belknap Press of Harvard University Press, 2007), 92–137; David Engerman, "Rethinking the Cold War University," *Journal of Cold War Studies* 5:3 (2004): 80–95.

[29] The groundbreaking study on émigrés and the OSS is Alfons Söllner, *Zur Archäologie der Demokratie in Deutschland*, vol. 2, *Analysen von politischen Emigranten im amerikanischen Außenministerium und Geheimdienst* (Frankfurt a.M.: Fischer, 1986). Joachim Radkau's classic study of German émigrés' efforts to shape U.S. foreign policy does not extend to the postwar era. See his

Beyond their fierce anti-communism, three key factors drove American diplomats and intellectuals to take such exceptional interest in German émigrés. Understanding these factors sheds light on broader transformations wrought by the Cold War. The first, as several scholars have noted, was the émigrés' international background. In the immediate postwar era, American policymakers lacked the systematic expertise to engage in large-scale alliance building and anti-Communist diplomacy. Unlike European empires, which had obsessively explored, mapped, and analyzed their colonized possessions for decades, the United States had not yet developed such an apparatus of global knowledge. With their language skills and knowledge of European history and politics, German émigrés were a rare asset. They were able to translate, analyze, and explain foreign cultures. Their experience in crossing national borders and enthusiasm for international cooperation made their work and advice indispensable to Americans desperate to build and maintain international hegemony.[30]

The second reason for the allure of German émigrés in the Cold War establishment stemmed from the dramatic expansion of the state. The Cold War solidified the rise of state power that had begun in the New Deal and advanced during World War II. The U.S. government aggressively intervened in the economy, expanded its military capabilities, and mobilized resources and people on an unprecedented scale. Crucial to this Cold War mobilization was the close cooperation that emerged between the state and private organizations. Countless philanthropists, academic institutions, and private associations came to view the state's interests as their own. They voluntarily joined forces with the government in suppressing Communist activities and forging bonds with foreign nations. The German thinkers at the center of this book provided both intellectual justification and practical models for such voluntary mobilization. Since their early years in Germany, they believed that the state was the natural vehicle for collective improvement. In their vision, institutions such as universities, labor unions, or philanthropies were not autonomous bodies; rather, they were organs of the democratic state. Whether working for government branches such as the State Department or mobilizing philanthropic foundations and universities to support state activities, these five émigrés helped expand the boundaries of state authority during the early Cold War. Historians have recently devoted much attention to nonstate actors as crucial agents of international

---

Die deutsche Emigration in den USA: ihr Einfluss auf die amerikanische Europapolitik, 1933–1945 (Düsseldorf: Bertelsmann Universitätsverlag, 1971). See also Barry Katz, *Foreign Intelligence: Research and Analysis in the Office of Strategic Studies* (Cambridge, MA: Harvard University Press, 1989).

[30] While my focus is different, my thinking about German émigrés and the opportunities that the Cold War opened up for them has been deeply influenced by Jeremi Suri's excellent *Henry Kissinger and the American Century*.

interactions. Yet the careers of these German émigrés demonstrate how such interactions did not undermine the American state's authority. On the contrary, the state became even more powerful by co-opting new actors for its own needs and goals.[31]

Finally, émigré influence was so profound because the mid-twentieth century was a time of extensive thinking about democracy. During the 1930s, the global Great Depression precipitated monumental and unprecedented threats to democracy. The economic catastrophe of the Depression, which brought about social upheaval and widespread misery, led to fears that elected institutions and the separation of power could not survive capitalism's failures. Moreover, the growing might and economic vitality of anti-democratic regimes in the 1930s, such as Italian Fascism, German Nazism, and Soviet Communism, seemed to confirm the inferiority of democracy and liberal-capitalism. The political scientist Pendleton Herring spoke for many when he nervously wondered in 1940: "Can our government meet the challenge of totalitarianism and remain democratic?"[32]

The shock of the Great Depression was quickly followed by the unprecedented mobilization of World War II and the threat of permanent conflict that came with the Cold War. Many Americans deeply feared these shifts, which demanded constant sacrifices from civilians, entailed ongoing confrontation with "subversive" enemies, and dramatically expanded the reach and responsibilities of the American state. In particular, they were concerned that, faced with the existential threat of the Cold War, democratic institutions would morph into a "garrison state" focused on a constant mobilization and militarization that would ruin the democratic and capitalist American values that it purported to protect. This anxiety over democracy's fragility generated substantial debates about the mechanisms that would guarantee its survival. Many U.S. leaders, scholars, and intellectuals sought to fashion new norms, institutions, and ideas that could enhance and protect American democracy. What constituted a healthy democratic regime was thus thrown open to debate.[33]

[31] On the cooperation between the State Department and independent groups, see, for example, Helen Laville and Hugh Wilford (eds.), *The U.S. Government, Citizen Groups, and the Cold War: The State-Private Network* (London: Routledge, 2006). On the rise of state power in the United States during World War II, see James T. Sparrow, *Warfare State: World War II Americans and the Age of Big Government* (New York: Oxford University Press, 2011). I discuss this issue in further detail throughout the book, and especially in chapters I and III. For the role of non-state actors during the Cold War, see Akira Iriye, *Global Community: The Role of International Organizations in the Making of the Contemporary World* (Berkeley: University of California Press, 2002); Nick Cullather, *The Hungry World* (Cambridge, MA: Harvard University Press, 2010).

[32] E. Pendleton Herring, *Presidential Leadership* (New York: Farrar and Rinehart, 1940), x.

[33] For a vivid description of these debates from the New Deal through the Cold War, see Ira Katznelson's magisterial *Fear Itself: The New Deal and the Origins of Our Time* (New York: Liveright, 2012). For a focus on the Cold War, see Michael J. Hogan, *A Cross of Iron: Harry Truman*

In this atmosphere of uncertainty, Friedrich, Fraenkel, Gurian, Loewenstein, and Morgenthau had much to offer. From Weimar they brought comprehensive theories on democracy and its enemies, institutional models for democratic education, and personal histories of living through democracy and its destruction. Many Americans saw these experiences as instrumental to their own quest to strengthen democracy. In the writings and narratives of German émigrés, they found helpful models for democratic renewal. During the 1930s and early 1940s, these émigrés' efforts concentrated on the United States' domestic sphere. Some German émigrés—especially Carl J. Friedrich—helped restructure U.S. bureaucracy and education in response to the Great Depression. But it was the outbreak of World War II, the reconstruction efforts that ensued in Europe and Asia, and the beginning of the Cold War that rendered the ideas of the émigrés especially influential. Their writings all sought to show how democracy and anti-Communist mobilization were not antithetical to each other but were, in fact, complementary processes. Both at home and abroad, U.S. leaders and diplomats sought their advice and invested substantial authority in them.

The intersection between Weimar democratic theory and U.S. diplomacy thus sheds light on the role of democracy in the early Cold War. Scholars of the era have frequently downplayed the United States' commitment to democracy at home and overseas. While American leaders and diplomats may indeed have been interested in democracy in the early years of occupying Germany and Japan, historians maintain that this interest was soon replaced by a focus on anti-Communist mobilization. In this narrative, American policymakers concluded that democracy provided an opening for subversive forces which, once in power, would dismantle Cold War alliances and even turn against the United States. It was therefore legitimate to limit democratic freedom and support authoritarian and despotic leaders in the name of anti-Communist security.[34]

Yet the intense attention paid to German émigrés and their theories demonstrates that American diplomats, scholars, philanthropists, and political leaders were often convinced that democracy played a crucial role in their domestic and international anti-Communist crusade. As historian Jennifer M. Miller has shown, they believed that effective anti-Communist mobilization required the willing consent of strong and vibrant societies,

---

and the Origins of the National Security State (Cambridge: Cambridge University Press, 1998); Melvyn Leffler, *A Preponderance of Power: National Security, the Truman Administration, and the Cold War* (Stanford: Stanford University Press, 1992).

[34] For representative works, see, for example, the essays in Ellen Schreck (ed.), *Cold War Triumphalism* (New York: New Press, 2004); Greg Grandin, *Empire's Workshop* (New York: Metropolitan, 2006). On how this point of view led several politicians and policymakers to claim that public participation in policymaking should be limited not only abroad but also in the United States itself, see Daniel Bessner, *The Rise of the Defense Intellectual: Hans Speier and the Transatlantic Origins of Cold War Foreign Policy* (Ithaca: Cornell University Press, forthcoming).

which could not be achieved exclusively through the coercive authority of dictators. To be sure, these aggressive American efforts to instill their version of democratic norms did not stem from benevolence. American leaders' conceptions of democracy rarely translated into a desire to build egalitarian societies or to empower people at the grassroots. Drawing on the émigrés' dualistic ideas, their visions of democracy were rigid, fixated on stability, and tragically paranoid. Like the architects of Germany's reconstruction, many Americans were convinced that those who challenged their militant understanding of democracy were necessarily cunning Communists, and they did not hesitate to vigilantly limit their rights at home or abroad, employing brutal violence. But it is impossible to fully comprehend their hysterical conduct and their conception of American self-interest without considering these genuine debates regarding democracy, their limits, and failures. Precisely because they inspired such disturbing actions and remained a crucial force in shaping policy, they must be fully understood.[35]

In the process of absorbing these German émigrés, the apparatus of American power did not remain unaltered. While German émigrés worked to promote and expand American power around the world, they also utilized their positions to implement and promote their own agendas. German émigrés drew on their earlier writings when they provided the language and ideas for the United States' global mission. The anti-Soviet "theory of totalitarianism," the theory of "militant democracy," and many other dominant Cold War concepts embraced by Americans were coined by Germans years before the global conflict with the Soviet Union had begun. Essentially, the agents who provided the language of democratization in West Germany were also instrumental in shaping the language of anti-Communist mobilization. Through their writings, these two intellectual projects became inseparable and inherently connected to each other. The symbiosis of German thought and American power shaped not only postwar Germany's reconstruction. It crossed the Atlantic and helped fashion American institutions, language, and self-understandings.[36]

These multidirectional influences offer a more nuanced portrait of Cold War politics, not only as a projection of American power but also as the

---

[35] My thinking about the place of democracy in the Cold War is deeply shaped by Jennifer M. Miller's work on this topic and on the role of democracy in the shaping of the U.S.-Japanese alliance. See her *Contested Alliance: The United States, Japan, and Democracy in the Cold War* (Cambridge, MA: Harvard University Press, forthcoming).

[36] Several scholars have begun to uncover the continuities between interwar-era central European theories and the Cold War paradigm, although these remain largely confined to a single individual or concept. The most important of these is Malachi Haim Hacohen's pioneering work, *Karl Popper, the Formative Years, 1902–1945: Politics and Philosophy in Interwar Vienna* (Cambridge: Cambridge University Press, 2000). See also William David Jones, *The Lost Debate: German Socialist Intellectuals and Totalitarianism* (Urbana: University of Illinois Press, 1999).

absorption and revival of European ideas and traditions. Although anxieties about communism were certainly crucial in shaping American thought and policy, the Cold War was more than an anti-Communist crusade. By uncovering the diverse ideological forces that drove American actions, historians have recently come to understand Cold War policies as the continuation and expansion of earlier American traditions, such as the spreading consumer culture, visions of "civilization," religious ideologies, and belief in progressive "development."[37] Alongside these forces, however, German thought and political traditions played a part in molding American Cold War hegemony. The writings and actions of German émigrés created an important channel through which the United States' engagement with the world returned to the United States itself. Their stories reflect how the global conflict was not merely a clash between polarized opponents that drew the world into its magnetic fields. It was also a space for the renewal and pursuit of European intellectual traditions, enabling foreign actors to shape the world.

In part, then, this is a book about the foreign impulses at the heart of the "American Century" and their role in charting the ideological and institutional contours of American global power after 1945. The stories of German émigrés do not by any means encapsulate all or even the most important forces that shaped U.S. outreach in the postwar era. But they do help to better understand the role of international experiences, the state, and democracy in this global conflict. They show how the Cold War provided unexpected opportunities to non-Americans, who had their own plans and goals. Through the institutions of U.S. power, they pursued intellectual projects that preceded the Cold War and were independent of American geopolitical considerations. German émigrés were always servants of U.S. institutions. Their influence both at home and abroad depended on the consent of their American superiors. Yet by injecting their own ideas into the Cold War, they made "the American Century" their own. In short, they made it also "the Weimar Century."

---

[37] On the role of consumer culture and free-market capitalism, see Victoria de Grazia, *Irresistible Empire: America's Advance through Twentieth-Century Europe* (Cambridge, MA: Belknap Press of Harvard University Press, 2005). On religious ideas, see Jonathan P. Herzog, *The Spiritual-Industrial Complex: American's Religious Battle against Communism in the Early Cold War* (New York: Oxford University Press, 2011). On the role of "development" and progressive ideas, see David Ekbladh, *The Great American Mission: Modernization and the Construction of an American World Order* (Princeton: Princeton University Press, 2010); and David Engerman, *Modernization from the Other Shore: American Intellectuals and the Romance of Russian Development* (Cambridge, MA: Harvard University Press, 2004).

CHAPTER I

The Search for "Responsible Elites"

CARL J. FRIEDRICH AND THE REFORM OF HIGHER EDUCATION

WHEN U.S. OCCUPATION FORCES ARRIVED in Germany in 1945, they confronted the daunting task of thoroughly rebuilding German thought and culture. After twelve long years of Nazi dictatorship, Americans believed that Germans needed not only new political institutions but also new values and norms to prevent them from reverting to violence and war. Nazism, however, had permeated every aspect of Germany society. Its racist and militarist ideology penetrated books, movies, art, and all major cultural institutions. Nowhere was this more apparent than in Germany's universities. In the late nineteenth and early twentieth centuries, Germany had built the most extensive and prestigious university system in Europe. Its scientists, political thinkers, and scholars drew admiration from around the world. By 1945, however, German universities were thoroughly Nazified, either by coercion or through professors' enthusiastic support for the Third Reich. The country's most renowned centers of thought had given their massive research, publishing, and teaching apparatus over to the service of Nazism's racist ideology, war, and genocide. In their mission to reshape German culture, U.S. diplomats, educators, and philanthropists thus stormed the campuses of Heidelberg, Munich, Göttingen, and the rest of Germany's institutions of higher education. They ushered in a plethora of new democratic curricula, research projects, and international student-exchange programs, seeking to instill values that would transform the postwar German state into a stable and peaceful democracy.

The U.S. occupation authorities did not focus on German universities solely to displace the Nazis, though this was a central goal. Rather, they saw higher education as the solution to a fundamental conundrum of democratizing Germany: how to build a stable democratic system that would not again fall prey to mass movements or charismatic dictators? In their eyes, the answer was the cultivation of new democratic elites, who had the breadth of knowledge, the skills, and the vision to manage democracy in the interests of the people. For U.S. authorities, universities were key to creating a democratic managerial class that would mold Germany's future and prevent a return to aggressive militarism. In this elitist conception of democracy, German universities had to quickly train thousands of teachers, bureaucrats, doctors, and lawyers and inculcate in them new values of peaceful political norms. These new norms, in turn, would trickle down to the rest of the population and foster democratic consensus. As economist and Rockefeller Foundation official Joseph Willits put it, "German universities ... [which] train talented individuals for active leadership in society, will shape the conditions, for good or ill, and the leaders of whatever new German society may emerge."[1]

In contrast to many scholars' claims, however, the educational revolution brought by the U.S. occupation was not merely an American response to war.[2] Rather, the massive reorganization of German higher education also resurrected intellectual programs, educational institutions, and international networks from the 1920s. The best embodiment of this continuation was the Calvinist political theorist Carl J. Friedrich. As a young intellectual in Heidelberg, Friedrich developed a highly idiosyncratic and pro-democratic theory of religion and politics. As part of his attempt to mobilize German Protestants in support of the Weimar Republic, he argued that democracy emerged from German Protestant Christianity, and specifically German Calvinism. Germany therefore had to join a democratic alliance with other Protestant republics, especially the United States. In this narrative, democracy was based not on individual rights and liberalism but on peaceful cooperation between Christian communities. Like the Calvinist concept of the "covenant"—a voluntary association of people—democracy drew from the people's consent. In Friedrich's vision, however, the people did not represent themselves. Rather, democracy was dependent on "responsible" elites who guided and represented these political communities. While "ordinary" people could easily fall prey to the pull of mass movements or charismatic leaders, which would destroy the covenant, well-trained and highly educated leaders would defy extremist politics to act in the broader interests of society. Democracy, then, was the work of elites who defended freedom from its reckless, plebian enemies.

Before World War II, Friedrich had claimed that the stability of democracy relied on higher education: German universities needed to support the Weimar Republic and train the responsible elite necessary for democracy.

---

[1] Joseph H. Willits, Report on Germany (24 May 1950), Folder 39, Box 7, Series 717, RG 1.1, Rockefeller Foundation Archive [hereafter referred to as RFA], Rockefeller Archive Center, Sleepy Hollow, NY [hereafter referred to as RAC].

[2] The most comprehensive works on the United States' role and de-Nazification during the occupation are Konstantin von Freytag-Loringhoven's monumental *Erziehung im Kollegienhaus: Reformbestrebungen an den deutschen Universitäten der amerikanischen Besatzungszone, 1945–1960* (Stuttgart: Steiner, 2012), and James Tent, *Mission on the Rhine: Reeducation and Denazification in American-Occupied Germany* (Chicago: University of Chicago Press, 1982). On U.S. influence on German higher education during and after the occupation, see Stefan Paulus, *Vorbild USA? Amerikanisierung von Universität und Wissenschaft in Westdeutschland, 1945–1976* (Munich: Oldenbourg, 2010).

During the 1920s, this was an exceptional vision among German academics. Since most professors and students came from conservative backgrounds and detested the new Weimar Republic, German universities were hubs of nationalist and anti-democratic fervor. Friedrich, however, sought to transform these centers of knowledge and teaching into an organ of the democratic state. In a series of bold endeavors, he founded educational institutions, curricula, and academic exchange programs in Heidelberg designed to create a democratic elite. As part of his goal to reform German academia, Friedrich fostered an unexpected alliance between American philanthropists from the Rockefeller Foundation, Weimar politicians, and German academics.

These visions and networks of elite democratic education did not collapse with Weimar in 1933. Rather, they also helped facilitate the epochmaking transformation of American higher education. After moving to the United States in 1926, Friedrich drew on the same top-down political visions to bring about unprecedented cooperation between American universities and the U.S. government. Throughout the 1930s and 1940s, he taught at Harvard University, where he re-created the programs and curricula that he had first developed in Heidelberg. Together with German and American educators and philanthropists he had come to know in Germany, Friedrich established a series of programs and institutions that included Harvard's Graduate School for Public Administration and later the School of Overseas Administration. These endeavors brought together policymakers, academics, and Rockefeller Foundation officials to train young men in the service of the U.S. government, military, and intelligence communities. This blurring of the boundaries between academia and state policy would become the norm during the early Cold War. Scholars continued to voluntarily cooperate with diplomats, policymakers, and intelligence officials, conducting research that would aid the struggle against domestic and international communism. Friedrich helped provide the language for this revolution. His writings explained why universities' cooperation with the state and voluntary suppression of Communist dissent were not a threat to academic freedom but essential for democracy. As in Heidelberg, American universities were not a site to critically assess the use of state power; rather, they were to serve as an organ of the state to train responsible democratic elites.

It was the same ideas and networks that Friedrich brought back to Germany after World War II. In the postwar era, his claim that democracy required responsible elites resonated with Americans and West Germans anxious to move beyond the trauma of Nazism. This was especially true during the 1950s, when fears of fascism were replaced by anxieties about Communist expansion. With the support of the Rockefeller Foundation, German intellectuals, and U.S. diplomats, Friedrich helped retool German higher education for the training of this elite. By resurrecting democratic curricula, research agendas, and exchange programs that he founded in Weimar and then expanded at Harvard, he helped transform West German universities into organs of the transatlantic alliance and anti-Communist mobilization. This time, German-American cooperation had lasting legacies. Rather than remaining an exception in German higher education, Friedrich's curricula, political theory, and exchange programs became the norm in postwar education. Like their counterparts in the United States, West German universities developed into organs of Cold War thought and politics. What was once on the margins of Weimar thought became the center of postwar order.

Protestant Legitimacy and Elite Education in Heidelberg

When the democratic revolution swept Germany in the fall of 1918, German Protestants reacted with shock, anger, and disbelief. Traditionally the most ardent supporters of German nationalism and imperialism, Germany's majority Protestant population had long associated the Protestant monarchy with their own "natural" hegemony in German life. In their eyes, democracy, with its political equality and seeming disregard for traditional authority, was a tool of foreign enemies, especially the French, to destroy Christianity and divide the German nation. This hostility toward democratic norms only intensified as the Weimar revolution seemed to realize Protestants' worst fears. After the first elections empowered a coalition of Socialists, Catholics, and liberals—all equally hated by Protestants—the new republic dismantled the imperial bond between "throne and altar" by removing Protestantism as the state religion. Protestant intellectuals and politicians responded by repeatedly attacking the Weimar Republic as a monstrous, secular, and foreign assault on German Christianity. As Lutheran theologian Emanuel Hirsch wrote, "Christian love ... must resist a democratic regime." Throughout Weimar's short existence, most Protestants flocked to nationalist right-wing parties and openly hoped the republic would be replaced by an authoritarian form of government. Their fierce opposition remained Weimar's Achilles heel.[3]

---

[3] On the intellectual and theological opposition to the republic, see Kurt Flasch, *Die geistige Mobilmachung: Die deutschen Intellektuellen und der Erste Weltkrieg* (Berlin: Alexander Fest Verlag, 2000); Jochen Jackem, *Kirche zwischen Monarchie und Republik: Der preussische Protestantismus nach dem Zusammenbruch von 1918* (Hamburg: Christians, 1976). On Protestants' political opposition, see Maik Ohnezeit, *Zwischen "Schärfster Opposition" und dem "Willen zur Macht": die Deutsch-Nationale Volkspartei (DNVP) in der Weimarer Republik* (Düsseldorf: Droste, 2011). Emanuel Hirsch is cited in Klaus Tanner, "Protestant Revolt Against Modernity," in Rudy Ko-

Yet a small group of Protestant thinkers challenged this political consensus. Under the leadership of Protestant priest and politician Friedrich Naumann, theologians such as Ernst Troeltsch and Otto Baumgarten vocally supported the new republic. In their minds, democracy was an inevitable product of modern society and rising mass involvement in politics. Germany had to embrace this transformation or face never-ending clashes between the people and the state. As Troeltsch anxiously pleaded, only by allowing all citizens to participate in democratic politics could Germany avoid "a volcano of misery . . . and civil wars."[4] The most important of these Protestant intellectuals was the sociologist Max Weber. A towering figure in German political thought, Weber argued that republican regimes were the best mechanism to ensure that leaders adhered to "the ethics of responsibility." He believed that the catastrophe of World War I had stemmed from the romantic and irresponsible tendencies that permeated the entire German political system and drove it to reckless political adventures. He therefore asserted that political institutions should facilitate the rise of talented and responsible leaders, who by the power of their natural charisma would guide the people through the "diabolical" temptations of politics. Despite his elitist distrust of the masses, which he shared with most German Protestants, Weber claimed that the electoral process was more likely to bring charismatic and responsible leaders to power than a hereditary monarchy. Before his untimely death in 1920, Weber institutionalized these ideas by participating in the drafting of the Weimar Constitution and by helping secure a strong executive branch. During the early 1920s, his followers worked to build Protestant support for the republic. Despite their small numbers, they remained among Weimar's most important architects and defenders.[5]

This dual campaign to recruit German Protestants in support of the republic and to produce "responsible" democratic elites stood at the core of Friedrich's early work. Born to a middle-class Calvinist family from Dresden, Friedrich began his career in Heidelberg, at Germany's oldest and most prestigious university. There he joined a group of ambitious young thinkers, such as Alexander Rüstow and Arnold Bergstraesser, who gathered around Alfred Weber, Max's younger brother and a renowned sociologist in his own right. Like his older brother, Alfred Weber was convinced that democ-

shar (ed.), *The Weimar Moment: Liberalism, Political Theology, and Law* (New York: Lexington, 2012), 3–16, here 8.

[4] Ernst Troeltsch, "Die deutsche Demokratie," in Hans Baron (ed.), *Spektatortriefe: Aufsätze über die deutsche Revolution und die Weltpolitik* (Tübingen: Mohr, 1924), 301–313, here 304.

[5] On the pro-democratic Protestants, see Bill Frye, *Liberal Democrats in the Weimar Republic* (Carbondale: Southern Illinois University Press, 1985). For Weber's theory of leadership, see Max Weber, *The Vocation Lectures* (Indianapolis: Hackett, 2004). On Weber and democracy, see Peter Breiner, *Max Weber and Democratic Politics* (Ithaca: Cornell University Press, 1996).

racy was the ultimate facilitator of elitist "creative genius." His students, who embraced the republic, became known as members of the "Weber School." During the Weimar period, Friedrich served as Weber's closest disciple and assistant, and in 1930 he completed his PhD dissertation on American politics and economy under Weber's supervision. After moving to the United States to accept a job offer in 1926, he began lecturing at Harvard University, but he remained involved in Heidelberg's programs and committed to Weber's political mission. Throughout the Weimar era, Friedrich expanded on Weber's pro-republic intellectual project as both a theoretician and an educator. He crafted a new theory on the republic's Protestant origins and helped establish a network of educational programs to train "responsible" democratic elites. The Nazis would abruptly crush these efforts in 1933. But the early ideas, networks, and organizations that stemmed from the "Weber School" would provide the blueprint for intellectual transformations in the decades to come.[6]

Friedrich's efforts to strengthen the Weimar Republic began by crafting a new political theory that framed democracy as the realization of Christian principles. Recasting Protestants' belief in their self-evident superiority, he claimed that Protestantism's genius was best reflected not in monarchy, but in republican institutions. According to Friedrich, the Weimar-era parliamentary system had not emerged from the secular Enlightenment and the anti-religious French Revolution, as most Protestants believed. Rather, its origins lay in the unique traditions of Calvinist Christianity first developed in German-speaking central Europe in the sixteenth and seventeenth centuries. It was no accident, Friedrich wrote, that "the centers of democracy are countries with a predominantly Calvinist tradition," such as "Switzerland, the United States, and Holland," rather than revolutionary France. There was an organic connection between Calvinism and democratic politics. By establishing an unexpected narrative that rooted the republic in the Calvinist creed, Friedrich believed he could dismantle Protestant objections to Weimar and channel their political energies toward democratic participation. He further hoped to guide German Protestants, who were mostly staunch nationalists, toward international cooperation with other democracies.[7]

---

[6] On Alfred Weber and his disciples, see Colin Loader, *Alfred Weber and the Crisis of Culture, 1890–1933* (New York: Palgrave Macmillan, 2012); Eberhard Demm, *Von der Weimarer Republik zur Bundesrepublik: Der politische Weg Alfred Webers, 1920–1958* (Düsseldorf: Droste, 1999). The biographical information on Friedrich is based on appointment records (15 September 1925) B-66801/1, IV, 3d, Nr. 22b, Universitätsarchiv der Ruprecht-Karls-Universität Heidelberg [hereafter referred to as UAH]; and on Hans J. Lietzmann, *Politikwissenschaft im Zeitalter der Diktatur: Die Entwicklung der Totalitarismustheorie Carl J. Friedrichs* (Opladen: Leske+Budrcih, 1999), 29–46.

[7] Carl J. Friedrich, preface to *Politica Methodice Digesta, Reprinted from the Third Edition of 1614*, by Johannes Althusius (Cambridge, MA: Harvard University Press, 1932), xvii.

At the center of this democratic genealogy, Friedrich placed the work of German Calvinist political theorist Johannes Althusius (1563–1638). A prominent lawyer in the independent German-speaking city of Emden, Althusius published a series of books on politics, religion, and law. While his writings received some attention during the imperial era, by the Weimar period he was largely forgotten and his works were out of print.[8] In Friedrich's eyes, however, Althusius was a giant of modern political and religious thought, "the clearest and most profound thinker which Calvinism has produced in the realm of political science and jurisprudence." For Friedrich, Althusius was the first to explain that political authority stemmed from the people, not from the monarchy, and that Protestant convictions were best embodied in republican regimes. In 1926 Friedrich embarked on a mission to restore Althusius and his ideas to the center of Western political theory. After long years of collecting rare copies, in 1932 he published a new version of Althusius's monumental 1614 *Politica Methodice Digesta* (Systematic analysis of politics). In a long introduction, Friedrich argued that Althusius's "Calvinist cosmology" opened the path to modern democracy. The seventeenth-century theoretician, he emphasized, explained democratic institutions "[i]n terms of [a] Protestant ethic" rather than by way of the hated French Enlightenment "humanitarianism."[9]

The goal of Althusius's theory was to establish a federal political regime: a system based on a *foedus*, the Latin word for "covenant," the spiritual bond between God and people. According to Althusius, the goal of politics was to create and maintain covenants between humans. These social and political agreements would be analogous to biblical covenants, such as that between God and Noah, or between God and the people of Israel. Unlike monarchies, these biblical bonds rested on citizen consent. Just as the people of Israel *chose* to enter into a covenant with God, people in the modern political era were free to enter as partners into a political bond. Althusius assumed that given the choice, every individual would voluntarily join a covenant instead of submitting to monarchical authority. He thus radically argued that political authority belonged not to the ruler but to the people. The right of sovereignty "does not belong to individual members, but to all members joined together.... [The state] can be constituted not by one

---

[8] Otto von Gierke, *Johannes Althusius und die Entwicklung der naturrechtlichen Staatstheorien* (Breslau: Verlag von M. & H. Marcus, 1913).

[9] Friedrich, preface, xviii and xv. The commencement of the project is mentioned in Letter, Friedrich to Gustav Braun (4 December 1926), Folder Book Sellers, Box 5, Carl J. Friedrich Papers, Harvard University Archive [hereafter referred to as HUGFP] 17.6. At Friedrich's insistence, the book was printed not in the United States but in Germany, and Friedrich immediately initiated a German edition, a plan that failed to materialize due to the rise of Nazism the following year. Letter, Friedrich to Duncker & Humbolt Publishing House (8 December 1932), Folder 4, Box 2, HUGFP 17.6.

member, but by all the members together." Covenants were therefore based on associations, or groups, in which individuals came together to cooperate on public matters. The goal of political theory was to offer models for the creation of such associations. It was these associations, rather than the king, that possessed the ultimate authority to legislate and create law. Only a regime based on such groups could create a political community that was "holy, just, comfortable, and happy."[10]

According to Friedrich, this focus on the group as the source of political authority was a profound innovation, unique to the Calvinist psyche. It was the product of Calvin's concept of predestination, the belief that God has preselected some souls for salvation while others were condemned to eternal damnation. According to Friedrich, "the awful terror of being among the damned" led Calvinists to seek earthly signs that they were among the selected few. Max Weber, in his famous theory of capitalism, argued that Calvinists looked to economic success as a sign of their felicitous fate. Friedrich maintained that Calvinists also sought such signs in their participation in political affairs.[11] Only by contributing to the prosperity of the political community, they believed, could they hope to be among the elect. According to Friedrich, "[t]his shows why the orthodox Calvinist must consider this [political] life in the community ... as the only valuable one.... [In Calvinism,] the social or political function has a religious significance, so that each function is permeated by an intensely religious spirit." The Calvinists were the first to portray the maintenance of a peaceful, just, and egalitarian political community as a sign of divine grace. Politics were a way to fulfill one's religious duty.[12]

Writing for a Protestant audience, Friedrich further emphasized Althusius's argument that a political covenant based on five key associations, in which political authority lay with the people, would be the most peaceful and harmonious. Two were private associations: the family and the *collegium* (based on one's profession, or guild); and three were public: the town, the province, and the commonwealth. In Althusius's vision, each of the public associations would be ruled by a council populated by representatives of the lower association. The town council, for example, would include representatives of its families and *collegia*; the representatives of several towns, in turn, would comprise the provincial council. Each council would

[10] Quotations from Althusius's book are from the English translation, which was initiated by Friedrich in 1965 and republished in 1995. See Johannes Althusius, *Politica* (Indianapolis: Liberty Fund, 1995), 18, 21.

[11] According to Weber's famous theory, the Protestant ethic's encouragement of work, trade, and the accumulation of wealth was the main force behind the development of capitalism. Max Weber, "The Protestant Ethic and the 'Spirit' of Capitalism," in *The Protestant Ethic and the "Spirit" of Capitalism and Other Writings* (New York: Penguin Books, 2002), 1–202.

[12] Friedrich, preface, lxxix.

have the autonomy to legislate and shape its own covenant in ways acceptable to its members. At the apex of this structure is the state, or commonwealth, which would mediate the relationships between all the associations. "[T]he members of the realm, or of this universal association," wrote Althusius, "[will be] many cities, provinces, and regions agreeing among themselves on a single body constituted by mutual union and communication." In this decentralized design, power would be diffused among different levels and institutions, always open to negotiation and debate.[13]

In Friedrich's story, then, it was this Calvinist model, rather than secular humanism, that gave birth to modern constitutional democracy, both in Europe and the United States. Althusius's claim that political authority lay with the people and his call for peaceful political cooperation between groups remained the intellectual foundation for modern-day democratic politics. Friedrich argued that *Politica*'s vision of nesting covenants had ultimately evolved into the modern separation of powers, electoral processes, and parliamentary politics. All of these were anchored not in individual rights or national sovereignty but in Althusius's religious defense of the covenant. These ancient ideas had propelled Calvinists in England and the United States to establish constitutional regimes and, ultimately, democracies. A "very definite road," Friedrich firmly concluded, "leads from Althusius' concept of a cooperative group to American institutions."[14]

With the enthusiasm of a political missionary, Friedrich contended that unearthing modern democracy's Althusian roots provided three bases for legitimizing the Weimar Republic. First, Althusius's work revealed that the republican system was not the product of destructive secularization, as many German Protestants believed. Instead, it was the fulfillment of Christian thought. "Nothing shows as clearly" as Althusius's work, Friedrich wrote, "that a ... cooperative commonwealth, a democracy, can last only among men motivated by Christianity." The republic preserved the noble Calvinist conviction that political authority lay in consenting communities, not in hereditary monarchy. Replicating his Protestant milieu's exclusionary vision of politics, Friedrich argued that the rise of democracy did not challenge Protestants' spiritual superiority. Rather than undermining their intellectual and religious hegemony, it reaffirmed and expressed their unique values in new political forms.[15]

---

[13] Althusius, *Politica*, 67.

[14] Friedrich, preface, lxxiv, xix. Similar arguments, which traced the institutions of American democracy to Calvinist theology and social norms, were presented by Alexis de Tocqueville a century earlier, in his famous study *Democracy in America*, although Friedrich did not refer to these in his own writings. Barbara Allen, *Tocqueville, Covenant, and the Democratic Revolution* (Lanham: Lexington Books, 2005).

[15] Friedrich, preface, lxxxii–lxxxiii.

Second, Althusius showed that political *groups*, and not individuals, were the foundation of political authority. Parties, labor unions, and political associations—and not an authoritarian leader like the German kaiser—could build a covenant. Friedrich consistently warned that *only* such a group of people could fulfill the spirit of a covenant. "[T]he group ... is composed of members, and these members together possess ... the unity of the group. Only what they jointly decide can be considered a realization of the collective unity of the group." The decentralized structure of the parliamentary system therefore did not embody destructive individualist liberalism. Rather, democracy was based on unified religious communities, which German Protestants cherished. Covenants and republics thus *weakened* individualism by strengthening communal bonds. In the "inclusive groups" that democratic life encouraged, "the individual tends to disappear," to become one with the community. Friedrich argued that the political concepts which undergirded the republic, such as equal political rights for all, were "not in any sense an individual right ... [but] rooted in the group.... This sort of idea has little to do with such ideas as the 'natural rights of man.'" The institutions of the republic, therefore, were not inherently tied to the ideologies of Western liberalism. German Protestants could embrace them even while rejecting secularism and individualism.[16]

Finally, Althusius's work provided Friedrich with intellectual proof that the Weimar Republic was not a foreign implant forced on Germany by its Western liberal enemies. According to Friedrich's narrative, democracy sprouted on German soil, formed by independent cities like Emden, decades before other nations embraced it. Althusius's theory had emerged organically from such early modern German city-states as Frankfurt and Nuremberg. These cities had been the first to develop the "complex institutions that are reflected in the theoretical propositions which Althusius expounds." The establishment of a republic in Germany therefore restored these home-grown traditions. After spreading to Britain and the United States with the Puritans, these traditions returned across the Atlantic to their German birthplace. As Friedrich stated in a lecture, the Weimar Constitution was the realization of German ideals. It should thus be "the source of pride of every German."[17]

Through this emphasis on the transnational flow of religious ideas, Friedrich also sought to bolster the Weimar government's search for peaceful international cooperation. The historical narrative Friedrich discovered

[16] Ibid., lxxiv–lxxv.

[17] The first quotation is from ibid., lxxiv. The second is from Manuscript, "Lecture on the German Constitution 1919" (1926), Folder the German Constitution of 1919, Box 8, HUGFP 17.60. This narrative appears also in Friedrich's "Deutsche Gedanken beim Aufbau des amerikanischen Staates," in Anton Erkelenz (ed.), *Carl Schurz: Der Deutsche und der Amerikaner* (Berlin: Sieben Verlag, 1929), 114–136.

in Althusius did not simply link Germany to its former Western enemies, especially the United States, through spiritual and intellectual affinities. Decades before the Cold War and West Germany's policies of "western integration," Friedrich argued that the two republics were part of an international, supranational covenant, which began in the seventeenth century and continued into the 1920s. In this internationalist vision, these two nations could deepen and strengthen their own democracies through cultural interaction. They had to join hands and establish a democratic alliance.

In seeking to guide German Protestants in a democratic crusade, Friedrich's thought challenged Protestant convictions while ironically reproducing some of their most exclusionary and anti-democratic sentiments. In its obsession with religiosity and an awkward historical genealogy, Friedrich's belief system reiterated an arrogant sense of Protestant superiority, elevating German Protestant history as the origin of celebrated political traditions. Friedrich's ideas adhered to Protestants' exclusionary image of themselves as the originators and defenders of all meaningful values, offering little room for German Catholics, Jews, or Socialists. They imposed strict limits on the possibility that other religions or secular ideas could ever generate productive political concepts. Yet at the same time, this thinking boldly challenged the Protestant political consensus. It was the most comprehensive attempt to reverse German Protestants' widespread hostility to the republic and to retool their religious and political identity toward an embrace of democracy. Even the few Protestants who supported Weimar, such as Alfred Weber or Ernst Troeltsch, did not see it as the full realization of Protestant traditions. In the following decades, Friedrich would slowly expand the scope of his ideas to include other religions as members of the democratic coalition. However, his idiosyncratic interweaving of religion, democracy, and Western international cooperation would remain at the core of his intellectual agenda and drive his energetic program building for years to come.

Responsible Elites and Higher Education

Friedrich's campaign to strengthen the Weimar Republic was not limited to his elevation of the Christian covenant. Equally important, he took part in broader debates about the role of leadership and education in a democratic society. Like most middle-class German Protestants, Friedrich and other members of the "Weber School" believed that the vast majority of citizens were unfit for leadership, lacking the knowledge and vision required for public office. As Friedrich acidly put it, Althusius himself, the father of democracy, recognized that "the average man" was "inconstant, violent, lacking in judgment, credulous, envious, wild, turbulent, seditious, frivolous, ungrateful, changeable, and aping those who govern." In light of this intense hostility toward "ordinary" people, the success of democracy rested on the ability of the covenant communities to produce visionary and responsible leaders. Althusius's vision of cooperating communities demanded that "learned men should govern states." These leaders, who pursued the community's interest on the local, regional, and national level, would help the masses transcend petty weaknesses and support the public good. Citizens could improve themselves through cooperation and public engagement, but it fell on leaders to navigate politics and help ordinary people choose the correct policies. Friedrich believed the creation of this elite was key to the survival of democracy, and this goal drove his institutional work in the Weimar years. In particular, he developed a decades-long fascination with democratic education and institution building, which led to the creation of some of Germany's most innovative educational programs. In Friedrich's eyes, a proper democratic education would instill the morality, ethics, and responsibility necessary to sustain a properly functioning covenant democracy.[18]

This patrician thinking drew from broader anxieties about "the masses" widely held by Germany's political and cultural elites. Since the nineteenth century, leading German politicians and intellectuals had feared that the growing involvement of ordinary citizens in politics threatened the "natural" order of society. The rise of mass politics threatened to destroy the influence of capable leaders and to subject politics to the domination of reckless, uneducated, and irresponsible crowds. These elitist anxieties were especially potent among the German Protestant middle class, which associated the "masses" with anti-religious Socialists. The hostility that many Protestants felt toward the Weimar Republic was thus fueled by their belief that democracy brought the irresponsible masses to power, especially the working class. Ernst Troeltsch spoke for many when he worried that Weimar's democratic system would bring "chaos and leveling . . . the artful spread of mediocrity that holds everything down." Alfred Weber, Friedrich's mentor, shared this disdain of the masses. Like his older brother, Max, his support of the republic stemmed from the belief that electoral politics would be better than the monarchy in bringing "responsible" leaders to power, who could tame the masses.[19]

In an attempt to mitigate these paralyzing fears, Friedrich argued that the training of a responsible and pro-democratic elite could counteract the dangers of the reckless masses and defend the covenant. In particular, it was crucial to train a cadre of unelected state officials, which Friedrich called a "responsible bureaucracy," who would use their position to balance the pres-

[18] Quotations are from Friedrich, preface, lxxi.

[19] The quotation is from Troeltsch, "The German Democracy," 90. These fears were of course widespread among many conservatives in Europe, and not only in Germany. For an overview, see Berghahn, *America and the Intellectual Cold Wars in Europe*, 77–91.

sures faced by elected politicians. Bureaucrats, unlike elected politicians, could transcend sectarian pressures. They could defend the integrity of the covenant by protecting the interests of *all* members of the community, not only those who won elections. In Friedrich's eyes, a "responsible bureaucracy" was necessary for covenant democracy. "Not only must we reject the idea that democracy is opposed to bureaucracy," he wrote, "but we must recognize that the future of democracy depends upon its ability to maintain a fully recognized bureaucracy."[20]

In this rigid vision, democracy was a top-down structure. Elites, not their constituencies, would guard the vigor of free interaction and develop ideal public policies. Politics and power had little room for the uncultivated masses; democracy was not designed to empower popular influence. Moreover, the purpose of electoral politics and free debate was to manufacture consensus, not to highlight fissures or disagreements. Leaders were necessary because only they could transcend the narrow emotionalism of the people and reach long-term and rational compromises. In Friedrich's Manichean thought, undermining the authority of unelected officials would thus not benefit the people, but lead them to the hands of uncompromising tyrants. "If popular government is incapable of maintaining a bureaucratic hierarchy," he scoffed, it is "bound to give way to dictatorship."[21]

The core model for the creation of this bureaucratic elite was found in Heidelberg. As a student of Alfred Weber, Friedrich found inspiration in the institution for political thought that Weber founded in 1918, where Friedrich both studied and later taught. During the 1920s, the vast majority of German academics—professors and students alike—remained hostile to democracy and the republic. Hoping for the return of the monarchy or the establishment of an authoritarian regime, German universities offered almost no education in democratic theory and history. Weber and his students were among the first to try strengthening the republic by designing a pro-republican teaching and research agenda. In the institute that Weber founded, members of the "Weber School"—including Friedrich—taught and researched democratic theory and history. In 1924 this institute became the Institut für Sozial- und Staatswissenschaften (Institute of Social and Political Science) and quickly became known by its acronym, InSoSta. Throughout the 1920s, InSoSta offered courses and facilitated research on German economics, political science, sociology, history, geography, and law, with the explicit intention of producing a skilled and democratically oriented elite. Thousands of students studied its curricula in preparation for careers in local and state-level administration. In 1924, for example, the

[20] Carl J. Friedrich, *Responsible Bureaucracy: A Study of the Swiss Civil Service* (New York: Russell and Russell, 1932), 14.
[21] Ibid., 28.

State of Baden's Ministry of Culture and Education endorsed the institute as the best center for training bureaucrats for the republic.[22]

To Friedrich, InSoSta's uniquely pro-democratic atmosphere both provided the model and served as the launching pad for a new educational vision. In his mind, InSoSta was to become the prototype for higher education across Germany, the heart of a new intellectual-political order. Only through robust democratic curricula and research could the covenantal democracy of the Weimar Republic find the responsible elite it needed to survive and thrive. The foremost role of academic education was not to foster the critique of power structures but to produce qualified state administrators, who by dint of judgment could balance the reckless conduct of elected politicians. Friedrich thus called for a close collaboration between the institutions of higher education and the democratic state. "[A] public school and university system," he wrote, "fulfills the function of integrating the educational agencies with the hierarchy" of the state apparatus.[23] Through rigorous curricula that explored democratic institutions, economics, and international cooperation, such as the programs offered at InSoSta, German universities could become the bastions of democratic stability. This was a vision that both affirmed and challenged German universities' self-perception. It maintained their elitist disdain for ordinary people but channeled their mission toward a new democratic mobilization.

What made InSoSta a crucial model for republican education, however, was not only the pro-democratic content of its courses but also its new institutional framework. Friedrich believed that the creation of a responsible elite could not to be left to state authorities or to the private market. Instead, it would be achieved through the cooperation of state officials, academics, and philanthropists, producing a hybrid matrix of thought and power. In 1920s Germany, this was a radically new idea. In both the imperial and Weimar eras, the state allowed some private investment in the fields of biology and chemistry but maintained a monopoly in designing education in law, political theory, and humanities. Friedrich therefore broke new ground by mobilizing philanthropic organizations and private benefactors to create a semi-independent academic center at InSoSta. Tapping into the

[22] The classic work on Germany's anti-democratic academic life remains Fritz K. Ringer, *The Decline of the German Mandarins* (Cambridge, MA: Harvard University Press, 1969). On InSoSta and Weber in general, see Reinhard Blomert, *Intellektuelle im Aufbruch* (Munich: Carl Hanser Verlag, 1999), and Reinhard Blomert (ed.), *Heidelberger Sozial- und Staatswissenschaften* (Marburg: Metropolis-Verlag, 1997). The statement on students taking classes as preparation for assuming positions in the state administration is from Memorandum, Dr. Gieseke to the Senate of the HU (17 November 1920), B-6680/1, IV, 3d, Nr. 22 g, UAH. The ministry's endorsement is in Letter, Ministry of Culture and Education in Baden to the Senate of the UH (23 May 1924), B-6680/1, IV, 3d, Nr. 22 g, UAH.

[23] Friedrich, *Responsible Bureaucracy*, 24.

networks of Alfred Weber's former students who were positioned across German industry, Friedrich promoted research projects on German politics and diplomacy and established dozens of courses on democratic political theory. The members of InSoSta were relentless in their search for new private donations. To Friedrich and InSoSta, the involvement of such wealth secured its independence from the state and, more importantly, linked the world of German industry and commerce with democratic education. This was to be the nucleus of a truly democratic German elite.[24]

InSoSta's most important support, however, did not come from private wealth in Germany. Rather, the institute's most energetic backers arrived from across the Atlantic, from the deep pockets of American philanthropists. Friedrich had long believed that Americans realized Althusius's vision of covenantal democracy, a regime based on the consent of the people, decentralized power, and cooperation between groups. Americans had an extensive tradition of successfully building the institutions and norms that the Weimar Republic had only begun to create. Friedrich therefore believed that American educators and philanthropists were natural allies in fostering democratic education and responsible elites in Germany.

With the arrival of the Rockefeller Foundation, these hopes for American support soon became reality. Founded in 1913, the Rockefeller Foundation sought to promote global cooperation and advance scientific education after World War I. In 1924, after several years of deliberations, its officers turned their attention to Germany. They sought to invest in institutions that would promote international understanding, democratization, and peace, which the foundation officers regarded as inherently intertwined. Through Friedrich, InSoSta became the gateway for this bold foreign intervention. In 1924 economist and Rockefeller Foundation officer John V. Van Sickle met Friedrich in New York, and then Alfred Weber and Arnold Bergstraesser in Heidelberg. Following these meetings, the foundation began to support InSoSta's activities with generous funding, hoping that its graduates would enhance republican institutions and would create similar endeavors across Germany. Decades before the 1940s and the creation of the Western Cold War alliance, a connection emerged between German democrats and American philanthropists.[25]

[24] Memorandum, JVS [John V. Van Sickle] visit to Heidelberg (13 May 1931), Folder 195, Box 21, Series 717S, RG 1.1, Rockefeller Foundations Archive [hereafter referred to as RFA], Rockefeller Archive Center [hereafter referred to as RAC]. Letter, InSoSta to the Ministry of Culture and Education Baden (9 August 1927); Letter, Josefine and Eduard von Portheim-Stiftung für Wissenschaft und Kunst, to the HU Senate (10 October 1927); both at B-6680/1, IV, 3d, Nr. 22 g, UAH.

[25] The information is based on Memorandum, JVS [John V. Van Sickle] visit to Heidelberg (13 May 1931), Folder 195, Box 21, Series 717S, RG 1.1, RFA, RAC. For more on the Rockefeller Foundation, its history, and especially its activities in Germany, see chapter III. On other at-

Throughout the 1920s, the Rockefeller Foundation's investment in In-SoSta increased exponentially. At first, the foundation helped InSoSta open a center for Anglo-American studies in Heidelberg, which offered courses on British and American democratic institutions, economy, and legal systems. These were the very first German programs for the study of English-speaking democracies. Within a few years, the foundation funded visits of InSoSta members for lectures in the United States, publication of the institution's books, and visits of American scholars to Heidelberg. It also backed the expansion of the institute's curricula to hire more assistants and expand its class offerings. Even when German politics fell into disarray during the Great Depression, one of the foundation's most senior officers concluded that "the decision to invest . . . [in InSoSta] has been an excellent one. . . . The Institute draws its student body from all over Germany so that its influence is nationwide." Through InSoSta, Heidelberg became the first locus of a pro-democratic symbiosis, in which German scholars and American wealth cooperated to promote a mutual agenda.[26]

Sensing that InSoSta was a striking success, the foundation expanded its intervention in German higher education and spread among an entire galaxy of new academic centers that promoted international understanding. After visiting Heidelberg, Rockefeller Foundation officials traveled to and invested in the Academy of Politics in Berlin, the Hamburg Institute of International Affairs, and the Kiel Institute for World Economy, all academic institutions that supported or were tolerant of the republic. Throughout the Weimar era, the foundation also sought to expand the InSoSta model by funding dozens of other smaller institutions and projects. It financed research and training programs in finance in Bonn, statistics in Leipzig, and international finance in Cologne. Rockefeller officials helped found an institute for the study of the modern press in Berlin, seminars on economic theory in Frankfurt, an institute of law and international law in Berlin, and an institute of international law in Cologne. By the time the republic collapsed in 1933, the foundation had poured over $1.5 million into Germany, its largest donation worldwide. Friedrich's belief in the inherent bond between German and American democracy thus played a key part in inaugurating new international interactions. These wide collabora-

---

tempts by German scholars to utilize U.S. philanthropic donations in order to promote their own educational agendas, see Malcolm Richardson, Jürgen Reulecke, and Frank Trommler, *Weimars transatlantischer Mäzen: Die Lincoln-Stiftung 1927 bis 1934* (Essen: Klartext, 2008).

[26] The information on the Anglo-American Studies is from Report, Entwurf zur Stiftungsurkunde des Anglo-Amerikanischen Institutes an der Universität Heidelberg (undated, probably winter 1924), B-6680/1, IV, 3d, Nr. 22 g (InSoSta, 1920–1929), UAH. The quotation is from Memorandum, JVS [John V. Van Sickle] visit to Heidelberg (13 May 1931), Folder 195, Box 21, Series 717S, RG 1.1, RFA, RAC.

tions would be the blueprint for similar educational programming after World War II.[27]

The crown jewel of InSoSta's projects was the creation of a new and bold experiment: an international academic exchange program. True to his internationalist vision, Friedrich believed that the future German elite was in desperate need of interaction with other countries, especially with the United States. Through exchange programs, future German leaders and bureaucrats would mingle with other elites, strengthening international stability and forging a transnational covenant. By participating in the building of an international bond, this German elite would bring home a new sensitivity for cooperation and peaceful negotiations, which would translate into supporting democratic politics. Friedrich envisioned a new form of diplomacy, in which scholars worked alongside diplomats and business leaders to import, adopt, and transfer democratic techniques of government. As with his thinking about domestic governance, this was a narrow and hierarchical vision where ordinary citizens played only a marginal role in forming policies. The vast majority of the people, especially the poor and uneducated, had nothing to contribute to politics, international bonding, or diplomacy. For Friedrich, only such an elite program could "go beyond passive pacifism and nationalism" to establish an international order of stability and peace. Just as elites were to produce consensus at home, they were to be the agents of peace abroad.[28]

Efforts to erect this international order first took institutional shape in 1922, when Friedrich and fellow members of the "Weber School," Alexander Rüstow and Arnold Bergstraesser, sought to bring together German and American students and faculty. These academics, they envisioned, would spend a year in a foreign country, learn its language and its governmental system, and forge social bonds with future elites. The creation of this experimental program involved all the major agents, institutions, and organs that defined InSoSta's unique structure—the German government, American philanthropists, and German universities. Eager to restore its reputation as an internationally esteemed seat of learning, the University of Heidelberg quickly agreed to host the exchange program. German state officials, too, backed this agenda, believing they would help stabilize the republic and break the diplomatic isolation that followed its defeat in World

[27] Report on the Rockefeller Foundation's Investment in Social Sciences in Germany (9 August 1932), Folder 36; and Annual Report, RF Appropriations in Germany (27 June 1933); Folder 37; John V. Van Sickle, Report on the Rockefeller Foundation's Activities in Germany (22 June 1933), Folder 36; all in Box 7, Series 717, RG 1.1, RFA, RAC.

[28] Quoted in Carl J. Friedrich, Report, "Der akademische Austauschdienst 1924–1926" (1926), B-8245/1, IX, 7, Nr. 34, UAH. The rest of the information is from Report, "Studie für Ausländer auf französische Schulen" (September 1920), B-0680/1, VII, 1, Nr. 83, UAH.

War I. Despite devastating hyperinflation and economic chaos, in 1923 both the State of Baden and the federal government in Berlin agreed to support this program despite shrinking resources. From the United States, Friedrich secured the support of the Institute of International Education (IIE), a philanthropic organization funded by the Rockefeller Foundation. After the institution's director, Stephen Duggan, visited Heidelberg in 1924, he reported to the Rockefeller Foundation that such an exchange program would be the best way to combat "the monarchist and reactionary element [that] is still in control of higher education in Germany." Following this desperate plea, the foundation contributed more than $20,000 to provide fellowships and traveling expenses for German students to come to the United States. Major figures in American education, such as philosopher John Dewey and political theorist Charles Merriam, also volunteered to take part in the program.[29]

In 1924, then, Heidelberg inaugurated a new era of democratic cultural diplomacy when it launched the first modern student exchange program, the Deutscher Akademischer Austauschdienst (DAAD), in cooperation with Cornell, Columbia, Yale, and Johns Hopkins Universities. The first group of 175 German students and professors—all selected by Friedrich and Bergstraesser—traveled to the United States for a year. At the same time, 155 Americans arrived in Heidelberg to stay for a year and take classes at InSoSta. Into the 1930s, hundreds of students traveled to and from Heidelberg, spreading InSoSta's reputation among proponents of global understanding. These students did not simply learn new languages and cultures for their own individual enrichment. For Friedrich, the Rockefeller Foundation, and German politicians, they were to be the vanguard in forging an international Western, democratic, elite identity.[30]

While probably oblivious to Friedrich's peculiar intellectual visions and belief in covenant democracy, the diplomats of the Weimar Republic soon grasped that this innovative program could enhance Germany's prestige

[29] The information on Heidelberg is from Letter, Senate of HU to the Ministry of Culture and Education in Baden (23 June 1922), FII-B-0682/1, Nr. 64, Heft 6, UAH; and Demm, *Alfred Weber*, 124–128. The information on Duggan's visit is from Report, Stephen Duggan to Administrative Board of the IIE (10 October 1925), Folder 134, Box 9, Series 1, Accession 26, Subseries 207, RFA, RAC. The American academics who joined the program are mentioned in Letter, Carl J. Friedrich to Edgar Salin (23 January 2914), Folder Salin, Box 39, HUGFP17.6.

[30] Arnold Bergstraesser and Carl J. Friedrich, Application Guidelines for the DAAD Program in the United States (29 October 1925), B-8245/1, IX, 7, Nr. 34; Letter, Alfred Weber to the Rector of the UH (10 September 1925), F-II-6680/1, IX, 3 Nr. 96; Report, "Der Akademische Austauschdienst" (October 1930), B-0680/1, VII, 1, Nr. 83; Letter, Captain AEW Thomas to Alfred Weber (24 April 1931), B-0683/2, I, 17, Nr. 80; all at UAH. Despite its importance, there is no comprehensive study of the history of the DAAD. The only account, which is fragmentary and partial, is by Giesela Schultz and Hubertus Scheibe, *Der deutsche Akademische Austauschdienst, 1925–1975* (Bonn: Deutscher Akademischer Austauschdienst, 1975).

both at home and abroad. German academics had participated in international conferences prior to World War I, but the scale and intensity of the DAAD was unparalleled, and German diplomats were eager to exploit Germany's academic reputation in their mission to break down the country's isolation. Once word of the new endeavor had spread, German diplomats from around the world flooded Friedrich and the authorities at Heidelberg University with requests to take part in this academic exchange. The German ambassador to Beijing offered to fund delegations of Chinese and German students. The German consul in Kobe, Japan, invited German professors to tour the country and sought to arrange for Japanese delegations to visit Heidelberg. Similar requests soon poured in from Argentina and other Latin American countries, generating an avalanche of lectures, publications, and mutual visits.[31]

German bureaucrats rejoiced at every account of the country's regained international stature. One gushing report to Berlin, for example, conveyed how biologist Wilhelm Kolle's lecture in Madrid, which the DAAD had sponsored, led to spontaneous outbursts of "Viva Spain, viva Germany!" The Spanish scholars, the report explained, "are not as productive as the nations of the north ... [so the lecture] made a deep impression, [showing] that we have changed our ways after the war." The Spanish people were "enthusiastic" to see Germany reengaged in international cooperation. Throughout the 1920s, the German government regularly sponsored such delegations and trips to Europe, Latin America, and Asia and sent members of InSoSta to lecture about Germany's commitment to international cooperation around the world. Universities and scholars became active members in the broader mission of elite cultural diplomacy.[32]

As the 1920s progressed and the DAAD's popularity exploded, the program opened branches on all major German campuses. One after the other, Berlin, Bonn, Breslau, Freiburg, Danzig, Frankfurt, Giessen, Göttingen, Halle, Hamburg, Jena, Kiel, Karlsruhe, Leipzig, Marburg, Königsberg, Munich, Stuttgart, and Tübingen all opened DAAD offices. Moreover, the program quickly expanded beyond the United States in an attempt to tie German elites into a truly global network. In 1926 Friedrich inaugurated the

---

[31] Letter, German Embassy in Peking to Dr. Linde, General Secretary of the Verbands Fernen Osten in Berlin (19 October 1922); Letter, German Consulate in Kobe to the Senate of the Heidelberg University (11 April 1923); Letter, German Consulate in Buenos Aires to the Auswärtige Amt, Berlin (11 May 1923); all in B-0680/1, VII, 1, Nr. 83, UAH.

[32] Letter, W Kolle to Baden Ministry of Culture and Education, Karlsruhe (26 June 1922); letter, Karlsruhe to Ministry of Foreign Affairs in Berlin (26 June 1922); Letter, German Consulate in Kobe, Japan, to the Senate of HU (29 December 1922); all in B-0683/1, I, 17, Nr. 76, UAU. On InSoSta's members' lectures, see Report, Stephen Duggan to the Rockefeller Foundation Board (10 October 1925), Folder 134, Box 9, Series 1, Accession 26, Subseries 207, RFA, RAC.

DAAD's first branches in Britain and France, both of which were visited by several dozen students each year. By 1930, the program had expanded German exchange programs to Austria, Ireland, Iceland, Hungary, Switzerland, Finland, Czechoslovakia, Canada, and Chile and planned to expand further to Sweden, Spain, Argentina, Australia, and Japan. A year later, in the midst of the Great Depression, the German government still saw it as a priority and expanded into Mexico, Denmark, Lithuania, and South Africa. Through the DAAD, Friedrich's and InSoSta's shared vision seemed to encompass the entire globe. German academia embraced this new role as the training ground of an international elite.[33]

Friedrich's campaign to rally German Protestants in support of the Weimar Republic thus gave birth to one of the era's most innovative educational endeavors. His attempt to show that democracy stemmed from German and Christian conceptions of the covenant, and his effort to train a "responsible" elite informed the creation of a new and unexpected coalition. Using InSoSta as a model, Friedrich helped bring together American wealth, German state officials, and pro-democratic academics in a joint effort to make Germany's higher education into an agent of democratic support at home and international collaboration abroad. The democratic vision that guided this collaboration was highly strict and elitist, in which "responsible" and educated men would lead the masses. In its top-down structures, democracy's success was measured through facilitation of consensus and order, both at home and overseas. Friedrich's theory placed little value in the critical expression of political strife, in challenging state power, or in including the poor and dispossessed in the political process. Yet even within these narrow confines InSoSta and its programs expanded the scope of German academia. By creating pro-republic curricula and fostering international exchanges, Friedrich and other members of the "Weber School" inaugurated a highly ambitious mobilization of higher education in the service of German democracy.

Despite their steady expansion, however, Heidelberg's intellectual and institutional initiatives ultimately failed to recruit German Protestants to support the republic and international cooperation. When the Great Depression hit Germany, the Protestant middle class led the country's shift to the right, embracing authoritarian and racist ideologies and supporting increasingly belligerent and imperialist expansion. Indeed, no other voting bloc supported Nazism with greater enthusiasm.[34] But InSoSta's mission to

---

[33] Memorandum (unsigned) (14 June 1921); Report (unsigned) (28 October 1929); Josy Schäfer, Report (10 October 1929); all in B-0680/1, VII, 1, Nr. 83, UAH. Also, a List of Students enrolled in the DAAD, 1931–1932 (undated, summer 1932?), B-8245/1, IX, 7, Nr. 34; and Report, "Der Akademische Austauschdienst 1924–1930" (undated, probably summer 1930), B-0680/2, VII, 1, Nr. 80; both in UAH.

[34] Manfred Gailus, *Protestantismus und Nationalsozialismus* (Cologne: Böhlau, 2001).

train responsible democratic elites did not disappear. Within a few years, Friedrich's democratic visions made their way to the United States, where the same individuals and institutions would again join hands to transform American higher education and, ultimately, to return to Germany itself.

THE HEIDELBERG MISSION IN THE UNITED STATES: THE CREATION OF A NEW AMERICAN ACADEMIA

The Nazi seizure of Germany's universities was swift and thorough. Within months of Hitler's appointment as chancellor in January 1933, the enthusiastic support of many nationalist and conservative scholars allowed the new regime to take over the entire system of higher education. The Third Reich fired all anti-Nazi and Jewish professors, shut down democratic programs, and imposed its racist ideology on academic curricula. German universities became the workshops of dark knowledge and teachings. Among the many victims of this assault was Heidelberg's InSoSta. For two years, its semi-independent status allowed it to continue operating, but in 1935 Nazi officials took over the institution and hung the swastika flag above its doors. On Berlin's direct orders, Nazi officials banned American funding, dismantled the DAAD, and forced Alfred Weber into retirement and his assistants into exile. Within two years, the "Weber School" was destroyed and its vision of a "responsible" democratic elite shattered. As Weber glumly put it, InSoSta's deserted building became a monument to the ruined republic, its empty hallways and torn books "lying as a beached wreck, rotting as sacrifices on the shore."[35]

This utter devastation, however, did not mark the end of InSoSta's mission to produce a democratic and responsible bureaucracy. Nor did it end its quest to build a triangular nexus of state, academia, and philanthropy. Rather, the dramatic transformation of U.S. politics in the following decades opened unexpected opportunities for Friedrich at the heart of the American educational system. The Great Depression and the New Deal inaugurated a massive reconfiguration of government's role in American life. U.S. politicians and bureaucrats feared that economic misery and social un-

---

[35] Quoted in Steven P. Remy, *The Heidelberg Myth: The Nazification and Denazification of a German University* (Cambridge, MA: Harvard University Press, 2002), 40. On Nazism and the universities in general, see Joachim Scholtyseck and Christoph Studt (eds.), *Universitäten und Studenten im Dritten Reich* (Berlin: Lit, 2008). On the Nazification of InSoSta, see Klaus-Rainer Brintzinger, "Die nationalsozialistische Gleichschaltung des InSoSta und die Staats- und Wirtschaftswissenschaftliche Fakultät," *Heidelberger Sozial- und Staatswissenschaften*, 55–81. Curiously, the Nazi authorities planned to revive the DAAD's framework in 1940 in an attempt to establish cultural exchange with the Soviet Union, although the program was soon canceled with the Nazi invasion of the Soviet Union in June 1941. Memorandum, Reich Minister für Wissenschaft, Erziehung und Volksbildung to Senate of HU (21 October 1940), FII—B-0682/1, Nr. 64, Heft 6 (DAAD 1922–1962), UAH.

rest would undermine American liberal-capitalist democracy. Therefore, many found Friedrich's call to train a responsible, unelected, yet democratic elite highly appealing. His writings and experience provided the blueprint for the creation of educational programs that would train such leadership, stabilize American society, and fend off challenges to its core social and political hierarchies. During the 1930s and 1940s, from his office in Harvard's Department of Government, Friedrich initiated a stream of projects that brought together academia, the U.S. government, and philanthropy, cooperation that transformed American academia into an organ of the democratic state. The programs that emerged from this collaboration revolutionized U.S. higher education. Far surpassing InSoSta's work in Heidelberg, they provided a model for the role of elite universities in decades to come.

During the 1930s, Friedrich gradually established his stature as a specialist in political theory at Harvard University. To his colleagues, however, his vision of a state-academia-philanthropy nexus seemed eccentric at best. As the country's most prestigious academic institution, Harvard prided itself on its insularity from everyday politics. The high walls surrounding its campus symbolized its active discouragement of engagement with contemporary social and political issues. While other academic institutions, especially state universities, often advised policymakers on science and education, Harvard, and many other American elite schools, considered collaboration with policymakers to be inappropriate and dangerous to intellectual independence. Robert Hutchins, president of the University of Chicago, spoke for many in such institutions when he claimed that scholars had to shield themselves from the temptation of cooperating with the government. It was doubtful, he famously wrote, whether scholars could create "any body of systematic knowledge" that would be helpful for government officials.[36]

These sentiments only intensified after Franklin Roosevelt initiated the New Deal. Like their counterparts at Princeton, Yale, and Stanford, most Harvard scholars viewed FDR's experimental and populist policies with disdain and did not seek to collaborate with his administration. Even when the Great Depression dramatically diminished revenues, they declined to accept the generous support that the U.S. government offered in hopes of recruiting elite universities to join its social and political experiments. Nothing illustrates this contempt for partnership better than Harvard's 1936 tercentenary celebration. When FDR, the university's most renowned graduate, arrived on campus, students, faculty, and alumni responded in a storm

---

[36] Cited in Morton Keller and Phyllis Keller, *Making Harvard Modern: The Rise of America's University* (Oxford: Oxford University Press, 2001), 131. The following relied substantially on Jeremi Suri, *Henry Kissinger and the American Century* (Cambridge, MA: Belknap Press of Harvard University Press, 2007), 92–137.

of protest and boycott. As another famous graduate, Arthur Schlesinger Jr., put it, Harvard of the 1930s "was a cocoon." Influencing politics and advising government, in the words of one historian, were "not on the agenda."[37]

In contrast, Friedrich's vision of elite education assumed close cooperation with the state. While mostly uninterested in the New Deal's focus on welfare, Friedrich quickly recognized that the newly activist U.S. government, and the enormous state apparatus it created, offered new possibilities for closer cooperation between scholars and administration officials. Despite the dramatically different intellectual and social traditions of the United States and Germany, Friedrich strongly believed in the universality of his theory. Responsible bureaucrats, trained by elite academic institutions, remained the key to healthy democratic political conduct and the global defense of the covenant. In a lengthy 1935 study designed for government officials, Friedrich resurrected his ideas from InSoSta in an attempt to provide the intellectual foundations for American thinking about bureaucracy. According to Friedrich, the dramatic increase in government authority during the New Deal posed a threat to democracy. By creating countless new social programs, planning boards, and government agencies, the president could acquire almost dictatorial powers. At the same time, however, the plethora of new state organs provided an opportunity for "responsible" elites to join democracy's defense. Well-trained bureaucrats could monitor these programs and ensure that they served the public good. Moreover, a network of wise elites would secure democracy from the reckless masses and the politicians who represented them. Unelected and thus shielded from special interests, they could provide the "neutral" perspective that public policy required.[38]

Reviving the zeal that powered his conduct in Weimar, Friedrich preached that the path to this elite lay in restructuring academic life. The United States had to look across the Atlantic, to the "government-supported system of schools and universities" that facilitated the production of a trained bureaucracy. The American system, which Friedrich claimed was "dominated" by private schools, lagged behind Europe. It failed to accept that the ever-growing need for government experts would ultimately require mutual dependence between the state and academia. Modern U.S. universities thus had to reconsider their role in society in order to develop responsible bureaucrats, and the government had to expand its investment in academic institutions. In this narrative, the rise of Nazism in Europe had shown that without such institutional blending, democratic society could

---

[37] Suri, *Henry Kissinger and the American Century*, 100, 101. On the tensions between U.S. universities and the New Deal administration, see Rebecca Lowen, *Creating the Cold War University* (Berkeley: University of California Press, 1997), 31–33.

[38] Carl J. Friedrich, *Responsible Government Service under the American Constitution* (New York and London: McGraw-Hill, 1935), 111.

collapse into a violent dictatorship. Only responsible bureaucrats possessed the power to prevent the "diabolical" forces of politics from "destroying the fundamental law of the land."[39]

For the scholars, state officials, and philanthropists who supported the New Deal, Friedrich's ideas provided a helpful framework for responding to the Great Depression. His vision of unelected yet responsible leadership resonated with many who believed that the economic catastrophe necessitated a dramatic expansion of government power and centralized planning. His theory explained why the work of an unelected and self-appointed elite did not contradict democratic principles but instead enhanced them. Moreover, Friedrich provided new language for those who believed that academic cooperation with the government was not a partisan act or the corruption of academic freedom. Rather, it served the national good and was a crucial step in the training of democratic leadership. Many agreed with Friedrich that the horrific Nazi overthrow of the Weimar Republic only proved the urgency of fostering cooperation between the academic establishment and democratic regimes. Stacy May, a senior official of the Rockefeller Foundation, wrote to Friedrich that the foundation was eager to bring home the programs that it had helped build in Heidelberg. Like Friedrich, the foundation's officials believed that "active cooperation of persons with academic experience and the government officials who are actually handling the problems should be helpful to both."[40]

Friedrich's blend of institutional ingenuity and social elitism thus quickly caught the attention of government officials and philanthropists, who sought new avenues of cooperation with the American academic elite. The first was Otis Wingo, who in 1933 founded the National Institution of Public Affairs in Washington, D.C., a private school for the training of government officials. While most people, Wingo wrote, responded "with amazement" to his call for the academic training of public officials, in Friedrich he found a rare ally.[41] In 1934 Wingo recruited Friedrich to serve on an advising committee to the FDR administration. For two years, Friedrich served as chair for the Commission of Inquiry on Public Service Personnel, a think tank created by the Social Science Research Council, an independent organ that provided research for government legislation. The figures appointed to serve on the commission—the first of its kind in American history—were indicative of Roosevelt's ambitious attempt to infuse the public sector with intellectuals and academics. Alongside Friedrich and

---

[39] Ibid., 68, 74. Friedrich further elaborated the role of bureaucracy in democracy in his *Constitutional Government and Politics* (New York: Harper, 1937), 20–40.

[40] Letter, Stacy May to James Conant and Carl J. Friedrich (18 April 1935), Folder 4106, Box 345, Series 200, RG 1.1, RFA, RAC.

[41] Otis T. Wingo, "Training for Public Administration," *The Journal of Higher Education* 8:2 (February 1937): 84–88, quote from 84.

Wingo, they included L. D. Coffman, president of the University of Minnesota, and Louis Brownlow, director of the Public Administration Clearing House in Chicago. After holding hearings across the country, the commission drafted plans for new programs to train administrators and state bureaucrats. These curricula would be offered to universities across the country, which would train unelected officials to provide politicians with "scientific" and "rational" policies in the era of the Great Depression.[42]

While Princeton, Yale, and other elite universities had little interest in the commission's plans, through Friedrich, Harvard created the first space for such collaboration. In March 1934 Friedrich proposed that Harvard establish an institute of public administration. The contours of this institute were to be identical to InSoSta, bringing together political theorists, government officials, and representatives of the Rockefeller Foundation to train men and women who would go on to take "responsible positions in public life." As Friedrich explained to the foundation's officials, the program's graduates would populate federal, state, and local governments, legislative and law enforcement organs, trade associations, magazine and newspaper boards. They were the United States' future responsible elite. Despite strong objections from the university board, in January 1935 Harvard inaugurated a Public Service Training program. Its students, including labor unionists, administration officials, and young college graduates, were to spend three years taking classes with Friedrich, attending lectures by Massachusetts politicians, and training in public institutions, such as public works departments and attorney generals' offices across the country. The Rockefeller Foundation quickly joined the initiative and eagerly agreed to sponsor the new program for half a decade. Together, Friedrich and the Rockefeller Foundation began rebuilding InSoSta in New England.[43]

The combination of private wealth and political pressure soon transformed Friedrich's budding experiments into a major institution. In November 1935 former Republican congressman and glove manufacturer Lucius Littauer unexpectedly supported the new program with a donation of two million dollars. Littauer believed that Harvard should establish a new graduate school of public administration, which would be "the best hope of avoiding disasters arising from untried experiments in government and administration," which he perceived in Roosevelt's New Deal, with its expan-

---

[42] On the new role of academics in the Roosevelt administration, see Elliot A. Rosen, "Roosevelt, the Brain Trust, and the origins of the New Deal," in Herbert D. Rosenbaum and Elizabeth Bartelme (eds.), *Franklin D. Roosevelt* (New York: Greenwood, 1987), 153–166. The information on the committee is drawn from materials in Folder Committee on Administrative Ability, Box 9, HUGFP 17.6.

[43] Friedrich's proposal is in Letter, Friedrich to Edmund Day (13 April 1934); the Foundation's support appears in Press Release (29 October 1934); both in Folder 4106, Box 345, Series 200, RG 1.1, RFA, RAC.

sion of state authority and empowerment of labor. In Friedrich's ideas, Littauer believed to have found the key to channeling government's energy away from welfare measures and toward strengthening elite institutions. After Harvard's board deliberated for a year, hesitant to expand the university's ties to government, politics tipped the scale. Roosevelt's landslide reelection in 1936 convinced the university's conservative board that Littauer was correct and that the New Deal could only be tamed through cooperation with federal power. In December 1936 Harvard announced the creation of a Graduate School of Public Administration, with Friedrich as its director. As the university's president, James Conant, mused, "the project of providing, at the graduate level, a program of training for the public service is a wholly new one. There is no successful experience to serve as a guide in this country and very little in other countries." The scholars, politicians, and philanthropists (both Littauer and the Rockefeller officials) who initiated this new school were entering uncharted waters. Harvard was opening its gates to the federal government.[44]

Ironically, the program that Harvard hoped would restrain the growing American state would dramatically expand its reach and resources. Indeed, the most forceful support for Friedrich's vision of training a democratic leadership came from the U.S. government. Like the officials of the Weimar state, American politicians and bureaucrats quickly recognized that the new graduate school presented a rare opportunity to draw the country's elite into the orbit of the state. High-ranking government officials therefore flocked from Boston, New York, and Washington, D.C., to take part in shaping the future training center. Henry Morgenthau, Roosevelt's powerful secretary of the treasury, contributed to the syllabus on federal spending. Rosewell Magill, undersecretary of the treasury, discussed his ideas about defects in the existing tax system. They were joined by Supreme Court justice Felix Frankfurter, who lectured on judicial training; journalist Walter Lippmann; State Department official Henry Parkman, who would later become director of the civil administration of the U.S. occupation of Germany and one of Friedrich's closest collaborators; and dozens of academics, state politicians, lawyers, and businessmen. For these officials and for the philanthropists who funded their cooperation with Friedrich, the dramatic expansion of state power had become a permanent feature of

---

[44] Littauer is cited in Keller and Keller, *Making Harvard Modern*, 132. Conant's quotation is from James Conant to Stacy May, Memorandum on the Projected Conferences in Connection with the Organization of the Graduate School of Public Administration and Harvard University (1 December 1936), Folder 4097, Box 344, Series 200, RG 1.1, RFA, RAC. The information on Harvard's deliberation is from Meeting Notes (7 December 1936), Folder School of Public Administration, Box 9, HUGFP 17.10. The information on the Rockefeller Foundation's support is from Memorandum re[garding] Harvard Project, Stacy May to the Rockefeller Foundation Board (31 December 1936), Folder 4097, Box 344, Series 200, RG 1.1, RFA, RAC.

modern politics. Academic training was the best tool for the management of such expansion.[45]

The students who arrived at the school in the late 1930s received a thorough political indoctrination to prepare them for unelected leadership and defense of the covenant. As Friedrich reported, training in political theory "is of essential importance in many governmental posts. The School does not attempt to prepare expert technicians for particular branches of the public service. It seeks rather to provide a thorough grounding in the fundamental principles and problems" of public life.[46] Students were therefore required to take numerous classes on politics, law, and history. They regularly traveled to Washington, D.C., to meet U.S. senators, bureaucrats, and federal advisers and to gain a broad understanding of government functions. At the decade's end, Rockefeller officials cheerfully noted that Harvard's new school surpassed InSoSta in its national reach. Its graduates assumed positions at the Department of Agriculture, the Treasury Department, the Tennessee Valley Authority, the National Youth Administration, the National Park Service, the Department of Commerce, the Board of Governors of the Federal Reserve, the Labor Relations Board of the State of New York, the State Department, the U.S. military, the New York State Department of Social Welfare, the Michigan Unemployment Commission, heads of business schools across the Midwest, or became lawyers or journalists at such leading magazines as *The Nation*. The school's graduates thus found positions in the fabric of democracy, both inside and outside the state. In this mission to integrate elite universities into the democratic order, one Rockefeller official noted, the school was "a massive success."[47]

Striking in an era of mass unemployment and widespread poverty, democracy's main enemy, for Friedrich and his allies at Harvard, was not social misery but political instability. Unlike some New Dealers, they there-

[45] Outline of Topics and Speakers at the Seminar on Fiscal Policy (17 November 1937), Folder 4097, Box 344, Series 200, RG 1.1, RFA, RAC; Tentative Suggestions for Agenda of General Session, March 1–27 (January 1937), Folder School of Public Administration, Box 9, HUGFP 17.10; Letter, Larris Lambie to Stacey May (8 January 1938), Folder 4107, Box 345, Series 200, RG 1.1, RFA, RAC.

[46] Friedrich, Report on Harvard Graduate School of Public Administration (November 1938), Folder 4104, Box 345, Series 200, RG 1.1, RFA, RAC.

[47] Quotation is from Memorandum, Research in Public Administration (undated, fall 1939?), Folder Graduate School of Public Administration, Box 4, HUGFP 17.10; Grant approval (20 May 1938), Folder 4097, Box 344, Series 200, RG 1.1, RFA, RAC. The information is based on information in Carl J. Friedrich, Report on Graduate School of Public Administration (22 March 1938), Folder 4104, Box 345; Report, Carl Friedrich to the Rockefeller Foundation Board (17 October 1939), Folder 4113, Box 346; Report, Carl Friedrich to the Rockefeller Foundation Board (14 November 1938), Folder 4107, Box 345; Press Release, David Puttinger of the Harvard University Press (22 January 1940), Folder 4100, Box 344; all in Series 200, RG 1.1, RFA, RAC.

fore did not seek to challenge the fundamental norms of capitalism or to reconfigure the relationship between citizens and their government. Rather, they hoped to curb the potentially transformative effects of the Roosevelt administration's policies, such as recognition of workers' unions or the creation of new welfare programs. Indeed, the programs at Harvard were meant to preserve social and economic reality as much as they were designed to change it. The officials they trained were supposed to solidify socioeconomic hierarchies and duplicate existing class stratification, not challenge them. In many ways, these unelected elites were to serve as agents in the restraining of radical forces. Their mission was to protect state institutions from irresponsible people rather than open up state power to popular participation. As was the case in Weimar, the responsible students that Friedrich and others sought to train were first and foremost agents of order.

Although this new relationship among universities, the government, and philanthropy addressed specific domestic pressures in the United States, it also provided an opportunity for European expertise. Friedrich believed that the successful integration of European scholarship into American higher education was crucial to the creation of the responsible bureaucracy necessary to build and guide covenant democracy. Both Friedrich and the Rockefeller Foundation viewed the re-creation of InSoSta in the United States as a mechanism for rescuing persecuted German scholars, and the Graduate School of Public Administration absorbed many of them into the fabric of American academia. Among the many European émigrés and visitors who joined the school's staff were Alfred Oppler, a former judge in the Prussian Supreme Disciplinary Court who would later serve in the U.S. War Department and helped draft the postwar constitution of Japan; Swedish politician Nils Herlitz; and Hungarian politician Joseph Vcsekloy. The most prominent of all was Heinrich Brüning, the archconservative former chancellor of Germany, who went into exile in the United States and became a Harvard professor and one of the school's main political educators. While Friedrich had disapproved of Brüning's anti-parliamentary measures and policies of economic austerity in the early 1930s, he came to view the former chancellor as a leader of rare intelligence. In fact, the two men briefly plotted to establish an official German government in exile and overthrow the Third Reich. The expansion of Harvard into public policy thus created new spaces for European émigrés to influence American policymaking. It provided channels to government officials that would have been extremely rare only a decade earlier.[48]

[48] During the 1930s, Friedrich cooperated with Rockefeller Foundation agents in establishing the American Committee for the Guidance of Professional Personnel, which helped relocate hundreds of German scholars who were persecuted by the Third Reich. The foundation invested more than $350,000 in the committee. These facts are drawn from Letter, Murrow to Stephen Duggan (2 May 1934); Letter, Murrow to Carl J. Friedrich (2 July 1934), both in Folder

This blurring of the boundaries between university and government prepared the ground for the unprecedented cooperation unleashed by World War II. With the United States' entry into the war in December 1941, universities like Harvard became indispensable components of the war effort. The U.S. government enlisted scholars not only to help develop new weapons, like napalm or the atomic bomb, but also for their knowledge of the languages, societies, governments, and institutions of enemy countries. Unlike European empires, which had developed a substantial apparatus of such knowledge over decades, the U.S. government had few people with language skills or expertise on foreign cultures. This was especially true for Asia, and in particular China and Japan, but also for Europe. From Harvard, the War Department therefore recruited hundreds of humanities and social sciences scholars. Working in both Washington, D.C., and on Harvard's campus, they analyzed intelligence data, developed propaganda campaigns, and drafted plans for postwar occupations. The government also poured millions into universities in support of research that it would incorporate into its diplomatic, military, and social plans. This federal funding put intense pressure on universities to develop new curricula and to modify the focus of their research and publications. It fostered a symbiotic relationship between universities and government, including the military, and government priorities and scholarly research agendas overlapped like never before. As one historian put it, "Harvard was now so deeply integrated in the war effort that it became difficult to distinguish where the authority of the government ended and that of the university began."[49]

Ultimately, however, it was not the war that revolutionized higher education. Rather, it dramatically expanded the curricula, personal contacts, and state-academy-philanthropy nexus developed at InSoSta and at Harvard in the decades before. Indeed, it was no accident that the people who led Harvard's entry into the war were those who had built its public policy programs. After decades of seeking to bring academia and government together in the defense of the covenant, Friedrich, Harvard president James Conant, and the Rockefeller officials who funded them were well positioned to re-

9, Box 178, Emergency Committee in Aid of Displaced Scholars [MssCol 922], Special Collections and Manuscripts, New York Public Library [NYPL]. The information on émigrés at Harvard is from John H. Williams, Annual Report of the Harvard Graduate School of Public Administration (August 1941), Folder 4104, Box 345, Series 200, RG 1.1, RFA, RAC. The information on Brüning and Friedrich is from Carl J. Friedrich, Diary entry (1 January 1939), Folder 1938–1949, Box 1, HUGFP 17.2.

[49] Quotation is from Suri, *Henry Kissinger and the American Century*, 102. Robin W. Winks, *Cloak and Gown: Scholars in the Secret War* (New York: William Morrow, 1987); Michael A. Bernstein, "American Economics and the National Security State, 1941–1953," *Radical History Review* 63 (Fall 1995): 8–17; Ellen Herman, "Project Camelot and the Career of Cold War Psychology," in *Universities and Empire: Money and Politics in the Social Sciences During the Cold War* (New York: The New Press, 1998), 97–134.

spond to the pressures of wartime mobilization. No institution better represents these long continuities than Friedrich's most ambitious educational project: the Harvard School of Overseas Administration (HSOA). Founded in 1942, the school trained hundreds of diplomats and military officials in preparation for postwar occupations. Directed by Friedrich, its deputy director was the Harvard sociologist Talcott Parsons, who had also studied with Alfred Weber in the 1920s. HSOA's purpose, Friedrich wrote to the War Department, was "to develop intensive programs of regional research and study, with a special attention to the training needs of Americans who go to fight overseas in connection with the war and postwar tasks America is facing all over the world."[50] Throughout the war years, military and government officials studied the politics, language, geography, history, economy, and culture of the countries they were about to occupy, and practiced techniques for the establishment of postwar democratic structures. Émigrés from Europe and former missionaries to Asia helped plan the establishment of civil administration structures, food supplies, and judicial systems. These programs provided the detailed plans for future foreign rule, and their graduates would later serve as occupation officers in Frankfurt, Tokyo, and Rome.[51]

Like the School for Public Administration that preceded it, HSOA was much more than a center for technical skills. It sought to instill the values of consensus building in future governing elites through rigorous classes on political theory. Under Friedrich's supervision, HSOA students were subjected to countless lectures and seminars by German émigrés Arnold Brecht, Karl Loewenstein, Heinrich Brüning, and Protestant theologian Paul Tillich on "the institutional structures" of Germany, "Nazi and democratic law," "the organization of religion," "Protestant-Catholic Relations," and "State and Church." Friedrich himself taught all the introductory lectures on political ideologies, liberalism, conservatism, and the origins of democracy. Without exception they all seemed unmoved by the glaring tension that stood at the heart of HSOA's work. Even as HSOA sought to pro-

[50] Appendix II, List of Courses (undated, spring 1942?), Folder 1, Appendices to Annual Report, Harvard School of Overseas Administration Collection I, 67.143.75.5, Harvard University Archive [hereafter referred to as HUE].

[51] Carl J. Friedrich, Annual Report 1 Feb. 1943–1 Feb. 1944 (undated, February 1944?), HUE 67 143.75 A; Military Government: Organization of Civil Affairs Staff (undated, fall 1943?), Folder Solutions to Military Government Problems Central Europe, Box Military Government Problems 1943–1945; Military Government: Civil Affairs Training Program (8 December 1943), Folder Solutions to Military Government Problems Central Europe, Box Military Government Problems 1943–1945; Civil Affairs Training Program Assignments, Folder Military Government Regierungsbezirke, Box Military Government Problems 1943–1945; all in Harvard School of Overseas Administration Collection II [UAV] 664.255, Harvard University Archive.

vide necessary and specific knowledge about distinct foreign cultures, it claimed that democracy was universal, that it could be imposed from the top-down, and that it was applicable to all states and cultures. As the responsible elites who would facilitate covenant democracy, its students would extend the Public Policy School's mission from the U.S. state to Germany, Italy, and Japan. The theory of responsible elites thus moved smoothly from the domestic to the international sphere. HSOA helped plan the foundations of U.S. global hegemony.[52]

As the war progressed, HSOA became the model for similar collaborations across American university campuses. The scholars, military officials, and Rockefeller officials who took part in its creation duplicated similar curricula, assignments, and training in Michigan, Virginia, and New York. In the summer of 1943, the Rockefeller Foundation brought together representative of sixteen colleges and universities and government and military officials to coordinate this expansion. At a conference in Washington, D.C., they agreed to embrace HSOA's curricula and create a dozen similar institutions on U.S. campuses. By 1944, professors had mentored thousands of U.S. diplomats and military officials in countless institutions of higher education. Friedrich's vision of responsible elite training became the wartime consensus.[53]

While many embraced these educational, institutional, and intellectual structures as something new, at both the theoretical and personal levels they expanded earlier initiatives. As at InSoSta, these educational programs stemmed from a highly elite conception of the democratic state. Scholars had to supply knowledge and teaching to unelected bureaucrats, who were to protect democratic institutions without public oversight. Indeed, ordinary citizens were almost completely absent from Friedrich's visions. Higher education was not meant to provide social mobility, only to prepare elites for policy; it is therefore not surprising that this program found a home at the United States' most elite educational institution. This privileging of stability and social hierarchy was precisely what allowed Friedrich to take part in the transformation of American academia. As the New Deal and World War II put unprecedented pressure on Harvard, his ideas inspired state-university collaboration without shaking the foundations of elite-driven political, economic, and social hierarchies. The university that emerged from the war drew heavily on InSoSta. But unlike its Heidelberg predecessor, the Great Depression transformed this model at Harvard into an engine for monumental mobilization.

[52] Classes curriculum, Folder SOA curriculum, Box 1, HUGFP 17.26; OA-Examination and problems, 1944–1945, Folder OA, Box 1, HUGFP17.26; Synopses of Courses (undated), Folder 4, Appendices to Annual Report, School for Overseas Administration, HUE 67.143.75.5.

[53] William Fenton, Reports on Area Studies in American Universities (April 1945), HUE 67 545 A.

Cold War Universities: "Responsible Elites" in Cold War United States and Germany

If the New Deal and World War II enabled Friedrich to mobilize American academia in the service of the state and the democratic covenant, it was the Cold War that made this collaboration permanent. As anxieties about Soviet power, fears of Communist infiltration in the United States, and a sense of perpetual threat spread among American diplomats, political leaders, and scholars, the Cold War became an enduring presence on U.S. campuses. Rather than demobilizing after World War II, professors, philanthropists, and state officials only tightened their cooperation. They devised new areas of study, language programs, institutional centers, and academic curricula for the training of state bureaucrats, for the creation of knowledge and capabilities to fight the Cold War enemy, and to understand Cold War allies. From their libraries and seminar rooms, scholars at Harvard and other universities produced a barrage of studies that would mobilize students at home and guide diplomats in responding to Communist expansion in Europe, Asia, and around the globe. The U.S. government forcefully encouraged this mission, pouring millions into new teaching programs, language training, and academic research agendas. Intellectuals and scholars who produced policy-relevant knowledge gained access to enormous funding, classified information, and often government positions. The global struggle with communism solidified universities' new role as engines for domestic mobilization, government service, and assertive diplomacy. This new institutional setting is what historians came to call "the Cold War University."[54]

Less noted by scholars, however, is the fact that the Cold War University was not merely an American peculiarity. Nor was it simply an expansion of InSoSta and Harvard's earlier projects of training responsible elites within the United States. It also became a powerful model for the reconstruction of postwar Germany. After helping build the Cold War University in the United States, Friedrich and other members of the "Weber School" sought to resurrect their Weimar-era models in Germany. As the U.S. occupation authorities began rebuilding Germany's institutions of higher education, dozens of educators and philanthropists descended on German campuses.

[54] See, for example, David Engerman, "Rethinking Cold War Universities: Some Recent Histories," *Journal of Cold War Studies* 5:3 (Summer 2003): 80–95; Joy Rhode, *Armed with Experience: The Militarization of American Social Research during the Cold War* (Ithaca: Cornell University Press, 2013); R. C. Lewontin, "The Cold War and the Transformation of the Academy," in Noam Chomsky et al. (eds.), *The Cold War and the University: Toward an Intellectual History of the Postwar Years* (New York: New Press, 1998), 1–34; Michael A. Bernstein and Allen Hunters (eds.), "The Cold War and Expert Knowledge," special issue of *Radical History Review* 63 (Fall 1995); Suri, *Henry Kissinger and the American Century*, 92–137.

Among them were Friedrich and many other veterans of the 1920s. Through these returnees, older visions of training responsible and unelected bureaucrats in defense of covenant democracy inspired new educational programs. With massive American support, the long-standing collaboration of state-philanthropy-academia again became the blueprint for German higher education, fusing German thought with Friedrich's hierarchical and rigid conception of democratic and Cold War order. Under the umbrella of the U.S. occupation, InSoSta returned from exile to play a central role in Germany's reconstruction.

The Cold War University at Harvard

More than any other institution of higher education, Harvard responded to the Cold War by extending its wartime collaboration with philanthropy and government. While other universities received more government funding, Harvard became the beating heart of government-academic policymaking. In the eyes of President James Conant, the university's earlier adventures in training public officials and participating in national defense now had to guide its core postwar mission. "The primary concern of American education today," Conant prophesized in his plans for educational reforms, "is not the development of the appreciation of the 'good life' in young gentlemen born to the purple.... Our purpose is to cultivate in the largest possible number of our future citizens an appreciation of both the responsibilities and benefits which come to them because they are Americans and are free." For Conant and countless other scholars and politicians, the Cold War tested Americans' resilience and commitment to their institutions and democratic norms. Communist propaganda, pressure, and subversion could potentially expose citizens' lack of understanding of democracy's benefits and values. Policymakers and scholars alike elevated this loss of national will as one of the biggest threats of the Cold War. Through courses and lectures, universities could foster an informed and unwavering commitment to democratic institutions and America's global mission. They were the vanguard in forging a widespread consensus.[55]

This renewed conviction about the United States' unique role and responsibilities was to undergird not only a commitment to the Cold War at home but also the formation of American hegemony abroad. In its efforts

---

[55] The quotation is from James Conant, *My Several Lives* (New York: Harper & Row, 1970), 368. As Suri mentions, this plan inspired curriculum changes in many other institutions in the United States during the Cold War. Suri, *Henry Kissinger and the American Century*, 103–105. On the crucial role played by this ethos of patrician service among unelected yet responsible elites in the U.S. foreign service in this period, and the place of gender norms of stoic masculinity in its formation, see Robert D. Dean, *Imperial Brotherhood: Gender and the Making of Cold War Foreign Policy* (Amherst: University of Massachusetts Press, 2001).

to foster an ethos of foreign service, Harvard dramatically expanded its courses in international politics and foreign cultures, emphasizing knowledge that would prepare its graduates to help contain Communist global power. Diplomats such as Paul Nitze and George Kennan often visited campus to meet young students and identify promising recruits for the State Department. The education of unelected officials became the driving mission of the elite university. This constant mobilization of academic prowess in the service of the state also shaped research agendas. Like their counterparts at Columbia, Yale, and other schools, Harvard scholars rushed to establish area studies programs, which emphasized the study of topics relevant to national security. Continuing the work of the HSOA, and funded by philanthropic foundations, scholars explored the culture, society, and policies of foreign leaders and societies. Central to these efforts was the study of the Soviet Union, whose structures and history scholars explored with feverish anxiety. But the growing notion that the Cold War was a global struggle, one where all countries were potential battlegrounds, led to the explosive production of studies, reports, and charts on Communist regimes in Europe, economic development in Asia, and social movements in Latin America and Africa. The Cold War University produced the precious knowledge required for the U.S. government's engagement with the rest of the world.[56]

Friedrich's theory was a potent force in shaping this environment. In their thirst for domestic strength and international knowledge, scholars and state officials valued his ideas and experience in program building. Like many Harvard scholars who despised communism's call to abolish all social hierarchy, Friedrich emerged from World War II with fierce anti-Communist and anti-Soviet convictions. In his eyes, the Soviet Union was a monstrous regime that sought to enslave the entire globe. Its leaders sought to eradicate all separation of powers and to dismantle covenant democracies. To Friedrich, the Soviet Union—and communism in general—was the incarnation of the "irresponsible" masses. By seeking to establish a social utopia, Communists fueled the "diabolical" forces of mass politics that responsible elites were meant to tame. In his dualist vision that divided human politics between democracies and their mortal enemies, there was no room for coexistence. The struggle against communism was not just about the United States' security or geopolitical interests. It was an effort to control domestic anti-democratic vulnerabilities, a struggle to prevent covenant democracy's destruction.[57]

---

[56] Engerman, "Rethinking Cold War Universities"; David Szanton, "The Origin, Nature and Challenges of Area Studies in the United States," in *The Politics of Knowledge: Area Studies and the Disciplines* (Berkeley: University of California Press, 2004), 1–33.

[57] The earliest expression of Friedrich's fierce anti-communism predated the war. See, for example, his "The Deification of the State," *Review of Politics* 1:1 (1939): 18–20.

1.1. Carl J. Friedrich at Harvard University (date unknown). Friedrich was among the most important figures in constructing the Cold War University. Courtesy of Su Friedrich.

Equally important, Friedrich's religious and eschatological political theory facilitated his vision of the Cold War as a religious struggle. As was the case before the war, Friedrich could not envision legitimate secular politics and automatically equated atheism with brutal enslavement. Communists, beyond being anti-democrats, were also atheists and thus agents of civilization's destruction. Drawing on his Weimar-era beliefs, Friedrich maintained that the United States was the defender of a broader Christian-democratic alliance that preserved Althusius's covenantal order. The experience of cooperating with U.S. officials in defeating Nazism solidified his conviction that the United States was the guardian of "the common religious heritage of modern civilization." It had to defend not only itself but also humanity and Western civilization from the specter of communism. If anything changed during World War II and the early Cold War, it was Friedrich's belief that not only Protestantism, but also Catholicism and Judaism, were part of the religious-democratic order. The experience of meeting Jewish and Catholic German émigrés who fled Nazism—as well as the violence of Nazi anti-Semitism—convinced Friedrich that democracy did not only belong to Protestants but was part of a broad "Judeo-Christian" tradition. The struggle against the Soviet Union was therefore a "a gigantic struggle ... around the spiritual destiny of the planet." The United States had "the right and duty to help all those in the world ... who are fighting the battle for the extension of democracy ... and for a kingdom of peace and heaven on earth."[58]

This perception of the Cold War as a total conflict with political, religious, and geopolitical consequences informed Friedrich's efforts to make Harvard's programs permanent. All the scholarly and institutional resources of the great university were to be put at the service of the democratic state and the larger anti-Communist crusade. In the spring of 1946, only months after the conclusion of HSOA's work, Friedrich joined a group of Harvard faculty in creating a "committee on international and regional studies." Composed of Talcott Parsons, economist Edward Mason, Japan scholar (and future ambassador to Tokyo) Edwin O. Reischauer, and others, the committee created a new academic program to respond to "our national need for broadly trained personnel to cope with current and future problems." They planned courses in international economics, political relations, diplomacy, and state administration. Students in the new program would learn about "recent trends in world community, whether strategic, economic, or constitutional." They would also take intensive courses in foreign languages, explore distant cultures, and write reports on their histories. Like the HSOA before it, the program was explicitly designed to feed policymaking institutions. As one scholar put it, "our hope is to form students who will later serve both academic circles and government policy."[59]

At their genesis, Harvard's programs focused mostly on China and Japan, two crucial countries about which policymakers felt they were in desperate need of knowledge. Friedrich, who with characteristic self-confidence mused that "all political concepts and history are essentially universal," designed and taught the first curriculum on China and Japan as well as lec-

[58] The quotations are from Carl J. Friedrich, "Anti-Semitism: Challenge to Christian Culture," in Isacque Graeber and Steuart Britt (eds.), *Jews in a Gentile World: The Problem of Anti-Semitism* (New York: Macmillan, 1942), 1–18, here 12, 13. On the emergence of "Judeo-Christianity" as an important trope in American thought during World War II and its popularity afterward, see Katherine Healan Gaston, "The Genesis of America's Judeo-Christian Movement" (PhD diss., University of California–Berkeley, 2008).

[59] Draft Program for International and Regional Studies (October 1946), Folder International and Regional Studies, Box 9, HUGFP 17.6.

tures on countries that were recently liberated from the Japanese empire, such as Korea and the Philippines.[60] As Cold War tensions rose in Europe, however, Friedrich and Harvard quickly expanded their scope to include the Soviet Union. In 1947 the committee inaugurated a comprehensive program in Russian and Soviet studies, recruited scholars and intelligence experts on the Soviet Union, and increased the fellowships it provided for the study of Russian. By 1948 these programs became the Russian Research Center, one of the country's most influential institutions for the study of the Soviet regime. In the following years, the center swelled in size, recruiting new scholars, diplomats, and hosting a plethora of lectures and seminars. Funded by the Rockefeller and later also the Ford Foundations, it analyzed Soviet politics, military capacities, cultural policies, and diplomatic strategies. This research agenda, one of its members wrote, was meant "to determine the mainspring of the international actions and policy of the Soviet Union." With its coalition of academics, philanthropists, policymakers, and intelligence officials, the Russian Center embodied Harvard's transmutation into a permanent organ of the American state. It exemplified both Friedrich's vision of responsible elite training and the Cold War University.[61]

The crystallization of the Cold War in Europe further fueled these endeavors. After a coup brought the Communists to power in Czechoslovakia in 1948 and Germany was divided into two antagonistic regimes in 1949, U.S. policymakers' desire for knowledge about European affairs only intensified. The subsequent division of the entire continent into two hostile military alliances, NATO in the West and the Warsaw Pact in the East, made U.S. diplomats eager to know more about Europeans, both allies and enemies. Friedrich headed the Area Studies program's European division at Harvard, designing classes and seminars on Britain, Germany, Poland, Hungary, France, and Italy. Alongside veteran German émigrés from HSOA, such as former chancellor Heinrich Brüning, he continued to train American diplomats in the histories of European politics and the most effective measures to combat communism. These diplomats then traveled to the embassies in

---

[60] Minutes of the Meeting of the Standing Faculty Committee on International and Regional Studies (9 December 1946), Folder International and Regional Studies 1949–1950, Box 9, HUFGP 17.6.

[61] Clyde Kluckhohn, "Russian Research at Harvard," *World Politics* 1:2 (January 1949): 266–271, here 266. The rest is based on Minutes of the Meeting of the Standing Faculty Committee on International and Regional Studies (25 October 1948); Minutes of the Meeting of the Standing Faculty Committee on International and Regional Studies (17 November 1950), Folder International and Regional Studies 1949–1950, Box 9, HUFGP 17.6. On the Russian Research Center, see David C. Engerman, *Know Your Enemy: The Rise and Fall of America's Soviet Experts* (New York: Oxford University Press, 2009), 43–70.

London, Copenhagen, Frankfurt, and Rome. From there, they would take part in the formation of a Western, anti-Communist alliance.[62]

Equally important to its training of diplomats was the Cold War University's production of knowledge. Across U.S. campuses, Friedrich and others orchestrated enormous projects of data collection and analyses on the world's cultures, societies, and regimes, all prepared for U.S. diplomats. The most ambitious of these was the Human Relations Area Files (HRAF) project, which began in 1948 and was headed from Yale by anthropologist Clellan Ford. Dividing the world among them, twelve of the United States' leading universities produced thick volumes of information and analysis on crucial Cold War battlegrounds. A group of historians and social scientists from the University of Chicago, for example, explored Poland, Laos, and India; their Stanford counterparts contributed eight volumes on China; the team from Indiana University produced detailed studies of Czechoslovakia, Hungary, and Finland; and a group from Cornell studied the Philippines. Funded by the Carnegie Corporation and the U.S. government, HRAF produced dozens of books for U.S. diplomats. Many, in shorter format, were distributed as background readings for thousands of U.S. military troops in Europe and in Asia.[63]

Friedrich spearheaded Harvard's participation in HRAF. Under his supervision, Harvard contributed a lengthy study on East Germany's Communist regime, the German Democratic Republic (whose sovereignty Friedrich insisted on denying by calling it "The Soviet Zone"). Based on both diplomatic reports and official publications, the 646-page study analyzed East Germany's domestic institutions, cultural policies, and economic development. It evaluated the country's potential military capacities and geopolitical value for the Soviets. As Friedrich noted, the report's explicit goal was to assess whether the United States could bring about the regime's demise. With persistent American pressure and radio transmissions to the East German public, he argued, "most of the institutions built by the present regime would fall like the walls of Jericho before the trumpet calls of . . . German democracy." Confident in the inevitable appeal and superiority of a democratic system, the study went on to provide recommendations for economic measures and educational programs "to assimilate the Soviet Zone's society to West German society." Friedrich's knowledge and teaching agenda thus articulated and reinforced the legitimacy of American faith in democratic transformation and anti-Communist propaganda. While never a policymaker himself, they made him an important member of the Cold

[62] Norman Burns (Direction of Foreign Service Institute, Department of State) to Carl J. Friedrich (30 May 1952); List of Vice Consuls studying with Professor Friedrich 1950/1951 (undated, probably late 1951); both in Folder Foreign Service Officers, Box 14, HUGFP 17.6.

[63] Clellan Ford, *Human Relations Area Files, 1949–1969* (New Haven, CT: Human Relations Area Files, 1970).

War establishment, and the report was distributed among State Department officials.[64]

Like the School of Public Policy and HSOA, the Cold War University was not a critical space. Its scholarly energies and the state and philanthropic funding that facilitated these area studies programs were not directed at those who critiqued power structures, challenged their legitimacy, or questioned the logic of the United States' new position as leader of the global struggle against communism. Indeed, the exact opposite was the case. In an era of intense anti-communism, best epitomized by the rise of Joseph McCarthy, Harvard and other universities joined the growing public intolerance of dissent. They voluntarily suppressed—and in several cases fired—those they suspected were "subversive" opponents of the Cold War. For Friedrich and others like him, this was exactly the role that universities were supposed to fulfill. In their hierarchical understanding of democracy, the mission of higher education was to empower elites who would serve the democratic state, not undermine it through critique. The inflexible dichotomy that Friedrich's thought helped inspire equated almost all critique with dangerous subversion. Challenging social hierarchies at home or anti-Communist actions abroad seemed like an existential threat to the covenant. The new opportunities that the Cold War University opened for Friedrich and other European émigrés thus came at the expense of more critical voices. The collaboration between scholarship, philanthropy, and government policymaking remained an agent of Cold War order and hegemony.[65]

No scholars better represent the Cold War University's role as an extension of U.S. policymaking and source of international knowledge than Henry Kissinger and Zbigniew Brzezinski, two young European émigrés who came to Harvard and studied with Friedrich. Kissinger, a young and poor German-Jewish refugee from Bavaria, arrived at Harvard after completing his U.S. military service in 1947 and spent the first decade of his academic career under Friedrich's tutelage. While completing his PhD in international politics, he also served as Friedrich's deputy-editor on his monumental study of East Germany. Perhaps more than anyone, Kissinger skillfully utilized the academic-diplomatic interconnection that Friedrich helped shape, establishing some of Harvard's most important institutions of international studies, such as its Center for International Affairs. After becoming a famous theoretician of international politics, he moved into diplomatic service and ultimately became Richard Nixon's secretary of state

[64] Carl J. Friedrich (ed.), *The Soviet Zone of Germany* (New Haven, CT: Human Relations Area Files, 1956), 9. The enormous correspondence regarding Harvard's participation in HRAF under Friedrich is in Box 8, HUGFP 17.16.

[65] Sigmund Diamond, *Compromised Campus: The Collaboration of Universities with the Intelligence Community* (New York: Oxford University Press, 1992); Ellen Schrecker, *No Ivory Tower: McCarthyism and the Universities* (New York: Oxford University Press, 1986).

in the 1970s. Brzezinski, a refugee from Poland, similarly arrived at Cold War Harvard and collaborated with Friedrich in writing highly influential anti-Communist books. He, too, would move from Harvard with ease, becoming a diplomatic consultant to John F. Kennedy and, later, Jimmy Carter's national security advisor. Like their mentor Friedrich, both Kissinger and Brzezinski understood democracy as a project of knowledgeable and unelected elites who would guard democracy against the weaknesses of mass politics. While serving different parties—Kissinger mostly Republicans, Brzezinski Democrats—both elevated and celebrated the United States as the defender of Western civilization against the Communist evil that sought to destroy it. For both, the structures created by Friedrich made the move from academia to policymaking easy, almost natural. Like an entire generation of bureaucrats and diplomats who passed through Harvard and similar elite institutions, they were the products of the Cold War University.[66]

The Cold War thus provided the final impetus for the broad implementation of Friedrich's democratic vision. For many, Friedrich's ideas and their institutional manifestation were a necessary response to the threat of Communist expansion. They provided the framework for the monumental mobilization of knowledge and extensive training required by a prolonged global conflict. Drawing on InSoSta, for Friedrich the deployment of academia in the service of the democratic state was the obvious solution to international instability. In the same manner that responsible elites had to stabilize covenant democracy in Weimar and during the New Deal, they now helped the state fend off its foreign enemies. By the mid-1950s, Harvard's transformation was complete, and its collaboration with the government had become the norm. Only the rise of a new generation in the 1960s and the Vietnam War would undermine this intellectual consensus and thereby transform universities into centers of critique toward U.S. government policy.

The Cold War University and Democratic Elites in Germany

When U.S. occupation authorities arrived in Germany in 1945, they did not only seek to replace the Nazi dictatorship with a democratic parliament, elections, and constitutions. Rather, they believed that German democracy—and world peace—would not survive unless they dramatically re-

---

[66] On Brzezinski's thought, as well as his collaboration with Friedrich, see Engerman, *Know Your Enemy*, esp. 108 on. The work on Kissinger is vast. The best account of Kissinger and the Cold War University, which deeply influenced my own work, is Suri, *Henry Kissinger and the American Century*. Kissinger was one of Friedrich's closest students, and the two remained in touch throughout Kissinger's academic and political career. Their correspondence on the editing of *The Soviet Zone of Germany* is in Folder Common Man, Box 9, HUGFP 17.12.

structured German culture, national character, and patterns of thought to instill democratic, anti-imperialist, and anti-authoritarian norms. Central to this ambitious project was the remaking of German universities. For twelve years, the universities of Tübingen, Heidelberg, Munich, and other institutions of higher learning had functioned as organs of the Nazi war machine. Their professors, publications, and curricula justified and helped craft the Third Reich's racist and imperialist agendas. As part of their vision of a democratic and anti-Nazi Germany, U.S. authorities therefore sought to de-Nazify the seven German universities they controlled. Under the guidance of Edward Hartshorne, a Harvard sociologist who studied in Weimar-era Heidelberg and helped Friedrich build Harvard's Public Policy Graduate School, the U.S. military assembled American philanthropists, education specialists, and anti-Nazi intellectuals to design a democratic German academia. After serving the Third Reich, these institutions were to become the motors of new society based on free elections, nonviolent citizen participation, and the rule of law. They were to train the new anti-Nazi, democratic, and responsible elite.[67]

At the same time, and much less noted by historians, these efforts were not simply the product of "Americanization." Germany's reconstruction also marked the resurrection of earlier educational models, most notably InSoSta. With the backing of the United States' diplomatic establishment, members of the "Weber School," including Friedrich himself, resumed the democratic theories and programs first developed in Weimar-era Heidelberg and realized in the United States. With striking confidence that what failed in the 1920s would now succeed, Friedrich returned to Heidelberg with the support of the Rockefeller Foundation to train responsible elites through democratic curricula, an academia-state-philanthropy bond, and international academic exchange. As part of this effort, he emerged as one of postwar Germany's most important democratic thinkers and educators. After the horrific violence and devastating defeat of World War II, his older ideas about the benefits of democratic elites—and the limits of mass democracy—resonated with many more Germans than they had in Weimar. In many ways, Friedrich's ideas marked both the scope and limits of Germany's postwar democratic consensus. They were a revolution after Nazism, but a revolution that privileged stiff social hierarchies and stability, not critical challenges to the state.

---

[67] See the scholarship cited in note 3, as well as Brian Puaca, *Learning Democracy: Education Reform in West Germany* (New York: Berghahn, 2009). On the tying of West German academia to the Western and anti-Soviet alliance, see Helka Rausch (ed.), *Transatlantischer Kulturtransfer im "Kalten Krieg"* (Leipzig: Comparativ, 2007); Annette Puckhaber, "German Student Exchange Programs in the United States, 1946–1952," *Bulletin of the German Historical Institute* 30 (2002): 123–141.

The rise of the Cold War prolonged and expanded these efforts beyond the end of occupation in 1949. Americans and Germans alike saw West German universities as not only a motor of democracy but also as necessary barriers against Communist subversion. As they did at Harvard, U.S. diplomats sought to incorporate the universities at Marburg, Heidelberg, and Frankfurt into their broader mission of Cold War mobilization and alliance-building. Through lavish investment, cultural programming, and curricular intervention, they hoped to make them into Cold War universities, bastions of democratic stability and anti-Communist recruitment. Few benefited more from these efforts than Friedrich's educational programs in Heidelberg. Friedrich's visions of elite democracy, fierce anti-communism, and his belief in a natural alliance between Germany and the United States made him the epitome of Cold War education. By the end of the 1950s, with massive American investment, Friedrich and his allies had once again transformed Heidelberg into a bustling intellectual center of anti-Communist democratic thought. The Cold War University was thus not just an American institution. Through Friedrich and others, it became a crucial model for West German education.

Friedrich's initial return to postwar Germany was not officially tied to education. In 1946 General Lucius Clay, the commander of the U.S. occupation of Germany, invited Friedrich to helped draft new democratic constitutions, first for the states of Bavaria, Baden, and Hesse, and in 1948 for West Germany's federal state. In all these positions, Friedrich sought to realize Althusius's covenantal model by creating a decentralized regime in which local and state governments held substantial authority over education, taxes, and cultural policies. He also helped secure the creation of an upper house alongside the Reichstag, the *Bundesrat*, whose members were to be appointed by the parliaments of the states (*Länder*). Its role was to balance the directly elected Reichstag and the reckless masses.[68] Friedrich saw these constitutions as the first steps in constructing a new political identity in Germany, one centered not on nationalism but on commitment to and active participation in democratic institutions. Drawing from his earlier ideas, he maintained that the survival of liberty depended on citizens' investment

---

[68] The information on Friedrich's participation in the drafting of states' constitutions is from Memorandum, Carl J. Friedrich to the Chief of Staff (4 March 1947); Memorandum on State Constitutions, Carl Friedrich to Deputy Military Governor (28 January 1947); both in Folder DR CJ Friedrich Adviser to Gen Clay, Box 93, OMGUS, RG 260, NARA. The information on his participation in the drafting of the federal constitution (the "Basic Law") is from Memorandum, Carl J. Friedrich to General Clay (3 September 1948), Folder II 44–3, Box 136, OMGUS, RG 260, NARA. For Friedrich's personal recollections on his role in drafting the *Grundgesetz*, see Carl J. Friedrich, "Rebuilding the German Constitution," *American Political Science Review* 43 (1949): 461–482, 704–720. See also Edmund Spevak, *Allied Control and German Freedom* (Hamburg: LIT, 2001), 275ff.

in democratic institutions. Through their active participation in political associations and by exercising their political rights, they would develop a sense of collective belonging through peaceful and self-ruling covenants, which would replace the primacy of such national concepts as language, race, folk culture, or ethnic identity. This was a democracy that sought not to empower civil society or grant social mobility but to establish loyalty between citizens and the constitutional state.[69]

For Friedrich, the key to assuring democracy in Germany was the training of a new democratic elite through the rebuilding of German higher education. This new democratic bureaucracy would defend the spirit of the covenant, of peaceful political interactions between groups of citizens; essentially, it would model the democratic norms, interactions, and practices necessary to displace both Nazi bureaucrats and authoritarian patterns of thought. As he wrote to U.S. occupation officials, through the training of a talented "responsible bureaucracy," the new democratic experiment would succeed where Weimar had failed. "The failure of the Weimar Republic," he warned, "was not due to specific constitutional problems" but to "the maintenance of power in the established [imperial-era] bureaucracy." It stemmed from the failure of democratic forces to dislodge the old personnel. "The situation was such as might have arisen in the United States if George Washington, after the revolution, had proposed to carry forward the American government with the British and Tory officials who had carried on the administration before."[70]

Friedrich therefore utilized his position in the U.S. occupation to intervene in the reform of German universities. Throughout the occupation era, he traveled between Heidelberg, Munich, and Berlin, organized scholarly groups, and met rectors and professors from German universities "to discuss the place of the university within the constitutional scheme as a whole." In 1948 he further helped coordinate the establishment of a new university in West Berlin, the Freie Universität Berlin (Free University of Berlin, or FU). Designed explicitly as a counterweight to the city's Soviet-controlled Humboldt University, the FU brought together Rockefeller officials, U.S. occupation personnel, and anti-Communist German intellectuals. Friedrich provided many of the syllabi on political theory, democracy, and communism, which were taken straight from his classes at Harvard. After 1949, these course plans were embraced by political science departments in Marburg, Cologne, and Hamburg. These were the first steps in reforming German academia into centers of "responsible" elites. As an extension of the Cold

[69] These ideas received their first systematic manifestation in Carl J. Friedrich, *Constitutional Government and Politics* (New York: Harper, 1937).

[70] Memorandum, Carl Friedrich to Henry Parkman, The Significance of the Constitutional Draft Prepared by the SED in 1946 (18 March 1947), Folder DR CJ Friedrich Adviser to Gen Clay, Box 93, OMGUS, RG 260, NARA. Emphasis added.

War University in Germany, many visitors celebrated Berlin's curricula as the model for pro-democratic and anti-Communist education not only for Germany but also for the rest of Europe.[71]

Nowhere was the role of the "Weber School" in Germany's reconstruction more prominent than in Heidelberg. The initial driving force behind this resurrection was Alfred Weber, Friedrich's mentor and the spirit behind InSoSta. In 1945, after twelve years of forced retirement, Weber was eager to resume his educational endeavors in support of a new republic. The trauma of war and total destruction had not weakened his firm belief in democracy's need for a talented elite, nor his conviction that only political education could prepare the "responsible bureaucracy" required to rule the country. The establishment of democratic structures without appropriate political education would lead to national decline and spiritual impoverishment. "The two great wars and the Nazi period deprived Germany of her best leaders," he despaired in a conversation with an American visitor, and there was an imminent danger that political power would fall into the hands of "mediocrities."[72]

As in Weimar, Weber was possessed by a deep anxiety that modern society had become too bureaucratized to allow human freedom. Industrialized economies and powerful state agencies had destroyed the freedoms of individuals and diminished the power of elected officials. In Weber's eyes, the Nazi regime was "a totalitarian bureaucracy," the most monstrous manifestation of these broad trends of modern society. It was the product of the masses' inability to recognize the value of democratic liberties. The aging Weber—now in his late seventies—therefore believed that the training of a responsible bureaucracy was the only bulwark against Germany's collapse into another dictatorship. From his home in Heidelberg, he began assembling old and new allies for the rebuilding of InSoSta. These included Dolf Sternberger, a rising star of legal democratic theory who arrived to serve as his assistant, and Karl Geiler, the State of Hesse's postwar prime minister (and Weber's former student) who came to lecture in Heidelberg. Together, this group of scholars and politicians established the first pro-democratic intellectual magazine in postwar Germany, *Die Wandlung* (Transformation), and began drafting programs for democratic curricula. In 1946 they proposed reopening InSoSta in Heidelberg. This training center, Weber

---

[71] Quotation is from Letter, Friedrich to Henry Parkman (April 1 1947), Folder Correspondence (out), Box 1, HUGFP 17.39.5. On the opening of the FU and Friedrich's role in it, see Siegward Lönnendonker, *Freie Universität Berlin: Gründung einer politischen Universität* (Berlin: Duncker & Humbolt, 1988). Friedrich was also a member of the 1949 conference that established political science as a discipline in German universities. His contribution is detailed in *Die politischen Wissenschaften an den deutschen Universitäten und Hochschulen* (Frankfurt a.M.: Neue Presse, 1950).

[72] Carl Schorske trip diary (June 1950), Folder 41, Box 7, Series 717, RG 1.1, RFA, RAC.

claimed, would help complete the democratic revolution that Weimar had begun.[73]

Given Germany's catastrophic postwar poverty, only American wealth could turn such dreams into reality. And as in Weimar, it was Friedrich who provided the link between Weber's educational visions and the officials of the Rockefeller Foundation. In the winter of 1948, the foundation's officials met with Friedrich and then traveled to Heidelberg to meet Weber and Sternberger. Impressed by Weber's plans and the enthusiasm of his students, they renewed the support that the Nazis had blocked a decade earlier. By year's end, InSoSta was officially refounded and its courses on democratic politics and international cooperation resumed. Through Friedrich's initiative, the U.S. government also invested in InSoSta's resurrection both before and after West Germany's independence. The Rockefeller Foundation and the U.S. government contributed tens of thousands of dollars to fund InSoSta's study of democratic institutions and leadership. In their mind, Heidelberg again was to become the intellectual center for pro-democratic and anti-Communist mobilization.[74]

U.S. authorities also began to reassemble InSoSta's old guard, who, like Friedrich, had spent the war in exile. In them, American diplomats saw the intellectuals who would mobilize German academia in the service of the Cold War. In 1948 Alexander Rüstow, Friedrich's partner in establishing the DAAD, returned from exile in Turkey and replaced Weber as InSoSta's director. In 1954 the philosopher Arnold Bergstraesser likewise returned from exile in Chicago to lead the reconstruction of the University of Freiburg, where he established what would become known as the pro-democratic "Freiburg School" of political thought. Together, these political theorists were among the leading figures in postwar Germany's intellectual reconstruction. Their writings and teachings called for rigorous German support of anti-Communist mobilization and for a deep, close alliance with the United States.[75]

---

[73] The quotations are from Alfred Weber and Alexander Mitscherlich, *Freier Sozialismus* (Heidelberg: Schneider, 1946), 5. On Weber's prominence in postwar Heidelberg, see Sean A. Forner, "The Promise of Publicness: Intellectual Elites and Participatory Politics in Postwar Heidelberg," *Modern Intellectual History* 9:3 (2012): 641–440; Freytag-Loringhoven, *Erziehung im Kollegienhaus*, 265–326.

[74] Robert Havinghurst, Interview Notes (9 October 1947), Folder 20, Box 4; Robert Havinghurst, Interview Notes (10 October 1947), Folder 20, Box 4; Memorandum, Friedrich to the Rockefeller Foundation Board (16 November 1951), Folder 197, Box 21; all in Series 717, RG 1.1, RFA, RAC.

[75] On Rüstow's postwar work, see Jan Hegner, *Alexander Rüstow: Ordnungspolitische Konzeption und Einfluss auf das Wirtschaftspolitische Leitbild der Nachkriegszeit in der Bundesrepublik Deutschland* (Stuttgart: Lucius & Lucius, 2000). On Bergstraesser, see Horst Schmitt, *Politikwissenschaft und freiheitliche Demokratie* (Baden: Nomos, 1995).

This resurrected collaboration between U.S. philanthropy and German scholars facilitated Friedrich's continued influence in Germany as a central figure in political education long after the end of the occupation. Once InSoSta reopened, Friedrich regularly traveled to Germany to teach at Heidelberg. In 1956, through the cooperation of the institute and the Rockefeller Foundation, Heidelberg University established its first chair of political education, which Friedrich held as a part-time position in addition to teaching at Harvard. In the 1950s and 1960s, Friedrich would divide his time between Heidelberg and Harvard. According to Alexander Rüstow, this return sparked "intense excitement" among Germany's anti-Communist theorists, who would now view Heidelberg, Rüstow hoped, as the "most important center of Political Science in West Germany." Throughout the decade, Friedrich published a stream of books and studies on constitutions, elections, and their religious origins. He also taught hundreds of German students about democracy and its Nazi and Communist enemies. Like their counterparts at Harvard, these students learned about parliamentary regimes, federalism and democracy, the nature of communism, Christianity and politics, theories of American government, American political thought, and, most important in Friedrich's eyes, Althusius's political theory of democracy's Calvinist roots.[76]

This mission to disseminate democratic language underpinned the refounded InSoSta's wide-ranging educational campaign during West Germany's formative years. Like Harvard, the Institute in Heidelberg (soon to be renamed the Alfred Weber Institute) became an arm of the state to promote stability and anti-Communist mobilization. Under Friedrich's and Dolf Sternberger's supervision, an army of young students and scholars embarked on the first major West German research project on the nature of democratic politics. During the project's first year alone, they generated a stream of short books and booklets designed for classrooms across the nation, bearing such titles as "The Nature of Parliamentary Groups," "The Formation and Forms of the Coalition Government," "The Character of Party Resolutions in Parliament," "The Behavior of Parliamentary Groups in Voting," and "The Structures of Parliamentary Politics," which served as

---

[76] Quotation is from Letter, Alexander Rüstow to Kenneth Thompson (16 July 1956), Folder 199, Box 21, Series 717S, RG 1.1, RFA, RAC. Friedrich's most important publications on democratic theory are his *Demokratie als Herrschafts- und Lebensform* (Heidelberg: Quelle & Meyer, 1959); *Föderalismus und Bundesverfassungsrecht* (Heidelberg: Quelle & Meyer, 1962); *Die Philosophie des Rechts in historischer Perspektive* (Berlin: Springer, 1955); and *Die Staatsraison im Verfassungsstaat. Politische Bildung* (Munich: Isar, 1956). The information on Friedrich's return to Heidelberg is from Letter, Rector of the HU to the HU Kasse (9 June 1950), FII-B-0682/1, Nr. 64, Heft 6 (DAAD 1922–1962), UAH, and Interview notes, Kenneth Thompson with Carl J. Friedrich (17 March 1958); Report, Carl J. Friedrich to the Rockefeller Foundation Board (16 October 1959); both in Folder 199, Box 21, Series 717S, RG 1.1, RFA, RAC.

reading texts in German high schools. The institute likewise organized a series of research groups on the "sociology of representation," "parliamentary opposition," and "studies of national elections." During the early postwar years, this reintroduction of democratic language was of profound importance in forming a new political identity that made parliamentary politics, the separation of powers, and the rule of law central to West Germany's self-perception.[77]

Aided by the influx of American funds, the Weber Institute expanded to become one of the country's leading centers of political studies. As its volume of activity gradually surpassed its Weimar-era endeavors, it hosted dozens of lectures, symposia, and international conferences on German democracy, religious history, and the evils of global communism. From across Europe and the United States, politicians, scholars, and philanthropists converged on Heidelberg to discuss how to strengthen Western integration. From 1953 until 1960, figures such as Baden-Württemberg's prime minister and the German president listened to the institute's students discuss their research on parliamentary systems, the electoral apparatus, and civil service training in Britain, Switzerland, France, and the United States. As the decade progressed, young businessmen and politicians flocked to Heidelberg. Among the young workers the institute hired and educated was Helmut Kohl, the future German chancellor from the conservative Christian-Democratic Party, who in 1957 completed a dissertation on the postwar rebuilding of the German parties. Many American observers believed that the institute was the "single biggest success" among the various programs intended to reconstruct German intellectual life. Like Harvard, its many publications and courses helped train a democratic and anti-Communist elite and put academia in the service of the democratic state.[78]

Heidelberg also welcomed the rebirth of Friedrich's most innovative prewar program of cultural diplomacy, the academic exchange program. As if three decades had not passed, academia mobilized to forge an international elite. In 1949 a group of British occupation officers, who were alumni of the program from the 1920s, decided to re-create the DAAD as a pan-European and transatlantic initiative geared to promote international understanding. In their mind, Heidelberg, its birthplace, was to be the first center to host the program, alongside the FU in Berlin and the prestigious University of Tübingen. In the summer of 1950, the first group of French students crossed

---

[77] Report, Götz Roth to Joseph Willits (24 January 1953), Folder 197, Box 21, Series 717S, RG 1.1, RFA, RAC. On Sternberger's importance in forming the concept of "constitutional patriotism," see Jan-Werner Müller, *Constitutional Patriotism*, 21–23.

[78] Quotation is from Letter, Kenneth Thompson to Carl J. Friedrich (24 February 1956), Folder 199, Box 21, Series 717S, RG 1.1, RFA, RAC. The information is based on Report (1 September 1953), Folder 198; Report, Dolf Sternberger to Kenneth Thompson (13 December 1957), Folder 199; both in Box 21, Series 717S, RG 1.1, RFA, RAC.

into Germany and arrived at Heidelberg to study at the Alfred Weber Institute. A year later, British and American students joined them and the first German group traveled to Harvard. By 1953, Baden's Ministry of Culture had expanded the DAAD at breakneck speed to include Italy, Sweden, Iran, Greece, and Israel, and by the end of the decade it had reached Japan. French, British, American, and German émigré scholars also utilized the DAAD framework to make their way to Heidelberg. They included Hannah Arendt, who lectured on Communist terror; Herbert Marcuse, who discussed his Freudian interpretation of Soviet "Totalitarian perversion"; and Arnold Brecht, who lectured on the values of German democracy. As it did three decades earlier, the DAAD sought to strengthen German democracy at home through intellectual exchange with other democratic states.[79]

By the late 1950s, Friedrich's work and the institute had surpassed even Harvard in their reach, when they became the foundation for the political education of millions of German high school students. In 1958, following a prolonged campaign conducted with his friend and colleague Bergstraesser, the two men helped institute "politics" (*Politik*) as an obligatory high school topic, and their writings heavily influenced the programs' curricula. Initially in the state of Hesse, and subsequently in Baden-Württemberg and other states, teachers, who were all trained by political scientists, taught classes about the nature of the democratic system, the parliamentary process, and constitutional reforms. As Heidelberg political theorist Klaus von Beyme later recalled, Friedrich's theories on democracy in the postwar era were "epoch-making ... the teaching of an entire generation." Beyme declared that Friedrich showed the young generation that "there was another, democratic tradition in Germany, which was the counter-image to the year 1933."[80]

Hyperbole aside, by 1960, Friedrich's vision of democratic, supranational, and elite education had entered mainstream West German thought.

[79] Memorandum, Rector of the HU to the Ministry of Culture and Education of Baden (7 February 1950), B-0680/2, VII, 1, Nr. 80, UAH; Memorandum, Rector of the HU to the Ministry of Culture and Education of Baden, "Promotion of the International Student Exchange" (10 April 1953), B-0680/2, VII, 1, Nr. 80, UAH; Letter, Rector of UH to the Ministry of Culture and Education in Baden (22 June 1951); Report, Eberhard Drees to the Senate of HU (5 January 1962), Letter, Rector of the UH to Universitätskasse (4 June 1956); List of Visiting Lecturers (14 May 1952); Letter, Rector of the UH to Universitätskasse (4 June 1956); all in FII—B-0682/1, Nr. 64, Heft 6, UAH.

[80] I am grateful to Noah Strote and his work on Bergstraesser for directing my attention to these facts about German education. Details on Friedrich's role in this process appear in Report, Carl J. Friedrich to the Rockefeller Foundation Board (16 October 1959), Folder 199, Box 21, Series 717S, RG 1.1, RFA, RAC. On the introduction of *Politik* as part of West German high school curricula, see Johann Zillien, *Politische Bildung in Hessen von 1945 bis 1965* (Frankfurt a.M.: Peter Lang, 1994). The quotation is from Klaus von Beyme, "Vorwort," *Theorie und Politik: Festschrift zum 70. Geburtstag für Carl Joachim Friedrich* (The Hague: Martisun Nijhoff, 1971), v–viii, here vi.

Powered by U.S. efforts to mobilize West German academia for the Cold War, his theories, personal networks, and decades of institutional experience helped establish a tight interaction between German academia and the democratic state. Like its American counterpart, the German Cold War University was not conceived with social mobility in mind. It was both created by and designed to train self-appointed elites, who were to guard democracy from reckless Nazis or Communists. In both the United States and Germany, universities became channels for the international circulation of such elites. They produced knowledge, curricula, and students that were supposed to bring the two countries together, marshaling them to combat communism at home and overseas. In this era of large-scale mobilization, InSoSta was no longer an idiosyncratic experiment of pro-democratic Protestants. On both sides of the Atlantic, it had become the intellectual and institutional mainstream of higher education.

In the early Cold War, political mobilization did not rest on anti-communism alone. Scholars, diplomats, and leaders across the political spectrum believed that a vigorous and strong democratic society was crucial to defeating the Communist enemy. It was thus imperative that both Americans and Germans be exposed to democratic visions. Democracy could only overcome its inherent weakness and adversaries through a strong commitment to democratic values. U.S. diplomat George Kennan expressed this prevailing sentiment when he warned in 1946 of the coming struggle against the Soviet Union:

> Much depends on [the] health and vigor of our own society.... This is the point at which domestic and foreign policies meet. Every courageous and incisive measure to solve internal problems of our own society, to improve self-confidence, discipline, morale, and community spirit of our own people, is a diplomatic victory over Moscow worth a thousand diplomatic notes and joint communiqués.

"Healthy" politics thus required a frantic quest for "vigor," "spirit," and voluntary action both at home and abroad. This conviction that democracy required new spiritual safeguards and leadership was key to a broader "Cold War consensus."[81]

The Cold War University was at the core of this consensus. Scholars had to both produce the knowledge necessary for waging a global Cold War and cultivate in students the values and responsibilities inherent in democratic citizenship. Moreover, higher education had to become the center for train-

---

[81] Kennan's quotation is from the famous "Long Telegram" (22 February 1946), http://www2.gwu.edu/~nsarchiv/coldwar/documents/episode-1/kennan.htm (accessed 9 October 2013). On the "Cold War consensus," see, for example, Wendy Wall, *Inventing the American Way* (New York: Oxford University Press, 2008); Benjamin O. Fordham, *Building the Cold War Consensus* (Ann Arbor: University of Michigan Press, 1998).

ing responsible elites who would harness democracy's instability and ensure it did not fall into the hands of extremists. Lecture halls and libraries were to be the spaces where capable leaders would acquire the knowledge and capabilities they needed. Academic centers would not produce free-floating thinkers for the purpose of individual self-improvement. Rather, they would be hubs for the training of democratic elites that would work within and alongside state institutions.

But like the broader political visions that shaped it, the Cold War University closed as many options as it opened. It had little room for dissent, opposition, or challenges to existing hierarchies and order. In its obsession with molding consensus, this intellectual space fostered an atmosphere of political hysteria. For Harvard's President Conant, Friedrich, and their allies, disloyalty to existing hierarchies and government policies could easily seem like a dark subversion against the essence of democracy. The new academic structure that emerged from the upheavals of the 1940s simultaneously extended and limited the scope of knowledge production and teaching. It was, like Friedrich's theory, both innovative and traditionalist, expansive and harshly exclusive.

Friedrich's international travels and his intellectual prominence on both sides of the Atlantic show that in both its origins and consequences, the Cold War consensus was not merely an American phenomenon. The intellectual foundations for a key institution of democratic mobilization—the Cold War University—lay in Weimar Germany, in religious and elitist visions and in centers such as InSoSta. Motivated by the conviction that democracy was authentically German and Protestant, Friedrich and others in Heidelberg sought to produce in the 1920s the capable elites that democracy required. They built new educational programs and crafted new curricula, seeking to train leaders who would guard democratic freedoms. At Harvard, Friedrich found the space to continue these early experiments. Drawing on the same connections and ideas, he expanded InSoSta through new schools and programs. It was thinkers like Friedrich who provided the vision, the networks, and the models that transformed the university into a central organ of a democratic Cold War state. Weimar ideas provided crucial foundations for the Cold War University.

The legacies of this transformation were not limited to the United States. Under the aegis of American diplomacy, Friedrich helped fundamentally shape the nature of postwar German democracy. Resurrecting InSoSta and its networks, Friedrich expanded its curricula and institutional models across West Germany. He helped transform German universities from hubs of authoritarian and Nazi dominance to centers of democratic development and citizenship. For Friedrich, American hegemony in Germany opened spaces to revive his international visions of the 1920s. As they did in the Weimar-era DAAD, educated men and women were again to carry the spirit of the democratic covenant across the Atlantic, strengthen their country's democratic edifice, and join the religious crusade of suppressing subversive and expansionistic enemies. During the period of Germany's reconstruction and the subsequent formation of the Cold War Western alliance, these ideas underpinned a vast international cultural exchange. Thousands of scholars and students crossed the Atlantic to visit, study, and learn from one another. Despite the idiosyncrasies and peculiar historical narratives of Friedrich's thinking, his work inspired a broad institutional transformation. German universities were to spearhead the shift from the nation as the ultimate source of political legitimacy to a commitment to a supranational, religious, and anti-Communist community. This conviction became a cornerstone for postwar German democracy.

Friedrich's success in carrying his ideas from Weimar to the Cold War highlights the unrecognized similarities between these two movements of democratic mobilization. When Germans and Americans came together to restructure Germany after World War II, the dilemmas they confronted were not entirely new. The postwar moment evoked challenges reminiscent of those that had arisen in the wake of the 1918 Weimar revolution. Once again, a republic had to be built following a humiliating military defeat and amid the shattered dreams of imperial glory. Proponents of democracy would have to convince the German population of the political legitimacy of this system after, and not before, the creation of democratic institutions. As in Weimar, a democratic state was to emerge in a society whose cultural, political, and economic institutions had not yet been democratized. And these democratic reforms would have to be put in place under the specter of Communist subversion and fears about the rise of the Soviet Union. During the early Cold War, democracy thus reverberated with ideas from the Weimar era, both in their exciting possibilities and their impoverished limits. To Friedrich, the covenant that was born in Weimar had survived Nazism and total war and emerged triumphant.

CHAPTER II

Socialist Reform, the Rule of Law, and Labor Outreach

ERNST FRAENKEL AND THE CONCEPT OF "COLLECTIVE DEMOCRACY"

IN THE 1950s, the German left went through a radical intellectual and political transformation. During the immediate postwar years, Social Democrats (or Socialists, as they were interchangeably called) had focused on rapidly rebuilding their party, the Social Democratic Party of Germany (SPD), and resuming their efforts to bring the working class to power. They adhered to a strictly Marxist ideology that opposed cooperation with the middle class and demanded the nationalization of all major industries. As their leader, Kurt Schumacher, proclaimed in fiery speeches, "true" democracy required breaking the power of big industrialists and capitalists, who exploited the people. Distributing that wealth through a centralized and planned economy was the path to Germany's democratization. In 1959, however, having suffered several electoral defeats, the SPD Congress gathered in Bad Godesberg to adopt an entirely new ideological platform. The party renounced Marxism, abandoned its traditional anti-clerical rhetoric, and sought to transform its class-based tactics. The SPD leadership instead embraced a vision of democracy that was based on a free-market economy and cooperation with the middle classes. In an emotional speech, Herbert Wehner, a senior Socialist leader and one of the new agenda's most vocal supporters, called on the delegates to leave the party's past behind them and to adopt a new vision of a multiclass society. The cheering crowd enthusiastically concurred. It endorsed the new program by a huge majority of 324 to 16 votes.[1]

This ideological reversal was paralleled by an equally striking transformation in the Socialists' view of international politics. Throughout the 1950s, the SPD had refused to support Germany's alliance with the United States and repeatedly called for Cold War neutrality. Socialist leaders as-

---

[1] For a detailed description of the Bad Godesberg Congress, see Kurt Klotzbach, *Der Weg zur Staatspartei: Programmatik, praktische Politik und Organisation der deutschen Sozialdemokratie 1945 bis 1965* (Berlin: Dietz, 1996), 433–53.

serted that only through negotiations with the Soviets, held beyond the reach of the North Atlantic Treaty Organization (NATO) and Western capitalist domination, could Germany achieve the full independence and reunification necessary to build a social-democratic planned economy. In a torrent of demonstrations, petitions, and campaigns, the party sought to detach Germany from the Western bloc. It further conducted an independent foreign policy, meeting with Communist leaders for negotiations, and mobilizing its supporters to oppose the West German government's policies of aligning with the West. Only in 1960, several months after declaring a new path in Bad Godesberg, did the SPD reverse its position on international diplomacy. Less remembered by historians, but equally important, Germany's second largest party proclaimed its support of NATO and embraced Germany's membership in the U.S.-led Western alliance.

The dual transformation of the German left, from a class-based party of international neutrality into a broad-tent party of Cold War conviction, has long puzzled observers. Historians have attributed this shift to electoral calculations, generational changes, and the influence of the American ideology of "consensus capitalism," which professed the ability of the free market to improve workers' conditions without a planned economy.[2] The SPD's shift, however, had deeper roots. Its dramatic change drew from intellectual projects rooted in the Weimar period. No one represents this continuity better than Ernst Fraenkel, one of the most important Socialist intellectuals in postwar Germany. As a young thinker in the 1920s, Fraenkel was a member of a unique intellectual school that sought to fuse Socialist and bourgeois theories of law, politics, and democracy. In this line of thought, it was incumbent on Socialists and middle-class liberals to join together in building a new kind of democratic regime, premised on equal respect for individual rights and social welfare. According to Fraenkel, the SPD had to renounce its belief that only the nationalization of the economy would bring about "true" democratic equality. Instead, Socialists had to embrace democratic visions that centered on individual rights, reach out to the middle class, and focus on welfare programs. In Fraenkel's mind, the true threat to this progressive vision was not the middle classes and industrialists, as many Socialists claimed, but ultimately communism. Therefore, the SPD's chief

---

[2] For scholarship that focuses on electoral considerations, see, for example, Helga Grebing, *Geschichte der deutschen Arbeiterbewegung* (Berlin: Vorwärts Buch, 2007); Franz Walter, *Die SPD: vom Proletariat zur Neuen Mitte* (Berlin: Alexander Fest, 2002); Diane L. Parness, *The SPD and the Challenge of Mass Politics* (Boulder: Westview Press, 1991). For emphasis on the generational dimension of the transformation, see Tilman Fichter, *Die SPD und die Nation* (Ulstein: Berlin, 1993); Peter Lösche and Franz Walter, *Die SPD: Klassenpartei-Volkspartei-Quotenpartei* (Darmstadt: Wissenschaftliche Buchgesellschaft, 1992). On U.S. influence, see Julia Angster, *Konsenskapitalismus und Sozialdemokratie: Die Westernisierung von SPD und DGB* (Munich: Oldenbourg Wissenschaftsverlag, 2003).

objective was to forge a broad coalition with the middle classes to crush the revolutionary and radical left.

As with Friedrich, it was the dramatic expansion of U.S. power after World War II and the rise of the Cold War that presented Fraenkel with an unexpected opportunity to bring his vision to the fore. And this cooperation with American institutions revealed both the progressive potential and oppressive narrowness of his politics. After fleeing the Nazis by emigrating to the United States and then working for U.S. intelligence during the war, Fraenkel sought to create a new Socialist democracy on the other side of the globe, in East Asia. In 1945 Fraenkel joined the U.S. troops occupying Korea and rapidly emerged as one of the occupation's most influential officials. Deeply convinced that his democratic theory was universal and thus applicable to all states and people, he sought to shape Korea according to his own ideology, one that was equally based on individual liberties and social equality. For five years, Fraenkel directed enormous U.S. financial aid to Korea, seeking to radically reform the Korean economy and educational system and to participate in the drafting of the South Korean constitution. Equally important, Fraenkel played an active role in the diplomatic drama that led to Korea's tragic partition. Fueled by a fierce anti-communism carried over from Weimar, he helped conduct the anti-Soviet strategy that put an end to U.S.-Soviet cooperation and disastrously divided the Korean nation. Just as Friedrich utilized U.S. institutions to reproduce his own elite visions from his Heidelberg days, so did Fraenkel use the U.S. military as the vehicle for his own theory of social democracy and vigilant anti-communism in Korea.

In 1951 Fraenkel returned to West Germany, where he resumed his attempts to reshape German Socialist views of democracy. After his long exile and work for the U.S. government, he was convinced that the United States was the fulfillment of his political vision and that an American alliance was the best tool to transform the German left. In particular, this bond would help delegitimize those who sought dangerous anti-capitalist and anti-democratic economic redistribution by excluding them from influencing policy. Fraenkel was therefore the most prominent West German Socialist intellectual to urge the SPD to abandon its focus on nationalization, embrace cross-class cooperation, and forge an anti-Soviet alliance with the United States. His intense outreach to German Socialists, combined with his highly influential writings, provided the language for those Socialists who sought to reform the SPD and make it into a welfare-based, pro-Western force. The transformation of the German left during the 1950s was thus not merely the product of "Americanization" or Cold War politics; it was deeply informed by intellectual projects that Socialists such as Fraenkel conceived decades earlier. Ultimately, Fraenkel utilized both his Weimar-era theory and his personal experience in the U.S. military to help bridge the gap between the German left and the United States. The alliance that he helped forge became the backbone of Cold War politics for decades.

DEMOCRACY, LABOR, AND LAW IN FRANKFURT AND BERLIN

For German Socialists, the democratic revolution that swept Germany in the fall of 1918 brought both exhilarating triumphs and disheartening compromises. Since its creation in the nineteenth century, the Social Democratic Party had demanded radical reforms, such as the redistribution of wealth, the nationalization of major industries, and the abolition of voting regulations that privileged citizens with high income. Despite state attempts at repression, the SPD became the country's largest party and the most vocal opponent of the imperial regime. After Germany was rocked by massive protests against World War I, it was SPD leaders who impeached the monarchy and proclaimed the establishment of a new republic. Socialist leaders Phillipp Scheidemann and Friedrich Ebert declared themselves Germany's new rulers in Berlin, and the SPD became the country's governing party. During the revolution's early days, the Socialists envisioned this new republic as the first step in the creation of a fundamentally new social order. Soon, they believed, they would establish a planned economy and bring about full economic equality. The Weimar Constitution, which they drafted in concert with other pro-democratic parties, reflected their vision of socioeconomic equality as the key for a true democracy. It established social security, imposed minimum wages, granted unions the right to participate in the running of factories, and turned countless other Socialist policies into foundational rights for all Germans.[3]

These elating dreams of total Socialist dominance were quickly shattered, however, when a radical wing of the party broke away from the SPD. Under the electrifying leadership of Rosa Luxemburg and Karl Liebknecht, the new German Communist Party (KPD) sought to destroy the young republic and its parliament, replace them with a workers' dictatorship, and abolish private property. In early 1919 the SPD joined forces with its former right-wing opponents in violently suppressing the KPD's armed Communist uprising. Communism, the Socialists believed, would not achieve true democracy but impose a party dictatorship and political terror. Scheidemann and Ebert therefore encouraged nationalist and monarchist militias to crush the KPD, leading to vicious street battles and bloodbaths that killed thousands. This violent schism fueled a deep animosity between the Socialists and the Communist Party that endured well into the 1920s. The

---

[3] For powerful overviews, see A. J. Ryder, *The German Revolution of 1918* (New York: Cambridge University Press, 2008); Pierre Broué, *The German Revolution* (Boston: Brill, 2005).

German left's traumatic division was one of the defining trademarks of politics in the Weimar Republic.[4]

This rift in the left forced many Socialists to reconsider their political alliances, in particular their attitude toward the bourgeois middle class. Due to the rupture with the Communists, the Socialists were unable to gain the decisive majority they had hoped for in local state parliaments and the Reichstag. They therefore joined middle-class, Catholic, and even nationalist parties in their endeavor to rule the republic and suppress communism, in what one historian called a "coalition of order."[5] These pragmatic politics of compromise were a new departure for the Socialists, who had never before been in power. It drove many SPD leaders and intellectuals to rethink their long-standing animosity toward liberal and middle-class institutions, such as the parliament, the universities, and the legal establishment. Across Germany, Socialists intensely debated whether such institutions could contribute toward the goal of achieving greater equality and help defeat the Communists. Some, such as the SPD's aging theoretician Karl Kautsky, clung to older visions of uncompromising class warfare and regarded cooperation with the middle class as a necessary but temporary evil. Yet others, such as the renowned editor (and later Israeli minister of welfare) Fritz Naphtali, began to argue that middle-class institutions could effectively serve the cause of economic equality and democracy. These debates were not unique to Germany and characterized social-democratic politics across countries and continents. But the SPD's self-appointed role as founder and protector of the republic lent them a special urgency.[6]

In these intense debates, Ernst Fraenkel emerged as one of the most outspoken supporters of cooperation with the bourgeoisie. The son of an assimilated Jewish family in Cologne, Fraenkel had served on the Western Front during the war. In the fall of 1918 his unit was among the first to mutiny and to take part in the democratic revolution. Fraenkel then joined a group of young Socialist students that included Franz L. Neumann and Otto Kahn-Freund. They gathered in Frankfurt to study law with Hugo

---

[4] Eric D. Weitz, *Creating German Communism* (Princeton: Princeton University Press, 1997); David Crew, "A Social Republic? Social Democrats, Communists, and the Weimar Welfare State," in Eric D. Weitz and David E. Barclay (eds.), *Between Reform and Revolution* (New York: Berghahn, 1998), 223–249.

[5] Weitz, *Creating German Communism*, esp. 100–101.

[6] Karl Kautsky, *Die proletarische Revolution und ihr Programm* (Berlin: Dietz, 1922); *Fritz Naphtali, Wirtschaftsdemokratie: Ihr Wesen, Weg und Ziel* (Berlin: Verlagsgesellschaft des allgemeinen deutschen Gewerkschaftsbundes, 1928). For more on these debates, see Bernd Buchner, *Um nationale und republikanische Identität: die deutsche Sozialdemokratie und der Kampf um die politischen Symbole in der Weimarer Republik* (Berlin: Dietz, 2001); Gerhard A. Ritter, *Arbeiter, Arbeiterbewegung, und Soziale Ideen in Deutschland* (Munich: Beck, 1996). On the SPD in a transnational, European context, see Sheri Berman, *The Primacy of Politics: Social Democracy and the Making of Europe's Twentieth Century* (New York: Cambridge University Press, 2006).

Sinzheimer, one of the leading intellectuals of the SPD and the founder of labor law studies in Germany. After earning a PhD in labor law in 1923, Fraenkel published popular books and essays in leading social-democratic journals, such as *Die Gesellschaft*, and helped establish Socialist educational programs for workers in Berlin, Leipzig, and Karlsruhe. In 1926 he and Neumann became the legal consultants to the Union of Metalworkers, Germany's largest and most powerful workers' union, and subsequently to the SPD itself. Widely considered one of the SPD's rising intellectual stars, in 1930 the party leadership considered appointing him Germany's minister of justice.[7]

From the beginning, Fraenkel immersed himself in Socialist calls for cross-class collaboration. In particular, he contributed to the Akademie der Arbeit (Academy of Labor), a new experimental education center in Frankfurt. Founded in 1921, the academy embodied the attempts of moderate Socialists to encourage pro-republican and anti-Communist collaboration between the working and middle classes by bringing together local labor unions, the University of Frankfurt, and Socialist intellectuals such as Fraenkel's mentor Hugo Sinzheimer. Each year, thousands of young students, older Socialist functionaries, and union leaders took courses in economics, law, history, and art, and attended special political seminars about the history of parliament, elections, and welfare legislation. In its effort to blend theory with practice, the academy also hosted intellectuals and political leaders from both the SPD and the more conservative Catholic labor unions, such as Socialist leader Erik Nölting, the renowned Belgian Socialist writer Hendrik de Man, and the Catholic leader (and future West German cabinet member) Jakob Kaiser. By virtue of its scope and novelty, the academy became one of the most celebrated institutions among moderate Socialists and inspired similar models in both Germany and the United States. Fraenkel joined the academy's staff before completing his dissertation, and over the course of a decade lectured to thousands of students on socialism, democracy, and law. The academy's vision of cross-class cooperation would shape his writings, thought, and policy recommendations for years to come.[8]

---

[7] These biographical details are based on Simone Ladwig-Winters, *Ernst Fraenkel: ein politisches Leben* (Frankfurt a.M.: Campus, 2009).

[8] On the Academy and its foundation, see Otto Antrick, *Die Akademie der Arbeit in der Universität Frankfurt a.M.: Idee, Werden, Gestalt* (Darmstadt: Eduard Roether Verlag, 1966). On Weimar labor education in general, see Lothar Wenzel, *Die Bildungsarbeit des Deutschen Metallarbeiter-Verbandes* (Frankfurt a.M.: Otto Brenner Stiftung, 1995). For an example of the academy's influence abroad, see Martha Anderson and Eduard C. Lindeman, *Education through Experience: An Interpretation of the Methods of the Academy of Labor, Frankfurt-am-Main, Germany* (New York: The Workers Education Bureau Press, 1927). The information on Fraenkel's participation in it is from "Programm des Arbeiterbildungsschule für November/Dezember 1932,"

Building a new political regime of cross-class cooperation, however, required more than new institutions. Fraenkel joined an ambitious intellectual project that sought to reconcile a major divide in German political theory, between the bourgeois and the Socialist conceptions of the law. At the center of this effort was the concept of the *Rechtsstaat*, literally translated as "state of the law" or "state under the law." German legal scholars employed the term *Rechtsstaat* to describe a legal-political order in which all citizens, and all components of political authority, were subject to the same rational, impersonal, and predictable laws.[9] The vast majority of bourgeois thinkers claimed that by establishing such a legal order in the nineteenth century, Germany had achieved one of the greatest accomplishments in modern politics. However, the rise of the Socialists, many of them feared, threatened the *Rechtsstaat*. In their eyes, by demanding special social programs and legal provisions that applied only to workers, such as minimum wages or unionization rights, the Socialists violated the principle of universal and abstract law. The great sociologist Max Weber gave voice to these worries by claiming that the Socialists' quest for "workers' rights" would revive the feudal system, in which each group was subject to its own laws, and thus ruin the *Rechtsstaat*. Socialist thinkers, for their part, originally took little interest in the concept of *Rechtsstaat*. While they supported legal equality, they believed that it was marginal to true economic equality, which could only be achieved through the nationalization of the economy. Socialists therefore often viewed the *Rechtsstaat* as a veil for the perpetuation of class exploitation.[10]

Folder 32, Box 2, Nachlass Ernst Fraenkel [hereafter referred to as NL Fraenkel], Archiv der Freie Universität Berlin [hereafter referred to as UFU].

[9] In translation, this term is sometimes equated with the British-U.S. concept of the "Rule of Law," and some historians use the two terms interchangeably. In Germany, however, the debates about the nature of this legal system were deeply connected to questions of political authority and were often reflections of wider debates about who should control the state. In order to reflect these distinct intellectual overtones, I use here the German original. On the emergence and development of the term in Prussia and later in Germany from the eighteenth to the twentieth centuries, see Michael Stolleis, *The Eye of the Law: Two Essays on Legal History* (New York: Birbeck, 2008), 1–52; Gustavo Gozzi, "*Rechtsstaat* and Individual Rights in German Constitutional History," in *The Rule of Law: History, Theory, and Criticism* (Dordrecht: Springer, 2007), 237–259.

[10] These ideas are best reflected in Max Weber, "Socialism," in Peter Lassman and Ronard Speirs (eds.), *Max Weber: Political Writings* (New York: Cambridge University Press, 1994), 272–303. On other occasions Weber expressed more sympathetic views of socialism. See John P. McCormick, *Weber, Habermas, and Transformations of the European State* (New York: Cambridge University Press, 2007), 70–125. An attempt to reconcile socialism and the *Rechtsstaat* was made by Ferdinand Lassalle, the founder of the German Socialist Party, already in the nineteenth century, but his publication's influence was marginal and it failed to generate much attention among theorists. Ferdinand Lassalle, *Das System der erworbenen Rechte: eine Versöhnung des positiven Rechts und der Rechtsphilosophie* (Leipzig: Brockhaus, 1861).

As part of the broader campaign to forge an alliance between the SPD and the middle class, however, Socialist intellectuals began to rethink the concept of the *Rechtsstaat*. At the forefront of this attempt were Hugo Sinzheimer, Fraenkel's mentor in Frankfurt, and Hermann Heller, a leading legal scholar from Berlin. Both Sinzheimer and Heller sought to show that the *Rechtsstaat* and socialism were in fact complementary. In their eyes, bourgeois thinkers were right to claim that the *Rechtsstaat* was a noble achievement. Any decent political society had to constrain itself through universal and predictable laws. However, the state also had to ensure the fairness of social relations and guard its weakest members against economic exploitation. In order to render legal equality meaningful, the state and the courts had to repair social inequality and conflict. Sinzheimer and Heller believed that the state should simultaneously protect the *Rechtsstaat* and actively promote social legislation and welfare programs. It had to defend private property from arbitrary confiscation by the government, but must also strive peacefully toward greater economic equality. In what would become a highly popular term, Heller called this hybrid regime a "social *Rechtsstaat.*"[11] According to this school of thought, Socialists had to abandon the Marxist vision of a classless and homogeneous society, in which the working class ruled the economy. Instead, workers should strive toward a social *Rechtsstaat* and embrace the institutions created by the bourgeoisie.[12]

As a young writer and Sinzheimer's protégé in Frankfurt, Fraenkel joined the intellectual campaign to create a social *Rechtsstaat*, quickly becoming one of its most articulate writers. In a stream of publications, he sought to recast Socialist thinking by asserting that the workers' struggle for social equality was not merely the consequence of economic and materialistic considerations. Rather, Fraenkel provocatively argued that the impulse behind Socialist politics was ultimately ethical and moral. Workers sought better wages, welfare programs, and unionization rights, not simply to build economic justice, but because they regarded these as the only *moral* measures to achieve a just society. Fraenkel thus maintained that both workers and the bourgeoisie were heirs to the tradition of a rational "natural law." Both believed that laws should reflect universal moral truths, not power relations or class interests. Consequently, workers were not as radically different from the bourgeoisie as Communists or Marxist Social Democrats often believed. While they disagreed on economic policies, they still shared

[11] Hermann Heller, *Rechtsstaat oder Diktatur?* (Tübingen: Mohr, 1930).

[12] On this school of thought, see Joachim Blau, *Sozialdemokratische Staatslehre in der Weimarer Republik* (Marburg: Verlag Arbeiterbewegung und Gesellschaftswissenschaft, 1980). On Sinzheimer, see David Kettler, *Domestic Regimes, the Rule of Law, and Democratic Social Change* (Cambridge: Galda and Wilch, 2001). On Hermann Heller, see David Dyzenhaus, *Legality and Legitimacy* (Oxford: Clarendon, 1997), 161–217.

a similar conviction that the *Rechtsstaat* had to serve universal justice. Workers, in this line of thought, were not obliged to overthrow the entire bourgeois legal system. They merely had to expand it to create what Fraenkel termed "proletarian natural law."[13]

In making this provocative critique of Socialist materialist ideas, Fraenkel referred to his own experiences as a lawyer, claiming that workers did not adhere to Marxism but rather to the *Rechtsstaat*. According to Fraenkel, the workers he frequently represented in court were routinely exploited by their employers and by conservative judges, who ruled against them in legal disputes. Despite this injustice, workers never renounced their conviction that the legal system could and should bring about social justice. To their mind, only the *Rechtsstaat* and the universal law it defended could be legitimate tools to solve social disputes. "I encourage anyone," Fraenkel mockingly challenged potential Communists readers, "to repeat an experiment that I have conducted dozens of times with groups of workers." Try to convince them that the legal system does not defend justice, Fraenkel speculated, but only the arbitrary forces of Capitalist elites. "You will not meet with understanding, only the echoes of a unified chorus: nonsense!" According to Fraenkel, these responses reflected workers' intuitive grasp that socialism's call for equality and the *Rechtsstaat*'s universal legal norms were inherently similar. The working class, he argued, "is filled with natural law ideals ... it believes in the law."[14]

The *Rechtsstaat* therefore did not have to be a source of tension between the working and middle classes but, rather, the basis for cooperation. Instead of striving to nationalize the economy, workers should peacefully legislate new social and economic policies. According to Fraenkel, the Weimar Constitution had begun this heroic process of merging the *Rechtsstaat* with Socialist programs. Alongside assuring individual rights, such as freedoms of the press, association, and religion, its clauses also enshrined collective rights for workers. Fraenkel especially celebrated the articles that his mentor Sinzheimer had helped draft, such as Article 151, which required that "the regulation of economic life must be compatible with the principles of justice"; Article 159, which stated that the freedom of labor association "is guaranteed to everyone and to all vocations"; and Article 165, which called on workers and employers to "cooperate, on an equal footing ... in the reg-

[13] Ernst Fraenkel, "Die Stellung des jungen Proletariers zum Recht" (1925), in Hubertus Buchstein, Alexander v. Brünneck, and Gerhard Göhler (eds.), *Ernst Fraenkel: Gesammelte Schriften* [hereafter referred to as *GS*], vol. 1 (Baden: Nomos, 1999), 135–138. See also Ernst Fraenkel, "Die politische Bedeutung des Arbeitsrechts" (1932), *GS* 1, 469–480.

[14] Ernst Fraenkel, "Zur Soziologie der Klassenjustiz" (1927), *GS* 1, 177–212, quotations are from 203, 200.

ulation of wages and of the conditions of labor."[15] According to Fraenkel, such articles demonstrated that the Weimar Republic was not, as the Communists alleged, a shameful compromise with conservatives and capitalists. Rather, it was a major Socialist accomplishment that would guide Germany into a postcapitalist era and toward "proletarian natural law."[16]

This early rethinking of the relationship between law and social equality soon blossomed into an ambitious intellectual campaign to reorganize Germany's democratic system. According to Fraenkel, the parliamentary system established in the Weimar Republic, like the *Rechtsstaat*, drew from nineteenth-century bourgeois principles and social conditions that predated the industrial revolution and the creation of the Socialist movement. Fraenkel therefore claimed that, like the *Rechtsstaat*, the German parliamentary system had to be reformed and fused with Socialist ideas to create a hybrid, Socialist-liberal democracy. Like Heller's social *Rechtsstaat*, this new democratic order would realize socialism's most important objectives. It would bring about greater economic equality, empower the working class, and create an economy not based on free-market capitalism.

In order to explain why the parliamentary system needed Socialist reform, Fraenkel borrowed heavily from Weimar's most influential anti-parliamentary thinker, Carl Schmitt, with whom he had briefly studied. Schmitt was deeply nationalist and conservative and hated the SPD. In his mind, the Socialist focus on the working class and economic policies destroyed the unity of the German nation and weakened the German state. Fraenkel, however, believed that Schmitt's writings best explained why the Weimar Republic had failed to establish cross-class cooperation among its diverse populations and parties. They identified the democratic weaknesses that Fraenkel sought to heal.[17]

According to Schmitt's aggressive critique, which Fraenkel reiterated in his own writings, the parliament had not originally been an institution of democracy and national politics. When first created in the nineteenth century, it was a distinctly bourgeois institution, open only to wealthy elites. Its

[15] "The Constitution of the German Republic," in Elmar M. Hucko (ed.), *The Democratic Tradition: Four German Constitutions* (Oxford: Berg, 1987), 150.

[16] Ernst Fraenkel, "Zehn Jahre Betriebsrätegesetz" (1929), *GS* 1, 384–397; Ernst Fraenkel, "Die politische Bedeutung des Arbeitsrechts" (1932), *GS* 1, 469–480.

[17] During the last years of the Weimar Republic, Fraenkel studied with Schmitt in a seminar in Berlin; Letter, Fraenkel to Laurens Seeleye (26 August 1941), Folder 28, Box 58, MssCol 922, NYPL. Throughout the 1920s and early 1930s, he sent Schmitt copies of his publications with warm dedications. See, for example, Ernst Fraenkel, "Die Krise des Rechtsstaats und die Justiz" (1931), RW 265–25054, Nachlass Carl Schmitt, Hauptstaatsarchiv Düsseldorf [hereafter referred to as HStAD]. On the relations between the two, see Michael Wildt, "Ernst Fraenkel und Carl Schmitt: Eine ungleiche Beziehung," in Daniela Münkel and Jutta Schwarzkopf (eds.), *Geschichte als Experiment* (Frankfurt a.M.: Campus, 2004), 35–48.

purpose was to provide a forum for capable and independent individuals to engage in free discussion and peaceful competition of ideas, then legislate laws for the benefit of the general public. In the Weimar Republic, however, this bourgeois institution had begun to unravel. The electorate now comprised not only wealthy individuals but also the masses, huge parties, powerful pressure groups, and private interests that no longer cared about the public good and sought only to serve their own constituencies. In Schmitt's narrative, celebrated by many anti-republican conservatives, this irreversible process had turned the German parliament, the Reichstag, into a pathetic institution, in which there was no free discussion or any form of cooperation. As he famously put it, "[s]mall and exclusive committees of parties or party coalitions make their decisions behind closed doors, and what representatives of ... interest groups agree to in the smallest committees is more important for the fate of millions of people, perhaps, than any political decision." Schmitt thus acidly dismissed the parliament as an empty shell that was irrelevant to modern politics. Germany had to dispose of it altogether and reconstitute itself as an authoritarian dictatorship.[18]

While Fraenkel agreed with the crux of Schmitt's painful critique, he strongly rejected his anti-parliamentary conclusions. Schmitt was correct in asserting that the Reichstag had emerged from a bourgeois worldview that sought to preserve individual liberties and free economic enterprise, one that was no longer attuned to the twentieth century. Indeed, the rise of the working class had introduced a new concept of rights to politics. Workers were not interested in individual rights but in what Fraenkel called "collective" rights, which were based on the identity of the group. According to Fraenkel, this concept of "group rights" had spread beyond the working class to religious, ethnic, and other groups. These groups were now demanding that the state represent their interests, not just as individuals, but also as members of collectives. "It has rarely been noticed before," he maintained, "that our era is experiencing the rudiment of a new social order ... [in which] not only the individual, but also associations *as such* engage independently in the creation of public affairs." It was this modern focus on group demands that had transformed the parliament into a stage for rival blocs. The difficulty that politicians faced in building coalitions between parties reflected the conceptual conflict between the individualist principles of bourgeois parliamentarianism and the collective nature of modern parties and politics.[19]

---

[18] Carl Schmitt, *The Crisis of Parliamentary Democracy* (Cambridge, MA: MIT Press, 1985), 49–50.

[19] Quotation is from Ernst Fraenkel, "Die Gewerkschaften und das Arbeitsgerichtsgesetz" (1927), *GS* 1, 255–262, here 259, emphasis added. See also his "Staat und Gewerkschaften" (1928), *GS* 1, 285–292; Ernst Fraenkel, "Kollektive Demokratie" (1929), *GS* 1, 343–357; "1919–

While these ideas drew from Schmitt's anti-republican tracts, Fraenkel vehemently argued that the parliamentary system was not doomed. Rather than negating each other, individual and collective rights could merge in a new system that Fraenkel called "collective democracy." Indeed, as they did for the *Rechtsstaat*, Socialists could join forces with the middle class and enrich the parliament with Socialist ideas and calls for collective rights. In a lengthy series of essays and booklets, Fraenkel called on Germans to expand the mechanisms of government by establishing a series of new legislative councils (*Räte*) that would operate alongside the Reichstag, which would continue to represent individual rights and interests. Each of these councils would have the authority to debate and approve potential laws in its own particular field. One council would be in charge of the economy, while others would legislate on religion, education, and other spheres. According to Fraenkel, unlike the delegates to the Reichstag, representatives to these councils would not be elected by individual votes. Instead, they would be chosen by collectives, by the groups that had the highest stakes in their policies. For example, the economic council would include representatives of the leading groups in the economic sphere, labor and business. The council on health would include the doctors' association and government officials. Moreover, Fraenkel suggested that decisions made in the councils should be reached by consensus. Only proposals that received the support of representatives of all the collectives in each council would be approved as law, though Fraenkel was never entirely clear on the relationship between council approval and Reichstag approval. Nevertheless, in Fraenkel's eyes, these councils would institutionalize the Socialist demand for "collective" representation. Just as the "proletarian natural law" enhanced the bourgeois *Rechtsstaat*, these councils would transform bourgeois democracy into a collective democracy.[20]

Fraenkel maintained that this hybrid system would invigorate democracy by including diverse groups and professions in the process of legislation. Rather than being solely dependent on party politicians in the Reichstag, citizens would also be represented in multiple councils through different collectives. This multifaceted representation would empower groups that were otherwise left out of the political process. Workers, for example, would not depend on the SPD to be part of a ruling coalition in order to have their interests represented, since their delegates would serve in the economic council. Fraenkel argued that such a system would likewise

1929, Zum Verfassungstag" (1929), *GS* 1, 358–364; "Um die Verfassung" (1932), *GS* 1, 496–509.

[20] Fraenkel, "Kollektive Demokratie" and "Um die Verfassung." Fraenkel occasionally used the term "dialectic" instead of "collective," but their meanings remained similar. See Hubertus Buchstein, "Von Max Adler zu Ernst Fraenkel: Demokratie und pluralistische Gesellschaft in der sozialistischen Demokratietheorie der Weimarer Republik," in Christoph Gusy (ed.), *Demokratisches Denken in der Weimarer Republik* (Baden: Nomos, 2000), 585–592.

alleviate some of the pressure on delegates in the Reichstag. Since the councils would operate through consensus, it would become easier for politicians to embrace compromises, rather than merely serving their narrow constituencies. Fraenkel believed that such a system would fulfill the original vision of the Weimar Constitution, which sought to establish a balance between individual liberties and social equality. Collective democracy would "complete" the parliamentary system.[21]

This new system would not only transform the political mechanisms of the Reichstag and the Weimar Republic. Equally important, it would lead the Socialists to abandon their vision of democracy as based on a homogeneous, classless society. According to Fraenkel, the SPD had to accept that society was composed of a heterogeneous amalgamation of conflicting groups. Instead of seeking to eliminate conflict between classes, the democratic system had to accept and manage social tensions, resolving them through cross-class cooperation. Fraenkel maintained that workers must recognize that their interests were not determined by class identity alone. They were simultaneously members of various social communities, and the democratic state had to reflect this multiplicity. Fraenkel therefore believed that by building collective democracy, the SPD would both promote social equality and defend the essence of democracy. It would integrate *both* individual rights and group interests into the fabric of politics. The Weimar Republic and the hesitant cooperation it forced on the SPD and bourgeois groups therefore signaled the dawn of a truly democratic age. The republic was a system that Socialists and the bourgeoisie alike should "defend to the death" when the time came to crush nationalist and Communist extremists.[22]

Like Friedrich's theory of Christian covenants, Fraenkel's conception of democracy sought to foster consensus about state institutions. The goal of democratic politics was not challenging power structures or restraining state authority but facilitating compromise and cooperation between groups and voting blocs within the state. In positioning cross-class collaboration at its center, Fraenkel's theory opened new vistas for Socialist politics but also sought to channel workers' energies away from radical challenges to existing social, political, and economic hierarchies. It portrayed traditional socialism and communism as inherently amoral and destructive, incapable of grasping the universal values that parliamentarism and compromise embodied. Indeed, while Fraenkel rarely wrote on communism, he referred to it as a barbaric idea that lay beyond the horizon of the "civilized

---

[21] Fraenkel, "Kollektive Demokratie," 352.

[22] Fraenkel, "Abschied vom Weimar" (1932), *GS* 1, 481–495, quote from 494. As Noah Strote notes, Fraenkel believed that a crucial ally in building such order would be Christian thinkers. See Noah Strote, "Emigration and the Foundation of West Germany, 1933–1963" (PhD diss., University of California–Berkeley, 2011), 12–52.

world [*Kulturstaaten*]." During Weimar, this hostility to competing ideas of working-class politics remained in the background. After the trauma of Nazism and the dawning of the Cold War, however, it would rise to the fore, leading to political tragedies of epic proportions.[23]

In the rich universe of Weimar social-democratic theory, Fraenkel stood out as one of the most original voices by envisioning new ways for Socialists to think about democracy. Instead of building a classless society through central economic planning, Socialists had to become protectors and rejuvenators of the bourgeois institutions like the *Rechtsstaat* and parliament, embracing society as a multifarious and ever-changing jigsaw puzzle of heterogeneous forces. During Weimar's last years, this call for cross-class cooperation failed to bring the Socialists and the middle classes together. In 1928 the SPD and middle-class parties joined hands to form a broad "Grand Coalition," but this coalition disbanded under the onslaught of the Great Depression, unable to agree on a cohesive response to such economic calamity.[24] The Weimar Republic's collapse in 1933, however, would not end Fraenkel's mission to reform modern democracy. After his emigration to the United States, his ideas became the guide to unprecedented diplomatic action.

SOCIAL DEMOCRACY AND U.S. POWER: FRAENKEL IN THE UNITED STATES AND KOREA

When the Nazis came to power in the winter of 1933, they immediately and violently suppressed the German left. The Nazis had long believed that both Social Democrats and Communists were part of a Jewish-led conspiracy to spread chaos and divide the German nation. As Hitler proclaimed on the day he took office, the Third Reich's first and principal goal was to prevent the Marxist "red flag of destruction" from flying over Germany.[25] The new regime thus swiftly unleashed a wave of brutal repression against this perceived existential threat. First targeting Communists and then trade unions and Social Democrats, storm troopers raided workers' offices, beat up labor activists, and shut down their newspapers. All Socialist-led organizations, such as Frankfurt's Academy of Labor, were quickly disbanded, and the leading Socialist intellectuals, such as Sinzheimer and Heller, fled into exile. Nazi officials either murdered labor leaders or placed them in concentration camps, and forced all workers' unions to operate under the Nazi-

---

[23] For Fraenkel's blunt attack on the Soviet Union and communism, see "Zur Soziologie der Klassenjustiz," 191.

[24] On this process, see Dona Donna Harsch, *German Social Democracy and the Rise of Nazism* (Chapel Hill: University of North Carolina Press, 1993), esp. 51–85.

[25] Adolf Hitler, "Proclamation of the Government of National Concentration," in Roderick Stackelberg (ed.), *The Nazi Germany Sourcebook* (London: Routledge, 2002), 126.

controlled "German Labor Front." By the summer of 1933, only six months after Hitler's appointment as chancellor, the world's largest labor movement lay in ruin. In June, Joseph Goebbels, the Nazi minister of propaganda, wrote jubilantly in his diary that the German left had been "dissolved. Bravo! The total state won't have to wait for long now."[26]

Yet the Nazis' devastating and violent seizure of power was not the end of Fraenkel's quest to reform democracy. Rather, the beginning of World War II and the subsequent eruption of the Cold War offered him unexpected opportunities to resume this project outside of Germany. After fleeing to the United States in 1938, Fraenkel joined dozens of social-democratic émigrés to help U.S. government officials draft plans for Germany's postwar reconstruction. This initial cooperation opened new vistas overseas: in 1945 Fraenkel joined the U.S. occupation forces in Korea as a senior official. As such, he participated in a broader American project to fundamentally restructure postwar Asia, one that sought to displace Japanese imperialism with American hegemony. Despite drastically different historical experiences and cultural, linguistic, and political traditions, Fraenkel remained convinced that the United States could fulfill Weimar's failed yet universal promise through an ambitious project of social-democratic and anti-Communist state-building in South Korea. In helping write South Korea's constitution, he implemented his concept of collective democracy by authoring provisions that balanced individual rights with social equality. In drawing from older Socialist ideas, however, Fraenkel also carried over an intense and virulent anti-communism, a conviction exacerbated by the growth of Soviet power in the Cold War. Indeed, as the Soviets engaged in their own process of Communist state-building in North Korea, Fraenkel violated initial plans for Korean unification by actively working for the peninsula's partition into Communist and anti-Communist blocs. Through Fraenkel, Socialist theory from Germany helped shape U.S. economic investment, political reforms, and anti-Soviet diplomacy. It merged with the ambitious American project of nation building and Communist suppression in East Asia, with destructive and tragic consequences.

Because he was a World War I veteran, Fraenkel was exempt from early Nazi regulations that prohibited Jews and Socialists from working in Germany's legal system. For five years, he continued to represent workers in German courts, witnessing the Nazi assault on the rule of law, organized labor, and the legal establishment. In 1938, however, after continual harassment by the Gestapo, Fraenkel learned from the Socialist underground that his arrest was imminent. With the help of family members, he fled to Brit-

---

[26] Quoted in Richard Evans, *The Coming of the Third Reich* (New York: Penguin, 2004), 359. On the suppression of the labor parties in Germany in general, see Weitz, *Creating German Communism*, 280–310.

ain and then to the United States. Assisted by a network of German émigrés and philanthropic organizations, Fraenkel began to work for Jewish labor organizations and taught several courses on labor law at the New School for Social Research in New York. He then studied at the University of Chicago for two years to acquire a second law degree.[27]

The years he spent under Nazism merely added urgency to Fraenkel's quest for an alliance between Socialist and bourgeois groups. While his former colleague, Franz Neumann, was radicalized by Weimar's collapse, calling for a united Socialist-Communist "Popular Front," Fraenkel continued to highlight intellectual similarities between Socialist and bourgeois thought. The best example of this effort is Fraenkel's study of the Nazi legal system, *The Dual State*, which became his most famous and often-cited work. Published in the United States in 1941, scholars praised Fraenkel's study as a detailed study and condemnation of Nazi jurisprudence.[28] Fraenkel, however, also reiterated his Weimar-era argument about the similarity between Socialist and bourgeois views of the law, maintaining that German Socialists and middle-class thinkers shared a commitment to universal norms and natural law. Both camps sought to build a society that would realize these norms through the creation of a *Rechtsstaat*. Fraenkel mocked those Socialists who continued to believe that the inevitable Socialist revolution predicted by Marxism would bring about social justice. As he sarcastically asserted, "no one has ever been willing to risk his life because of his belief in the [Marxist] 'laws of social development.'" *The Dual State* thus advocated a broad coalition between Socialists and bourgeois activists against the Nazi regime. In his eyes, "[t]here can be no objection to the affiliation of the German Marxists with the United Front, which is composed of groups whose ethical demands are based on Natural Law."[29]

While the crux of his political theory remained the same, Fraenkel's exile spurred a thorough transformation in his interpretation of the United States. Like many European Socialists, prior to his immigration Fraenkel had conceived of the United States as a symbol of advanced capitalism, free-market forces, and plutocratic rule. As he later recalled, in his eyes the United States was "the most reactionary country in the world."[30] While in

[27] For a more detailed account of Fraenkel's immigration, see Ladwig-Winters, *Ernst Fraenkel*, 127–134.

[28] My description here relies on both Strote, "Emigration and the Foundation of West Germany," and William E. Scheuerman, "Social Democracy and the Rule of Law," in Peter C. Caldwell and William E. Scheuerman (eds.), *From Liberal Democracy to Fascism: Legal and Political Thought in the Weimar Republic* (Boston: Humanities Press, 2000), 74–105.

[29] Ernst Fraenkel, *The Dual State* (New York: Oxford University Press, 1941), quotations from 131 and 129, respectively.

[30] Letter, Fraenkel to Kahn-Freund (1 October 1947), Unmarked Box, Kahn-Freund Papers [hereafter referred to as OKFC]. London School of Economics Archives [hereafter referred to as LSEA].

exile, however, under the influence of U.S. legal scholars in Chicago, Fraenkel came to think of his host country as the most progressive force in world politics. According to Fraenkel, the New Deal had radically transformed the United States from a capitalist powerhouse to the center of social-democratic politics. Franklin Roosevelt's bold intervention in the social and economic order, the creation of Social Security, the legalization of unionization rights, and the development of new welfare programs were not merely emergency measures to stabilize capitalism but constituted the beginning of a new social-democratic order. In this narrative, the New Deal had unleashed a "peaceful revolution" and created a new blend of liberal and Socialist democracy, committed to both individual liberties and social equality. Under Roosevelt's leadership, the United States had become the collective democracy that Weimar Socialists had for so long sought to establish.[31]

Fraenkel argued that the response of U.S. legal elites to Roosevelt's revolutionary New Deal had allowed the United States to succeed where Weimar had failed. In contrast to Weimar Germany, the American legal establishment had realized that its former belief in bourgeois law could no longer assure justice in the modern industrial age. Under the leadership of Supreme Court justice Louis Brandeis, American judges recognized that in order to preserve democracy, the state had to take bold steps to regulate the economy while at the same time defending the rule of law. Despite early conflicts between the Supreme Court and the FDR administration (writing in vague terms, Fraenkel ignored Roosevelt's controversial and failed attempt at "court-packing" in 1937), the justices ultimately relented and affirmed the constitutionality of the New Deal's most important programs, such as the National Labor Relations Act. By doing so, the United States accepted collective agreement as being equivalent to individual rights. In a clear projection of his own visions, Fraenkel claimed that thanks to the court, "all constitutional misgivings regarding laws of workers' time and protection, coalition rights, labor struggle and payments, as well as modern legal social insurance were radically removed."[32] This was far more than an intricate legal debate about the limits of state authority. By accepting collective and individual rights as equal, the court had radically recast American legal thought. In a dramatic and somewhat fantastical transformation, Fraenkel now saw the United States as the guardian of his own ideas, the

---

[31] See his 1944 article "Die geplante Wirtschaft," *GS* 4, 156–161. While Fraenkel expressed his views on the New Deal in a more systematic and detailed manner only after his return to Germany in 1951, his wartime publications and manuscripts reveal that his evaluation of the United States had begun to change already in the early 1940s.

[32] Ernst Fraenkel, "Das richterliche Prüfungsrecht in den Vereinigten Staaten von Amerika. Eine Untersuchung unter besonderer Berücksichtigung des Arbeitsrechts" (1953), *GS* 4 (Baden: Nomos, 2000), 49–141, here 122.

embodiment of democratic social justice. In this telling, only workers mattered to the achievement of this democratic social justice, which existed despite the legalized repression and violent persecution of racial minorities, an issue that Fraenkel rarely discussed. As he wrote later to his Socialist friend Otto Suhr, explaining his admiration of the United States, "we had the luck to immigrate to FDR's America, and not to that of Harding, Hoover, or Coolidge."[33]

The United States' entry into World War II transformed these sentiments into policy. Among the vast transformations brought about by Pearl Harbor and the creation of a massive wartime bureaucracy was the entry of scores of Socialist émigrés into U.S. intelligence bodies. Most famously, the Office for Strategic Services (OSS), the War Department's central intelligence organ, quickly enlisted dozens of social-democratic émigrés. These included radical Marxist thinkers such as Hebert Marcuse and Fraenkel's former associate, Franz Neumann. While they did not necessarily share their political leanings, U.S. diplomats and wartime planners now regarded these reliably anti-Nazi activists as an arsenal of knowledge on Germany. Throughout the war, then, former Socialist scholars and lawyers advised U.S. diplomats on the Third Reich's legal system and economic structures, and helped draft plans for the future occupation and de-Nazification of Germany. Many émigrés would continue this cooperation well after the war was over.

While scholars have focused almost exclusively on Marcuse's and Neumann's work in the OSS, the war effort also drew many other émigrés into the orbit of the U.S. intelligence apparatus.[34] Among them was Fraenkel, who was recruited to the OSS's Foreign Economic Administration (FEA) in Washington, D.C., by Hedwig Wachenheim, a former SPD activist. As a specialist on both German and U.S. law, Fraenkel's job was to lay the groundwork for the legal aspects of postwar reconstruction. Throughout the war, he drafted plans for the de-Nazification and reestablishment of the German courts, municipalities, and police. As in Weimar, Fraenkel was guided by the conviction that Germany's reconstruction would not be achieved through the smashing of capitalist power and the formation of a planned economy, as many former SPD members continued to believe. The future American occupiers could not reverse the Nazi revolution merely by nationalizing key industries. In a series of memoranda, Fraenkel instead maintained that U.S.

---

[33] Letter, Fraenkel to Otto Suhr (8 February 1952), Folder 1, Nachlass Fraenkel [hereafter referred to as NL] 1274, Bundesarchiv Koblenz [hereafter referred to as BAK].

[34] The most renowned study of German émigrés in the OSS remains Alfons Söllner (ed.), *Zur Archäologie der Demokratie in Deutschland*, vol. 2 (Frankfurt a.M.: Fischer, 1986). A selection of the reports by the Frankfurt School members is collected in Raffaele Laudani (ed.), *Secret Reports on Nazi Germany: The Frankfurt School Contribution to the War Effort* (Princeton: Princeton University Press, 2013).

officials would have to focus their energies on the reestablishment of the *Rechtsstaat*, an order based on a universal and equal legal code. In particular, they would have to purge the German courts of the conservative judges who had subverted the law to crush German workers.[35]

Fraenkel thus joined a large group of Socialist émigrés who hoped to enlist the United States in the mission of rebuilding a social-democratic Germany. Fraenkel contributed to the major publication that Wachenheim's group prepared for the War Department, which argued that "German labor was the strongest democratic force in prewar Germany; if it is able to organize, it will become the pillar of democracy again.... The redemocratization of Germany must be started with the reorganization of the labor movement." The group produced detailed plans for the reestablishment of local unions, immediate elections in municipalities, and the recreation of welfare authorities. In all these plans, unions and the Socialist Party were to be the bedrock of post-Nazi reform.[36] For Fraenkel, however, the rebuilding of organized German labor was inseparable from the reestablishment of the social *Rechtsstaat*. "Only where a *Rechtsstaat* exists," Fraenkel explained, "are free unions possible. Only when free unions rise again can a *Rechtsstaat* blossom in Germany. A clear line runs from the rebuilding of the unions, through the reconstruction of the *Rechtsstaat*, to the guarantee of world peace." To Fraenkel and émigrés like him, the future occupation was to be the fulfillment of Weimar's incomplete achievements.[37]

If true democratization required a robust social and legal revolution, it was also threatened by socialism's old nemesis: communism. Drawing on the bitter memories of Weimar's violent clashes, Fraenkel and other Socialists predicted that the war's end would reignite the battle between the moderate and radical left. The greatest danger after the war, Fraenkel wrote in a lengthy 1944 report, would be posed neither by a Nazi underground nor right-wing fanatics, as many feared. The true threat lay in the Communists' plans to disseminate the Bolshevik model across Europe and Germany, which would constitute "the replacement of one form of totalitarianism by another." Fraenkel maintained that labor, the backbone of democratization,

[35] Ernst Fraenkel, Memorandum, "A Casebook on German Government and Administration," Folder 164, NL 1274, BAK; Memorandum, Fraenkel to David M. Leviten (26 April 1944); Memorandum, Ernst Fraenkel to A. R. Rosenberg (13 September 1944); both in Folder Foreign Economic Administration II Extra, Box 707, NL Fraenkel, UFU.

[36] Hedwig Wachenheim (ed.), *Germany in the Transition Period: Studies of Postwar Reconstruction* (New York: The American Labor Conference on International Affairs, June 1944), 11.

[37] Fraenkel, Memorandum, "Der Neuaufbau des Rechtsstaats in nach-Hitlerischen Deutschland" (undated), Folder 164, NL 274, BAK. The most detailed study that Fraenkel composed during this period, and which was intended to serve as a guide in the reestablishment of a *Rechtsstaat* in Germany after the end of the war, was his *Military Occupation and the Rule of Law: Occupation Government in the Rhineland, 1918–1923* (New York: Oxford University Press, 1944).

was ironically the most likely group to fall prey to communism's allure. After the trauma of depression and war, German workers could easily believe Soviet claims that "the Western 'plutocracies' [would] perpetuate rather than remove the National Socialist incubus and that Bolshevism is identical with freedom and democracy."[38] Believing in the masses' democratic potential yet fearing their possible failure to support democracy, Fraenkel warned that the Allies' ability to recruit German workers to a robust anti-Communist social democracy was crucial for Europe's survival. Their success would determine whether "Europe will be either Cossackian or republican."[39] In fact, the conflict between social democracy and communism was of global proportions. If the Communists were to succeed in their plan to create a Bolshevik revolution, it would not stop in central Europe, but would spread across the world and would "endanger democracies in their own countries."[40]

Fraenkel's time in the U.S. intelligence community thus helped complete a recasting of his thought. By the time World War II drew to a close, his visions of a virulently anti-Communist collective democracy had been projected from the domestic sphere onto the world stage. Having worked intimately with U.S. intelligence officers for three years, Fraenkel became convinced that the United States' dramatic victories in both Europe and Asia made it the ultimate vehicle for the building of a postcapitalist democracy. Equally important, thanks to its enormous military power, the United States was the only force that could defend social democracy from the Communist enemy that had sabotaged it in Weimar. But unlike the vast majority of his Socialist colleagues at the OSS, Fraenkel at first refused to participate in the rebuilding of the country that had exterminated millions of Jews. As he put it to a friend,

> take that army of *Schleimscheisser* (ass-kissers), *Postenjäger* (office-hunters), *Opportunisten* (opportunists), who backed, invented, glorified and enforced all those measures which finally, step by step, brought about Auschwitz and all the other extermination camps. They are no "war criminals" and they will not be hanged or imprisoned. You meet them every day on the street, in your office and in society. That is unbearable to me; no Jew should be exposed to such an experience.[41]

In 1945 Fraenkel therefore chose to serve the United States in Asia, hoping to bring collective democracy to the Pacific sphere. Working in Korea, he

[38] Ernst Fraenkel, Memorandum, "The Future of German Labor Organizations" (undated, 1944), Folder 164, NL 1274, BAK.
[39] Letter, Fraenkel to Kahn-Freund (25 December 1942), Unmarked Box, OKFC, LSEA.
[40] Fraenkel, "The Future of German Labor Organizations."
[41] Letter, Fraenkel to Otto Kahn-Freund (25 May 1946), Unmarked Box, OKFC, LSEA.

would take part in one of the earliest and most crucial battlegrounds of the Cold War.

It was the dramatic changes unfolding in postwar Korea that gave Fraenkel his first opportunity to actively realize his vision of democracy, with both its possibilities and destructive limits, under the umbrella of U.S. power. In the summer of 1945, its cities destroyed by U.S. bombings and threatened with a large-scale Soviet invasion that ended all hopes of negotiation, Japan finally surrendered. As part of disbanding the Japanese empire, U.S. officials hastily divided Korea, which had been a Japanese colony since 1905, between Soviet troops that invaded it from the north and U.S. troops that entered from the south. The division and occupation of Korea was supposed to be temporary, and was remarkably unplanned on all sides. While both Franklin Roosevelt and Harry Truman had declared their commitment to eventual Korean independence during the war, they had no clear plans for the duration and nature of the occupation, a stark contrast to the extensive wartime planning and training for the occupations of Germany and Japan. Throughout 1945 and early 1946, each country's occupation forces operated autonomously, but both American and Soviet occupation officers believed that Korea would soon become independent and they would return home.[42]

Within a year, however, rising tensions in Asia drew increasing American attention and investment in Korea. In 1946 U.S. diplomats and military leaders grew suspicious that Soviet investment in their northern occupation zone was part of a broader strategy to spread communism across East Asia. Figures such as diplomat Edwin Pauly and General Albert Wedemeyer, both of whom traveled to Korea as Truman's envoys, called the Soviet Union "an immense amoeba-like organism which surrounds and digests any object incapable of offering sufficient resistance." The resumption of the civil war in China between the Nationalists and the Communists greatly intensified this panic. As the specter of a Chinese Communist triumph loomed in 1947 and 1948, U.S. politicians and diplomats were deeply worried that an alliance of Asian Communists and Soviets would take over East Asia and threaten the United States' own security, especially its hold over Japan.[43] In

---

[42] On the last stages of the war in East Asia and the end of the Japanese war efforts, see Richard B. Frank, *Downfall: The End of the Imperial Japanese Empire* (New York: Random House, 1999); Tsuyoshi Hasegawa, *Racing the Enemy: Stalin, Truman, and the Surrender of Japan* (Cambridge: Harvard University Press, 2005); Ronald H. Spector, *In the Ruins of Empire: The Japanese Surrender and the Battle for Postwar Asia* (New York: Random House, 2007).

[43] Cited in David Ekbladh, *The Great American Mission: Modernization and the Construction of an American World Order* (Princeton: Princeton University Press, 2010), 125. On Japan's centrality to U.S. thinking about Pacific security, see John Lewis Gaddis, *Strategies of Containment* (New York: Oxford University Press, 2005 [new editions]), 75ff.

the shadow of these anxieties, the Korean peninsula became the center of intense American attention, and diplomats and policymakers elevated a prosperous, stable, and anti-Communist Korean state as a crucial bulwark against Communist aggression. Under General John Hodge, the commander of the occupation, U.S. authorities began supporting local conservative and anti-Communist forces. They flew in Syngman Rhee, a Korean nationalist and anti-Communist who spent the war in exile in the United States, and funded his building of an anti-Communist Korean party. Korea became a crucial test for American resolve. As Harry Truman put it with characteristic hyperbole in a letter to Pauly, Korea was "an ideological battleground upon which our entire success in Asia may depend."[44]

In response to growing tensions in Asia, U.S. military officials and diplomats sought to hurriedly transform Korea's postcolonial and largely agricultural economy into a fully industrialized and "modern" society. By introducing new technologies, building a new education system, and creating a system of public administration, the United States could launch the "backward" Koreans, stifled by forty years of Japanese imperial repression, into a "developed" and stable ally in the Cold War. These efforts in Korea were in many ways an extension of earlier ideas about international liberalism and "development," which evolved in the 1920s and during the New Deal. Like many of their counterparts in Germany and Japan, the Americans who flocked to Korea had long believed that the United States stood as a universal model of prosperity and stability, which could spread around the globe to prevent challenges to an "American way of life." By duplicating the American modernization projects, such as the New Deal–era Tennessee Valley Authority, Americans could "uplift" the Koreans to ward off Communist expansion and subversion. In the eyes of many policymakers, philanthropists, and academics, only a massive modernization project could secure Asia from falling to communism. Alongside Germany and Japan, Korea emerged as a central test for American superiority and benevolence. In the words of Paul Hoffman, a senior U.S. diplomat, Korea was to be "the proving ground" for the United States' ability to modernize and build stable societies around the world.[45]

[44] Cited in David M. Edelstein, *Occupational Hazards* (Ithaca: Cornell University Press, 2008), 64. On the beginning of occupation, see Gregg Brazinsky, *Nation Building in South Korea: Koreans, Americans, and the Making of a Democracy* (Chapel Hill: University of North Carolina Press, 2007); Bruce Cumings, *The Origins of the Korean War*, 2 vols. (Princeton: Princeton University Press, 1981, 1991); James Matray, *The Reluctant Crusade: American Foreign Policy in Korea* (Honolulu: University of Hawai'i Press, 1985).

[45] Quotation is from Ekbladh, *The Great American Mission*, 131. See also Robert A. Packenham, *Liberal America and the Third World* (Princeton: Princeton University Press, 1973). Ekbladh claims that U.S. reconstruction efforts in Korea were substantially different than their counterparts in Germany and Japan, since U.S. policymakers observed it as premodern and even primitive. Yet many of the policies in these three occupations were remarkably similar.

While both diplomats and scholars believed that these efforts embodied a uniquely American mission, the U.S. occupation of Korea also became a crucial space for Fraenkel's own vision of democracy. Like the many diplomats, occupation reformers, and military officers who worked across the peninsula, Fraenkel was convinced that his democratic theory was self-evidently universal and transferable to all parts of the world. The United States, he believed, had embraced his own vision of socialist democracy during the New Deal and could now bring social equality, the rule of law, and democracy to East Asia. In Fraenkel's mind, the United States was the ideal power to build a collective democracy in Korea. Through forceful leadership, economic development, and the suppression of Communist activities, Americans would create a Korean state that would embrace Weimar's blend of individual rights and social equality. U.S. diplomats quickly recognized the overlap between Fraenkel's vision and their own; Fraenkel's comprehensive democratic theory and his fierce anti-communism made him an ideal participant in the transformation of Korea.[46]

Initially, Fraenkel's work was limited to legal advising. The Japanese empire's legal code, which included Korea, had been based on German law. The U.S. occupation's legal division therefore hired Fraenkel, a specialist of German law, to help reform Korea's legal code. Within a year, however, Fraenkel's reputation as a formidable political thinker spread among U.S. occupation authorities. In the winter of 1946, after several U.S. officials read his wartime studies on the occupation of Germany, General Hodge appointed Fraenkel to serve on the joint American-Soviet commission that was to plan the future of the Korean peninsula.[47]

The commission's main task was to resolve a fundamental disagreement between the U.S. and Soviet authorities regarding the first postwar Korean elections. At the Potsdam Conference in July 1945, which laid out goals for the occupations of Japan and Korea, the Allies had declared that all "democratic forces and organizations" would be permitted to participate in Korea's political life. In 1946 the U.S. and Soviet occupation authorities established a joint commission to prepare the country for its first election and to review the "democratic credentials" of potential contenders. But the two sides could not agree on what qualified as a "democratic force" or "organization." While U.S. representatives demanded that all parties be allowed to participate, the Soviets insisted that only Socialist organizations could be trusted. With their memories of Japanese attacks on the Soviet Union's eastern borders in the 1930s, including Japan's failed invasion of Mongolia in 1939, Soviet officials feared that a non-Communist

[46] Letter, Fraenkel to Marta Fraenkel (22 January 1946), Folder 4, Box I, AR 4348, Leo Baeck Institute New York [hereafter referred to as LBINY].

[47] Letter, Fraenkel to Kahn-Freund (1 March 1946), Unmarked Box, OKFC, LSEA.

2.1. Ernst Fraenkel (third from right) in a meeting of the U.S.-Soviet Joint Commission on Korea, 1946. Drawing on his Weimar-era hostility to communism, Fraenkel was one of the most anti-Soviet members of the U.S. delegation. Courtesy of Wolfgang Müller.

Korea would become a base for anti-Soviet attacks. For over a year, the members of the joint commission were locked in negotiations over how to define "democratic."[48]

Fraenkel, who was one of the two nonmilitary personnel on the commission, was also the U.S. delegation's most vocally anti-Communist and confrontational member. As he complained to his superiors, the two superpowers held such incompatible worldviews on politics and law that negotiations were bound to fail. In this dualistic perspective, the United States believed in the existence of political plurality and in the free competition of political ideas. The Soviets, on the other hand, adhered to a lawless worldview, where any opposition to the government's brute force was illegitimate. The Soviets were therefore guided by a political theory that rendered agreement and negotiations impossible. "For the Communists," Fraenkel scoffed, "there could be no 'friendly' country that is not governed

[48] Letter, Fraenkel to Marta Fraenkel (22 January 1946), Folder 4, Box I, AR 4348, LBINY. On the diplomatic efforts and agreements regarding Korea before the beginning of the U.S. and Soviet occupations, see Cumings, *The Origins of the Korean War*, 1: 101–131. On the joint commissions, see 238–266.

by a Communist party, and which does not submit its will completely to the Soviet Union." From this point of view, European history seemed to be repeating itself in Asia. Communists would seek to tear down a new Korean republic, just as the Communist Party did in Weimar. Fraenkel therefore called for a unilateral end to the negotiations. By participating in a futile back-and-forth with the Soviets, American diplomats were only weakening their position. In light of these strong anti-Communist sentiments, some have blamed Fraenkel for the failure of U.S.-Soviet negotiations. Alfred Oppler, another German Jewish émigré who served in the U.S. military occupation of Japan, later claimed that Fraenkel had personally advised South Korean leader Syngman Rhee to boycott the joint commission.[49]

Though Fraenkel's ultimate responsibility is debatable, the collapse of U.S.-Soviet talks in the fall of 1947 only further expanded his influence in the peninsula. After a year and a half of futile discussions, the U.S. and Soviet authorities officially concluded that they could not find a mutually acceptable formula for jointly held elections. The growing tensions of the Cold War solidified each side's conviction that the other sought to transform Korea into a base for future aggression. In November 1947, at the request of both Washington and Moscow, the newly founded United Nations appointed an international delegation to determine Korea's fate. The delegation members traveled through the peninsula to determine whether elections should be held. While U.S. officials demanded an immediate transfer of sovereignty to the Korean people, the Soviets threatened to prevent elections in their occupation zone. The approval of "premature" elections, they warned, would lead to the peninsula's partition.

Fraenkel emerged as one of the key players in the diplomatic campaign to shape the delegates' opinions, with tragic consequences. Since he spoke multiple European languages and possessed intimate knowledge of European politics, U.S. officials believed that he was uniquely positioned to influence the European members of the committee. Moreover, as the only non-American in the occupation's highest echelons, his anti-Soviet sentiments would seem less tainted by U.S. power calculations. Fraenkel therefore testified for the delegation dozens of times. The Soviet Union, he repeatedly explained, sought to impose its monstrous Communist dictatorship around the globe and would never allow democracy to prevail in its occupation zone.[50] Equally important from U.S. officials' point of view,

---

[49] Quotation is from Ernst Fraenkel, "Report on sub-commission #3" (20 April 1946), reel 2, Records of the American Delegation U.S.-U.S.S.R Joint Commission on Korea (March 1946–July 1947), published by the U.S. Department of State. On Fraenkel and the negotiations, see Alfred C. Oppler, *Legal Reform in Occupied Japan* (Princeton: Princeton University Press, 1976), 70. Due to the destruction of Fraenkel's records during the Korean War, it is impossible to verify these claims.

[50] Memorandum, Fraenkel to John Weckerling (27 February 1948), Box 296, Entry A1 1399,

Fraenkel proved especially effective in informal meetings with the delegation's European members. Throughout the winter of 1948, he continued his advocacy by meeting with the Belgian, French, and Dutch representatives in Seoul's restaurants and bars. The social ties between the German émigré and the Europeans became so close that the committee's chair, Holland's Petrus Johannes Schmidt, sought to impose restrictions on their meetings.[51] Despite such hurdles, in February 1948 Fraenkel gleefully reported to his superiors that his efforts had borne fruit. Several delegation members, who at first opposed the U.S. requests for immediate elections, had now changed their minds and supported this step, even at the price of the peninsula's partition. Three months later, the UN embraced the delegation's recommendation, and two antagonistic Korean states would declare independence.[52]

This debate over Korea's future revealed the tragedies of anti-Communist fixation and belief in American Cold War hegemony. For all its celebration of collaboration and negotiation, Fraenkel's thinking could not envisage coexistence, let alone a long-term compromise, between democracy and communism. Despite his seeming emphasis on mass representation in collective politics, both Fraenkel and the American officials who invested him with authority showed shockingly little regard for the price that their diplomatic maneuvers would inflict on the Korean people. That Korea's partition would lock the nation into hostile states, break families, and divide communities was not a cause for hesitation. Rather, it was communism, with its disregard for individual rights and the rule of law, that was beyond the horizon of political engagement. The misery of Koreans was a price worth paying for communism's defeat.

For all its tragic consequences, however, Fraenkel's influence was not confined to Korea's division or anti-Communist sentiments. Ironically, he passionately believed that the division of Korea presented a golden oppor-

UN Temporary Mission on Korea, United States Army Forces in Korea [USAFIK], RG 554 [Records of General Headquarters, Far East Command Supreme Commander, Allied Powers and United Nations Command], National Archives II, College Park, Maryland [hereafter referred to as NARA].

51 Memorandum, Fraenkel to Brigadier General John Weckerling (22 January 1948), Folder Chronological Lists of Papers 1, Box 295; Memorandum, Brigadier General John Weckerling to General Hodge (9 February 1948), Folder Chronological Lists of Papers 1, Box 295; Memorandum, Charles Pergler to General Weckerling (25 March 1948), Folder Correspondence and Memoranda 1948, Box 296; Memorandum, Chronological Listing of Events (unsigned) (1 May 1948), Box 296; Memorandum, "List of events," unsigned (25 March 1948), Folder Chronological Lists of Papers 1, Box 295; all in Entry A1 1399, UN Temporary Mission on Korea, USAFIK, RG 554, NARA.

52 Memorandum, Fraenkel to General Weckerling (18 February 1948), Folder Chronological Lists of Papers 3, Box 295, Entry A1 1399, UN Temporary Mission on Korea, USAFIK, RG 554, NARA.

tunity to bring democracy, the rule of law, and social equality to Asia. Fraenkel's efforts began in the early months of the occupation while serving in the legal division, where he focused on the empowerment of labor unions. Many officials in the legal department had little interest in the role that unions would play in the future of Korea. Concerned primarily with political stability, these officials sought to limit union influence by excluding foreign—mainly Chinese—workers from membership in labor organizations, thus creating a competing and cheaper workforce. In contrast, Fraenkel believed that the core objective of the U.S. occupation was to strengthen labor. In a series of legal memoranda, he repeatedly warned his supervisors that limiting the rights of organized labor would endanger the structures of democracy. Any attempt to split the worker population or limit the autonomy of the unions by imposing government control appeared to him to run "against the recognized political aim of Military Government in Korea" and to be "inconsistent with the policy of encouraging the formation of trade-unions."[53] As Charles Pergler, the head of the legal department, noted, Fraenkel's arguments convinced his superiors, who embraced his recommendations. The U.S. authorities supported unionization and codified the right of trade unions to engage in bargaining through legislation.[54]

As the occupation progressed, Fraenkel also became involved in the large-scale project of modernizing Korea's economy. Alongside American liberals and veterans of the New Deal, Fraenkel joined the U.S. occupation mission to create a more "developed" and equal Korean economy. These efforts included a vast investment in Korean primary education. The U.S. authorities built hundreds of new primary schools across the southern peninsula and distributed new textbooks nationwide. Discarding the Japanese-enforced curricula that focused on Confucian teachings and contained authoritarian and militarist values, Fraenkel and others helped prepare new educational programs that emphasized modern technologies and democratic politics. In the same manner, U.S. occupation authorities engaged in a large-scale attempt at land reform. After selling and distributing large swaths of land that had been owned by the Japanese imperial authorities, Fraenkel joined U.S. officials who sought to empower poor peasants by distributing fertilizers, increasing electricity production in the countryside, and introducing new agricultural technologies. In Fraenkel's mind, all these efforts served the broader goal of establishing the economic and, especially, the social equality required for modern democracy. If Korea was the prov-

---

[53] Quotations are from Ernst Fraenkel, "Opinion #306 (6 May 1946)," "Opinion #359 (20 June 1946)," Selected Legal Opinions of the Department of Justice, United States Army Military Government in Korea, 1946–1948 (Seoul: Department of Justice, 1948), 70 and 98 respectively. On his objection to government supervision of unions, see "Opinion #128 (27 March 1946)," 26–28. The collection includes many other similar opinions.

[54] Charles Pergler, foreword to Selected Legal Opinions, page h.

ing ground for American liberalism, it would also prove the universal validity of German Socialist democratic theory.[55]

Nowhere was Fraenkel's conviction in the broad applicability of his ideas more apparent than during the drafting of the South Korean Constitution in the spring of 1948. In May of that year, the U.S. occupation zone held its first elections. Under the supervision of U.S. authorities, a South Korean national assembly convened to draft a constitution, and in August 1948 it declared South Korea's independence under the leadership of the anti-Communist Syngman Rhee. During the months between the elections and the declaration of independence, General Hodge appointed Fraenkel to supervise the drafting of the South Korean Constitution. As the most accomplished legal scholar serving with the U.S. authorities, Fraenkel mediated between the U.S. commander and the small group of Korean scholars and politicians that drafted the state's founding document. During the drafting process, Fraenkel insisted that the new constitution's rights include welfare and group empowerment. Collective and social rights, he explained, could not be achieved merely through economic development or private contracts. They had to be enshrined in law and accorded a status equal to that of individual rights, such as freedom of speech, assembly, or religion.[56]

Like the Weimar Constitution, the constitution ratified by the South Korean national assembly bore the clear imprint of social-democratic principles. Article 16 granted equal and affordable education to all; Article 17 guaranteed all citizens the right to work and minimum payment; Article 18 guaranteed the "freedom of association, collective bargaining, and collective action of laborers"; and other articles secured minimum wages and economic support for the ill and elderly. Such articles encompassed the key principles of collective democracy, and Fraenkel openly took credit for their inclusion in the constitution. As he stated in a report to his superiors, with these clauses, he believed he had brought "the spirit of Western democracy" to the shores of East Asia.[57]

[55] On educational reforms, see Noel F. McGinn et al. (eds.), *Education and Development in Korea* (Cambridge, MA: Harvard University Press, 1980). On land reform, see Brazinsky, *Nation Building in South Korea*, 18–23; Elkbadh, *The Great American Mission*, 129–131. Fraenkel's work is mentioned in Memorandum, Eric H. Biddle to Paul G. Hoffman, Staffing for ECA Mission to Korea (20 November 1948), Folder Draft Program for Economic Aid to the Republic of Korea, Box 2, Records Relating to Korea, MLR 271C, RG 469, NARA.

[56] Memorandum, Principal Secretary to Members of the UN Temporary Commission on Korea (3 June 1948), Folder Reports and Memoranda (UN Temporary Commission) 1947–1948, Box 297A, Entry A1 1399, RG 554, NARA. See also Memorandum (unsigned), "Observation of Election in South Korea" (22 July 1948), Box 299, Entry A1 1400, U.S. Army Forces in Korea (USAFIK), RG 554, NARA.

[57] This quotation is from Memorandum, Fraenkel to Weckerling (11 May 1948), Folder Reports and Memoranda (UN Temporary Commission) 1948 1, Box 297A, Entry A1 1399, RG 554, NARA. Fraenkel's role in enshrining these rights in the South Korean Constitution is also

2.2. Ernst Fraenkel (center), his wife, Hanna, and an unidentified U.S. official during a trip to the Korean countryside, 1948. Fraenkel was a senior agent in the American mission to "modernize" and "develop" South Korea. Courtesy of Wolfgang Müller.

If the occupation era fueled such visions of social democracy, then the years that followed witnessed their explosive expansion. As was the case in Germany and Japan, the establishment of South Korean independence in August 1948 did not end U.S. involvement. In their conviction that Rhee's regime would be a bulwark against Soviet and later Chinese aggression, U.S. policymakers continued to pour extensive energy and resources into the South Korean state, seeking to bolster its industry, economy, and education. In 1948 U.S. diplomats expanded the Economic Cooperation Administration (ECA), originally founded to carry out the Marshall Plan's reconstruction of Europe, to Korea. With a massive investment of $100 million, the ECA mission in Korea ballooned exponentially. The U.S. Embassy in

mentioned in Memorandum, Fraenkel to Headquarters of the XXIV Corps in Seoul (30 June 1948); Memorandum, Fraenkel to Headquarters of the XXIV Corps in Seoul (6 July 1948), both in Folder Korean Election (Constitution of Republic of Korea) 1948 4, Box 306, Entry A1 1403, RG 554, NARA. The description of the constitution is based on "The Constitution of the Republic of Korea," in Peter L. Lee et al. (eds.), *Sources of Korean Tradition* (New York: Columbia University Press, 2000), 2: 382–384

Seoul, partially because it hosted the ECA, grew to a staff of two thousand, one of the largest in the world. Working feverishly to modernize Korea, the ECA personnel used this windfall to build bridges, electrify remote villages, and expand Korea's educational system. South Korea became one of the largest U.S. investments in civil government in the world.[58]

This large-scale effort also marked the apex of Fraenkel's participation in U.S. policymaking in Korea. In June 1948, a month after the end of the military occupation, the U.S. ambassador appointed Fraenkel one of the most senior officials in Seoul's ECA headquarters, in charge of planning and organizing the budget. For two years, Fraenkel supervised the promotion of housing projects, electricity implementation, and industrial training. Traveling across South Korea's villages and towns, he helped build and manage public administration programs, railway development, book fairs, public health clinics, academic exchanges, and agricultural reforms. By 1950, these projects far surpassed the programs initiated by the military occupation. Millions of South Korean children enrolled in U.S.-built schools, thousands of farmers received U.S. fertilizer, and hundreds of Korean students joined exchange programs with the United States. The U.S.-led project of modernizing South Korea into a stable and prosperous anti-Communist state thus brought Fraenkel unprecedented authority. No such opportunity had presented itself during the Weimar period or while Fraenkel was engaged in wartime planning in Washington.[59]

Despite the high hopes held by both Fraenkel and other U.S. diplomats, they were aware that the new South Korean regime was far from a vibrant democracy. Immediately upon coming to power, Rhee concentrated authority and developed an autocratic government. After appointing personal allies to law enforcement positions, the president suppressed opposition, arrested leftist politicians, and violently dispersed political gatherings. Like the rest of the U.S. staff in Seoul, Fraenkel had little doubt that Rhee was an aspiring dictator. In 1949, for example, after thirteen members of the national assembly were arrested for treason, Fraenkel warned his supervisors

---

[58] Adwin Wigfall Green, who was one of the occupation officials and a judge in Korea, estimated U.S. support to Korea during 1948–50 at $300 million. See his *The Epic of Korea* (Washington, D.C.: Public Affair Press, 1950), 119. On the ECA in Korea, see Bruce Cumings, *Korea's Place in the Sun* (New York: Norton, 2005), 252–255.

[59] ECA Budget Estimate Assistance to the Republic of Korea, Fiscal Year 1949 (12 December 1948), and ECA Budget Estimate Assistance to the Republic of Korea, Fiscal Year 1950 (30 January 1951), both in Folder Budget—Korea, Box 1, Records Relating to Korea, MLR 271C, RG 469 [Records of the U.S. Foreign Assistance Agencies 1948–1961], NARA. On Fraenkel's responsibilities, see Memorandum, Eric H. Biddle to Paul G. Hoffman, Staffing for ECA Mission to Korea (20 November 1948), Folder Draft Program for Economic Aid to the Republic of Korea, Box 2, Records Relating to Korea, MLR 271C, RG 469, NARA. Some of this information is also based on Anne O. Krueger, *The Developmental Role of the Foreign Sector and Aid* (Cambridge, MA: Harvard University Press, 1979).

that the accused were targeted for their opposition to Rhee, that the trial was visibly biased, and that evidence was extracted through torture. Like many others in the U.S. embassy, however, Fraenkel believed these actions did not make U.S. involvement in Korea futile, nor did they disprove the universality of its attempt to democratize and modernize the country. Replicating older American claims that authoritarian leadership could be a way station to democracy by allowing economic development, Fraenkel asserted that the United States' efforts to facilitate social equality and prosperity would ultimately transform Rhee's anti-Communist dictatorship into a robust democracy. Fraenkel had little doubt about his own—or the United States'—capabilities for global transformation. In this worldview, the only question was whether the Koreans were willing to accept his superior wisdom.[60]

In both its coercive and progressive components, then, the architecture of U.S. power in Korea was not simply the product of U.S. Cold War strategy or American liberal internationalist traditions. While these ideas deeply shaped U.S. policies, the occupation also reflected German Socialist visions. As the United States engaged with new enemies—first the Third Reich, and then the Soviet Union and soon-to-be Communist China—and erected enormous new war bureaucracies, many military officials and diplomats began to appreciate the value of German émigrés. Thinkers such as Fraenkel combined anti-Nazi and anti-Soviet credentials with the legal knowledge and familiarity with international politics that U.S. officials sometimes lacked. But by recruiting Socialist émigrés, U.S. officials also allowed ideas and visions carried over from previous decades to take part in shaping U.S. policy. Fraenkel quickly utilized his position as a valuable asset for U.S. diplomats to resurrect his own campaign to build a social-democratic and anti-Communist state.

In 1950 these attempts collapsed when war tragically erupted between South and North Korea. Within a few months, the United States, under the auspices of the United Nations, and Communist China had both joined the conflict, leading to the violent death of hundreds of thousands and leaving the country permanently divided. Like all U.S. civilian personnel, Fraenkel was forced to evacuate the country in haste, leaving behind all the programs and bureaucracies he had helped establish. But the synergy of the American leviathan and German Socialist theory had not come to an end. Within a year, it would resume in Germany, and collective democracy would return to its birthplace.

[60] On Rhee's consolidation of authoritarian power, and on Fraenkel's influential report (which was distributed in both Seoul and Washington, D.C.), see Cumings, *Korea's Place in the Sun*, 185–236, esp. 216–217. On American support for dictators, see David F. Schmitz, *Thank God They're on Our Side: The United States and Right-Wing Dictatorships, 1921–1965* (Chapel Hill: University of North Carolina Press, 1999), 3–8.

The German Left and the Cold War

When Fraenkel returned to West Germany in 1951, the German left was embroiled in a fierce campaign against the country's alliance with the West. Since the occupation's end and the beginning of West Germany's independence in 1949, no major political camp had rejected the United States' call for international anti-Soviet mobilization more fiercely than the Socialists. This was not due to a lack of anti-Communist fury. Socialist activists, who rebuilt and expanded the postwar SPD into West Germany's second largest party, emerged from war and occupation as fiercely anti-Communist as they had been in the Weimar years. Their visions of democracy, however, led them to understand cooperation with the Western alliance as detrimental to liberty and social justice. Following the more hard-line Socialist sentiments from the Weimar era, leading SPD politicians and intellectuals believed that only a large-scale nationalization of the economy and centralized economic planning could secure democracy. Embracing the same platform that the party first wrote in 1925, they claimed that democracy necessitated breaking the economic power of industrialists and capitalists. SPD leaders therefore utterly rejected the New Deal model of free-market capitalism balanced by welfare programs. A German-American alliance would block their plans to aggressively nationalize major industries and prevent the SPD from fulfilling its vision. As SPD chairman Kurt Schumacher proclaimed in bellicose rhetoric, social democracy's goal was to complete the Weimar revolution by building a new economic order. The SPD had to find a "third way" between Soviet "monopolistic dictatorship" and the West's liberal capitalism, both of which were equally "foreign to the German people."[61]

In the first decade of West German independence, the SPD thus mobilized its energies and supporters in a long campaign to achieve German unification and to separate Germany from the Western alliance. SPD representatives conducted independent diplomacy in East Berlin and Moscow and regularly filled Germany's streets with millions of protesting workers, intellectuals, and unionists. These protesters sought to block all major Cold War policies, such as the reestablishment of German military forces in 1952, the country's entry into NATO in 1955, and its nuclear armament in 1957. Throughout the decade, opposition to the Cold War was one of the German left's chief political motors. The Western alliance was an obstacle, not a support, for "true" democracy.[62]

---

[61] The quotation is from Kurt Schumacher, *Reden, Schriften, Korrespondenzen* (Berlin: Dietz, 1985), 771.

[62] For more on the SPD opposition, see Dietrich Orlow, "Ambivalence and Attraction: The German Social Democrats and the United States, 1945–1974," in Reiner Pommerin (ed.), *The American Impact on Postwar Germany* (Providence, RI: Berghahn, 1995), 35–51; Andrei S. Mar-

The United States' efforts to reverse this opposition were wide and ambitious. Anxious U.S. diplomats feared that the SPD might succeed in removing West Germany from the Western alliance. These fears were especially strong for John J. McCloy, who as allied high commissioner continued to officially supervise the West German government after the end of the military occupation. They therefore unleashed a slew of cultural outreach programs, exhibitions, and lectures to German workers, seeking to recruit them to the U.S.-led international bloc. Fraenkel was a key agent in this mobilization effort. As one of few people who enjoyed a reputation as a leading Socialist intellectual and who was also intimately familiar with the U.S. establishment, he was in a unique position to facilitate engagement between the SPD and the United States. But unlike what some scholars have argued, these efforts were not solely an attempt to "Americanize" the SPD.[63] As he had done in Korea, Fraenkel utilized the United States' vast outreach and mobilization campaign to resume his own Weimar-era intellectual and political projects. He believed that by embracing the United States as an ally, the German left could abandon Marxism and embrace his own vision of democracy. The Western alliance would allow the SPD to conceive democracy not as synonymous with a state-planned economy and the redistribution of wealth but, first and foremost, as a combination of the rule of law and limited welfare measures, a simultaneous embrace of both individual-bourgeois and collective-socialist principles. After a decade of frantic public outreach, in the late 1950s Fraenkel's ideas provided the language for both domestic and international transformations. By helping to recast the SPD's vision of politics, he helped bridge the gap between the German left and the United States.

Despite his earlier refusal to return to Europe, after evacuating from Korea and failing to secure an academic position in the United States, Fraenkel changed his mind. In 1951 he accepted an invitation from Otto Suhr, a Socialist friend from the Weimar period who was now West Berlin's popular mayor. Joining Suhr's attempt to resurrect social-democratic education, Fraenkel took a teaching position at the newly reopened Socialist-leaning Hochschule für Politik (Academy of Politics), an independent institution of political education that operated alongside the city's Free University.[64] Within only a few years, the returning émigré emerged as one of West Ger-

---

kovits and Phillip S. Gorski, *The German Left: Red, Green and Beyond* (New York: Oxford University Press, 1993); Marc Cioc, *Pax Atomica: The Nuclear Defense Debate in West Germany during the Adenauer Era* (New York: Columbia University Press, 1988).

[63] See, for example, Angster, *Konsenskapitalismus und Sozialdemokratie*; Orłow, "Ambivalence and Attraction."

[64] Fraenkel mentioned Suhr's role in his own return to Germany in the eulogy he wrote upon Suhr's death. Ernst Fraenkel, Manuscript "Geleitword zu Otto Suhr" (31 August 1957), Folder 18, Box 2, NL Fraenkel, UFU.

many's most influential and admired political theorists. In a stream of publications, he introduced theories that explained the function of the parliamentary system, judicial review, coalition building, and party politics. German universities embraced these writings for their curricula with striking speed, followed by many of Germany's high schools. As one scholar stated, Fraenkel became an immediate "classic" of postwar German democratic thought. In many Socialist circles, Fraenkel was considered one of the most important social-democratic theoreticians of the postwar decade. Socialist leaders and scholars, some of whom had known him since the Weimar era, often wrote to consult him on burning legal matters.[65]

More than any other Socialist thinker in Germany, Fraenkel put this formidable prestige and democratic theory in the service of the United States. Alongside dozens of American labor activists and former New Dealers, he joined the massive cultural campaign that U.S. diplomats unleashed to bring the German left into the Western alliance. John McCloy—who, like Fraenkel, had arrived in Europe after serving in Korea—poured considerable energy into these efforts. Under his leadership, the United States sponsored thousands of visits and exchange programs between German and American labor activists and leaders. The main avenue for this operation were the cultural centers that U.S. diplomats opened across West Germany, which soon became known as "America Houses" (*Amerikahäuser*). Spread across twenty-seven cities, these centers built libraries, organized concerts, and funded sports events, all designed to introduce American culture to the German population. The enormous resources that U.S. diplomats poured into the America Houses elevated them into one of the most popular and vibrant cultural forces of the early post-occupation years. Each month, over a million Germans visited them.[66]

In Fraenkel's hands, this massive cultural apparatus also became a tool to modify the German left's conception of democracy. As he stated in a 1955 memorandum to U.S. diplomats in Frankfurt, domestic reform was a prerequisite to forging an international alliance. According to Fraenkel, the

[65] On Fraenkel's status as a classic, see Hubertus Buchstein, "Ernst Fraenkel als Klassiker," *Leviathan* 26:4 (1998): 458–482. On Fraenkel's importance in establishing pro-democratic education, see Alfons Söllner, *Deutsche Politikwissenschaftler in der Emigration* (Opladen: Westdeutscher Verlag, 1996); Hubertus Buchstein, *Politikwissenschaft und Demokratie* (Baden: Nomos, 1992).

[66] On McCloy's focus on cultural exchange, see Thomas Alan Schwartz, *America's Germany: John J. McCloy and the Federal Republic of Germany* (Cambridge, MA: Harvard University Press, 1991). On the America Houses, see Axel Schildt, "Die USA als Kulturnation: Zur Bedeutung der Amerikahäuser in den 1950er Jahren," in Alf Lüdtke (ed.), *Amerikanisierung: Traum und Alptraum im Deutschland des 20. Jahrhunderts* (Stuttgart: Steiner Verlag, 1996), 257–269. On the enormous U.S. propaganda campaign throughout the 1950s, see Kenneth Osgood, *Total Cold War* (Lawrence: University Press of Kansas, 2005). On the programs designed specifically for the German left, see Angster, *Konsenskapitalismus und Sozialdemokratie*, esp. 179–270.

SPD's opposition to collaboration with the West had little to do with its proclaimed adherence to Germany's unification. Rather, it was the product of Socialists' insistence on representing only the working class and their adherence to the Marxist obsession with the nationalization of major industries. According to Fraenkel's harsh assessment, the SPD's focus on the working class as the sole agent of progress and democracy showed that it was ultimately a "ghetto party." It was self-absorbed and obsessed with workers' issues, whereas it should be engaging with the middle class in coalition building. Fraenkel went so far as to argue that the SPD was preserving a feudal "caste-system" from the Middle Ages in the modern world. Its activists and leaders lived in a "pre-capitalistic ... self-created political ghetto, in which overlapping loyalties ... were frowned upon as a kind of treason." As long as the SPD remained locked in the rigid belief that only workers truly represented democracy, U.S. diplomats would simply be unable to channel the party's anti-Communist sentiments into a unified alliance.[67]

American cultural efforts therefore had to focus on the SPD's domestic outlook just as much as its international agenda. The enormous web of America Houses, exchange programs, and exhibitions were utilized to convince German workers of the value of pluralist politics and coalition building. According to Fraenkel, the German left suffered from a "split personality." On the one hand, it sought to achieve social equality through aggressive planning of the economy, but on the other hand, as its firm defense of the Weimar Republic had shown, it was "the guardian of a truly democratic constitution." The United States must therefore actively encourage Socialist activists who believed in cooperation with non-Marxist groups. It should sponsor meetings, seminars, and journals that would enable Socialists to meet conservative, religious, and liberal leaders and foster cross-class cooperation. The initiation of such a transformation would have repercussions far beyond the German left itself. Should the SPD fail to end its isolationism and continue to refuse to cooperate with other parties, the entire democratic system might collapse, as had happened in Weimar. Reaching out to German labor thus transcended the objective of anti-Soviet mobilization. It stood at the very heart of Germany's political reconstruction.[68]

For all its democratic zeal, Fraenkel's thinking about German postwar politics reflected the same militant inflexibility as his anti-Soviet work in Korea. Elections, party politics, and state institutions were meant to bring about consensus and collaboration, not allow a radical restructuring of economic inequalities. In Fraenkel's eyes, the "orthodox" Socialist ideas that

---

[67] Memorandum, "Caste Structure, Caste Spirit, Ghetto Parties and the Future of German Democracy," Ernst Fraenkel to the Research Division of the New School (undated, probably summer 1955), Folder 16, NL 1274, BAK.

[68] Ibid.

privileged aggressive economic nationalization over interclass cooperation were not merely unhelpful but an existential danger for democratic conduct. Like Weimar-era Communists and the Soviets in Korea, ardent Socialists undermined the entire project of erecting a modern collective democracy. For both Fraenkel and his American superiors, it proved impossible to envision a social democracy that was not committed to compromise with conservatives and the Cold War fight. Traditional Socialist worldviews could only be the product of primitive "medieval" politics or Communist subversion, and were not legitimate building blocks for a new German democracy or a transatlantic alliance.

This underlying anxiety about the threat posed by Socialist resistance explains the tremendous urgency that U.S. diplomats placed on bringing together Fraenkel and the network of America Houses as a base for their outreach operation to the German people. Each year, Fraenkel and U.S. diplomats worked together to organize exhibitions and concerts on American culture, history, and politics. More important, Fraenkel embarked on a soon to be famous annual lecture tour to explain U.S. diplomacy and its anti-Soviet efforts. Traveling through Hanover, Hamburg, Bremen, Kassel, Berlin, and dozens of other cities, he lectured to thousands on NATO (Germany was not yet a member), the Korean War, and Communist policies.[69] German audiences quickly recognized Fraenkel's unique intimacy with U.S. power and took note of his service on the front lines of the Cold War in Asia. With the similarities between their own divided country and the Korean peninsula in mind, thousands flocked to the America Houses to learn about their own place in the bipolar world.[70] As Fraenkel explained to his U.S. supervisors, this public advocacy was aimed at clarifying the benefits of joining the crystallizing Western alliance to an ambivalent audience. "Special emphasis," he wrote,

> will be laid on the purely defensive character of Nato [sic] and the origins of the idea of having Germany join this organization after the outbreak of the Korean war.... I intend to deal in these lectures with the global aspects of Soviet imperialism and to show how the Russians shifted in the course of the last thirty-five years their offensive back and forth from Central Europe to East Asia.

[69] For reports on his lectures at the America Houses, see Letter, Fraenkel to U.S. HICOG, Office of Public Affairs (2 February 1955); Letter, George D. Henry, Director of Amerika Haus Berlin, to Fraenkel (13 February 1955); both in Folder 1; Letter, Herwin Schaefer (Chief Exhibition Section, U.S. Office of Public Affairs) to Fraenkel (14 December 1953), Folder 10; Letter, Fraenkel to Harry Pross (11 May 1958), Folder 26; all in NL 1274, BAK.

[70] Letter, William Dietz to Fraenkel (6 May 1952), Folder 1; Letter, Bart N. Stephens (Director of the Amerika Haus Nürenberg) to Fraenkel (1 February 1956), Folder 14; Letter, Helen J. Imrie (Director of the Amerika Haus Hamburg) to Fraenkel (23 October 1951), Folder 1; all in NL 1274, BAK.

Regarding his principal message, he concluded, "I will try to explain the defensive methods used by the Western democracies to 'contain' Soviet Russia in those areas." The United States' hegemony was purely defensive, guarding the existence of European democracy.[71]

At the heart of this outreach effort were labor unions and the SPD. As he had advocated in his reports during his service at the OSS, U.S. outreach endeavors in Germany had to focus on the German left. The leaders of the SPD might be anti-Communist, but their followers across Germany were vulnerable to the Soviet promise of a classless and utopian society. Fraenkel therefore utilized the America Houses to lecture to thousands of labor unionists, Socialist women's organizations, and SPD youth movement members, seeking to mitigate their suspicions toward the United States. The Western superpower, he explained, was not the obstacle to German unification nor the opponent of labor that leaders like SPD chairman Kurt Schumacher claimed. Instead, it was the protector of social justice and workers' rights, goals the SPD had been striving for since its inception. By sending its troops around the globe and building military bases in Germany, the United States was merely seeking to expand the reach of social-democratic principles, such as welfare and the rule of law. In its essence, Cold War was about the U.S.-led promotion of social equality and democracy.

The historical narrative that Fraenkel constructed for these lectures became one of his most popular theories in the postwar era. In Fraenkel's telling, throughout the twentieth century, the nations of Western Europe and the United States had slowly adopted one another's democratic institutions and ideas. Through this long process of conversion, they had become profoundly similar to one another, all representing variations of the same "Western democracy," a variant on the widespread concept of "Western civilization." In this process of international transmission, each country had contributed a single fundamental concept. Britain, for example, had developed the concept of indirect representation, while France had perfected the notion of individual legal equality. According to Fraenkel, Germany's contribution to Western democracy was the boldest and most revolutionary: the idea of collective rights and social legislation. The Weimar Constitution and the numerous programs established by the SPD in the 1920s were the boldest realization of this concept. Drawing on work from his period of exile, Fraenkel claimed that Weimar's Social Democrats had inspired the welfare legislation of the New Deal. As he put it, "an astonishingly high number of social political scholars from Western nations followed with intense attention and inner enthusiasm the [intellectual] agitation that took place under the regime of the Weimar Constitution." The United States had merely reproduced what the SPD itself had begun to create before the Nazi

---

[71] Letter, Fraenkel to William Dietz (13 September 1952), Folder 1, NL 1274, BAK.

dictatorship. By allying with the United States, then, German labor would be empowered to fulfill its own earlier political mission.[72]

This awkward story proved to be a powerful tool of cultural outreach to the German left. By presenting the United States in familiar terms, as part of a social-democratic tradition that SPD members cherished, Fraenkel's lectures provided workers with a fresh perspective on the Atlantic giant. The directors of the America Houses were quick to appreciate Fraenkel's rare qualities and the effectiveness of his message. His unassailable social-democratic credentials and intellectual authority made SPD functionaries visibly receptive to his lectures. Throughout the 1950s, U.S. diplomats distributed Fraenkel's printed lectures among German workers and showered him with urgent requests for his service. They were eager to utilize him as a channel through which to reach audiences that had remained largely unmoved by their previous efforts. From the America House in Berlin, one diplomat admitted to Fraenkel that workers' unions presented "the hardest challenge" that he had encountered, and that Fraenkel's lectures had proved to be the best vehicle by which to engage with them. In Tübingen, another State Department official reported that "[y]our lecture enabled us for the first time to reach the labor union leaders in the Tübingen area and to interest them in the activities of the America House." Would Fraenkel be willing, he implored, to return for such lectures at "Reutlingen, Friedrichshafen, Schwenningen, and Tuttlingen, all of which are important small industrial centers?" "We have seldom, if ever," mused a third, "seen such wholeheartedly favorable, such enthusiastic responses" as those elicited by these lectures.[73] In the U.S. campaign to win over German labor, Fraenkel was a rare bridge figure; his lectures provided the language through which German workers could recast their views of international politics and see the United States as the new leader of older German policies and traditions.

As a key component of this outreach campaign to workers and SPD activists, Fraenkel sought to recruit leaders of the German left to a new universe of international Cold War elites. During the 1950s, in conjunction with NATO and with generous American support, a network of newly formed organizations brought together intellectuals, policymakers, and jour-

[72] Fraenkel, Report on activities, Fraenkel to John Brown Mason (HICOG) (14 September 1951), Folder 71; Letter, Robert T. Curran to Fraenkel (16 October 1957), Folder 20; Letter, Fraenkel to Theodore L. Eliot (25 January 1954), Folder 1; all in NL 1274, BAK. These lectures were later published as Ernst Fraenkel, "Deutschland und die westliche Demokratien" (1960), GS 5, 74–90, quotation from 75–76. On the popularity of Fraenkel's theory during the 1950s, see Arndt Bauerkämper, "Demokratie als Verheissung oder Gefahr? Deutsche Politikwissenschaftler und amerikanische Modelle 1945 bis zur Mitte der sechziger Jahre," in Konrad H. Jarausch et al. (eds.), Demokratiewunder (Göttingen: Vandenhoeck & Ruprecht, 2005), 253–280.

[73] Letter, Edwin C. Pancoast to Fraenkel (30 March 1954), Folder 1; Letter, Theodore L. Eliot, to Fraenkel (27 September 1954), Folder 1; Letter, William E. Dietz to Fraenkel (29 September 1954), Folder 1; all in NL 1274, BAK.

nalists to strengthen the bonds between the members of NATO. Organs such as the German Atlantic Society, the British Atlantic Treaty Association, and the Congress for Cultural Freedom routinely orchestrated meetings and discussions attended by social, cultural, and political leaders who exercised, as one member put it, "an influence both on public opinion and, directly or indirectly, on shaping governmental policies."[74] Through his extensive ties with U.S. diplomats, Fraenkel joined such politicians as French minister of foreign affairs Robert Schumann and political theorists like Harvard's William Elliot in planning anti-Soviet mobilization. The discussion groups they formed, called "Atlantic Futures" or "Atlantic Values," spent days and weeks discussing topics such as "the North Atlantic and totalitarianism," "scientific and technological advances of Western civilization," and "the North Atlantic and the underdeveloped world." Fraenkel was instrumental in arranging the initial contact between many SPD officials and this remarkably broad and powerful network of Cold War leaders. The chairmen of labor union branches, and parliamentary leaders such as Adolf Arndt, hesitantly accepted his invitation to join these networks, discreetly defying the party line that remained hostile to such events. Throughout the 1950s, their participation became increasingly frequent and provided rare opportunities for them to meet with pro-American labor activists from France, Britain, and Italy. Through Fraenkel, U.S. diplomats found a rare link to both rank-and-file activists and the SPD leadership. As Melvin Lasky, editor of the influential anti-Communist journal *Der Monat*, wrote, Fraenkel's rare intellectual gravitas "made it possible for you to do and say things which could not go down as easily from others. When you spoke against communism ... [and] called for a deeper, more intelligent understanding of the United States, its history and its problems—all this carried an authority which was a distinctive contribution to Berlin's democratic fight."[75]

At the same time, Fraenkel utilized the America Houses and elite networks to promote his own agenda of reforming the SPD's domestic priorities. In a series of U.S.-funded lectures and discussion groups, he reached out to thousands of workers, union leaders, SPD parliamentary delegates, and intellectuals in his effort to convince them of the value of cross-class

[74] Letter, Hendrik Brugmans to Fraenkel (19 September 1957), Folder 20, NL 1274, BAK. On the construction of these elite networks, see Thomas W. Gijswijt, "Beyond NATO: Transnational Elite Networks and the Atlantic Alliance," in Andreas Wenger, Christian Nuenlist, and Anna Locher (eds.), *Transforming NATO in the Cold War*, 15–30.

[75] Quotation is from Letter, Melvin J. Lasky to Fraenkel (2 February 1955), Folder 3, NL 1274, BAK. The rest is based on Letter, D. N. Chester (Nuffield College, Oxford) to Fraenkel (26 March 1956), Folder 20; Letter, John Epstein to Fraenkel (29 August 1960), Folder 37; Letter, Richard Jaeger to Fraenkel (15 March 1963), Folder 43; List of participants, Conference of European Political Scientists (25–26 June 1956), Folder 20; all in NL 1274, BAK. The lengthy correspondence between Arndt and Fraenkel is in Folder 9, NL 1274, BAK.

cooperation. In Frankfurt and Düsseldorf, Kiel and West Berlin, thousands of SPD members heard Fraenkel's musings on the urgency of abandoning Marxism in favor of adopting more moderate welfare programs. Moreover, he spearheaded a variety of gatherings, organizations, and activities that facilitated new spaces for Socialist leaders to engage with new partners and form coalitions. Procuring American funds, he initiated discussion groups and seminars that brought labor union leaders, such as Walter Freitag, chairman of the powerful federal labor union, together with leading free-market economists such as Wilhelm Röpcke and political theorists such as Helmut Schlesky and fellow returning émigré Carl J. Friedrich. At these seminars and meetings, this broad coalition discussed techniques that would encourage the working class to abandon Marxism and radical economic reform. Instead, as one speaker suggested, the energy of social-democratic politics should be channeled into the project of "Western and European integration."[76] In Fraenkel's urgent call, labor's democratic aspirations could only be achieved through cooperation with the middle class and the creation of a hybrid, Socialist-liberal state. As he put it in a lecture to union activists in Bochum, "only through such cooperation could the SPD rightfully achieve our democratic will and our democratic aspirations ... in the political, educational, and social spheres." Cooperation should not be equated with compromise or defeat; it would facilitate the realization of German socialism's historical mission of building a collective democracy.[77]

The culmination of this Cold War cultural campaign took place in West German universities. Both Fraenkel and the U.S. diplomats who supported him quickly sought to incorporate Fraenkel's ideas into the fabric of West German higher education. During the 1950s, the cooperation between the Socialist émigré and John McCloy gave birth to "American Studies" as an educational field, through which thousands of German students could familiarize themselves with the United States' new image. In 1952, supported by U.S. government funding, Fraenkel was the first faculty member at West Berlin's Academy of Politics to introduce courses on U.S. politics and his-

---

[76] Letter, Fraenkel to Theodore L. Eliot (25 January 1954), Folder 1; Letter, Studiengemeinschaft der evangelischen Akademien (unsigned) to Fraenkel (26 November 1953), Folder 2; Letter, Walter Freitag to Fraenkel (20 June 1956), Folder 17; all in NL 1274, BAK. On the significance of such forums in fostering new political collaboration, see A. J. Nicholls, *Freedom with Responsibility* (New York: Oxford University Press, 1994), 380–389.

[77] The quotation is from the manuscript "Startgleichheit und Klassenschichtung" (undated, 1956?), Folder 17, NL 1274, BAK. The lecture was later published under the same title in the union journal *Gewerkschaftliche Monatshefte* 7 (August 1956): 457–460. The many events that Fraenkel organized are mentioned in Letter, Kurt Mattick to Fraenkel (26 February 1952), Folder 8; Letter, DGB Kiel (unsigned) to Fraenkel (3 March 1954), Folder 1; Letter, Friedrich Sitzler to Fraenkel (8 December 1954); Letter, SPD Prenzlauberg to Fraenkel (14 December 1951), Folder 5; Letter, H. Imig to Fraenkel (4 December 1954), Folder 1; all in NL 1274, BAK.

tory. As part of this project, Fraenkel also initiated a series of German translations of what he deemed the "American intellectual canon," from *The Federalist Papers* to John Dewey's writings on education.[78] In 1963 Fraenkel's lobbying efforts led to the opening of the first center of North American studies at the Free University of Berlin, with generous American support. There, under Fraenkel's directorship, students could learn about the history, geography, literature, sociology, and science of the United States. Within four years, the center (soon to be renamed after John F. Kennedy) had cloned its curriculum and agenda across West Germany's universities. Its members—mostly Fraenkel's students—organized courses, lectures, exhibitions, and events on American culture, politics, and law in Hamburg, Frankfurt, Cologne, Giessen, Nuremberg, Heidelberg, Mainz, and numerous other cities across West Germany. These programs represented the most systematic and extensive project of U.S. cultural outreach. What began as a series of lectures at the America Houses was expanded into a comprehensive academic education for tens of thousands of young Germans.[79]

By the end of the 1950s, this breathless stream of writings, lectures, outreach efforts, and educational programs both prepared and provided the model for the radical transformation of German Socialist thinking about democracy. As the years progressed, Fraenkel's writings and initiatives helped Socialist activists, journalists, and leaders articulate a new program for the SPD, which no longer viewed the working class as the exclusive agent of democratic politics, nor championed bold economic reform as its primary objective. The SPD's heavy defeats in the 1953 and 1957 national elections empowered these reformist activists to promote their visions. At the groundbreaking SPD congress at Bad Godesberg in 1959, party representatives from across the country voted to replace the 1925 Heidelberg Program, abandon the nationalization of key industries as their major objective, and to eschew all anti-bourgeois rhetoric. In its place, the platform adopted at Bad Godesberg explicitly endorsed the party's commitment to cooperation in the exercise of political power and vowed to collaborate with middle-class groups. Despite the frustration felt by some older SPD members, who regarded the new agenda as an opportunistic attempt to woo voters, the vision outlined at Bad Godesberg would prove to be resilient. During the 1960s, it would open the door for the SPD to join multiple coalitions with conservative parties and would remain the SPD's platform for decades to come.

[78] Letter, Michael Weyl to Fraenkel (19 March 1956), Folder 17; Letter, Fraenkel to Gottfried Dietz (16 February 1958), Folder 23; both in NL 1274, BAK.

[79] Hubert Wurmbach, Mitteilungsblatt der deutschen Gesellschaft für Amerikastudien, Heft 14 (summer 1967), NL Fraenkel, Box 44, Folder 269, NL Fraenkel, UFU. On the history of American studies in Germany in general, see Gunter J. Lenz and Klaus J. Milich (eds.), *American Studies in Germany* (Frankfurt a.M.: Campus, 1995).

Equally important and deeply connected, Fraenkel's ideas and efforts helped bring support for the Western alliance into the SPD's political mainstream. He provided the intellectual framework for Socialist activists and leaders who relinquished their quest for German unification and sought a new alignment with the Western bloc. Headed by the parliamentarian Herbert Wehner and West Berlin's young mayor, Willy Brandt, a growing wing within the SPD came to embrace NATO and the United States as a natural ally. After several years of internal debates, this camp triumphed in 1960, when the party embraced the pro-American stance as its official platform. In a dramatic speech at the Reichstag, Wehner declared that the SPD had renounced its neutrality in the Cold War and would end its decade-long negotiations with the Soviet Union. "We now acknowledge," he said, that "the European Community and the Atlantic alliance [are] the prerequisites for the preservation of freedom." In a drastic shift that few could have envisioned a decade earlier, American power was no longer perceived to be a foreign capitalist threat but, rather, the defender of equality and democracy. Fraenkel's ideas, once controversial, now represented a new consensus.[80]

Fraenkel's public campaign to resurrect his Weimar-era theory thus stood at the center of the broad forces that transformed the German left in the 1950s. His theory of collective democracy provided theoretical legitimacy to nervous U.S. diplomats, who were determined to recruit the German left to the anti-Soviet alliance. It helped give voice to German Socialist reformers, who sought to shift their party away from Marxism toward cooperation with the middle class. As a unique boundary figure, familiar with both the U.S. Cold War establishment and the German social-democratic world, Fraenkel became the glue that joined the two campaigns for reform into a comprehensive project. He claimed that only through the Western alliance could Germany fulfill its social-democratic destiny; his cultural outreach campaign argued that radical changes to international and domestic agendas were inseparable and mutually reinforcing. In doing so, Fraenkel also helped delegitimize other Socialist theories. Drawing on the traumatic experiences of the 1920s, he tarred the advocates of nationalization as anti-democratic and ultimately similar to their hated Communist opponents. U.S. cultural outreach to the German left thus empowered older German Socialist-Democratic theories, which helped amplify the message of the U.S. cultural apparatus. By the late 1950s, the nexus of U.S. outreach and German Socialist reformists had successfully promoted the agendas of both its participants. The Cold War also marked the triumph of collective democracy.

[80] Quoted in Stephen J. Artner, *A Change of Course: The West German Social Democrats and NATO, 1957–1961* (Westport, CT: Greenwood, 1985), 151. For more on this process, see also Wayne C. Thompson, *The Political Odyssey of Herbert Wehner* (Boulder: Westview Press, 1993).

The theory of labor, rights, and democracy that Fraenkel carried from Weimar Germany into exile failed to become part of mainstream American thought. Unlike Friedrich's writings about democratic elites and higher education, Fraenkel was rarely published in English and received scant attention from American politicians and scholars.[81] This lack of attention may have stemmed in part from growing tensions about labor's place in the domestic postwar order. While countless American labor activists voluntarily joined American outreach efforts to workers in Europe and Asia, they faced growing backlash at home. Many American politicians and business leaders perceived organized labor as a threat to prosperity, liberty, and Cold War security. They sought to reverse New Deal–era labor gains. In 1947 the U.S. Congress passed the Labor Management Relations Act (colloquially known as the Taft-Hartley Act) by a large majority, drastically limiting the rights of workers to join trade unions, declare strikes, and engage in collective bargaining. Despite Fraenkel's unwavering conviction that the United States remained the beacon of collective democracy, his ideas found little resonance there. Few saw his Socialist-inspired writings and theories as a blueprint for democratic politics.[82]

Yet the Cold War created new spaces where Fraenkel could pursue his political vision. U.S. diplomats backed Fraenkel's efforts with authority and resources far beyond the borders of the United States, as part of American attempts at international transformation and Cold War hegemony in both Asia and Europe. The immediate impetus for this collaboration was anxiety about Communist expansion. Drawing on widespread Socialist hostility from the days of Weimar, Fraenkel believed that communism presented an overriding danger because it opposed the essence of collective democracy, the concept of individual liberties, and the necessity of cross-class collaboration. Communists—whether in Asia or Europe—therefore had to be crushed, a goal worth the high and tragic price of dividing both Korea and Germany. But the alliance between American diplomacy and German Socialist theory was based on more than anti-Communist frenzy. It also drew from conceptions of democracy and collective rights that Fraenkel developed in Germany and then projected onto American international power.

---

[81] The only exceptions are *The Dual State* (1941), which readers at the time (and often since) mistakenly read as a theory of the Third Reich and not for its insights on capitalism and law. Fraenkel's wartime publications regarding military occupations were also read by military strategists and forgotten immediately after the war (see note 37).

[82] On the complex relationship between labor and the U.S. government during the Cold War, see, for example, Landon R. Y. Storrs, *The Second Red Scare and the Unmaking of the New Deal Left* (Princeton: Princeton University Press, 2013); Quenby Olmsted Hughes, *In the Interest of Democracy: The Rise and Fall of the Early Cold War Alliance between the American Federation of Labor and the Central Intelligence Agency* (New York: Peter Lang, 2011); John Fousek, *To Lead the Free World* (Chapel Hill: University of North Carolina Press, 2000), esp. 55–62.

In South Korea, Fraenkel's ideas merged with other theories of modernization and development and helped shape massive American investment in the peninsula. His belief that democracy must empower workers fueled his campaign to modernize Korean industry, education, and legal order. The same was the case in West Germany, where Fraenkel's agenda merged with anxious American efforts to mobilize German labor. Under the umbrella of American Cold War power, Fraenkel resurrected his campaign to transform the SPD's conception of democracy.

As Fraenkel's story shows, in both East Asia and Europe, Americans were not always trying to impose and duplicate familiar sociopolitical models, whether visions of "development" or "consensus capitalism." They did not simply replicate domestic American political sentiments. Rather, they opened space for, and even promoted, foreign ideas, as long as those ideas contributed to their overall Cold War efforts to mitigate global communism and secure a domestic American "way of life." Paradoxically, Fraenkel served U.S. diplomacy in order to promote values that the American government did not support at home. Yet by reading and misreading his own visions onto American power, he could utilize the United States' enormous resources to put forward his own agenda.

CHAPTER III

Conservative Catholicism and American Philanthropy

WALDEMAR GURIAN, "PERSONALIST" DEMOCRACY, AND ANTI-COMMUNISM

THE YEARS AFTER World War II witnessed not only democratic rebuilding but also an unprecedented outburst of Catholic activity. Across Germany and Western Europe, Catholic communities emerged as a commanding force in postwar reconstruction. They feverishly built new cultural centers and formed powerful political organizations. For U.S. occupation officers in Germany, this vibrancy raised both hopes and concerns. German Catholics had not been among Hitler's most enthusiastic supporters, leading some U.S. officials to proclaim that they would act as "the spiritual foundation of the new democracy."[1] Yet historically, German Catholics had an uneasy relationship with democratic politics. Many of them had regarded the Weimar Republic as a secular threat to their values and instead supported authoritarian leaders and ideas. Moreover, as Cold War tensions rose in the late 1940s, numerous Catholic politicians and journalists declared that Germany should look not to a secular and materialist United States but should ally itself only with other European countries as part of the *Abendland* (European and Christian West). Throughout the early Cold War, Catholic ambivalence cast a shadow over American reconstruction efforts in Europe and the emerging transatlantic alliance.[2]

German Catholic émigrés stood at the heart of attempts to bridge this gap. Having spent the war in exile, they returned to Europe under the auspices of American power and worked to create a democratic and anti-

---

[1] Cited in James Chappel, *The Struggle for Europe's Soul: Catholicism and the Salvation of Democracy, 1920–1960* (Cambridge, MA: Harvard University Press, forthcoming). For an overview of Catholics' attitudes toward democracy and authoritarianism, see Jay P. Corrin, *Catholic Intellectuals and the Challenge of Democracy* (South Bend: University of Notre Dame Press, 2002), esp. 188–219.

[2] On the tension between the concept of *Abendland* and "the West," see Vanessa Conze, *Das Europa der Deutschen: Ideen von Europa in Deutschland zwischen Reichstradition und Westorientierung* (Munich: Oldenbourg, 2005); Axel Schildt, *Zwischen Abendland und Amerika: Studien zur westdeutsche Ideenlandschaft der 50er Jahre* (Munich: Oldenbourg, 1999).

Communist bond between the United States and the Catholic community. The best example of their influence can be found in political theorist Waldemar Gurian, who in 1948 was among the first Catholic émigrés to return from exile to visit Germany. During the occupation period and the early 1950s, Gurian utilized U.S. wealth to fund a stream of publications, lectures, and educational programs intended to establish a union between the United States and Europe's Catholics. His writings depicted the United States as the guardian of Catholic ideals, autonomy, and communities and insisted that an alliance with the United States presented the only effective path toward defeating Catholicism's ultimate enemy, the Soviet Union. With the massive support of the American diplomatic and cultural apparatus, Gurian and other émigrés worked to popularize these ideas among German Catholics. By the mid-1950s, their efforts helped forge an alliance between Catholics, West Germany, and the United States, a bond that became the backbone of the Cold War effort in Europe.[3]

While U.S. officials envisioned the Catholic émigrés as a channel for American conceptions of democracy, Gurian and others like him were motivated by a much older agenda. Like their Protestant and Socialist counterparts, their goal was to resurrect their own cultural project, a deeply reactionary and anti-liberal ideology first envisioned during Weimar-era debates about politics, nationalism, and communism. As a young journalist and thinker, Gurian participated in a Catholic group that sought to build a religious social order based on small, traditional, "natural" communities, such as the family, the village, professional associations, and the Catholic Church. The mortal enemies of this order, he warned, were the radical left and right—communism and hypernationalism—which he depicted as all-consuming, secular, modern, and destructive revolutions. During Weimar's final years, Gurian developed an idiosyncratic theory that identified liberal democracy as Catholicism's most natural ally in the struggle to protect these "organic" communities. He was among a tiny minority that called on other Catholics to recast their hostility to secular ideas by embracing democratic politics and vigilantly combating communism and extreme nationalism. Like Friedrich and Fraenkel, Gurian saw American reconstruction efforts as far more than a response to the trauma of Nazism and war. Rather, they were a renewed opportunity to reintroduce old spiritual visions from the 1920s and help shape Catholics' crucial participation in postwar reconstruction.

---

[3] On Catholics' role in the reconstruction of Germany and West Germany's Cold War, see Maria Mitchell's excellent *The Rise of Christian Democracy: Politics and Confession in Modern Germany* (Ann Arbor: University of Michigan Press, 2012); Joachim Kohler and Damian van Melis (eds.), *Siegerin in Trümmern: die Rolle der katholischen Kirche in der deutschen Nachkriegsgesellschaft* (Stuttgart: Kohlhammer, 1998). For a focus on Catholics and the German-U.S alliance, see Ronald J. Granieri, *The Ambivalent Alliance: Konrad Adenauer, the CDU/CSU, and the West, 1949–1966* (New York: Berghahn, 2002).

While this cooperation between German Catholic conservatives and the Americans had important legacies in Germany, it also left its mark on the United States. In particular, it deeply shaped the emergence of a new field of knowledge: Soviet studies. During his time in exile, Gurian built upon his early writing to develop the famous "theory of totalitarianism," which claimed that Nazism and communism were essentially identical. Both, he despaired, were twin secular monstrosities that sought to eradicate religion and obliterate autonomous and "natural" communities. Communism therefore could not be simply contained; like Nazism, it had to be destroyed. In the late 1940s, the Rockefeller Foundation invested some of its enormous resources in the endeavor of popularizing these extreme anti-Communist theories. Rockefeller officials, who met Gurian in postwar Germany and voluntarily joined the United States' anti-Soviet mission, provided the Catholic émigré with the financial means to organize a bevy of publications, conferences, and cultural programs. This support helped integrate Gurian's ideas into academic research and teaching across the United States, elevating Gurian as a central authority on Soviet studies. His theory of totalitarianism therefore became one of the key mobilizing concepts of the Cold War, electrifying the minds of many.

Like Friedrich and Fraenkel, Gurian's theories from the Weimar era fueled intellectual projects on both sides of the Atlantic. By providing a theoretical edifice that called for the total destruction of communism, Catholics ideas from Europe shaped not only American Cold War scholarship but fundamentally undergirded the United States' own understanding of its political mission in the world. Yet like his Protestant and Socialist counterparts, the Catholic émigré utilized American money, power, and institutions to promote his own conceptions of a Christian, communitarian, and anti-Communist order. The symbiosis between German Catholic thought and U.S. power was not an obvious one, and one that neither party could have anticipated during the 1930s. Yet its evolution helped shape culture and thought into the 1950s.

CATHOLICISM, "PERSONALISM," AND DEMOCRACY IN THE RHINELAND: THE ORIGINS OF GURIAN'S THOUGHT

No group in Germany awaited the coming of the Weimar Republic with greater confusion and bewilderment than German Catholics. The democratic revolution that swept through Germany's cities in the fall of 1918 brought both promises and anxieties for Germany's largest minority, which had long held an ambiguous view of democratic principles. On the one hand, as a hated and often persecuted minority during the imperial era, most German Catholics recognized the benefits of civil liberties and parliamentary representation vis-à-vis the Protestant majority. Unique in Europe's Catholic culture, some German Catholics enthusiastically embraced parliamentary politics and elections, leading several historians to call them (somewhat tongue-in-cheek) "the era's true liberals." On the other hand, many Catholics feared that the march toward democracy would advance secularism, individualism, and materialism, leading to an assault on the Catholic community and its institutions. The fact that the German republic was ushered in by Socialists, many of whom were fiercely atheist and anticlerical, led conservative Catholics to keep their distance. This duality manifested itself during World War I. Catholics joined Socialists and liberals in brazenly defying the monarchy's authority, demanding democratization, and calling for an end to the war, but did not join the revolution in 1918. Instead, they approved the creation of the new republic only after it was a foregone conclusion.[4]

As was the case for Protestants and Socialists, the arrival of democracy spurred fierce intellectual and political debates that tore at the Catholic community from within. After decades of marginalization, German Catholics could now enter the country's institutions of power and even assume positions of leadership. Defining their place in the new republican order therefore became a matter of grave urgency. The key debate centered on who would be the best ally for the Catholic political party, known as the Center (*Centrum*) Party. From the Center's left wing, politicians such as Matthias Erzberger and Joseph Wirth called for a firm coalition with the Social Democrats and saw the republican system as a new opportunity to exert Catholic influence. From the party's right, Cardinal Michael von Faulhaber, Hermann Port, and Ludwig Kaas sought cooperation with conservative Protestants to replace the republic with an authoritarian state, one that would weaken the parliament and concentrate power in the hands of the executive. These conflicting forces meant that the Center's political position remained in constant flux, caught up in a series of shifting and contradictory alliances. At both the local and federal level, the Center was often simultaneously a member of pro- and anti-republican coalitions. This political ambiguity was so glaring that some thought Catholics should give up

---

[4] The quotation is from Noel D. Cary, *The Path to Christian Democracy: German Catholics and the Party System from Windhorst to Adenauer* (Cambridge, MA: Harvard University Press, 1996), 3. For a similar focus on Catholics' embrace of democratic norms, see Margaret L. Anderson, *Practicing Democracy: Elections and Political Culture in Imperial Germany* (Princeton: Princeton University Press, 2000), esp. 69–151. On German Catholics during the war, the revolution, and the creation of the Weimar Republic, see Heinz Hürten, *Deutsche Katholiken, 1918–1945* (Padeborn: Schöningh, 1992), 13–62. On their ambivalence toward the republic, see Karsten Ruppert, *Im Dienst am Staat von Weimar: das Zentrum als regierende Partei in der Weimarer Demokratie* (Düsseldorf: Droste, 1992); Jürgen Elvert, "The Centre Party in Germany," in Wolfram Kaiser and Helmut Wohnout (eds.), *Political Catholicism in Europe*, vol. 1 (New York: Routledge, 2004), 46–64.

on unified political action altogether. In 1925 the Catholic journalist Heinrich Teipel raised a brief firestorm when he called for the Center to disband itself and to quit the political arena. Throughout the Weimar years, the quest to define their enemies, allies, and their place in the new German republic dominated Catholic thought.[5]

It was in this context of furious debates on Catholic alliances that Waldemar Gurian developed his conservative and anti-liberal thought about Catholicism, democracy, and their enemies. Born in 1902 in St. Petersburg, Gurian came from a family of Russian Jews who fled to Germany in 1911 in the wake of ethnic violence. After converting to Catholicism, the family settled in Düsseldorf, one of the country's Catholic centers, and from 1917 until 1923 Gurian studied in Berlin, Breslau, Cologne, and Bonn. As a student, he was a member of Romano Guardini's new Catholic youth movement, which sought to revitalize Catholic life through novel liturgy, rituals, and country hikes. After completing his studies, Gurian moved between Cologne and Frankfurt, working as an editor and writer for the era's foremost Catholic newspapers, magazines, and publishing houses, such as *Heiliges Feuer, Abendland, Kölnische Volkszeitung*, and the Center's official organ, *Germania*. Throughout the 1920s and early 1930s, these were the platforms in which he published his explorations of Catholicism's enemies and allies.[6]

In particular, Gurian's work was shaped by the reformatory impulses of the Rhineland and the University of Cologne. In contrast to Bavaria—Germany's other major Catholic region, which remained largely hostile to the republic—the Rhineland was home to the most innovative and pro-republican Catholic journals and organizations. Even under the foreign occupation sanctioned by the Treaty of Versailles, Catholic thinkers and politicians sought to rejuvenate Catholic cultural life and open new paths for Catholics in Germany's innovative political landscape. The crown jewel of the reformatory attempts was the creation of the University of Cologne in 1919. Spearheaded by the city's ambitious mayor, Konrad Adenauer, the newly founded university was billed as the German Catholic contribution to the post–World War I world. Its founders hoped that the university would

[5] Heinrich Teipel, *Wir müssen aus dem Turm heraus* (Berlin: Selbstverlag, 1925). On the discussions sparked by the pamphlet, see Cary, *The Path to Christian Democracy*, 106–109. For a good overview of Catholic political debates, see Reinhard Richter, *Nationales Denken im Katholizismus der Weimarer Republik* (Münster: Lit, 2000). On left-leaning Catholics, see Cary, *The Path to Christian Democracy*, esp. 101–124. On right-wing Catholics, see William Patch, *Heinrich Brüning and the Dissolution of the Weimar Republic* (New York: Cambridge University Press, 1998).

[6] These biographical details are based on Heinz Hürten, *Waldemar Gurian: Ein Zeuge Krise unserer Welt in der ersten Hälfte des 20. Jahrhunderts* (Mainz: Grünewald Verlag, 1972); and Ellen Thümmler, *Katholischer Publizist und amerikanischer Politikwissenschaftler: Eine intellektuelle Biographie Waldemar Gurians* (Baden: Nomos, 2011).

solidify internal bonds among Catholics while strengthening the community's position within the new democratic order. Gurian arrived as a student at the university in 1921 and completed his dissertation on the Catholic Youth Movement in 1923. His central mentors were Max Scheler and Carl Schmitt, two of Weimar's most innovative Catholic thinkers. Their teachings, and Cologne's mission to define Catholicism's role in the modern world, shaped Gurian's works for decades to come.[7]

Gurian's early anti-individualism and anti-Communist ideas emerged from a reactionary school of thought called personalism, which crystallized in the years after World War I.[8] Its founder in Germany was philosopher Max Scheler, a Catholic convert from Judaism, who during the war emerged as Catholicism's leading intellectual voice. At the core of Scheler's theory stood the distinction between the "individual" and the "person." According to the personalists, since the Enlightenment, modern secular thinkers had mistakenly taken the "individual" to be the basic unit of morality, philosophy, and social theory. In their obsession with creating a rational, scientific, and universal society, they sought to mold individuals who were liberated from society and spiritual traditions. In this telling, however, by reducing humans into "individuals," the modern era had shattered all tradition and healthy social relations. Rather than liberating humans, the Enlightenment led them into a state of impoverished isolation and atomism. In contrast to the individual, personalists advocated a spiritual entity they called the "person." The "person" was a human embedded in a web of natural and historical communities, such as family, village, profession, and nation. In contrast to the Enlightenment individual, guided only by science and reason, the person drew from multiple sources of traditional authority. He or she embraced moral values that stemmed from religion and tradition. The personalists maintained that only the person could lead a spiritual and moral life. As the movement's most famous spokesperson in France, Emmanuel Mounier, put it, only the person had "a spiritual value ... at the heart of all other human reality."[9]

While French personalism drew from a variety of intellectual traditions, in Germany it was decisively Catholic.[10] According to Scheler, the

---

[7] On the role of the Rhineland in German Catholic culture, see Chappel, *The Struggle for Europe's Soul*; Cary, *The Path to Christian Democracy*. On Cologne and the university, see Erich Meuthen, *Kölner Universitätsgeschichte*, vol. 2 (Cologne: Böhlau, 1988); Hans-Peter Schwartz, *Konrad Adenauer* (Providence, RI: Berghahn, 1995), 161–162, 195–197.

[8] The following is deeply influenced by the work done by James Chappel, especially "The Catholic Origins of Totalitarianism Theory in Interwar Europe," *Modern Intellectual History* 8:3 (2011): 561–590. While some of my emphases, particularly on the issue of democracy, are different, Chappel's work deeply informs my own analysis here and in the following section.

[9] Cited in John Connelly, "Catholic Racism and Its Opponents," *The Journal of Modern History* 79:4 (December 2007): 813–847, here 826–827.

[10] On the varied origins of personalism in France, which included Thomist philosophers,

Catholic community was the ideal group for the realization of the "person." Unlike German Protestants, he claimed German Catholics resisted secularization and materialism and preserved the traditional communities of family and church as the center of moral life. Most important, Scheler asserted that Catholics resisted the nation-state's demand for absolute loyalty. Unlike Protestants, who glorified the nation and saw it as "the only path to God," Catholics maintained their loyalties to the family, profession, and their Catholic community, which preserved a healthy distance from the nation.[11] During World War I's final stages, Scheler called on Catholics to lead Germany's spiritual reconstruction. Only Catholics, he anxiously wrote, could strengthen the role of family, church, and local communities and counteract the Protestants' glorification of the nation-state. With the war's catastrophic end and the collapse of the monarchy in Berlin, Scheler's message resonated widely across Germany's Catholic regions. His theory allowed Catholics to move beyond their historic marginalization and envision themselves as the vanguard of Germany's spiritual rejuvenation. After the war, Scheler became known as the "black [i.e., Catholic] Nietzsche," and young Catholic intellectuals, such as Dietrich von Hildebrand, gathered around him in Bonn. Among them was the young Gurian, one of Scheler's most enthusiastic students.[12]

While Scheler believed that the spiritual content of personalism was clear, its concrete political implications remained obscure. Beyond its fixation with "organic" communities and multiple loyalties, the theory never provided a clear guide to the economic, social, and political structures that would realize the "person." Indeed, like the Catholic community as a whole, adherents of the personalist school failed to agree which political structures would best serve their purposes. While Scheler hesitantly supported the Weimar Republic and even approved of Catholic cooperation with Socialists, others adhered to authoritarianism and even monarchism. Personalist theory was, however, unequivocal in the way it defined its political enemies. According to the personalists, the secular atomization of humanity into isolated individuals led directly to dangerous forms of collectivism,

---

Russian émigrés, and Jewish followers of Nietzsche, see John Hellman, *The Communitarian Third Way* (Montreal: McGill-Queens University Press, 2002); John Hellman, *Emmanuel Mounier and the New Catholic Left, 1930–1950* (Toronto: University of Toronto Press, 1981).

[11] Cited in Chappel, "The Catholic Origins of Totalitarianism Theory," 596.

[12] For more on Scheler, see Peter H. Spade, *Scheler's Ethical Personalism* (New York: Fordham University Press, 2002); Wolfhart Hennckmann, *Max Scheler* (Munich: Verlag Beck, 1998). Scheler's reputation as the "black Nietzsche" is cited in Heinrich Lutz, *Demokratie im Zwielicht: Der Wer deutsche Katholiken aus dem Kaiserreich in die Republik* (Munich: Kösel Verlag, 1963), 23. According to Gurian's university records, he took at least seven courses and seminars with Scheler. Study Records for Waldemar Gurian, years 1920, 1921, 1922, Box 18, Folder 4, Waldemar Gurian Papers [hereafter referred to as WGP], Library of Congress [hereafter referred to as LoC].

such as nationalism or communism. Disconnected from their traditional communities by liberalism, humans were enslaved to anti-religious forces that demanded their total obedience, such as the nation, the class, or the state. Personalists thus boldly bundled all modern sociopolitical systems into one, claiming that capitalism, liberalism, and communism were essentially the same. All were equally destructive and materialist; in fact, no secular social and political ideology could sustain decent human relations. Throughout the 1920s, this focus on a singular enemy—secular individualism—was personalism's trademark and often its source of appeal. As one historian states, "the ambiguity of personalism was, in a sense, its genius; it signaled the identity of the opposition clearly, while leaving flexibility about what the alternative program was."[13]

As a young writer, Gurian joined the personalist movement and became one of its most eloquent and popular advocates. His first book, a 1924 study of the German youth movements, echoed the personalist celebration of organic communities and Scheler's call for Catholics to lead Germany's spiritual renewal. It was a blockbuster that generated extensive discussions among Catholic readership. Yet Gurian's contribution to personalism, and his reputation as a rising talent in European Catholic thought, rested mainly on his detailed study of the person's secular enemies. During the Weimar era, he was the first personalist to embark on the ambitious project of systematically mapping the existence, nature, and history of Catholicism's political opponents in the modern world. According to Gurian, Catholicism faced three key enemies: liberalism, nationalism, and communism. The first, liberalism, was Catholics' earliest and oldest foe, and the source of the modern era's spiritual decline. Echoing Scheler's earlier writings, Gurian bemoaned that since the French Revolution, liberal thinkers had led humans to deify reason and reject any belief in salvation or transcendence. This elevation of reason fostered perverse materialism, by which Gurian meant an obsessive preoccupation with money and earthly pleasures. The society created by the bourgeoisie—liberalism's ultimate agent—was ruled by greed, bodily pleasures, and selfishness. It was the cradle of the modern era's assault on community and spirituality.[14]

Gurian further expanded on Scheler's theory to claim that Catholicism's second enemy was conservative nationalism. According to Gurian, modern

---

[13] The quotation is from Sammuel Moyn, "Personalism, Community and the Origins of Human Rights," in Stefan-Ludwig Hoffmann (ed.), *Human Rights in the Twentieth Century* (New York: Cambridge University Press, 2011), 85–106, here 88. Scheler's most famous essay in support of the republic was "Der Mensch im Weltalter des Ausgleichs," *Gesammelte Werke* (Bern: Francke, 1954–1997), 7: 145–170. On the personalists' support for authoritarianism and monarchism, see Chappel, *The Struggle for Europe's Soul.*

[14] Waldemar Gurian, *Die deutsche Jugendbewegung* (Habelschwerdt: Frankes Buchhandlung, 1924). On its reception, see Thümmler, *Katholischer Publizist*, 27–28.

nationalism was a blasphemous ideology. Like the liberal glorification of reason and science, nationalists celebrated a human creation, the nation-state. They elevated the nation as the source of all authority and sought to subjugate all other communities to its power and domination. In Gurian's eyes, even though nationalists often claimed to be the defenders of tradition, they in fact sought to secularize the public sphere and eliminate religious authority. Like liberals, their goal was the creation of a "secularized Catholicism," a perverse deification of humans and their earthly life, at the expense of true spirituality. Gurian accused nationalist thinkers, such as the German Oswald Spengler and the French monarchist Charles Maurras, as dangerous nihilists who had "no interest in dogma, and least of all ... in Christianity." Their vitriolic hatred of liberalism only hid the essential sameness of the two ideologies. When Catholic leaders such as Faulhaber and Kaas sought to cooperate with nationalists, they were in fact supporting their enemy. Catholics had to keep their distance from nationalists and their misleading claims of defending tradition.[15]

No work, however, resonated more widely than Gurian's critique of Catholicism's third and most devastating enemy: Bolshevism. In 1931 Gurian published *Bolshevism: Theory and Practice*, the first personalist study of the Soviet regime. The book became a touchstone throughout the Catholic intellectual world, and by 1933 had appeared in French, Italian, Dutch, and English, enjoying an enthusiastic reception throughout Europe.[16] While Catholic hostility to the explicitly secular Soviet Union was nothing new—the pope had condemned the new regime in 1917—Gurian's book provided fresh theoretical ammunition for the church's international campaign against Bolshevism. It offered an original and innovative theory of communism's origins and goals and helped fuel the Church's obsessive campaign to mobilize Catholics against rising Communist power.[17]

[15] Quoted in Waldemar Gurian, "Die Kirche und die Action française: eine prinzipielle Darlegung," *Heiliges Feuer* 14 (1926/1927): 330–345, here 343. See also Waldemar Gurian, "Der säkularisierte Katholizismus," *Heiliges Feuer* 15 (1927/1928): 442–448. Most of Gurian's writings revolved around the case of the French nationalist Maurras and his movement Action française, which was condemned by the pope in 1926 as heresy. For a few examples (out of many), see Waldemar Gurian, "Charles Maurras," *Der Gral* 21 (1926): 236–244; "Die Abendlandideologie als Maske des französische Nationalismus," *Abendland* 2 (1926/1927): 277–279; "Welt und Kirche," *Abendland* 2 (1926/1927): 362–366.

[16] Gurian published essays on the Soviet Union earlier and was considered an authority on the Soviet regime by Catholic publishers. See, for example, his "Die russische Revolution als Ausdruck des russischen Wesens," *Orplid* 1 (1924/1925): 47–51; and "Die sozialistische Aufbaupolitik Sowjetsrussland," *Abendland* 2 (1926/1927): 208–211. The information on its reception is from Review clipping, Folder 3, Box 11, WGP, LoC.

[17] On the Vatican's campaign against Bolshevism, see Giuliana Chamedes, "The Vatican, Nazi-Fascism, and the Making of Transnational Anticommunism in the 1930s," *Journal of Contemporary History*, forthcoming; Frank J. Coppa, *Politics and the Papacy in the Modern World* (Westport, Conn.: Praeger, 2008), 86ff.

According to Gurian, contemporary observers failed to recognize the essence and appeal of Bolshevism (he used Bolshevism, communism, and socialism interchangeably). They often misunderstood its ideology, claiming it was only a link in Russia's chain of authoritarian regimes, or focused on its campaign to abolish private property. But Russia's despotic history and the Marxist obsession with property were in fact marginal to Bolshevism's toxic intellectual essence. The motor behind the Soviet evil was the Communists' attempt to establish a society devoid of any transcendental sources of authority or legitimacy. It was this mission, rather than hostility toward capitalism, that truly guided the Bolshevik revolutionaries. "[Bolshevism's] mechanical conception of society," Gurian explained, only reproduced liberalism's and nationalism's secular assault on the family and organic communities. Like them, Bolshevism created atomized individuals with no social bonds or spiritual sources of inspiration. It was the extremist and "inevitable product of a world for which Christianity with its transcendental orientation has become a matter of private faith which no longer influences the organization of public life."[18]

Bolshevism's universalism made it especially perverse and dangerous to Catholics. Unlike liberalism's focus on the isolated individual and nationalism's glorification of concrete nation-states, Bolshevism sought to bring its secular mission to all of humanity. Like the Catholic Church, it offered salvation to all, regardless of class, nation, or sex. It claimed to bring peace to individuals and groups regardless of their past or specific cultural heritage. Unlike the church, however, Bolshevism's salvation was based on materialist conditions, money, and earthly possessions. It could not accept the person's overlapping membership in communities; people had to subject their entire being to its ideology. In a Communist society, "the entire man must be embraced and occupied by Bolshevism." By both emulating the church's universal message and perverting it, communism became for Gurian not only the church's enemy but also its dark mirror image. Communism, Gurian fumed, was the "anti-church, which seeks to erect a new tower of Babel on earth ... and will have no need of a redeemer." Gurian's writings thus embodied personalism's obsessive exploration and demonization of its enemies. They reflected the broader Catholic fears of modern politics and ideologies.[19]

During the 1920s, Gurian's writings positioned him as one of the most prolific and systematic thinkers of the personalist school and as a popular and influential German Catholic voice. By celebrating Catholicism's commitment to organic communities and attacking liberalism, nationalism,

---

[18] Waldemar Gurian, *Bolshevism: Theory and Practice* (London: Sheed & Ward, 1932), 228, 253.

[19] Ibid., 246, 244.

and Bolshevism, his writings helped crystallize German Catholic political philosophy. During Weimar's late years, however, a rift had begun to emerge between Gurian and the Catholic community. While Catholics began to embrace authoritarian and anti-democratic politics, Gurian both radicalized his conservative attacks on political extremists and called on Catholics to embrace the Weimar Republic as a bulwark against the twin threats of nationalism and communism. These shifts in the early 1930s launched Gurian to prominence but also isolated him from Catholic thought. While his anti-Communist writings continued to receive enthusiastic attention, his embrace of democracy was almost universally ignored. Yet despite this failure, Gurian's ideas would prove to be crucial in years to come. By tying democracy to anti-nationalism and anti-communism, they would fuel a broad intellectual realignment in later decades.

The key background behind Gurian's embrace of democracy was a broader German Catholic shift to the right in the late 1920s. In 1928 the Center Party's annual gathering in Cologne appointed as leader the arch-conservative priest Ludwig Kaas, who openly called for "leadership on a grand scale," the weakening of the parliamentary system, and the institution of authoritarian rule. Weimar's weakness in the face of the Great Depression accelerated this trend, as Catholic politicians and intellectuals decisively broke with liberal politics. Theologians such as Friedrich Muckermann called for the creation of a Catholic monarchy, while in Berlin, Catholic chancellor and Center member Heinrich Brüning led the assault on parliamentary power. Most personalist thinkers took part in this attack on liberal institutions, calling for the dismantling of political parties and universal suffrage. From Munich, Dietrich von Hildebrand supported the establishment of a Christian order based on class and profession, while in France, the personalist Emmanuel Mounier led a campaign against the Third Republic. Catholicism's ambiguity toward democracy seemed to crystallize into decisive hostility. Guarding organic communities and crushing communism seemed to be possible only through authoritarian and anti-democratic politics.[20]

For Gurian, the dangerous consequences of this shift were epitomized by Carl Schmitt's theory of the "total state." During Gurian's years in Cologne, Schmitt had been an influential mentor. In the early years of his journalism career, Gurian remained deeply influenced by Schmitt's thinking, which aggressively condemned liberalism and individualism as weak and soulless. As the 1920s progressed, however, this admiration morphed into enmity, as

[20] Kaas's quotation is from Hans Mommsen, *The Rise and Fall of Weimar Democracy* (Chapel Hill: University of North Carolina Press, 1996), 262. On the Catholic shift to the right, see Robert A. Krieg, *Catholic Theologians in Nazi Germany* (New York: Continuum, 2004), esp. 40–41. On Hildebrand, see Alice von Hildebrand, *The Soul of a Lion: Dietrich von Hildebrand: A Biography* (San Francisco: Ignatius Press, 2000), esp. 197–258; and Chappel, *The Struggle for Europe's Soul*; on Mounier, see Hellman, *Emmanuel Mounier and the New Catholic Left*.

Schmitt began supporting authoritarian and even fascist models for Germany.[21] Schmitt hoped that such a regime would break the autonomy of communities, parties, and churches and subject them to a strong and centralized state. In 1931 Schmitt coined the term that captured this vision, calling on Germans to replace parliamentary democracy with a "total state." In the modern era, Schmitt explained, countries had to choose between two options: to let the domestic struggle between parties and groups paralyze policymaking and thus tear states apart from within, or to transfer all power to a strong leader, who would disband the parliament, abolish opposition, and have the authority to impose economic and political policies. In Schmitt's anti-liberal theory, such an authoritarian state would have unrestricted power and would therefore be "total." Only this kind of regime would overcome the internal divisions of society and save Germany from disintegration and chaos.[22]

For Gurian, Schmitt's theory exemplified the danger in Catholics' turn toward authoritarianism. In their frustration with democratic politics, he believed, Catholics like Schmitt dangerously and ignorantly embraced secular and earthly institutions like the state and forgot the supremacy of spiritual organic communities. Gurian therefore appropriated the term "total state," using it not as a desirable political model but as the manifestation of the church's enemies, especially their adherence to earthly and secular ideas. By reversing Schmitt's term to describe Catholicism's opponents, Gurian hoped to alarm Catholics who might have found Schmitt's theory appealing. Indeed, in the first pages of his book on Bolshevism, which appeared only a few months after Schmitt first used the term, Gurian sarcastically claimed that the total state's most explicit manifestation was not Italy's authoritarian regime, which Schmitt lauded, but its enemy, the Soviet Union, which Catholics abhorred. "The fascist state," he declared, mocking his former mentor, "is far and away less 'total' than the Bolshevik."[23]

In 1932 Gurian used the concept of the total state to reiterate his claim that nationalism and communism were fundamentally similar. In a book

[21] As the personal and intense correspondence between them shows, Gurian and Schmitt were close to each other from 1924 until 1926. Folder 13, Box 7, WGP, LoC. In the foreword to the book, Gurian thanked Schmitt for "countless discussions" during the years 1924–26. Gurian, *Die Politische und Sozialen Ideen*, vii.

[22] Carl Schmitt, "Die Wendung zum totalen Staat," in *Positionen und Begriffe im Kampf mit Weimar-Genf-Versailles, 1923–1939* (Berlin: Duncker & Humblot, 1988), 146–157. On Schmitt's thought in the context of Catholic debates of the interwar period, see Manfred Dahlheimer, *Carl Schmitt und der deutsche Katholizismus, 1888–1936* (Padeborn: Schöningh, 1998).

[23] Gurian, *Bolshevism*, iv. The English translation used the term "totalitarian," one of the very first times the term appeared in print in English. In the original German, however, Gurian used "total." This brief comment was not the first time Gurian compared the two regimes to each other; see Waldemar Gurian, "Faschismus und Bolschewismus," *Heiliges Feuer* 15 (1927/1928): 197–203.

entitled *On the Reich's Future*, which Gurian published under a pseudonym, he argued that the Nazi movement—nationalism's most extreme manifestation—represented secularism's final revolution. Like all of liberalism's intellectual offshoots, the Nazis glorified earthly concepts—blood and race—as the source of all human values. Nazism was a secular and "nihilist religion" that employed Catholic terminology in its search for earthly salvation. For example, the Nazis' longing for a new "Reich" was a secular emulation of the Church's medieval order of *Sacrum Imperium* (the Holy Roman Empire). Moreover, in seeking to create a secular religion, the Nazis were emulating their declared enemy, Bolshevism. Both movements held a fanatical belief in secular redemption through complete politicization of society, the belief that the "total state" could redeem its followers on earth. As Gurian wrote to his friend Karl Thieme, "Nazism . . . is today [for us] what Marxism was before." By embracing authoritarian ideas like Schmitt's total state, Catholics were opening the door for a secular and Communist-like revolution. They were preparing the ground for Catholicism's demise.[24]

This intellectual assault on Nazism revealed the deep oversights and ironic consequences of personalist ideology. Gurian sought to bolster Catholic opposition to Nazism by equating it with Bolshevism, but in doing so, he often overlooked the most fundamental and disturbing elements of Nazi ideology. Gurian had virtually nothing to say about the Nazis' perverse anti-Semitism, intense militarism, or imperialist aspirations, all of which were core tenets of Hitler's political vision. Rather than develop a broader moral critique, he could only channel existing Catholic fears of communism against a new political target. Like other Catholics, Gurian seemed unaware of the bitterly ironic connections between personalism's obsessive anti-communism and the rise of Nazism. Even though Hitler built much of his appeal on his promises to suppress communism and ultimately destroy the Soviet Union, Gurian did not reflect on how the personalists' promotion of anti-Communist fever might have helped spur the Nazis' popularity. While personalism was not a racist ideology, dissociating it from the radical right required considerable intellectual acrobatics.

Despite these intellectual limitations, the fear that the total state was encroaching on Catholicism from both left and right led Gurian to offer one of the boldest suggestions in German Catholic thought: democracy was the only political system that could preserve Catholic autonomy. In his 1931 book on Bolshevism, Gurian advocated that Catholics overcome their natu-

---

[24] The quotation is from Walter Gerhart, *Um des Reiches Zukunft: Nationale Wiedergeburt oder politische Reaktion?* (Freiburg: Herder, 1932), 120–121. Second is from Letter, Gurian to Karl Thieme (15 December 1931), Band 28, Nachlass Karl Thieme [hereafter referred to as ED 163], Institut für Zeitgeschichte, Munich [hereafter referred to as IfZG]. It is unclear why Gurian published the book under a pseudonym. As Hürten speculates, in 1932 he might have been concerned about attacks by the Nazis. See Hürten, *Waldemar Gurian*, 72.

ral distaste for liberalism and consider an alliance with liberals in order to defeat the Communist threat.[25] A year later, in *On the Reich's Future*, he went further to recommend that Catholics actively embrace the Weimar Republic. Gurian called on Catholics to join hands with other pro-republican forces to reform the republic's parliamentary system, which had proven to be dysfunctional and broken after years of interparty strife. In its place, he claimed, they had to create a new democratic system, which he termed "authoritarian democracy." In using the term "authoritarian," Gurian was not calling for a dictatorship or corporatist state but rather a democratic system that could resist the weaknesses endemic to the Weimar Republic. Indeed, in contrast to the dictatorship envisioned by Schmitt, "authoritarian democracy" would not limit the power of parliamentary interest groups, nor would it seek to curb them. Rather, this future system would expand parliamentary democracy by allowing groups and communities to participate in the democratic process alongside existing political parties. Gurian envisioned a system that gave churches, labor unions, and other social organizations an opportunity to voice their interests independently of political parties by endowing them with equal recognition within the structures of the state. Only such a system, he wrote, would protect Catholic autonomy and would allow the person to flourish.[26]

In keeping with the elusiveness of personalist political thinking, Gurian remained vague about the specific mechanisms of such a system. He did not provide a clear blueprint for its institutions and procedures. He was clear, however, that "authoritarian democracy" would be based on its parliamentary predecessor. It would have to develop more effective mechanisms for governing, but it would continue to rely on the parliamentary and representative principles of the Weimar state. In stark contrast to growing Catholic hostility toward the republic, Gurian claimed that any system which defended traditional communities and Catholic autonomy "could not abolish the parliament and the parties . . . [which are] the essential forces of the political unifying process. . . . Without parliament and parties, there can be no political system in Germany that responds to the people's will." German Catholics, Gurian warned, therefore faced a dire choice: "either the total state or the 'authoritarian democracy,' which will develop and expand the world of Weimar." The meaning of the "total state" was clear: the end of all

---

[25] Gurian, *Bolshevism*, 256. In fact, some of the reviewers of the book believed that this claim was its most important contribution to Catholic thought. See, for example, Otto Forst-Battaglia, "Waldemar Gurian: Der Bolschewismus," *Jahrbücher für Kultur und Geschichte der Slaven* 7:4 (1931): 459–460; Otto Auhagen, "Der Bolschewismus," *Vierteljahrschrift für Sozial- und Wirtschaftsgeschichte* 25:4 (1932): 391–393.

[26] While these ideas seem remarkably similar to Ernst Fraenkel's theory of "collective democracy," there is no evidence they were aware of each other's work. The lack of interaction between Catholic and Socialist milieus in the Weimar era makes it unlikely that they ever met or read each other's publications.

traditions, the destruction of all spiritual independence, and the enslavement of communities to secular authority. Whoever opposed this night-
mare must work "for the imminent authoritarian democracy."[27]

While the horizons of his thought remained hamstrung by anti-secular
dogma, Gurian was among the very first personalists to explicitly embrace
liberal democracy by claiming that it was the guardian of Catholic autonomy. In his mind, the rise of the total state and the growing power of extremism showed that the liberal republic possessed the only mechanisms to
resist secularization and realize the person. Even though it was created by
liberals, the pluralist nature of the parliamentary system—with its multiple
parties and distribution of power on many levels—accommodated each person's overlapping loyalties to manifold communities. It was only through
such a system that each person could be a member of the polity without
being subjected to the autocratic powers of the "total state." While Gurian
continued to reject the individualist intellectual principles of liberalism, he
now claimed that its political structures were consistent with personalism.
In the early 1930s, no other major personalist figure expressed such a clear
defense of democracy.

By the end of the Weimar era, Gurian had come to hold a contradictory
position in the tremulous world of German Catholic culture. On the one
hand, his personalist celebration of organic Catholic communities, and his
attacks on liberalism, nationalism, and Bolshevism as the manifestations of
soulless modernity, resonated widely across Germany's Catholic regions
and beyond. Gurian's work helped facilitate an anti-Soviet intellectual energy that became the trademark of the era's Catholic culture, and his writing helped reinforce Catholics' inability to fully grasp the nature of Nazism.
At the same time, his writings dramatically broke with most German Catholics. As increasing numbers of Catholics turned to the authoritarian right
in Germany and across Europe, Gurian explicitly embraced the democratic
system as the defender of the person. During the Weimar period, this support of the republic left him on the margins of Catholic thought. Yet with
the backing of American wealth after World War II, these ideas would serve
as the intellectual foundation for Germany's pro-democratic cultural and
political realignment and the emerging transatlantic alliance.

THE PATH TO THE "THEORY OF TOTALITARIANISM": THE PERSONALIST
CAMPAIGN AGAINST NAZISM IN EXILE

The Nazis' rise to power in 1933 initiated an explosive controversy among
Catholics in Germany and across Europe. While some Catholic leaders

[27] Gerhart, *Um des Reiches Zukunft*, 207–208.

were uncomfortable with the new regime's obsession with racism and eu-genics, many of their followers were impressed by its swift destruction of the German left, its dynamism, and its claim to revive conservative values. The brutal swiftness with which the Nazis crushed the Communist Party— destroying its infrastructure and murdering or arresting its leaders—only furthered this impression. The Holy See in Rome did little to clarify Catho-lic attitudes toward the new regime, keeping its diplomatic options open by neither condemning nor supporting Hitler's Third Reich. In July 1933 Ger-many and the Vatican signed a highly publicized concordat that purported to guarantee the church's autonomy in Germany, but this did little to dispel this uncertainty. Throughout the 1920s, the Vatican had signed similar agreements with a score of regimes—both democratic and authoritarian— and explained that these did not imply endorsement of any particular po-litical ideology. This ambiguity left Catholic politicians, intellectuals, and clergy to bitterly clash over Catholicism's response to the Third Reich. Throughout the 1930s, this was the most acute debate in European Catholic thought and politics.[28]

During the course of these heated arguments, Gurian emerged as one of Europe's foremost anti-Nazi Catholic thinkers. First in Germany, and then from exile in Switzerland, he organized anti-Nazi émigré networks and publications and crafted anti-Nazi theories. In the short term, the success of these efforts was meager; Gurian and his allies failed to mobilize Catholics in Germany, the Vatican, and throughout Europe to declare war on Nazism. Yet by engaging in these battles, Gurian and others drew on his earlier ideas and laid the intellectual groundwork for dramatic transformations in the Catholic world. They provided the language and theories—most famously, the theory of totalitarianism—that, in the aftermath of World War II, led the church and Catholic communities around Europe to embrace democratic politics as a vehicle of their conservative values and join the Western alli-ance in a global crusade against the Soviet Union.

Like his defense of the Weimar Republic, Gurian's campaign against the Third Reich placed him far from the center of Catholic consensus. While many Catholic bishops, theologians, and thinkers felt little sympathy to-ward the Nazis, others saw the Third Reich as the beginning of Christian-ity's rejuvenation and sought to reconcile Nazi racial precepts with Catho-lic beliefs. From the country's Catholic seminaries, publishing houses, and churches, these pro-Nazi Catholics endeavored to prove that Catholicism and Nazism shared a deep spiritual affinity. Würzburg historian and chap-

---

[28] The literature on the Vatican and Nazism is enormous. For an excellent overview, which situates the Vatican's attitude in the broader context of its diplomacy, see Giuliana Chamedes, "The Vatican and the Making of the Atlantic Order" (PhD diss., Columbia University, 2013). See also Hubert Wolf, *Pope and Devil: The Vatican's Archives and the Third Reich* (Cambridge, MA: Belknap Press of Harvard University Press, 2010).

lain Joseph Lortz, for example, claimed that Nazism was creating the conditions for a spiritual revival by reversing the tide of secularization, liberalism, and Marxism. In Tübingen, renowned theologian Karl Adam wrote that divine grace was dependent on racial purity, and that only the German *Volk*, with Hitler as its leader, constituted the mystical body of Christ. Even Scheler's student and Gurian's close friend, theologian Karl Eschweiler, shocked his colleagues by embracing the new regime as the only guardian of the person.[29] While the Nazis regarded Catholicism as a despised remnant of "Jewish morality" and an obstacle to the "scientific" order they strove to create, they sought to exploit Catholic support in their campaigns against homosexuals, criminals, Jews, and other "enemies of the race." In the long run, the gap between Nazism and Catholicism proved to be too large, and by the end of the 1930s most Catholics had abandoned their attempt to reconcile the two. But during the regime's early years, Catholic supporters of Nazism appeared to be on their way to revolutionizing Catholic German thought.[30]

Horrified by what he perceived as the pollution of the Church's doctrines, Gurian quickly sought to bolster Catholic cultural resistance to Nazism. In the months following Hitler's 1933 appointment as chancellor, he published a series of essays under various pseudonyms and edited several Catholic newspapers in which he warned that the new regime would crush the church and eliminate Catholic autonomy. Within a year, however, the Nazi regime's tightening control over the media made it impossible for Gurian to operate in Germany. Nazi officials strictly censored his essays, and Nazi authors accused him of participating in the "Judaization of German Catholicism." Because of his status as a "non-Aryan"—due to his Jewish ancestry—officials declined his requests for assistance and strongly urged him to emigrate abroad. Following a visit to Rome in 1934, Gurian decided to leave Germany for Switzerland, where he thought he could continue his anti-Nazi efforts with more success. Over the next four years, he cooperated

[29] On Lortz, see Michael B. Lukens, "Joseph Lortz and a Catholic Accommodation with National Socialism," in Robert P. Ericksen and Susannah Heschel (eds.), *Betrayal: German Churches and the Holocaust* (Minneapolis: Fortress Press, 1999), 149–168. On Adam, see Lucia Scherzberg, *Kirchenreform mit Hilfe des Nationalsozialismus: Karl Adam als kontextueller Theologe* (Darmstadt: Wissenschaftliche Buchgesellschaft, 2001). On Eschweiler's support of Nazism, see Thomas Marschler, *Karl Eschweiler (1886–1936): Theologische Erkenntnislehre und nationalzozialistische Ideologie* (Regensburg: Friedrich Putest, 2011), 217–376. Throughout the 1920s, Gurian and Eschweiler corresponded and met frequently and planned several joint projects and translations of French Catholic thought. Their correspondence is kept in Folder 6 Box 3, WGP, LoC.

[30] John Connelly, *From Enemy to Brother: The Revolution in Catholic Teaching on the Jews* (Cambridge, MA: Harvard University Press, 2012), 36–93; Kevin P. Spicer, *Catholic Clergy and National Socialism* (DeKalb: Northern Illinois University Press, 2008); Richard Steigmann-Gall, *The Holy Reich: Nazi Conceptions of Christianity* (New York: Cambridge University Press, 2003), 51–85.

with other writers to produce a wide array of arguments against the racist Nazi state.[31]

In Switzerland, Gurian used his position and contacts as a writer and journalist to organize Catholic opposition to the Nazis, urging the clergy to end their silence on the regime's brutality. He was especially enraged by the events of 30 June 1934—the so-called "Night of the Long Knives"—during which SS men assassinated over a hundred journalists, politicians, and militia members who did not fully accept Hitler's authority.[32] In a small booklet entitled *Ambrosius and the German Bishops*, Gurian evoked the figure of St. Ambrosius (Ambrose), the bishop of Milan who excommunicated Emperor Theodosius in 390 C.E. for a massacre committed by his troops. Gurian reminded his readers that despite the might of the Roman Empire, Ambrosius stood firm by his decision while the emperor spent months in penance. Gurian used this comparison to highlight the shameful silence of German bishops, especially since Catholics were among those murdered. As he stated, "the silence of the bishops is perhaps the worst of all things that happened on June 30th." Gurian argued that the bishops' passivity compromised the church's moral authority and threatened to corrode the Catholic community from within.[33]

This booklet, which Catholic activists smuggled into Germany and circulated in their communities, provided the springboard for Gurian's larger project: the establishment of the weekly journal *Deutsche Briefe* (German Letters), known as *DB*. *DB* soon became one of the few mouthpieces for anti-Nazi writing in Catholic Europe. First published in September 1934, the journal was written and edited by Gurian and Michael Knab, another German Catholic journalist in Switzerland. *DB* contained accounts of Nazi harassment of Catholic institutions and leaders as well as reports of rare instances in which Catholic leaders condemned the Third Reich. Gurian also used *DB* to recycle his personalist arguments against Weimar's radical right.[34] In the journal he repeatedly warned his readers against the regime's

[31] Correspondence with the Nazi "Council for the promotion of German literature," Folder 1, Box 6. For Nazi attacks on Gurian, see Albert Wiedemann, "Stimme aus der katholischen Jugend," *Deutsches Volkstums* (1933), 567. For an example of Gurian's essays against the Third Reich, see Walter Gerhart, "Bundesgenossen: Alter und neuer Nationalismus," *Junge Front* 2:14 (1933): n.p. On the Catholic press under Nazism and Gurian's role as an editor, see Klaus Gotto, *Die Wochenzeitung Junger Front/Michael* (Mainz: Matthias-Grünewald, 1970).

[32] On the bishops' silence, see Ludwig Volk, "Nationalsozialistischer Kirchenkampf und deutscher Episkopat," in Klaus Gotto and Konrad Repgen (eds.), *Die Katholiken und das Dritte Reich* (Mainz: Matthias-Grünewald, 1990), 49–92.

[33] Stefan Kirchmann [Waldemar Gurian], *Ambrosius und die deutsche Bischöfe* (Lucerne: Liga Verlag, 1934), 6.

[34] All issues of *DB* were edited and republished in two volumes by Heinz Hürten as *Deutsche Briefe, 1934–1938: Ein Blatt der katholische Emigration* (Mainz: Matthias-Grünewald, 1969), vol. 1, 1934–1935, vol. 2, 1936–1938. On the Catholic émigré press, see Elke Seefried,

"total" nature, reminding them that despite its pretense of reviving Christian values, the Nazi state sought to destroy all autonomous groups, communities, and institutions and disable "its moral opponents through cooperation and embrace." By analyzing Nazi books and speeches, especially those by Nazi ideologue and leader Alfred Rosenberg, *DB* sought to demonstrate that the regime's racist obsession had eliminated the concepts of morality and divine grace. In its essence, Nazism was "self-deification, which ... must reject humanity's salvation through Jesus Christ." It was therefore the duty of all Catholics to fight against the Nazi state. *DB* and a handful of other Catholic organs—including *Die Christliche Ständestaat*, edited by Dietrich von Hildebrand in Vienna, and *Der Deutsche Weg*, edited by Friedrich Muckermann in Holland—were smuggled into Germany to help mobilize Catholic opposition to Nazism.[35]

By 1935, however, Gurian's campaign seemed to be falling on deaf ears. It was clear that the German bishops, and German Catholics more broadly, were not going to rise up against the Nazi regime. As his close friend Karl Thieme lamented, "from the German bishops ... nothing will emerge."[36] This failure led Gurian and his fellow exiles to shift their efforts in a new direction, targeting the Vatican and the people of Europe. The word of the Holy See, they believed, could mobilize the continent's Catholics in a broad alliance with other political forces to crush Nazism and reverse the gains of the radical right. In turning to this new audience, Gurian hoped to transform an internal German debate into a campaign of global proportions. Politically, this campaign, too, would prove a failure. Yet in exposing non-German readers to Weimar-era ideas, Gurian would produce the first comprehensive articulation of the theory of totalitarianism.

The opening salvo of Gurian's campaign to rouse the Vatican—the appearance of his 1935 book *Bolschevismus als Weltgefahr* (Bolshevism as world menace)—was one of the most important intellectual events in the interwar Catholic world. As historian James Chappel explains, the book "sent shock waves through Catholic intellectual culture" and electrified readers in

---

"Reich und Ständestaat als Anthithesen zum Nationalsozialismus: Die katholische Zeitschrift der christliche Ständestaat," in Michel Grunewald and Wilfried Loth (eds.), *Das katholische intellektuellenmilieu in Deutschland* (New York: Lang, 2006), 415–438.

[35] First quotation is from *DB* 48 (30 August 1935), 1: 540–551. The second is from *DB* 34 (24 April 1935), 1: 379. The third is from *DB* 34 (24 April 1935), 1: 379. Use of the term "total state" or "totality" to describe the Nazi regime appeared countless times in the journal. See, for example, *DB* 32 (10 May 1935), 1: 356–357; *DB* 49 (6 September 1935), 1: 552–553; *DB* 164 (12 November 1937), 2: 954–955; and many others. References to Rosenberg appeared frequently in *DB*; for further examples, see *DB* 1 (5 October 1934), 1: 21–23; *DB* 7 (16 November 1934), 1: 77–80. Gurian was personally very interested in Rosenberg as the representative of Nazi thought and wrote several manuscripts on him, which he did not publish. Waldemar Gurian, "Alfred Rosenberg," Folder 9, Box 10, WGP, LoC.

[36] Letter, Karl Thieme to Gurian (28 August 1935), Folder 5, Box 8, WGP, LoC.

3.1. Waldemar Gurian after his exile from Germany (date unknown). Gurian's writings were crucial in shaping Catholic thinking about communism and democracy. University of Notre Dame Archives.

France, Britain, Italy, Austria, Poland, and the United States. Within just a few years it was translated into eight languages and reviewed in dozens of journals around the world. So intense was the buzz surrounding the book that the era's most renowned French Catholic thinker, Jacques Maritain, facilitated the French publication of an essay-length version to maximize its distribution among hundreds of thousands of Catholic readers. Friends in the Vatican also reported to Gurian that the clergy was "very pleased" with his "superb work," and encouraged him to continue his endeavor.[37]

[37] Chappel, "The Catholic Origins," 579. Information about the book's translation is from Interview (undated, 1938?), Folder 11, Box 12, WGP, LoC. The Gurian collection includes clippings of reviews in five languages, Folder 7, Box 11, WGP, LoC. The first quotation is from Letter, Friedrich Muckermann to Gurian (26 January 1937), Folder 14, Box 1; the second is from Letter, Peterson to Gurian, 5 December 1935, Folder 15, Box 6, both in WGP, LoC.

Repackaging and expanding his Weimar-era personalist ideas for a broader audience, Gurian maintained that Bolshevism had gone through a radical metamorphosis and embraced a new ideological cover: one of racist and conservative nationalism. According to Gurian, Bolsheviks were no longer committed to communism's social and economic goal of universal equality. Rather, they sought only to establish a "total state" of the kind Carl Schmitt envisioned in 1931, to fully politicize human life and eliminate all competing sources of authority beyond the state. In this quest to create this "total state," the Bolsheviks in Germany had abandoned their Communist convictions and adopted the rhetoric of nationalism. The Third Reich, for all its anti-Soviet rhetoric, was ultimately a *Bolshevik* regime. According to Gurian, the Nazis, like the Soviets before them, sought only to eradicate traditional communities and to rule by isolating humans into helpless individuals who "cannot develop a common purpose." In Gurian's words, the "National Socialist state is just as much an educational dictatorship interfering in every department of life as its Communist opponent." Gurian maintained that both of these regimes were best understood, not through their official ideologies, but through their mutual and identical vision of a "total state." He therefore termed them both "totalitarian" (in German, *totalitär*), the twin incarnations of the same secular and destructive revolution.[38]

In Gurian's eyes, the term "totalitarian" grasped Bolshevism's frightening appropriation of national rhetoric. Indeed, it was this metamorphosis—from the language of economic equality to one of nation and tradition—that transformed Bolshevism into a "world menace." While Communist rhetoric failed to capture the hearts of Europeans beyond the Soviet Union, the Nazi regime demonstrated that celebrating nationalism could deceive millions into the Bolshevik project of total politicization. By filling their rhetoric with a celebration of the community, the family, and the organic nation and seeking to defend traditional gender roles, the Nazis appropriated traditional values for their own nihilist goals. Indeed, Gurian claimed that compulsive lying and deception were the essence of the totalitarian phenomenon. In totalitarian regimes, he wrote, "*all concepts are transformed* and lose their previous significance. They continue to be employed as instruments of propaganda but simply as such for the sake of the emotions which, obviously as a result of traditional associations, they evoke." In totalitarianism, "[j]ustice becomes the maintenance in power of a particular party."

---

[38] The English translation of Gurian's book, from which the quotations are taken, appeared as *The Future of Bolshevism* (New York: Sheed & Ward, 1936). Quotations are from 27, 63, and 34. Historians have been unable to trace the origin of the words "totalitarian" or "totalitarianism." Gurian himself did not use the term before going into exile, even in his works warning against the "total state." The English translator of his first book on Bolshevism, which appeared in 1933, did use the term "totalitarian," even before Gurian expanded on its meaning in his subsequent book in 1935.

Liberty means the control of public life by the Bolshevik party ... a contemptible device to enslave and deceive humanity. ... Humanity means the inhuman annihilation, the "liquidation" of all those who are branded as enemies of the state and the workers. ... Free choice is the same as acting under compulsion. ... Truth means whatever the state prescribes; falsehood everything which is opposed to the state, to the party which controls it.

Totalitarianism could mask itself under any appealing rhetoric in its quest to annihilate all tradition and authority beyond the state. Even the fiercest anti-Communists could misrecognize its diabolical core and join its campaign to eradicate the person.[39]

In this eschatological and apocalyptic worldview, totalitarianism was not simply a political regime but a nihilist intellectual movement that continually expanded by exploiting its enemies' spiritual weaknesses from within. After conquering Germany, the next targets on its list were the Western liberal countries, especially Britain and France. But Gurian feared that the European middle class, after decades of secularization, material success, and individualism, had become spiritually anemic and atomized, without convictions. The Western European world, Gurian complained, "is inferior to National Socialism, for it has lost its primitive faith." The nations of Western Europe, while building powerful states and enormous empires, thus failed to recognize the nature of totalitarianism and had no intellectual resources to resist it. Like their German counterparts, Western Europeans were successful in rejecting communism but could not suggest an alternative to totalitarianism's newer Nazi incarnation, which presented its nihilism as the defense of traditional values.[40]

In articulating the theory of totalitarianism, Gurian therefore had two goals. First, he hoped to reach beyond his Catholic audience to inspire a moral rejuvenation in Europe's middle class. The Nazi triumph, he claimed, revealed a "moral crisis." Gurian therefore called on Europe's middle class to recognize that their survival depended on Catholic beliefs to resist the Nazis' claim as the defenders of "tradition." Only by accepting the teachings of the church, and arming themselves with its spiritual mission, could European liberals prevent the complete disintegration of their countries and their transmutation into totalitarian regimes. As he wrote, "[t]he vital issue is whether or not there are moral forces [within society] sufficiently strong to oppose the Bolshevising process, of which the Soviet Union and the Third Reich are representatives in our contemporary world."[41] In making this claim, Gurian relied on what he believed was the self-evident superiority of Catholic faith and culture. Indeed, in its inability to imagine a legiti-

---

[39] Ibid., 40–41. Emphasis in the original.
[40] Ibid., 114.
[41] Ibid., 120.

mate secular politics, Catholic thought had a difficult task in building bridges to liberalism. For Gurian, the liberal state remained a tool for combating Christianity's enemies and had little value in and of itself.

Gurian's second goal was to shock Catholic readers across Europe into resetting their political priorities. Unlike other personalists, Gurian no longer argued that *every* modern and secular movement was equally dangerous to the Catholic Church. Indeed, a lengthy section of the book explained why other nationalist movements, such as Italian fascism or Action française, were not totalitarian, since in their ideology, "[t]he totalitarian authority of the state is limited by traditional institutions such as the monarchy and the Church." Rather, Nazism was totalitarianism's apotheosis, its most radical manifestation, and therefore Catholicism's chief enemy. By presenting Nazism as the most virulent manifestation of Bolshevism, Gurian intended to undercut its appeal to Catholics and channel Catholic anti-Communist sentiment into the campaign against the Third Reich.[42]

Viewed in light of Gurian's intentions, *Bolshevism as World Menace* was both strikingly successful and dishearteningly disappointing. On one level, its pairing of communism and Nazism under the rubric of "totalitarian" galvanized Catholics throughout Europe. Catholic thinkers of all political inclinations—from supporters of Austria's authoritarian regime to those sympathetic toward liberal structures—saw in the new theory a key framework in their struggle for Europe's soul. One after the other, Catholic writers such as Dietrich von Hildebrand and Jacques Maritain used it to articulate their call for a Catholic renewal. Within months of the book's publication, "totalitarianism" had spread across the continent's Catholic journals and books, inspiring countless reiterations.[43] In March 1937 the Vatican itself signaled its receptiveness by issuing dual condemnations of the Nazi and Communist regimes. Despite his refusal to declare an all-out conflict with Germany or abolish the concordat he signed in 1933, Pius XI issued the anti-Nazi *Mit brennender Sorge* (With burning concern) and the anti-Communist *Divin redemptoris* (Divine redeemer) almost simultaneously, decrying both regimes as hostile to Catholicism, organic communities, and the autonomy of the family. The language of anti-totalitarianism spread across Catholic circles and became a fundamental organizational concept behind Catholic political thinking.[44]

Yet to Gurian's disappointment, even as European Catholics increasingly embraced his ideas in expressing their disdain for the Third Reich, they did not actively organize themselves against it. Most Catholics did not join anti-

[42] Ibid., 105.

[43] On the spread of the theory in Europe, see Chappel, *The Struggle for Europe's Soul*.

[44] As Chamedes shows, this dual condemnation, which was followed by a condemnation of the Mexican Socialist government, was part of the Vatican's attempt to claim a leading role in the defeat of communism (*The Vatican and the Making of the Atlantic Order*, 184–218).

Nazi networks, nor did they advocate for diplomatic sanctions against the Third Reich. Even the pope's dual statements left some room for ambiguity. While he reaffirmed anti-communism as fundamental to the church's teaching, his statement on Germany mostly complained about Hitler's encroachment on Catholic education and did not fully condemn Nazism's ideological foundations. For all their dislike of Nazi eugenics, many Catholics continued to hope that Hitler's regime would preserve Catholic cultural autonomy. During the 1930s, Gurian's personalist theory of totalitarianism was a popular term but not yet a mobilizing one. Only later, with the support of American might, would it inspire wide-scale political action.[45]

Despite this partial embrace, Gurian's theory offered the template for a Catholic approach to modern politics. It tied a variety of events, phenomena, and trends into one term—*totalitarianism*—and presented a coherent agenda for Catholic thinking about its global enemies. Gurian's most important contribution, often overlooked by historians, was his emphasis on totalitarianism's ability to transform, to adopt opposite ideological languages, and to infiltrate the workings of all political structures. According to his theory, no existing institutional mechanism could counteract the spread of totalitarianism. In their mission to create a "total state," totalitarian agents would relentlessly deceive, subjecting all modern societies to the totalitarian menace. Perhaps most crucial, Gurian's framework explained why the totalitarian enemy's military and economic powers were mostly irrelevant to its ability to threaten civilization. Even without such might, it could deceive its opponents into submission and then consume their states from within. This claim was Gurian's most important influence on political theory, and it appealed to readers around the world. Forged in Weimar's domestic Catholic debates, it became a crucial intellectual component of European Catholic thought.

Gurian's years in exile marked German personalism's darkest hour. Expelled from Germany, conservative émigrés such as Gurian were distressed by their community's submission to Nazism in the face of Vatican and international passivity. Indeed, in 1937 Gurian began to seek refuge beyond Europe's Catholic regions, translating his works into English in the hope of finding allies in Britain and the United States. Despite the failure to mobilize Catholics, however, these years solidified his Weimar-era theories and expanded their scope beyond Germany. The terms and concepts that emerged provided the intellectual lenses through which many Catholics would observe the coming war and, later, the clash with the Soviet Union. After 1945, these ideas would break out of their isolation to shape the postwar world.[46]

---

[45] This interpretation of the pope's dual statements relies substantially on Chamedes (ibid.).

[46] Letter, Hermens to Gurian (2 September 1935); Letter, Hermens to Gurian (18 July 1935), Folder 3, Box 4, both at WGP, LoC.

PERSONALISM AND AMERICAN PHILANTHROPY: TRANSATLANTIC
DEMOCRACY AND ANTI-COMMUNISM

At the end of Gurian's time in Switzerland, the personalist project lay in
ruins across central Europe. When, in the spring of 1938, Nazi troops entered Vienna, the center of personalist networks, all personalist activity—
and all anti-Nazi Catholic activity—was brutally suppressed. The Nazis dismantled personalist periodicals, destroyed publishing houses, and forced
leading personalists to flee to France, Britain, and the United States.[47] Only
a decade later, however, personalists would become the leading figures in
the Catholic renaissance that drastically reformulated European thought
and politics under the banner of "Christian Democracy." Working with
Catholic activists, politicians, and parties, they formed coalitions and cultural networks that reshaped Europe as a federal, integrative, and suprana-
tionalist entity. In Germany, conservative Catholic ideas about small communities and Christian dogma as the source of spiritual renewal became a
crucial force in shaping post-Nazi culture. Enduringly anti-secular and anti-
Communist, Catholic politicians and thinkers emerged as dominant figures in Germany's postwar reconstruction.

A key force in this revolution was cooperation between Catholic émigrés
and American philanthropy, especially the Rockefeller Foundation. Little
noticed by historians, the foundation's enormous capital and well-
established organizations were fundamental to reviving German Catholic
activities in the immediate postwar years. As part of the foundation's quest
to supplement U.S. government efforts toward Germany's reconstruction,
its officials recruited thinkers such as Gurian, who then utilized the foundation's resources to resurrect old ideas and networks. This cooperation in
postwar Germany provided Gurian the opportunity to distribute his ideas,
not only in Europe, but also in the United States on an unprecedented scale.
With the active support of the Rockefeller Foundation, his theory of totalitarianism reached beyond Catholic circles to become one of the most popular and respected theories among U.S. intellectuals and diplomats. Like
Friedrich and Fraenkel, Gurian and Catholic émigrés like him served the
dramatic expansion of American power abroad by participating both in
Germany's occupation and Cold War mobilization. In doing so, they integrated their own reactionary agendas, blind spots, and contradictions into
the fabric of postwar thought in ways no one could have envisioned only a
few years earlier.

When Gurian left Switzerland in 1937, he did not anticipate that his
migration would mark the beginning of a mass exodus of Catholic thinkers

[47] On the destruction and exile of these groups and thinkers, see Seefried, *Reich und Stände*,
425–458.

to the United States. Arriving at the University of Notre Dame in Indiana, where President John F. O'Hara—later a Philadelphia archbishop and cardinal—sought to recruit European scholars to enhance the Catholic institution's academic reputation, Gurian anticipated a period of loneliness and isolation in the unfamiliar country. Despite the attempts of several American Catholic organizations to recruit and assist refugee scholars, the vast majority of anti-Nazi Catholic thinkers preferred to remain in Europe, where they could steer Catholic opposition to the Third Reich. Yet the fall of Austria in 1938 and France in 1940 brought many more to the United States. By the end of 1940, all of Gurian's allies in the anti-Nazi Catholic community, including such thinkers as Johannes Oesterreicher, Dietrich von Hildebrand, Yves Simon, Ferdinand Hermens, Jacques Maritain, and Otto Knab, had found refuge in U.S. universities and seminaries across the East Coast and the Midwest.[48]

Within a year of his arrival at Notre Dame, Gurian resumed his anti-totalitarian campaign. While his friend Karl Thieme doubted that Catholic ideas and messages "would be of interest to those of the Anglican tradition," Gurian was determined to win over new global audiences.[49] In a series of lectures to political theorists, addresses to Catholic organizations, and essays in the Catholic press, Gurian introduced his theories on totalitarianism and its secular roots, inherent expansionism, and aggressive nature. "The political totalitarianism of the Nazis," he warned in a lecture, meant "the rise of a new, anti-Christian conception of life."[50] Totalitarianism's inherent evil, however, posed an existential threat not only to Christianity but to all democratic systems, including that of the United States. "[T]he totalitarian regimes destroy all real stabilizing forces. . . . The strength of the totalitarian state has to be in the long run demonstrated in the destruction of the non-totalitarian states."[51] In 1939 Gurian created a permanent stage for thinking about totalitarianism by founding *The Review of Politics*. Among the journal's many contributors were Jacques Maritain, Talcott Parsons, and Carl J. Friedrich, who published his first systematic discussion of totalitarianism in the journal's pages. Hannah Arendt, who developed a close friendship with Gurian and was deeply impressed by his political theory, also sent the *Re-*

---

[48] Robert E. Burns, *Being Catholic, Being American*, vol. 2 (South Bend: University of Notre Dame Press, 1999).

[49] Letter, Karl Thieme to Gurian (22 December 1935), Folder 5, Box 8, WGP, LoC.

[50] Waldemar Gurian, Lecture, "The Current Crisis in Europe" (undated, 1938?), Folder 4, Box 10, WGP, LoC. For similar texts, see Gurian's "The Totalitarian State," *Proceedings of the American Philosophical Association* 15 (1939): 50–66; "On National Socialism," *Review of Politics* 4 (1942): 347–350; "The Fifth Annual Convention," *American Catholic Sociological Review* 3:4 (1942): 244–247.

[51] Waldemar Gurian, "Trends in Modern Politics," *Review of Politics* 2:3 (July 1940): 318–336, here 330.

3.2. Waldemar Gurian (center) celebrating the publication of *The Review of Politics* with philosophy teacher Frank O'Malley (left) and historian Thomas McAvoy (right), 1945. The Review was crucial in the popularization of the theory of totalitarianism in the United States. University of Notre Dame Archives.

view drafts of her work on "totalitarian terror," which she subsequently developed in her postwar writing.[52]

As was the case for other members of Gurian's Catholic milieu, the experience of exile and migration accelerated three parallel intellectual transformations. First, Gurian now claimed that personalism and democracy were not only allies against totalitarianism but necessary for each other's survival. On the one hand, the creation of a "New Christendom, destined to be the interior mover of the personalistic, pluralistic, and humanistic new civilization," was dependent on the mechanisms of elections and individual rights. On the other, only personalist convictions could prevent democracy from disintegrating into atomization and individualism. According to Gurian, personalism's focus on religious spirituality and the autonomy of organic communities would inject democrats with the ideological conviction

[52] For more on the evolution of *The Review of Politics*, see A. James McAdams, "The Origins of *The Review of Politics*," in *The Crisis of Modern Times: Perspectives from the Review of Politics* (South Bend: University of Notre Dame Press, 2007), 1–28. Arendt's intense correspondence with Gurian is available in Hannah Arendt Papers, LoC [accessed through the Manuscript Room's online service].

required for their regime's survival. People's participation in political life, especially representative politics, "are based ... on the Eternal Law of the Creator ... democracy is inspired by Christianity." Gurian argued that personalism had to categorically reject all authoritarian regimes, including those explicitly sympathetic to the Catholic Church, such as Franco's regime in Spain. Only a bond between elective democracy and true Christianity could guarantee religion's survival.[53]

Second, in addition to these changing ideas about democracy, growing anti-Semitic violence in Europe propelled Gurian to proclaim that the future personalist order would be accessible to all religious denominations. While his earlier writings celebrated Catholicism as the only community that could realize the person, after migrating to the United States, Gurian envisioned a society in which Catholics would freely cooperate with other religions to defend organic communities. Such cooperation would not undermine Catholic self-evident superiority; instead, it would strengthen its political mission. "This New Christendom," he wrote, "will recognize the existence of different religious beliefs and corresponding religious groups as a fact which has to be accepted."

> That, of course, does not mean a dogmatic toleration in which no dogma matters, because all can be true or all can be wrong. But the civil toleration does not exclude the orientation of all communities towards the temporal common good.... [O]nly the Christians who are citizens of the one *supratemporal* polis, the Church, know about the deepest foundation and ultimate finality of this common good, but it remains open to all groups, though in a more or less imperfect way and not as an expression of a minimum of theoretical philosophical agreement, but as a common duty and work.

In Gurian's opinion, this personalist society would be guided "by friendship and the will to mutual understanding and cooperation." Long before the Catholic Church accepted the principle of religious freedom, Gurian's personalism embraced religious pluralism.[54]

Finally, these shifts coincided with a new understanding of the United States as the guardian and enabler of personalism. Throughout the 1920s and 1930s, personalists, and Catholic writers in general, had paid little attention to the United States, which they saw as the incarnation of secularist and liberal forces, the originator of spiritual decay, and the symbol of materialist obsession.[55] By 1940, however, Gurian was promoting the United

[53] Waldemar Gurian, "On Maritain's Political Philosophy," *Thomist: A Speculative Quarterly Review* 5 (1943): 7–22, here 17.

[54] Ibid., 16.

[55] Heinz Hürten, "Der Topos vom christlichen Abendland in Literatur und Publizistik nach den beiden Weltkriegen," in Albrecht Langner (ed.), *Katholizismus, nationaler Gedanke und Europa seit 1800* (Paderborn: Schöningh, 1985), 131–154.

States as the true embodiment of Christian values. Like Friedrich, Gurian now claimed that American democracy owed little to the Enlightenment's secular traditions. Rather, its pluralism stemmed from "the spiritual essence of the New Christendom." Therefore, the United States was destined to lead the crusade against totalitarianism and bring about a Christian revival in Europe. Years before the United States entered the war, Gurian was confident that its involvement was a foregone conclusion. In 1940 and 1941 he repeatedly asserted that only the United States could ensure that the Nazi and Soviet "deification" of the state would "break down and be replaced as after the breakdown of the Roman Empire by a new discovery of the real center of human life."[56]

For all their broadening of Catholic political horizons, these ideas remained confined within the narrow and exclusionary limits of Weimar-era personalism. Gurian and other émigrés still could not envision a legitimate secular culture, let alone one that would resist and defeat totalitarian forces. Secular political institutions remained dependent on religious visions to infuse them with life and meaning. Equally glaring, Gurian and other Catholic émigrés continued to imagine Christianity as the main victim of Nazi brutality. Even though the Third Reich's most extreme policies and rhetoric were directed at the Jewish communities, for Gurian and others, anti-Semitism remained a manifestation of a more profound anti-religious sentiment, whose worst manifestation was anti-Christianity. Personalist imagination, then, remained self-absorbed and vehemently anti-secular. What changed was its democratic sensitivity and geopolitical strategy.

In light of both these changes and continuities, Gurian and his Catholic allies believed that the United States' entry into the war in December 1941 represented the continuation of their ongoing mission to erect "New Christendom" and destroy totalitarianism. While the Vatican itself never officially backed any side in the war, the émigré community had no doubt where Catholicism's allegiance should lie. Nothing better represented this merging of personalist ideology with new visions of democracy and a new admiration of the United States than the *Manifesto on the War*, a collective declaration by forty-three Catholic intellectuals. The *Manifesto* brought together thinkers of varied intellectual tendencies, among them Dietrich von Hildebrand, Otto Knab, Jacques Maritain, Yves Simon, and Johann Oesterreicher. Despite voicing reservations about some of the specific wording,

---

[56] First quotation is from Gurian, "On Maritain's Political Philosophy," in Hubert Gruber (ed.), *Katholiken, Kirche, und Staat als Problem der Historie* (Padeborn: Schöningh, 1994), 131–154. The second is from Waldemar Gurian, Manuscript, Reflections on the European Crisis (undated, 1940?), Folder 6, Box 10, WGP, LoC. Gurian also expressed similar sentiments in his correspondence with Yves Simon, cited in Kathleen Mary Connelly, "Catholic Witness: The Political Activities of Five European Christian Democratic Scholars while in Exile in the United States, 1938–1945" (PhD diss., Boston College, 1995).

Gurian too agreed to join the group.[57] Though work on this essay began in February 1942, it was only published in the Catholic journal *Commonweal* after a long delay. Nevertheless, it became one of the most important Catholic texts of the era, providing a blueprint for Catholic rhetoric that was embraced by the Vatican itself only two years later.

In language that became a consensus among Catholic émigrés, the *Manifesto* presented World War II as the culmination of secularism's inner decay. The war marked totalitarianism's final assault against Christianity, "the most irremediable outcome of the process of corruption so long at work in modern history." The *Manifesto* likewise decisively embraced a personalist democracy as the war's goal. According to the authors, universal suffrage, equality under the law, and citizens' fundamental rights were expressions of personalism and the Gospels' message and were "one with the Christian ideal of civilization." The war in Europe and Asia, the *Manifesto* argued, "is not an economic or political war, it is a war of civilization, and by virtue thereof, because it involves the spiritual and religious principles of the civilized order, it is also a religious war." With this simultaneously reactionary and revolutionary manifesto, a wide coalition of Catholic thinkers followed Gurian's footsteps and embraced the democratic electoral process as the manifestation of personalist ideals. Even those who earlier supported authoritarian regimes, such as the Austrian dictatorship that was toppled by the Nazis, now agreed that liberal mechanisms, such as universal suffrage and the rule of law, were not the enemies but the defenders of Catholicism. Gurian's language of democracy, which in the 1920s and 1930s had been on the very margins of Catholicism, had now become integral to its global outlook.[58]

Perhaps the most striking feature in the *Manifesto* was its ire toward the Soviet Union. The authors reminded their readers that although the United States and Soviet Union were allies, the spiritual essence of the Soviet Union "requires the destruction of religion, of the family, of everything which protects the human person and prevents its absorption into the social mass." The *Manifesto* stated that one goal of the war should be to dismantle the Soviet Empire and replace it with a Christian, democratic regime. By fighting alongside the Soviet Union, they believed the Christian West was inviting the Russian people to begin "the process of re-entering the Western community, and that in itself enlarges the possibilities of civilization's victory." Echoing Gurian's fierce anti-Bolshevik writings, the *Manifesto* claimed that belief in Christianity never left this people, despite Soviet anti-religious

---

[57] Gurian's discontent is mentioned in Chappel, "The Catholic Origins of Totalitarianism Theory," 588.

[58] "In the Face of the World's Crisis: A Manifesto by European Catholics Sojourning in America," *Commonweal* (21 August 1942): 415–421, here 415.

propaganda. With the right policies, the West could salvage Russia "from the spiritual and political evils from which [its people] now suffer." To Gurian, Maritain, and the others who formulated and signed the text, neither the exigencies of the war, nor even the defeat of Nazism, could suspend the mission to combat and defeat the Communist regime. Years before the Cold War, they cast the mission to destroy communism and the creation of Christian democracy as one and the same.[59]

By the mid-1940s, Gurian's ideas from the Weimar era had become the consensus of the Catholic camp in exile. A growing number of Catholic émigrés embraced the connections he established between the defense of "natural" and autonomous communities, the democratic process, and fierce anti-communism. Gurian's early writings thus provided the intellectual framework for a sea-change in Catholic thought. Now, personalist émigrés observed U.S. democratic institutions as the vehicle for their own religious visions and anxiously awaited American victory as the path to their own participation in the future reconstruction of Europe.

This proposed relationship between contemporary Catholic thought and U.S. democracy might have remained a mere idea had it not been for the emergence of the Rockefeller Foundation as a crucial organ shaping the postwar order. While most of the foundation's international projects collapsed during World War II, in 1945 its trustees decided to resume their efforts in cooperation with U.S. diplomats and military officials. After decades of working in separation, and even in conflict with the U.S. government, the foundation's officials believed that their mission "to support undertakings that would help 'steady' democratic forms of government" was now in concert with their government's view of the world.[60] At the heart of this new cooperation was the reconstruction of Germany. Many in the foundation believed that the future of European peace and stability lay in rebuilding Germany from its physical and spiritual ruins to prevent the eruption of chaos, extreme ideologies, and a new war. Under the supervision of Robert Havinghurst, a renowned professor of education at the University of Chicago who studied in Germany during the Weimar period, the foundation

---

[59] Ibid., 415, 417–418.

[60] The quotation is from Memorandum, "History of the Rockefeller Foundation's Investments in the Social Sciences through the War and Post-War Period (1939–1948)," Folder 19, Box 3, Series 910 Social Sciences, Rockefeller Foundation Archive [hereafter referred to as RFA], Rockefeller Archive Center, Sleepy Hollow, NY [hereafter referred to as RAC]. On the foundation's attempts to shape U.S. foreign policy, see Inderjeet Parmar, *Foundations of the American Century: The Ford, Carnegie, and Rockefeller Foundations in the Rise of American Power* (New York: Columbia University Press, 2012); Frank A. Ninkovich, *The Diplomacy of Ideas: U.S. Foreign Policy and Cultural Relations, 1938–1950* (New York: Cambridge University Press, 1981), esp. 14–15, 110.

established a gigantic "Emergency Project for German rehabilitation." In 1948 alone, it poured hundreds of thousands of dollars into Germany, initiating youth leadership programs, personnel exchanges, exhibitions, and art and music events, which sought to supplement the U.S. occupation efforts.[61] With this bold program, which the German press enthusiastically called "a spiritual Marshall Plan," the Rockefeller Foundation became the first U.S. philanthropic organization to initiate contact with Germany after World War II. While scholars have focused on the Ford Foundation's cultural diplomacy, which began years later, it was the Rockefeller Foundation's work that remained the blueprint for private cultural diplomacy for years to come.[62]

The foundation's officials envisioned their mission as spreading American liberal-democratic ideology, which they considered self-evidently universal, to a broad array of Germans. Yet it was Catholics who quickly emerged as the program's main beneficiaries; no other group recognized as quickly the unique opportunities presented by the foundation's program in Germany to promote its own agenda. After World War II, Gurian and other Catholics searched for ways to resurrect their prewar networks, yet their distrust of the nation-state made them hesitant to work directly with the U.S. government, preferring instead to work through a private organization. In the foundation they found such an avenue, and in 1947 they began to coordinate their reconstruction efforts with Rockefeller officials. When they received word of Havinghurst's visit and the foundation's arrival in

[61] Despite its importance, scholarship on the foundation's work after World War II has focused almost exclusively on its activities in the United States, Africa, Asia, and Latin America, and only scant attention has been paid to its efforts in Germany. The description here is based on Memorandum, Records of Allocation for the European Rehabilitation Program, 1 January–15 November 1948 (November 1948), Folder 89, Box 10, Series 700, RG 1.2; Memorandum, Progress Report on the Program of Cultural Rehabilitation in Central Europe (21 May 1948), Folder 87, Box 10, Series 700, RG 1.2; Minutes of the Rockefeller Foundation's Officers' Conference (15 April 1948), Folder 86, Box 10, Series 700, RG 1.2; Robert J. Havinghurst, "Recommendation for Program" (November 1948), Folder 95, Box 11, Series 700, RG 1.2, all at RFA, RAC.

[62] The quotation is from an article in the *Neue Zeitung*, quoted in Report, The Foundation's Program to Help Europe (October 1948), Folder 89, Box 10, Series 700, RG 1.2, RFA, RAC. The significance of Havinghurst and his educational theory on the Rockefeller Foundation's work in Germany is charted in Caitlin O'Neil, "Robert Havinghurst, the Rockefeller Foundation, and the Re-Education of Germany" (undergraduate thesis, Dartmouth College, 2012). The most important study on the Ford Foundation's cultural diplomacy is Volker Berghahn, *America and the Intellectual Cold Wars in Europe: Shepard Stone between Philanthropy, Academy, and Diplomacy* (Princeton: Princeton University Press, 2001). Military authorities in all Western occupation zones mentioned that they had forwarded the foundation's models to other philanthropies and that they were following them in their own operations. Interview, Edward F. D'Arms with General Robert McClure (29 September 1948), Folder 88, Box 10, Series 700, RG 1.2, RFA, RAC.

Germany, German Catholics began to flood the Rockefeller headquarters with requests that Gurian and others be sent to help rebuild Catholic culture. Franz Joseph Schöningh, a friend of Gurian's since the 1920s and publisher of the newly founded newspaper *Süddeutsche Zeitung*, wrote that Gurian would be a key agent in the re-creation of a democratic Catholic press. The dean of the newly founded School of Law in Bonn, Ernst Friesenhahn, hoped that his old friend would be able to participate in devising new educational programs for international politics. According to Friesenhahn's gushing plea, Gurian was among the very few scholars who could communicate new ideas on totalitarianism and democracy to the university's students. As a former student who had maintained his ties to the region, "Dr. Gurian has maintained friendly contacts with certain members of the faculty. His earlier work was closely connected with political and church circles in the Rhineland."[63]

At Havinghurst's invitation in the spring of 1948, Gurian returned to Europe as one of the Rockefeller Foundation's first fellows in Germany, traveling for months throughout the French, British, and U.S. occupation zones. Under the foundation's aegis, he embarked on an intensive series of lectures and exhibitions, reaching out to nascent Catholic associations and organizations across the country. In Bonn, he taught students and faculty in a series of courses and seminars on the Soviet Union and totalitarianism. His lectures took him to student organizations at the University of Frankfurt, the Pedagogical Academy of Bonn, Stuttgart's Technische Hochschule, the Catholic Cultural Association of Münster, and the Catholic Publishers Association in Munich. The foundation further funded and arranged meetings between Gurian and Catholic journalists, politicians, and clergy across the country, as well as his lectures in Kiel, Stuttgart, and Frankfurt. As enthusiastic letters from Germany reported to the foundation, Gurian's lectures propelled Catholic organizations and activists to mobilize behind electoral processes. Dean Friesenhahn from Bonn believed that these lectures had had "an immediate influence" in leading students to form a university-wide electoral society and to engage in organization of the city's democratic processes. The foundation's work, he claimed, had "a great deal of good [impact] on the political education of the young German generation," and he requested that visits by former Rhinelanders become a permanent fixture of the foundation's program.[64]

---

[63] Quoted in Letter, Ernst Friesenhahn to Havinghurst (12 March 1948), Folder 773, Box 64, Series 200, RG 1.1, RFA, RAC. The rest is based on Letter, Schöningh to Gurian (20 January 1934); and Letter, Schöningh to Gurian (8 January 1947), both in Folder 14, Box 7, WGP, LoC; and Letter, Aloys Wenzl (Office of Rector, University of Munich) to Franz Joseph Schöningh (22 April 1948), Folder 773, Box 64, Series 200, RG 1.1, RFA, RAC.

[64] Letter, Ernst Friesenhahn to Havinghurst (6 October 1948), Folder 773, Box 64, Series

In all these engagements, Gurian presented the process of democratization, the promotion of hegemonic Christianity, and the alliance with the United States as integral to the traditions of German Catholicism. American troops in Germany, he explained in talks in Frankfurt and Cologne, were not the agents of a brutal foreign occupation. Rather, their Christian convictions and adherence to democracy made them the protectors of local Catholic ideas and natural allies in the efforts to "reverse the process of secularization."[65] According to Gurian, Catholics had little reason to fear that rising American power in Europe would compromise their own autonomy. The United States was not "too imperialist, on the contrary, it is not imperialist enough." Indeed, it was the only political force that could enable the promotion of the church's universal message of spiritual salvation. As he put it in a later essay, "[t]he United States does not fight for the United States alone; it represents the cause of mankind."[66]

As a continuation of the decades-long personalist (and, more broadly, Catholic) campaign to build a Christian polity, however, this new order could not be separated from anti-Communist fervor. As Cold War tensions erupted in Europe, Gurian rekindled his intellectual assault on the Soviet Union, claiming that Europe's reconstruction necessitated the total defeat of communism. Rebuilding Germany could only be accomplished "without Russia and against her will and hope."[67] In contrast to the failures of the 1920s and 1930s, however, Catholics had a new opportunity to bring their war against communism to a triumphant conclusion. Gurian prophesied that with the full might of the United States on their side, German Catholics could finally and decisively reverse the tide of totalitarianism. As several observers reported, this recasting of Catholic anti-communism as a transatlantic and democratic project received enthusiastic response among Gurian's audiences. Several German publishers wrote to him in hopes of republishing updated versions of his anti-Bolshevik books of the 1930s that would include references to the United States' new mission.[68]

The tremendous appeal of such ideas to Catholic communities in postwar Germany reflected profound intellectual lacunae. They allowed Catho-

---

200, RG 1.1, RFA, RAC. The details of Gurian's activities are detailed in Waldemar Gurian, Report: My Trip to Germany (August 1948), Folder 5, Box 16, WGP, LoC.

[65] Waldemar Gurian, Manuscript, "Political Religions," Folder 6, Box 10, WGP, LoC. Gurian mentioned this theme as the topic of his lectures in Germany in Letter, Waldemar Gurian to Hannah Arendt (8 September 1950), Hannah Arendt Papers, LoC.

[66] Waldemar Gurian, "Die Weltpolitik der USA," *Rheinischer Merkur* 5:37 (9 Sept. 1950): 5; Waldemar Gurian, "Peace Ideals and Reality," *Annals of the American Academy of Political and Social Science* (1948): 72–75, here 74; Waldemar Gurian, "Defeat in Korea," *Commonweal* 52 (1950): 259–262, here 259.

[67] Gurian, "Peace Ideals and Reality," 74.

[68] Letter, Gurian to Philip Mosely (28 April 1949), Folder 5034, Box 588, series 200, RG 1.2, RFA, RAC; Gurian, Report: My Trip to Germany.

lics to recast their long-held belief in the superiority of their religious community and resume the anti-Communist struggle without reflecting on the role they played in the rise of Nazism and the catastrophe of war. As historian Maria Mitchell has shown, German Catholics emerged from the war with a deep sense of self-victimization. The Nazis, many now claimed, were the agents of "materialist," individualist, and secular barbarity, and Christianity was their main casualty. This belief conveniently absolved Catholics from any responsibility for Germany's anti-Semitism and violent atrocities in Germany and throughout Europe. It facilitated their disregard for the enslavement of other European nations and the extermination of the Jews, which Catholic leaders and politicians almost universally ignored in their postwar meetings and statements. As the bishop from Münster, Clemens von Galen, famously put it, "we suffered more under the Nazis than others."[69] Gurian's ideas encouraged and reinforced such sentiments while channeling them toward a new bond with the United States.

American officials in the foundation and the U.S. occupation were not unaware of the disturbing strands in Catholic thought. In internal correspondence, they more than once commented on Catholics' previous support of authoritarian politics and indifference to many Nazi atrocities. But they were anxious to find new allies and quickly recognized Gurian's unique ability to reach Catholic crowds while merging Catholic convictions with American hegemony. They therefore turned his visits into an annual occurrence. In the summer of 1949, he returned to Frankfurt to teach classes on democracy and religion, then continued to deliver lectures on Catholicism and international politics in Munich, the Bavarian Ministry of Education, the University of Wurzburg, the University of Freiburg, the University of Münster, and to the Catholic Students Association in Westphalia. In 1950 his lectures on U.S. diplomacy and the Soviet Union took him beyond Germany to Paris, Zurich, and Innsbruck.[70] As the 1950s progressed, this resurrection of old ideas found new allies in the publishing world. Melvin Lasky, editor of the journal *Der Monat* and one of Europe's foremost anti-Communist activists, began distributing *The Review of Politics*, Gurian's books on Bolshevism, and other essays among his journal's staff. By 1953,

---

[69] Mitchell, *The Rise of Christian Democracy*, esp. 76–104, here 80. As Mitchell notes, historians often refer to a 1948 statement by Catholic bishops that expressed guilt for anti-Semitism as a symbol for the broader Catholic turn away from anti-Semitism, but this statement remained a clear exception to otherwise deafening silence on the topic.

[70] Both of Gurian's biographers wrongfully claimed that Gurian traveled to Germany only twice, in 1948 and again before his death in 1954, for personal visits. As the following paragraphs show, however, this was not the case. Thümmler, *Katholischer Publizist und amerikanischer Politikwissenschaftler*, 187; Hürten, *Waldemar Gurian*, 170–172. The information on the trips is from Letter, Gurian to Philip Mosely (28 April 1949); Committee on International Relations Activity Report (1 July 1950), both in Folder 5034, Box 588, series 200, RG 1.2, RFA, RAC.

the two men had created a list of works to be published in Germany, including reissues of Gurian's previous works in their original language.[71]

Beyond promoting his own ideas, Gurian utilized the foundation's wealth to help support countless Catholic thinkers, seminars, and journals that had been allies since the Weimar period. When Havinghurst requested his help in recruiting thinkers that would be "particularly valuable for the building up of German-American cultural relations," Gurian targeted those who had long sought the creation of a personalist order. Reaching back to his networks from the Weimar era and his years in exile, he recommended Karl Thieme, Johannes Maassen, Eugen Kogon, and other Catholics who had spent the war in Europe and were now eager to bring about a Catholic revival.[72] He also expanded his recruiting mission to the United States, encouraging Catholic émigrés to join in the construction of a new Christian order. The most important of these was philosopher Eric Voegelin, then living in exile in Louisiana. The son of German converts to Catholicism, Voegelin was among the most ardent anti-racist Catholic writers of interwar Austria and shared Gurian's belief that Nazi racism and communism were perverse "secular religions." Since Voegelin's arrival as a refugee to the United States in 1938, the two searched for ways to disseminate their ideas about communism as a global menace beyond the American press. The arrival of the foundation presented such opportunities, and Gurian moved quickly to allocate its resources to support Voegelin. After sponsoring a series of lectures on the importance of a Western and anti-Communist alliance, the foundation funded Voegelin's return to Munich for a permanent position in political theory.[73]

---

[71] Letter, Melvin Lasky to Gurian (28 August 1952); Letter, Melvin Lasky to Gurian (17 September 1952); Letter, Gurian to Melvin Lasky (15 September 1953); all in Folder 15, Box 5, WGP, LoC.

[72] Quoted in Letter, Havinghurst to Gurian (17 February 1948), Folder 773, Box 64, Series 200, RG 1.1, RFA, RAC. The recommendations are from Waldemar Gurian, Report: My Trip to Germany. Gurian and Maassen corresponded from 1934 onward, and their correspondence is kept in Folder 15, Box 5, WGP, LoC.

[73] Voegelin greatly admired Gurian's works on Bolshevism; on Gurian's 1935 *Bolshevism as World Menace*, he wrote that "nothing has been published in recent years that even faintly resembles it as a systematic exposition and critique of the problem of Bolshevism." Letter, Eric Voegelin to Gurian (10 July 1946), Folder 27, Box 15, Eric Voegelin Papers [hereafter referred to as EVP], Hoover Institution Archives, Stanford University [hereafter referred to as HIA]. The two men corresponded continuously after 1938, sharing essays, drafts, and ideas. Voegelin published some of his most important essays in Gurian's *Review of Politics*. In 1946 and again in 1949, the two discussed various ways of bringing Voegelin to lecture in Austria and Germany. For example, Letter, Gurian to Voegelin (12 July 1946), and Letter, Voeglin to Gurian (10 May 1949), both in Folder 27, Box 15, EVP, HIA. I am grateful to Arie Dubnov for helping me find these materials. Voegelin reported on his lectures to Gurian in Letter, Eric Voegelin to Gurian (20 November 1950), Folder 27, Box 15, EVP, HIA. Material on his activities with the foundation in Munich are in Folder 19, Box 4, EVP, HIA. His lectures in the America Houses in Darm-

Gurian's growing influence manifested itself in the foundation's increasing investment in German Catholic culture, and its officers' conviction that Catholics were the key to both democratic reconstruction and anti-Communist alliances.[74] After distributing Gurian's reports among the foundation's board and officials, Havinghurst gained their authorization for an ongoing investment in Catholic publications, exchange programs, and cultural exchange. Within a few months of Gurian's report, the foundation began funding the Catholic-led *Frankfurter Hefte*, *Hochland*, and *Rheinischer Merkur*; these publications had hundreds of thousands of readers, who read new calls for cooperation with the United States. It funded conferences organized by Thieme for the promotion of Protestant-Catholic dialogue, resurrecting Thieme's Weimar-era project of interfaith collaboration. It likewise fostered the publication of Catholic books, invited leading Catholic thinkers such as Eugen Kogon for visits in the United States, and organized a series of lectures in Salzburg given by Gurian, Dietrich von Hildebrand, and Erik Peterson. Like Gurian, all these thinkers were driven by a long entrenched hostility to the nation-state, which they observed as a secular enemy, and sought to utilize the foundation's support to promote their own intellectual agenda of Catholic revival.[75]

The culmination of this cooperation between the Rockefeller Foundation, the U.S. state, and German Catholic émigrés was an enormous cultural education program that brought German Catholics for lengthy visits in the United States. From 1948 on, hundreds of Catholic thinkers, journalists, intellectuals, religious leaders, and teachers traveled to the United States for a period of three to four months to observe its political, spiritual, and educational institutions. The goal of this effort was to foster a natural spiritual kinship between the two countries. The German guests visited Rosary College in Chicago, Catholic University in Washington, D.C., St. Benedict College in Minnesota, and finally Notre Dame University, where Gurian welcomed them. The countless reports documenting their experiences reveal

---

stadt, Essen, Hanover, Munich, Nuremberg, and Tübingen are kept in Folders 9–15, Box 38, EVP, HIA.

[74] As Chappel and Chamedes show, similar sentiments were also common among many U.S. military occupation officials at the same time. Chappel, *The Struggle for Europe's Soul*; and Chamedes, *The Vatican and the Making of the Atlantic Order*.

[75] Letter, Robert Havinghurt to Gurian (11 August 1948), Folder 31, Box 3, WGP, LoC. The quotation is from Chappel, *The Struggle for Europe's Soul*. Gurian himself published in all these journals, explaining the values of U.S. foreign policy to his German audience. See, for example, his "Amerika und Sowjetrussland," *Rheinischer Merkur* 38 (18 November 1948), 6–7; "US-Aussenpolitik," *Frankfurter Rundschau* (12 September 1949): 202–204. Material on these publications is kept in Folder 1, Box 18; material on the lecture tour is kept in Folder 11, Box 17; both at WGP, LoC; information on Kogon's visit is from Memorandum, Grants Approved Under European Rehabilitation Program (2 April 1948), Folder 86, Box 10, Series 700, RG 1.2, RFA, RAC.

that the trip had a substantial impact on these visitors. As one of the participants reported, "I have always thought of America as cultureless.... But now I see the Christian forces [that dominate its life] ... and how deeply it is formed by European traditions."[76]

This enormous and multifaceted collaboration helped ideas from Weimar mold the contours of Catholicism's political revival in postwar Germany. With active American support during the Allied occupation, Catholics joined hands with religious Protestants in mobilizing against communism and in forming a new Christian party, the Christian Democratic Union, or CDU. Under the leadership of Konrad Adenauer, the chief Catholic proponent of parliamentarism in the 1920s, the CDU emerged as the most dominant force in postwar German politics, leading the country well into the 1960s. Echoing the visions that Gurian and other personalists had charted in Weimar and in exile, the CDU blended fierce anti-secularism, a burning hatred of communism, and support for parliamentary mechanisms. Its rhetoric lambasted Nazism and communism as the product of "secular materialism" and celebrated Christianity, the family, and small communities as the bedrock of healthy politics. Under its influence, the West German Constitution included special conservative provisions allowing religious education in schools and declared that the "family and community" were under the special protection of the state. For the CDU, the lessons of Nazism and war were an urgent need to Christianize Germany and defend parliamentarism. Only a Christian democracy could prevent the triumph of godless totalitarianism.[77]

The intense campaigns of U.S. philanthropists and Catholic émigrés also helped many German Catholics embrace a supranational and transatlantic vision as West Germany fused itself into the American-led anti-Communist bloc. With Adenauer's firm advocacy, the CDU steered West Germany not only into collaboration with other European countries but also into membership in NATO and other transatlantic organizations. This was a remarkable transformation less than a decade after Hitler's quest for total German domination of the European continent. Gurian's and the Rockefeller Foundation's work was crucial in recasting the United States not just as a protector against the Soviet Union but also as a natural ally in the creation of a Christian order. The publications, lectures, and teachings funded by the foundation tied the mission of domestic reconstruction, Christian rejuvena-

[76] The individual records from hundreds of trips can be found in Box 201–203, Records of the Catholic Affairs Section, Records of the Religious Affairs Branch, Records of Education and Cultural Relations Division, RG 260, NARA. The quotation is from Report by Wilhelm Ludwig (undated), Folder Ludwig, Wilhelm, Box 202, Records of the Education and Cultural Relations Division, Records of the Religious Affairs Branch, Records of the Catholic Affairs Section, RG 260, NARA.

[77] Mitchell, *The Origins of Christian Democracy*; Chappel, *The Struggle for Europe's Soul*.

tion, and the Atlantic alliance into a single, inseparable matrix, where all parts depended on the others. Certainly some anti-American sentiments remained, with some Catholics continuing to exclude the United States from their vision of a unified West, but this hostility dissipated as time passed. Following the footsteps of Gurian and other émigrés like him, a growing number of Catholic journalists and politicians came to include the United States in the anti-materialist and anti-secular camp. When, in 1953, Adenauer praised "the United States'...Occidental Christian spirit," his was not a lone voice. Such statements reflected years of efforts by intellectuals, journalists, and scholars. By the late 1950s, the alliance between the United States and German Catholics became a permanent feature of Cold War politics. Even Adenauer's most ardent opponents embraced it, and for a generation of Germans, it became an accepted fact of postwar German life.[78]

The emerging symbiosis between Catholic émigrés and the Rockefeller Foundation did not only influence Germany. In an overlooked yet equally striking development, personalist theories also helped shape one of the foundation's most important intellectual campaigns in the United States itself: the creation of Soviet studies or, as it soon became known, Sovietology. Through multiple channels, the foundation promoted Gurian's ideas as the key for understanding the United States' new global foe. It helped frame the Cold War as a battle between Christian civilization and its evil and uncompromising destroyer.

The growing popularity of Gurian's concept of totalitarianism predated the beginning of the Cold War. In the years after his arrival in the United States, the term spread like wildfire beyond the Catholic community, circulating among American and émigré journalists, politicians, and thinkers. It was a powerful term to express the anxiety that many felt about the rise of aggressive anti-liberal regimes like the Third Reich and the Soviet Union, and the danger that they might inspire anti-democratic forces in the United States itself. Journalist Eugene Lyons echoed widespread sentiments when in 1937 he wrote about the "totalitarian insanities" that grew out of "the moral collapse of Europe" and claimed that there was no difference between Stalin's and Hitler's brutal dictatorships.[79] Yet it was the rise of global ten-

---

[78] The quotation is from Konrad Adenauer, "Christian Civilization at Stake," *World Indivisible: With Liberty and Justice for All* (New York: Harper & Brothers, 1955), 11–15, here 12. For more on this process, with emphasis on its inner tensions and conflicts, see Granieri, *The Ambivalent Alliance*. On the role of Christian democracy in building trans-European collaboration, see Wolfram Kaiser, *Christian Democracy and the Origins of the European Union* (New York: Cambridge University Press, 2007).

[79] Eugene Lyons, *Assignment in Utopia* (New York: Harcourt, 1937), quotations from 611 and 621. On the rising popularity of the term in American culture in the 1930s, see Benjamin L. Alpers, *Dictators, Democracy, and American Public Culture: Envisioning the Totalitarian Enemy*

sions with the Soviet Union that fostered totalitarianism's spectacular ascendance as the era's most important political phrase. Across political camps and ideological convictions, it reflected the growing belief that the Soviet Union was not just an anti-democratic regime but a perverse monstrosity that could not coexist with democracy. Gurian's term simultaneously nurtured and captured the intense anxiety that foreign threats could morph into destructive subversion at home; totalitarianism's most disturbing feature was its ability to deceptively weave itself into the tissue of democratic society. The postwar years therefore witnessed an explosion of publications, conferences, discussions, and speeches on the origins and nature of totalitarianism. It was no accident that when President Harry Truman, in his famous address to the joint session of Congress in March 1947, envisioned a newly assertive American foreign policy, he did not mention the Soviet Union but called on the United States to stand against "aggressive movements that seek to impose totalitarian regimes." Like Gurian, Truman and his aides believed that the term best captured the diabolical and all-encompassing nature of the Communist threat.[80]

Gurian's portrayal of the Cold War as a Christian crusade further dovetailed with a growing persuasion that the United States was leading a struggle not merely for democracy but also for Christian civilization. American thinkers and politicians of all religious persuasions increasingly claimed that monotheistic religion, Christianity in particular, was the spiritual source of American greatness. Theologians such as Reinhold Niebuhr and diplomats such as George Kennan declared monotheism the source of political liberties and the driving force behind democracy. In this view, international communism, with its secular creed, posed an existential threat to democracy's oldest roots and its claims to religious freedom. Harry Truman, whose worldview was soaked in Christian terminology, spoke for many when he said that "our American heritage of human freedom is born in the belief that man is created in the image of God and therefore capable of governing himself." In his mind, Christians across the globe had to join hands in a global struggle. As he wrote in 1946 to Pope Pius XII, striving

---

(Chapel Hill: University of North Carolina Press, 2003), especially 67ff. As Alpers notes, the term itself appeared in the U.S. press in 1933, but it was only in the late 1930s that it came to signify the similarities between the extreme right and left.

[80] Harry Truman, "Special Message to the Congress on Greece and Turkey" (12 March 1947), in Denise M. Bostdorff (ed.), *Proclaiming the Truman Doctrine* (College Station: Texas A&M University Press, 2008), 1–7, here 5. On the rise of totalitarianism as the Cold War's most important doctrine, see Abbott Gleason, *Totalitarianism: The Inner History of the Cold War* (New York: Oxford University Press, 1995), 72ff., and William David Jones, *The Lost Debate: German Socialist Intellectuals and Totalitarianism* (Urbana: University of Illinois Press, 1999). As Chappel correctly notes, both, like most historians of the theory, overlook the importance of Catholic thought to the development of the theory. See also Anson Rabinbach's reflections in "Moments of Totalitarianism," *History and Theory* 45 (2006), 72–100.

for anti-Communist cooperation, "[n]o peace can be permanent which is not based upon Christian principles."[81] In this cultural environment, the global struggle with communism depended on religious commitment just as much as the force of arms. As Truman hyperbolically asserted, the United States' "quest for righteousness" could succeed only if, "in St. Paul's luminous phrase, [we] put on the armor of God."[82]

A crucial force in shaping and perpetuating this cultural environment was the Rockefeller Foundation's and Gurian's joint quest to expand knowledge of the Soviet Union and communism. In 1946 the Rockefeller Foundation had funded the opening of a Russian Institute at Columbia University, the first of its kind in the United States. By the early 1950s, the foundation poured millions into the creation of forty additional centers at campuses across the United States. Bustling with energy and flush with funds, these institutions produced countless conferences, journals, and books. They also trained thousands of students, diplomats, and soldiers in the history, economy, languages, and politics of the new enemy. Despite the foundation's "apolitical" pretenses, its officers were well aware that its postwar mission ran parallel to the U.S. government's anti-Communist campaign, and foundation officers were intimately acquainted with U.S. policymakers. They took pride in providing the government with knowledge it needed, and they labored intensively to promote further cooperation. As one official proudly reported, "[n]ot only the State Department but the War Department and the Navy send their people there [to the centers the foundation funded] to be trained." Nowhere was this cooperation between philanthropy and government more intense than in the creation of postwar Sovietology.[83]

[81] Letter, Harry Truman to Pius XII (19 April 1946), in Myron C. Taylor (ed.), *Correspondence between President Truman and Pope Pius XII* (New York: n.p., 1953), 9–10. On the Truman administration's cooperation with the Vatican, see both Chamedes, *The Vatican and the Making of the Atlantic Order;* and George J. Gill, "The Truman Administration and Vatican Relations," *Catholic Historical Review* 73:3 (July 1987): 408–423.

[82] On the rising role of religious ideas and rhetoric in the United States during the early Cold War and from Truman in particular, see, for example, Andrew Preston, *Sword of the Spirit, Shield of Faith: Religion in American War and Diplomacy* (New York: Knopf, 2012), 411–464; Dianne Kirby, "Harry Truman's Religious Legacy: The Holly Alliance, Containment, and the Cold War," in *Religion and the Cold War* (London: Pagrave Macmillan, 2003), 77–102; as well as Jonathan P. Herzog, *The Spiritual-Industrial Complex: America's Religious Battle against Communism in the Early Cold War* (New York: Oxford University Press, 2011).

[83] The quotation is from History of RF on SS through the War and Post-War Period (1939–1948), Folder 19, Box 3, Series 910 Social Sciences, RG 3, RFA, RAC. On the rise of Sovietology, see David Engerman, *Know Your Enemy: The Rise and Fall of America's Soviet Experts* (New York: Oxford University Press, 2009). On cooperation between Sovietologists and British and U.S. diplomats at the beginning of the Cold War, see Marc J. Selverstone, *Constructing the Monolith: The United States, Great Britain, and International Communism, 1945–1950* (Cambridge, MA: Harvard University Press, 2009). For a detailed study of the Rockefeller Foundation and Sovi-

Gurian quickly recognized the opportunities that this new web of money, institutions, and knowledge presented for his own brand of anti-totalitarianism. Upon his return from Germany in 1948, he utilized his relationship with the foundation to suggest that it finance a new institution at the University of Notre Dame. Gurian envisioned a Catholic institution for the study of international politics, the Soviet Union in particular, that would produce relevant knowledge on "the interrelations of religion, democracy and international order ... the relations of Church and State, the role of religion in educational systems ... [and most important,] the threat of totalitarianism in its manifold forms." In his mind, such an institution could provide a unique Catholic perspective on communism and help mobilize the Catholic community against the totalitarian enemy it failed to fight during the 1930s.[84]

Philip Mosely, founder of the center at Columbia and a specialist of Russian culture who had orchestrated the foundation's efforts in the field, was ecstatic about Gurian's participation in the mission. While largely oblivious to Gurian's personalist theories, he believed that the émigré's Catholic bona fides and ties to the Catholic intellectual community could expand both Sovietology and the foundation's reach. Gurian's work on Bolshevism, he wrote to the foundation's board, "is one of the most intelligent long-range interpretations and is accepted as objective by most non-Communist scholars." In 1949 the foundation agreed to invest tens of thousands of dollars in the creation of Notre Dame's Committee of International Politics, a new institution of research. This center, the board hoped, would become the center of the foundation's Sovietology project in the Midwest. Gurian was appointed to lead this new Catholic institution and all its activities. From this position, he disseminated his Weimar-era anti-communism on a scale that dwarfed the personalists' earlier campaigns in Europe.[85]

In the sprawling empire of the foundation's Soviet studies, the committee at Notre Dame soon emerged as a humming center of scholarship and as the only Catholic academic institution. Alongside Gurian, its second senior member was Ferdinand A. Hermens, another German Catholic émigré who had supported democracy since the Weimar era and fled the Third Reich to Indiana.[86] The Committee at Notre Dame also included military

---

etology, see Tim Müller, *Krieger und Gelehrte* (Hamburg: Hamburg Edition, 2010). As Engerman shows, the foundation's investment began in 1942 when the Soviet Union was still an ally of the United States, but the expansion of its investments was deeply tied to the Cold War.

[84] Letter, Gurian to Philip Mosely (28 March 1949), Folder 5034, Box 588, Series 200, RG 1.2, RFA, RAC.

[85] Mosely's evaluation is from Evaluations of the Committee (20 June 1949), Folder 5034, Box 588, series 200, RG 1.2, RFA, RAC. The creation of the committee is from Grant approval (17 June 1949), Folder 5034, Box 588, Series 200, RG 1.2, RFA, RAC.

[86] Gurian and Hermens had corresponded since 1935; upon Hermens's arrival in the

scholar William Shanahan, historian Matthew Fitzsimons, and Stephen Kertesz, a former Hungarian diplomat who fled the Communist revolution and became a scholar of Bolshevism. In the span of four years, this group convened several international conferences on the Soviet Union and its ideology. These conferences assembled Russian specialists from Yale, Harvard, Columbia, and Fordham, diplomats from the State Department, and Russian refugees to discuss the "aims and methods of Soviet Terrorism" and the "methods of Soviet penetration in Eastern Europe." Similar events included the conference "Who Is the Enemy—Russian Imperialism or Soviet Communism?" and symposia attended by Hans Morgenthau and Kertesz on "The U.S. Weaknesses in Today's World Crisis." In 1952 the Notre Dame center convened a conference on "The Fate of Central Europe: Hopes and Failures of American Foreign Policy," which included Mosely; Alvin Bentley, a member of the U.S. House Committee on Foreign Affairs; and numerous scholars. By 1953, the committee had expanded by founding a graduate program, funded by the foundation, where graduate students supervised by Gurian and Kertesz wrote works on Soviet ideology, with a focus on its "methods of expansion and operation." The Committee on International Politics' reputation as a tower of knowledge on Soviet affairs even caught the attention of the FBI. The bureau's director, J. Edgar Hoover, lauded its symposia as "a contribution to every segment of our American society."[87]

While the Rockefeller Foundation never adhered to religious politics, the committee provided Gurian with a stage to promote and expand the reach of his anti-secularist theory of totalitarianism. In a flurry of journal essays, collections, and monographs, Gurian provided a platform for numerous religious scholars, such as N. S. Timasheff and Yves Simon, who called for uncompromising confrontation with the secular Eastern Bloc and even for military intervention against the Communist regimes of Eastern Europe. The most popular of these publications were by a renowned scholar of nationalism, German-Jewish émigré Hans Kohn. With the committee's help, in 1953 Kohn published a vitriolic attack on Soviet diplomacy entitled *Pan-Slavism*. Based on lectures delivered at Notre Dame, Kohn's book claimed that Soviet policies were the continuation of aggressive Russian nationalism that could never coexist peacefully with the West. As the

---

United States, Gurian repeatedly proposed that they cooperate, but it was not until the establishment of the committee that the two men worked together on a joint project. Letter, Hermens to Gurian (29 March 1938), Folder 3, Box 4, WGP, LoC.

[87] Conference Program—The Soviet Union (7–8 February 1950); Committee on International Relations Activity Report (1 July 1951), both in Folder 5034, Box 588; Conference Plan, "The Fate of Central Europe: Hopes and Failures of American Foreign Policy" (11 February 1955), Folder 5036, Box 589; both in Series 200, RG 1.2, RFA, RAC. The information on Hoover is from a news clipping (16 April 1950), Folder 15, Box 12, WGP, LoC.

foundation's officers reported, the publications sponsored by the committee were widely circulated and applauded throughout U.S. universities.[88]

At the center of this stream of publications stood Gurian, who used the committee's platform to recycle his earlier ideas. In 1952 the committee republished a new and condensed version of his 1931 work *Bolshevism*, changing only the subtitle and leaving entire sections of the text untouched. In the following years, it also sponsored several new works in which Gurian reiterated his depiction of the Soviet Union as a "total state" that sought the destruction of all communities, traditions, and religion. If anything had changed over time it was his rhetoric, which continued to intensify as the Cold War wore on. Years before rumors about the scale of Stalin's crimes began to circulate in the West, Gurian claimed that the Soviet Union was not only aggressively seeking to expand but that it was also embarking on a genocidal plan that would surpass that of the Nazis. "The ruthless planning and industrialization of totalitarian methods," he wrote in 1953,

> [are] used to obliterate national boundaries ... whole nations and groups are deported. Today the Jews are threatened with extermination or loss of all rights because they are condemned as bourgeois nationalists and as cosmopolitans....
> The totalitarian ruthlessness of the Soviet regime permits methods far more systematically brutal and efficient than ever before.

Gurian spelled out the implications of this argument in no uncertain terms: "Should not the fight against the totalitarian Soviet system become at the same time a campaign of liberation from any rule by Moscow? Should not the totalitarian Soviet Union ... cease to exist in order to make a lasting peace possible?" These ideas were not isolated publications. They sold thousands of copies and were widely distributed on American campuses.[89]

The committee's mission, however, was more ambitious than the dissemination of anti-totalitarian propaganda. Both Gurian and the foundation envisioned it as a center for Catholic thought, broadly conceived. The committee thus became a hub for international scholarship on contempo-

---

[88] Waldemar Gurian (ed.), *The Soviet Union: Background, Ideology, Reality* (South Bend: University of Notre Dame Press, 1951); Waldemar Gurian (ed.), *Soviet Imperialism: Its Origins and Tactics* (South Bend: University of Notre Dame Press, 1953). Hans Kohn, *Pan-Slavism: Its History and Ideology* (South Bend: University of Notre Dame Press, 1953). The lectures on which the book was based are mentioned in Letter, Hans Kohn to Waldemar Gurian (6 February 1952), Folder 27, Box 4, WGP, LoC. The information about their circulation is from Philip Mosely, Memorandum "Evaluations of the Committee for International Politics" (20 June 1949), Folder 5034, Box 588, series 200, RG 1.2, RFA, RAC.

[89] Quotations are from Waldemar Gurian, "Introduction to Soviet Imperialism," in *Soviet Imperialism*, 1–16, here 12, 13. Waldemar Gurian, *Bolshevism: An Introduction to Soviet Communism* (South Bend: University of Notre Dame Press, 1952).

rary politics and religion, duplicating Catholic convictions with all their inner tensions and contradictions. It organized conferences and symposia on "Catholicism and the Vatican in World Affairs," brought over German philosophers to discuss "World Government and Christian Hope," and gathered Italian political theorists to address "Christian Democracy in Western Europe." It organized a lecture series on Catholic theology, designed to bring Catholic ideas to "the wasteland of Europe, Asia, and the great wilderness of civilization in our American cities." All these were hastily published as collections and monographs for popular and scholarly audiences. The Notre Dame committee sponsored talks by the philosopher Hannah Arendt, who discussed her recent work on "Totalitarian Terror and Organization," French philosopher Bertrand de Jouvenel, who lectured on "The United States and Europe," and the diplomat-turned-scholar Robert Byrnes, who discussed international law. It established a permanent visiting program, which brought Catholic professors from Germany and France for research at Notre Dame, and funded trips for Catholic intellectuals to lecture in Europe. Year after year, the foundation's investment in the committee continued to grow, further expanding its activities and the reach of its publications.[90]

This intersection of Catholic thought, private philanthropy, and international politics further guided the committee's most ambitious mission: to insert its graduates into the fabric of diplomatic service. As Gurian stated to the foundation, the committee's Catholic students formed the vanguard of the mission to "defend the true values of secular civilization and of its liberties against secularist pseudo-religions." While Gurian and other committee members never quite explained why secular civilization, the source of modern politics' destruction, merited Christianity's defense, they nevertheless directed their students to serve it. During its first two years of operation, they introduced a series of new courses at the University of Notre Dame, emphasizing "Papal teachings on international order, the peace efforts of the Catholic Church ... methods of Soviet expansion, and the religious

[90] The information on events is from Committee on International Relations Activity Report (1 July 1950), Folder 5034, Box 588, series 200, RG 1.2, RFA, RAC; Announcement (undated), "The Ageless Witness Lecture Series," Folder 1, Box 18, WGP, LoC. For publications, see, for example, F. A. Hermens, *Europe between Democracy and Anarchy* (South Bend: University of Notre Dame Press, 1951); Mario Einaudi, *Christian Democracy in Italy and France* (South Bend: University of Notre Dame Press, 1952); Gurian (ed.), *The Catholic Church in World Affairs* (South Bend: University of Notre Dame Press, 1954). The information about lectures is from Committee on International Relations Activity Report (1 July 1951), Folder 5034, Box 588; Symposia Sponsored by the Committee on International Relations (28 February 1955), Folder 5036, Box 589; Committee on International Relations Activity Report (1 July 1950), Folder 5034, Box 588; Expenditure Summary Committee on International Relations Report (7 September 1950); Committee on International Relations Activity Report (1 July 1951); Grant approval (22 May 1952); all in Folder 5034, Box 588, all in Series 200, RG 1.2, RFA, RAC.

policies of the Soviet Union." These were followed by evening classes on "Communism in Theory and Practice" and "Today's World Crises" that drew laymen and advanced students. As time passed, the committee merged its efforts with a small program founded by the Department of Political Science at Notre Dame, which trained students explicitly for diplomatic service with the support of the State Department. All of this program's graduates took classes with Gurian on the Soviet Union, the Vatican, and international politics in the twentieth century. In 1955 Rockefeller Foundation president Dean Rusk, a former diplomat (and future secretary of state) chose the committee to host his lectures on U.S. foreign relations in the postwar era. Through Gurian's work, the committee transformed Catholic education and scholarship into one of the pillars of the Cold War establishment. With Rockefeller support, it continued to operate well after Gurian's death, organizing conferences, publications, and educational programs on religion and international politics into the 1960s.[91]

In the years before his premature death in 1954, Gurian brought his personalist ideas to the heart of American Sovietology and emerged as one of the field's most important figures. Alongside Hannah Arendt, Philip Mosely, Carl Friedrich, and Hans Morgenthau, his opinions helped shape the Rockefeller Foundation's intellectual, institutional, and investment agenda. His reputation spread to other philanthropies, and the Ford Foundation, the Carnegie Foundation, and the American Council of Learned Societies each sought his advice on how to invest in Soviet studies. As one Rockefeller Foundation officer wrote, "I must confess to a certain admiration of the work of the committee ... [Gurian] is a man of integrity and a first-class scholar of the Soviet Union," adding that the studies his committee produced were among the most "important addition[s] to the literature on international politics." While American philanthropies absorbed German émigrés of diverse ideological leanings and even sponsored studies on the Soviet Union by Marxist authors such as Herbert Marcuse, none mobilized their frameworks on the same scale as Gurian.[92]

[91] This first quotation is from Five Year Plan for the Committee on International Relations (28 February 1955), Folder 5036, Box 589, Series 200, RG 1.2, RFA, RAC. The information on the committee's activities is from Project Proposal, A Study of International Relations Submitted to the Board of Directors of the Rockefeller Foundation, 20 June 1949, Folder 5034, Box 588; and Committee on International Relations Report 1952–1955, Folder 5035, Box 589, both in Series 200, RG 1.2, RFA, RAC; Report on the Foreign Service Program of the Department of Political Science of the University of Notre Dame (undated, 1950?), Folder 7, Box 18, WGP, LoC. The information on Rusk is from Letter, Dean Rusk to Stephen Kertesz (6 December 1955), Folder 5036, Box 589, Series 200, RG 1.2, RFA, RAC. The information on further approval is from Grant approval (25 February 1955), Folder 5034, Box 588, Series 200, RG 1.2, RFA, RAC.

[92] A description of Gurian's role in the foundation's programs and an assessment of his work's value are to be found in Interview Report, KWT with Waldemar Gurian and Hannah

The Rockefeller Foundation's outreach program in Germany and its support of Sovietology in the United States were not just a product of postwar reconstruction and the divisions of the Cold War. Nor were they merely the realization of the foundation's brand of liberal internationalism, despite the idiosyncrasies that guided some of its officers' principles. Rather, they also constituted the reemergence of a unique strand of German Catholic conservatism, which had survived in exile and entered the fabric of the United States' philanthropic, intellectual, and educational worlds. Through the foundation, Gurian and other Catholic émigrés promoted their antisecularist visions of Catholicism and its totalitarian enemy and spread them in both West Germany and the United States. Despite the many blind spots and limits of Gurian's thought, the wealth and connections of the foundation helped him reach audiences on a scale that he could not have envisioned during his early years as Catholic journalist and anti-Nazi activist. After the destruction brought by war, it was ideas like his that provided the theoretical language for Catholicism's participation in democratic reconstruction and the formation of the Atlantic alliance. His writings also helped shape American thinking about communism, international politics, and the Soviet Union. The terms that Gurian helped coin, his embrace of democratic structures, and the diabolical qualities he attributed to the Soviet Union became common on both sides of the Atlantic. By the mid-1950s, these ideas became so widespread that few could remember they were once controversial.

Of the many alliances fostered by the Cold War, the one between Catholic personalists and American internationalist philanthropists was perhaps the least expected. A wide intellectual divide separated the Rockefeller Foundation's vision of a liberal "civilizing mission," confidence in the superiority of American knowledge and scholarship, and belief in progressive and scientific education and Gurian's conservative search for traditional, Catholic, organic, and anti-individualist communities. Indeed, during the Weimar era, Rockefeller officials and European personalists had largely ignored one another. While they shared a deep disdain for communism, no one could have envisioned collaboration between them. But the shock of Nazism and World War II, the perils and opportunities of exile, and intense fears of rising Soviet power brought them together. With the shared belief that only

Arendt (29 July 1954), Box 589, Folder 5035, Series 200, RG 1.2, RFA, RAC. The information on his influence on other organizations is based on Grant Report to the Carnegie Foundation (undated), Folder 11, Box 17; Letter, Pendleton Herring (president of ACLS) to Gurian (3 November 1953), Folder 8, Box 1; Letter, Alexander Dallin (associate director of the Ford Foundation's "Research Program on the USSR") to Gurian (25 March 1952), Folder 25, Box 2; all in WGP, LoC. On the foundation's cooperation with Marxist German thinkers, mostly former members of the Frankfurt School, see Müller, *Krieger und Gelehrte*.

liberal democracy could prevent social chaos, and in their commitment to the crusade against communism, they came to recognize one another as valuable allies.

This cooperation was part of a monumental transformation generated by the Cold War, manifested in the voluntary self-mobilization of individuals and private organizations in the service of American state goals. During the 1920s and 1930s, the Rockefeller Foundation operated separately from the U.S. government. While it invested in the promotion of scientific education, health initiatives, and political theory, it did so without consulting government officials. Catholic personalists were even more suspicious of government organs. Their veneration of small communities was, in part, a protest against the power of the modern state, which they viewed as a potential agent of secularism. Yet by the time the Cold War began, both philanthropists and personalists believed that their own missions ran parallel to that of the U.S. government. The new superpower was the only force that could block communism and could enable non-Communist communities to flourish. This form of voluntary self-mobilization behind the expansion of state power was one of the Cold War's most profound legacies. It put enormous wealth and intellectual energy in the service of state goals and often endowed American power with crucial ideological legitimacy.

The theory of totalitarianism was in many ways the glue that held this symbiotic partnership together. Through the works of Gurian and other European émigrés, totalitarianism became the single most popular framework for the interpretation of communism as a diabolical, uncompromising, and ever-expanding global menace. Drawing on its religious and eschatological origins, this theory positioned totalitarianism as not only a foreign threat but also a potential danger rooted in the heart of modern society. Hiding their true nature, totalitarian agents could exploit the perceived cultural weakness of democracy to take over democratic institutions from within. The intense fears fostered by these paranoid views meant that the campaign against communism required constant cultural mobilization, both in the United States and abroad. Victory in the Cold War could only be achieved through the large-scale production of cultural ammunition, by repeatedly if not compulsively reminding readers and students of the values of democracy and the evils of communism. Both Gurian and Rockefeller officials recognized their overlapping commitment to such mobilization and worked together to achieve it. Acting in consort, their campaigns provided important concepts and ideas for the promotion of West German Catholics' turn toward democracy, the creation of Sovietology in the United States, and the broader solidification of the Western alliance.

While this self-mobilization was crucial to U.S. Cold War diplomacy, it empowered visions that far preceded the Cold War. Throughout their evolution, Gurian's ideas and work remained linked to his Weimar-era roots and to the project of securing the realization of the person—a human embedded in a web of traditions and communities. Forged in the 1920s, Gurian's intellectual efforts were consistently directed at mapping the person's enemies and its potential allies. Participating in Weimar's Catholic debate on politics and autonomy, he forcefully maintained that, despite its many flaws and secular origins, only democracy could protect the spiritual integrity of organic communities and families. While he was never able to respect secular politics as legitimate or liberating, he insisted that the institutions of liberal democracy were the only ones that could resist the nihilist destruction threatened by the "total state," the total politicization and secularization promoted by the radical right and the left. The advent of American wealth after World War II enabled Gurian and others to disseminate this message, providing the global stage they had sought since the 1920s and leaving their mark on thought and culture on both sides of the Atlantic.

CHAPTER IV

Individual Liberties and "Militant Democracy"

KARL LOEWENSTEIN AND AGGRESSIVE LIBERALISM

IN AUGUST 1956 the West German Supreme Court handed down one of the most dramatic rulings in its history. After years of deliberation, the justices granted the West German government's long-standing plea to ban the Communist Party. The Communists, the court ruled, opposed the fundamental principles of democracy and had thus lost their right to participate in political life. As its rationale, the court cited the theory of "militant democracy" (*wehrhafte* or *streitbaredemokratie*), which asserted that the liberal and democratic state must deny freedom of expression, association, and opinion to anti-democratic forces. The justices explained that the integrity of democratic institutions was more important than full popular representation, and that the state therefore had the right to deny political existence to the Communists. The German government implemented this historic ruling with fierce determination, swiftly disbanding the party, all Communist youth movements and clubs, and confiscating the party's property. West Germany became the only European state to officially ban communism. Some observers expressed astonishment that Germans believed that such "militant" measures protected, rather than limited, democratic life. After all, only two decades earlier, the Nazis had begun their campaign of political repression by similarly suppressing the Communist Party and confiscating its property. East Germany's official newspaper, *Neues Deutschland*, noted this blatant irony with a headline declaring that West Germany had now "followed Hitler's path."[1]

This dramatic limitation of political rights was facilitated by the broader postwar transformation of German liberals, one of the country's largest political camps. Since the nineteenth century, the German liberal parties had advocated the protection of the individual from the state and for equality under the law, regardless of religion, profession, or class. Supported primarily by the educated and urban middle classes, liberal politicians advocated "classical" political liberties, such as freedom of expression and religious

---

[1] "Adenauer geht den Weg Hitlers," *Neues Deutschland* (18 August 1956), 1. For more on the ruling, see Svetlana Tyulkina, "Militant Democracy" (PhD diss., Central European University, 2011), 11–115.

worship and the sanctity of private property. Before World War II, most liberals believed that these rights were valid for all Germans, even those who opposed democracy. Yet during the Cold War, liberals turned their back on this conviction. In the 1950s liberal politicians, intellectuals, and jurists widely welcomed the theory of militant democracy and claimed that political rights were dependent on loyalty to democratic institutions. They became ardent advocates of limiting rights and energetically supported Germany's participation in Cold War anti-Communist suppression.[2]

Scholars have often attributed this combative attitude toward democratic rights to the trauma of Nazism. In this telling, German liberals were horrified that Nazi abuse of political freedom had destroyed democracy from within, especially by using unfettered political speech and parliamentary mechanisms in its rise to power.[3] But intellectually, the transformation of German liberalism and the rise of militant democracy drew from older experiences. They were deeply shaped by the resurrection of a Weimar-era theory promulgated by Karl Loewenstein, the liberal émigré who coined the term "militant democracy." As a young legal scholar, Loewenstein celebrated democratic institutions, such as the parliament and political parties, as the guardians of individual liberties. These institutions, he maintained, were *not* intended to reflect the will of the people but rather to prevent the masses from abusing democratic freedoms and supporting dictators. In Loewenstein's eyes, individual liberties had to supersede the larger "will" of the people, and the rights liberals cherished depended on loyalty to the democratic state. The state therefore had the authority and even the duty to deny the freedoms of speech and political organization to anyone who threatened these rights, including Communists and Fascists. During the Weimar period, Loewenstein called on German liberals to abandon their support of universal freedoms. In order to defend itself, the Weimar Republic had to vigilantly curb anti-democratic parties.[4]

---

[2] Peter Lösche and Franz Walter, *Die FDP: Richtungsstreit und Zukunftszweifel* (Darmstadt: Wissenschaftliche Buchgesellschaft, 1996).

[3] See, for example, Karrin Hanshew, *Terror and Democracy in West Germany* (New York: Cambridge University Press, 2012); Peter L. Lindseth, "The Paradox of Parliamentary Supremacy: Delegation, Democracy, and Dictatorship in Germany and France, 1920s-1950s," *Yale Law Review* 113:7 (May 2004): 1341–1415; Jan-Werner Müller, "Compromised Republicans: The *Vernunftrepublikaner* and the Transformation of Liberal Thought from Weimar to the Federal Republic," in Henning Tewes and Jonathan Wright (eds.), *Liberalism, Anti-Semitism, and Democracy* (New York: Oxford University Press, 2001), 127–147.

[4] A vast amount of scholarship, much of it written by political scientists, explores the concept of "militant democracy." While scholars all recognize Loewenstein as its first theoretician, they generally attribute its origin to the experience of exile and universally ignore Loewenstein's pluralist and democratic theory during the Weimar period, thus overlooking the context of its creation. For selected examples, see the essays in Markus Thiel (ed.), *The "Militant Democracy" Principle in Modern Democracies* (Burlington, VT: Ashgate, 2009); András Sajó (ed.),

While these ideas failed to save Weimar, they crossed the Atlantic during World War II, with unexpected and dark consequences. Officials in the U.S. Justice Department, anxious that anti-democratic activists were working to undermine the United States, found much to admire in Loewenstein's political vision. They recruited him to conduct a massive international campaign, which coordinated the capture, incarceration, and deportation of "subversive" agents across the United States and Latin America. In one of the most expansive—and largely forgotten—experiments of U.S. foreign policy, American diplomats joined forces with their counterparts in Brazil, Chile, Honduras, Mexico, Venezuela, and other countries to build a network of concentration camps across the Western hemisphere. They arrested and even deported thousands of political prisoners deemed to be enemies of the democratic order. This brutal campaign allowed Lowenstein to implement his vision of a "militant" international organization, in which democracies actively overpowered anti-democratic activities. It also convinced him that the United States offered the most useful vehicle for the realization of his combative democratic theory. As was the case with Ernst Fraenkel in Korea, Loewenstein claimed that his democratic ideas were universal; U.S. power thus opened up new spheres for the implementation of older ideas far beyond American and European shores. And as in Korea, the tragic consequences of these ideas were disgraceful violence and large-scale suppression.

After the war, Loewenstein resumed his campaign to build a militant democracy in Germany, with the backing of U.S. occupation authorities. American officials, who believed that his plan would promote democratization and strengthen anti-Communist sentiments, sponsored his writings, lectures, and speeches. Lowenstein spoke to thousands of scholars, students, and politicians across the country. This U.S. support helped him turn "militant democracy" into a popular phrase and framework among German intellectuals and politicians, ultimately helping inspire the 1956 Supreme Court ruling that banned the Communist Party. For many, Loewenstein's theory explained why political persecution and the limitation of liberties did not undermine democracy but, in fact, was necessary to secure its integrity. It provided a comprehensive vision of rights and their limits in a liberal state. It soothed widespread fears that the security demands of the Cold War would destroy what it sought to protect.

Like Friedrich, Fraenkel, and Gurian, Loewenstein was a crucial agent in the creation of the Cold War alliance. In promoting his own liberal ideas

---

Militant Democracy (Utrecht: Eleven, 2004); and the scholarship cited later in this chapter. For an excellent overview of the concept and the debates it has sparked since World War II, see Jan-Werner Müller, "Militant Democracy," in Michael Rosenfeld and András Sajó (eds.), *The Oxford Handbook of Comparative Constitutional Law* (New York: Oxford University Press, 2012), 1253–1269.

from the Weimar era, he helped shape U.S. foreign policy and mobilize German liberals in support of anti-Communist suppression. His visions offered an important response to the seemingly existential threats against democracy that shaped the midcentury world, setting stiff boundaries for postwar democratic tolerance. On both sides of the Atlantic, militant democracy became a guiding principle for Cold War democracy.

THE INTERNAL STRUGGLE OF LIBERAL DEMOCRACY

Like German Socialists and Catholics, German liberals met the creation of the Weimar Republic with a mixture of triumph and fear. The democratic revolution of 1918 had fulfilled liberal visions of a state based on individual liberties and the rule of law. Under the guidance of Hugo Preuss, one of Germany's most eminent liberal legal scholars, the Weimar Constitution enshrined cherished liberal principles, such as freedom of the press, freedom of association, and the protection of private property. The heads of Germany's liberal party, Deutsche Demokratische Partei (German Democratic Party, or DDP), assumed leading roles in both state and federal governments and energetically utilized them to promote equality for women and liberal education.[5] At the same time, the Weimar era also exposed liberals to intense hatred and violence. Leaders of nationalist and monarchist militias continually called for the overthrow of democracy and encouraged violence against liberals and their allies. During Weimar's early years, this vitriolic campaign inspired countless terrorist attacks and failed coups. Most famously, in 1922 right-wing activists assassinated Walther Rathenau, the DDP's most senior politician and Germany's minister of foreign affairs. In the early 1930s anti-democratic violence and subversion became an even more potent force in German life. In particular, the Nazi and Communist parties, both of whom had parliamentary representation and flourished under the Weimar Constitution's protections on speech and assembly, openly plotted to overthrow the regime. Democracy's success therefore paralleled the growth of liberalism's worst enemies. The question of whether the republic could endure under such threats was a burning political and intellectual question.[6]

---

[5] On the role of the DDP and Preuss in shaping the Weimar Constitution, see Detlef Lehnert, *Verfassungsdemokratie als Bürgergenossenschaft* (Baden: Nomos, 1998). On DDP politics in general, see Volker Stahlmann, "Einleitung," in *Linkliberalismus in Preussen* (Düsseldorf: Droste, 2009), xi–cviii; Bill Frye, *Liberal Democrats in the Weimar Republic: The History of the German Democratic Party and the German State Party* (Carbondale: Southern Illinois University Press, 1985); and Lothar Albertin, *Liberalismus und Demokratie am Anfang der Weimarer Republik* (Düsseldorf: Drost, 1972).

[6] Dirk Schumann, *Political Violence in the Weimar Republic* (New York: Berghahn Books, 2009).

The sense that the republic paradoxically empowered its own enemies was the backdrop for Loewenstein's combative ideology. Specifically, the city of Munich shaped much of his early experiences and thought. In the initial Weimar years, the capital of Bavaria was the site of extensive political violence, failed coups, and bloody clashes between the young republic, Communists, and extreme nationalists, including the nascent Nazi Party. At the same time, the University of Munich served as a center for democratic-leaning liberal scholars, who gathered to promote democratic theory and international cooperation. They included Karl Neumeyer, a founder of the study of international law and an advocate of international liberal coopera-tion; Robert Piloty, a scholar of British politics and an enthusiastic sup-porter of the parliamentary system; Albrecht Mendelssohn-Bartholdy, a re-nowned expert in international cooperation, later to become Germany's delegate to the League of Nations and the International Arbitration Tribu-nal at the Hague; and, for a brief period, the great sociologist Max Weber. With its blend of anti-democratic upheaval and democratic optimism, Mu-nich was a microcosm of German liberalism's dilemmas.[7]

Born to a German-Jewish family in Munich in 1891, Loewenstein stud-ied law and economics with these scholars in Munich and also briefly in Heidelberg, where he became one of Max Weber's young protégés.[8] After serving in the Munich office of the military's legal division during World War I (under the supervision of Wilhelm Frick, the future Nazi minister of the interior), and observing Nazi and Communist violence on the city's streets during Weimar's early years, he joined Munich's liberal circles, first as a student and then as an increasingly renowned scholar. In the fall of 1932, the University of Munich appointed him as a lecturer of international and comparative constitutional law, and the city's liberal party considered nominating him for elections to the Reichstag.[9]

Throughout the Weimar period, Loewenstein sought to provide a de-fense for the fragile republic by formulating a new liberal theory of rights and democratic protection. In his eyes, German liberals had failed to recog-nize the true political and intellectual forces that shaped democratic poli-

[7] For an overview of Munich in this period, see Heinrich Hillmayr, *Roter und weisser Terror in Bayern nach 1918* (Munich: Nusser, 1974).

[8] On Loewenstein's relationship with Max Weber, see his eulogy: "Persönliche Erinnerun-gen an Max Weber" (1920), in René König and Johannes Winckelmann (eds.), *Max Weber zum Gedächtnis* (Cologne and Opladen: WestdeutscherVerlag, 1963), 48–52.

[9] This biographical background is based on Loewenstein's unpublished memoirs, which he composed in the late 1960s. See Karl Loewenstein, "Das Lebens Überfluss: Erinnerungen eine ausgewanderten Juristen," 1–158, Folder 10, Box 3, Karl Loewenstein Papers, Amherst College Archives and Special Collections, Amherst College [hereafter referred to as KLP]; and Markus Lang, *Karl Loewenstein: Transatlantischer Denker der Politik* (Stuttgart: Franz Steiner, 2007), 88–171. Records of Loewenstein's cooperation with liberal politicians in Bavaria are in Folder 80, Box 50, KLP. Records of his classes at the University of Munich are in Folder 13, Box 1, KLP.

tics, and thus misunderstood the nature of their enemies. Determined to correct these misconceptions, he embarked on a study of the historical origins of democracy and the mechanisms it had developed across Europe and the United States. Such a study was to point the way toward a more robust intellectual foundation for German liberalism and mobilize German liberals to take action against their enemies across the political spectrum. From the beginning, then, Loewenstein's thinking about democracy was inseparable from his awareness of democracy's foes. Therefore, his study made two important contributions. First, it helped him formulate a liberal theory of democratic rights and institutions. Second, it led him to articulate why democratic states had the right—even the obligation—to take aggressive action to repress their enemies. During the 1920s and early 1930s, these ideas were not fully formed and did not gain widespread attention. But in the following decades, they came to serve as the basis for both influential theory and diplomatic action.

The immediate target of Loewenstein's Weimar-era writings was German liberal thought on the anti-democratic challenges. During the Weimar era, the vast majority of German liberals believed that the nature of democracy precluded any action to curtail anti-extremists' violence. In the eyes of Germany's leading liberal scholars and politicians, democracy was founded on political relativism, the conviction that in a secular world no political ideology was superior to any other. As a result, democracy had no right to limit any action or opinion, even those who called for its destruction. Gustav Radbruch, the legal scholar and German minister of justice, claimed that "since no political view can be proven, none can be refuted," adding that liberals were not entitled to ban or restrict opinions they disliked.[10] Hans Kelsen, central Europe's foremost liberal thinker, maintained that what differentiated democracy from autocracy was its willingness to recognize that absolute truth did not exist. The "absolutist worldview," he wrote, "translates into an autocratic stance, [while] the critical and relativist worldview [translates] into a democratic stance."[11] According to Kelsen and his students, the republic's mission was to represent the will of the people, broadly defined, and it therefore bore the "tragic fate" of allowing anti-democrats to participate in its institutions. Liberals could hope to convert citizens to democracy through education but could not coerce them. If the republic failed to gain support, its advocate could only "remain true to his flag, even when the ship is sinking."[12]

[10] Gustav Radbruch, "Parteienstaat und Volksgemeinschaft" (1929), *Gesamtausgabe* 12 (Heidelberg: Müller Verlag, 1992), 94–99, here 95.

[11] Hans Kelsen, *Vom Wesen und Wert der Demokratie* (Aelen: Scientia Verlag, 1981 [1929]), 100.

[12] Hans Kelsen, "Verteidigung der Demokratie," *Blätter der Staatspartei* 2 (1932): 90–98, quotations from 98. For an excellent analysis of Kelsen's theory during the Weimar era, see David Dyzenhaus, *Legality and Legitimacy* (Oxford: Clarendon, 1997), esp. 132–149.

Loewenstein believed that these views were misguided and dangerous. Democracy, he claimed, relied not on relativism but on a firm belief in the importance of democratic institutions. According to Loewenstein, all modern regimes had evolved through a continual struggle between two opposing democratic ideologies: "representative" democracy and "radical" democracy. Both claimed that "the people" were the ultimate source of political authority, but their proponents had developed a completely different set of political institutions and values. By explaining the difference between these two ideologies, Loewenstein sought to remind liberals of the origins of their values. He also hoped to illuminate the nature of liberalism's enemies and to explain why they must be suppressed.

Loewenstein identified "representative" democracy as the model to which all Germans should aspire. During the seventeenth century, Britain and the United States had gradually developed a new and unprecedented idea: the concept of "representation." Anglo-Saxon politicians and political thinkers argued that political leaders were bound to serve the interests and will of the "people." This challenged traditional sources of power and redistributed it among different classes and groups. By referring to the entire population of Britain (and later the American colonies) as the source of political authority, British and American thinkers limited the power of the monarch and forced the crown to share political power. Loewenstein contended that this Anglo-Saxon conception of representation fostered the evolution of governing institutions that diffused the state's power, including parliaments, local councils, and judicial reviews. These institutions counterbalanced one another to prevent the accumulation of power in a single center. Furthermore, this desire to limit power gave birth to a series of individual liberties, such as equality under the law and freedom of religion. The Anglo-Saxons, then, were the first modern people to seek the dispersal of power at the expense of unity. They embraced division, heterogeneity, and individual liberty as their foundational principles.[13]

Like many German liberals (and like Carl J. Friedrich), Loewenstein was convinced that democratic institutions flourished only under the guidance of a wise and responsible political elite. This class of highly skilled and well-educated politicians, who were deeply committed to individual liberties, would make sure that power did not become concentrated in the hands of an autocratic ruler. Like other liberal scholars, including Richard Thoma and Gerhard Anschütz, Loewenstein held a highly elitist and suspicious view of the "masses." Most citizens, he believed, were prone to primitive emotions and irresponsible demagoguery. They lacked the capacity to fully appreciate the liberties granted by the liberal state. In this top-down model,

---

[13] Karl Loewenstein, *Volk und Parlament nach der Staatstheorie der Französischen Nationalversammlung von 1789* (Munich: Drei MaskenVerlag, 1922), esp. 44–89.

representative democratic institutions were not designed to encourage the "people" to actively participate in politics but to help responsible elites preserve individual liberties and the separation of power.[14]

In this telling, the greatness of the British and American systems stemmed from their recognition that representative democracy must maintain this suspicious attitude toward the people. Both British and American elites understood that a democracy should include its citizens in the political process but must also prevent the masses' dark energies from abusing democratic liberties. The Americans, Loewenstein gleefully observed, had drafted their state and federal constitutions in secrecy, without input from their constituencies. Even when they presented these constitutions to the people for ratification, they did not permit amendments or changes. Similarly, early British parliamentarians actively sought to limit public knowledge of their debates by holding secret meetings and hiding information from journalists. These historical examples proved to Loewenstein that in the representative system, the *institutions* of democracy ultimately stood above the will of the people. The parliament, elections, and constitutions had to shape public life regardless of whether they enjoyed the people's support. German liberals such as Radbruch and Kelsen were therefore wrong to believe that democratic institutions must reflect what the people wanted. As the British and American founders of democracy recognized, these institutions defended universal liberties and had to remain vigilant against the irrationalism of ordinary citizens.[15]

Representative democracy, however, was not alone. In Loewenstein's daunting story, a parallel and independent regime evolved, one he deemed "radical" democracy. This alternative democratic vision could be traced to Jean-Jacques Rousseau and the radical revolutionaries of the French Revolution. Rousseau and his followers introduced the concept of undivided sovereignty. In this theory, political legitimacy stemmed from the community as a unified organism—the "general will." Loewenstein argued that the main mission of radical democrats was to form political organs that would integrate the entire community into the state. State institutions had to reflect the will of the masses as directly as possible and allow them full control over both domestic and diplomatic policies. In Loewenstein's narrative, the key institutions of radical democracy were direct election of the executive— for example, the popular election of the president in France's Third Republic—and referendums, which afforded citizens complete supervision over decision making. These institutions sought to channel the political energy

---

[14] On this tradition in Weimar liberal thought, see Arthur J. Jacobson and Bernhard Schlink (eds.), *Weimar: A Jurisprudence of Crisis* (Berkeley: University of California Press, 2000).

[15] Karl Loewenstein, "Zur Soziologie der parlamentarischen Repräsentation in England vor der ersten Reformbill," in Melchior Palyi (ed.), *Hauptprobleme der Soziologie: Erinnerungsgabe für Max Weber*, vol. 2 (Munich und Leipzig: Duncker & Humbolt, 1923), 85–110, esp. 105.

of the people by unifying them around one leader or a particular political decision. According to Loewenstein, this radical idea of democracy politicized the masses and made them highly involved in state affairs. Radical democracy had powered all modern revolutions in Europe and was irreversible.[16]

If radical democracy was a permanent feature of modern politics, its disturbing consequence was the rise of brutal tyrannies. In their urge to achieve unity, radical democrats suppressed domestic divisions, sacrificed all liberties, and reversed the liberal separation of powers. It made little difference how radical democrats defined the "people," whether they saw the nation, class, or race as the basic category of political identity. They all sought to create a homogeneous community, abolish the difference between elites and the people, and erase individual liberties. Both the Soviet Union's classless utopia and fascist Italy's extreme nationalism, for example, were variations of radical democracy. Loewenstein asserted that a "long and unbroken thread" led from Rousseau's vision of a collective and participatory state to Lenin's and Mussolini's oppressive regimes. Just as the French revolutionaries sought to represent all the French, the Bolsheviks sought to embody the entire working class and the Fascists hoped to reflect the unified Italian nation. In Loewenstein's narrative, Rousseau and his followers had unleashed a destructive political vision into the world. By seeking to mold entire nations and states into uniform entities, the regimes they created replaced the responsible elites of representative democracy with mass enslavement.[17]

Loewenstein argued that this universal story of the constant clash between representative and radical visions of democracy explained the evolution of modern politics. Since the American and French revolutions, all the countries that viewed "the people" as the ultimate authority labored under hybrid, contradictory regimes that locked liberal and radical ideas into a struggle for dominance. For example, many local governments in the

[16] Karl Loewenstein, *Volk und Parlament*, esp. 89–224.

[17] Ibid., esp. 3–38, here 6. While this book was completed before the Fascist revolution and thus included references only to Bolshevism, the pairing of communism and fascism was repeated in Loewenstein's writings and teachings throughout the Weimar era. See, for example, his *Minderheitsregierung in Großbritannien: Verfassungsrechtliche Untersuchungen zur neuesten Entwicklung des britischen Parlamentarismus* (Munich: Schweitzer, 1925), 2. The most elaborate comparison is in Karl Loewenstein, "Apologie des liberalen Staatsdenkens" (unpublished manuscript, 1932), Folder 3, Box 24, KLP. German conservative scholars had long attacked Rousseau's writings as dangerous. In the eyes of many German monarchists, Rousseau's obsession with the "general will" gave birth to parliamentarism, which they saw as destructive to the unity of the nation. Loewenstein, however, maintained that French radicals did not shape the parliamentary system, which instead was a product of representative democracy. On this tradition of German thought and politics, see Mark Hewitson, *National Identity and Political Thought in Germany* (Oxford: Clarendon Press, 2000), esp. chapters 2–3.

United States violated their supposedly representative ethos by allowing citizens to propose and vote on constitutional amendments. The French Third Republic, despite the authority it gave to a representative parliament, also created the powerful position of a directly elected president.[18] The Weimar Constitution had replicated this wider struggle between the uncontrollable impulses of radical democracy and the taming influence of representative traditions. It granted the parliament ultimate authority and recognized many individual liberties, but it also allowed citizens to demand direct plebiscites and created the position of a directly elected president. According to Loewenstein, this blend of representative and radical institutions demonstrated the failure of Weimar liberals to implement their full vision. It provided radicals with the tools to undermine the liberal order. Weimar's weaknesses were thus endemic to its democratic structure.[19]

For Loewenstein, this historical narrative demonstrated that the weakness of German liberals in the face of anti-democratic aggression stemmed from the intellectual confusion between these two conceptions of democracy. When politicians and thinkers such as Radbruch and Kelsen argued that democracy must represent the people's will, they were confusing the representative and radical ideologies. They forgot that liberal institutions were designed not only to defend citizens from state coercion but also to protect the liberal structure of divided government from attack by the anti-democratic masses. According to Loewenstein, the tragedy of liberal democracy was that its core institutions and principles—"the people," elections, and representative politics—held the potential for its destruction. Like liberals, radical Communists and Fascists invariably claimed that by mobilizing their supporters and contesting elections, they were acting in the spirit of democracy. This meant that the assault on liberalism was not an exceptional event that occurred only in moments of crisis. Rather, it was rooted in the democratic vocabulary itself, a danger that constantly lurked behind the façade of liberal ideas.[20]

Throughout the Weimar era, Loewenstein explored British and American models that he believed would help the German republic tame the "radical" masses. In his eyes, the British and Americans had grasped that democratic institutions transcended the sovereignty of the nation and successfully integrated the masses into politics without undermining personal liberties. One such institution, for example, was the North American "town hall meeting," in which members of Congress routinely met their constituencies and listen to their frustrations and wishes. Such forums allowed the

---

[18] Loewenstein, *Volk und Parlament*, 46–53.

[19] Karl Loewenstein, *Erscheinungsformen der Verfassungsänderung* (Tübingen: Mohr Siebeck, 1931).

[20] Ibid., esp. 191–232.

masses to vent and express anger but did not force members of Congress to impulsively enact popular desires, since they were shielded from their constituencies for the duration of their terms. Another such institution was political parties, which channeled popular energies into parliamentary debates. Rather then seeking to represent the entire nation, parties reflected the will of specific groups and interests and were thus forced to engage with one another and build coalitions. German liberals needed to emulate these models.[21]

In Loewenstein's eyes, the most inspiring model for strengthening the republic and taming the masses was the new British theory of "pluralism," which had sparked intense debates among political theorists in the early 1920s. As championed by Harold Laski, a young political scientist and a friend of Loewenstein, pluralism held that liberal democracy was best served by distributing its authority to as many centers as possible. According to the pluralists, the state's willingness to share power with local organizations, such as churches, associations, and labor unions, assured the security of individual liberties.[22] Loewenstein maintained that such a diffusion of power would allow responsible elites to emerge in Germany. By including the leaders of clubs, towns, and unions in decision making and encouraging them to serve the public good, the republic could train leaders who would defend individual liberties while also taming the masses. In this process, Germans would slowly learn to view the state not as the political realization of a mystical and "organic" nation. Instead, they would recognize the values of individual liberties and representative institutions. From the beginning, then, Loewenstein's thought was filled with a glaring tension. While celebrating representative institutions, his theory rooted their legitimacy in subverting and restraining popular will.[23]

As he confronted Germany's growing political crisis in the early 1930s, Loewenstein began to move in a more extreme direction. Following the calamity of the Great Depression, the Nazi party experienced meteoric growth in the 1930 elections; it skyrocketed from 12 to 107 delegates in the Reichstag and became the country's second largest party. The Communist

[21] Karl Loewenstein, *Minderheitsregierung in Großbritannien*; see also his "Verfassungsleben in Großbritannien," *Jahrbuch des öffentlichen Rechts* 10 (1932): 195–319. As part of the effort to "import" British ideas to Britain, Loewenstein also translated James Bryce's monumental three-volume study of liberal democracy from 1921, *Modern Democracies*. It was published as *Moderne Demokratien* (Munich: Drei Masken, 1924–1926).

[22] Harold Laski, *The Foundations of Sovereignty, and Other Essays* (New York, Harcourt, Brace, 1921). The correspondence between Laski and Loewenstein, which shows much mutual respect and exchange of ideas, began in 1924 and continued into the 1930s. It is located in Folder 8, Box 51, KLP.

[23] Karl Loewenstein, "Das Problem des Föderalismus in Großbritannien," *Annalen des deutschen Reichs* 55 (1922): 1–95; Loewenstein, "Zur Soziologie der parlamentarischen Repräsentation in England."

Party, the liberal republic's other mortal opponent, also gained power. Meanwhile, Loewenstein's DDP was obliterated. Over the next three years, the Reichstag became a site of brazen anti-democratic action; the extreme right and left prevented the creation of any coalitions, forcing cabinets to rule by emergency decrees. The foundational institutions and organizations of German liberalism appeared to be doomed.[24]

In response to these desperate political times, Loewenstein produced a series of bellicose writings and speeches. He sought to save German liberalism by asserting that representative democracy had both the right and obligation to crush the representatives of radical ideologies. The time had come, he boldly proclaimed, for representative democracy to confront the Fascists and Communists undermining the liberal state. In order to secure the parliamentary system, the German republic had to deny radicals the liberties it granted to all citizens. In October 1931, for example, the association of German legal scholars met in Halle to discuss the constitutional crisis and consider potential remedies for Weimar's political paralysis. Many of the era's leading legal scholars, such as Georg Jellinek, Richard Thoma, and Ernst Jacobi, attended the meeting. In the heated debate that followed, Loewenstein claimed that the republic "had an obligation of self-preservation." Despite their massive popularity and support, parties whose programs and actions repudiated the Reichstag must be denied the right to operate within it. The Nazis and the Communists should therefore be banned from running for office, prevented from distributing political propaganda, and perhaps even denied the right of free speech. The republic should likewise consider allowing only parties with democratically elected leaders to run for parliament and even ban state workers from holding memberships in radical parties. Facing off with Radbruch and Kelsen, Loewenstein argued that democratic institutions did not represent relativism but empirically valid and superior liberties. Moreover, these liberties did not exist independently of the representative state: they were part of the unique bond that liberal regimes forged with their citizens. Liberals were thus entitled to use state institutions to "strike back" at their inferior and violent enemies.[25]

In the rapidly shrinking world of German liberalism, such ideas offered a bold adaptation of the liberal creed. While the vast majority of his intellectual milieu continued to believe that liberties and individual rights were

---

[24] For an excellent overview of the parliamentary crisis, see Richard Evans, *The Coming of the Third Reich* (New York: Penguin, 2005), 247–288. On liberals' failed attempts to respond to this crisis by seeking new political coalitions, see Frye, *Liberal Democrats in the Weimar Republic*, 178–194.

[25] Loewenstein, "Diskussionsbeitrag," in *Veröffentlichungen der Vereinigung der Deutschen Staatsrechtslehrer* (Berlin and Leipzig: Walter de Gruyter, 1932), 192–194, here 193. See also Hans-Jürgen Papier and Wolfgang Durner, "Streitbare Demokratie," *Archiv des öffentlichen Rechts* 128 (2003): 340–371.

universal, Loewenstein framed them as part of the liberal state's struggle against its radical enemies. By projecting his own visions of democracy on Great Britain and the United States, Loewenstein framed the Western powers as the natural associates of German liberals. Decades before the Cold War and the Western alliance, he called on German liberals to look to the West in order to strengthen their own democratic institutions. During the Weimar period, these ideas gained little traction. While his prestige grew as a scholar, the republic's supporters in the Reichstag ignored his calls and made no attempt to utilize legal or political mechanisms to halt the rise of extremist parties. Within a few years, however, these theories would elicit a surprising response across the Atlantic. From Washington, D.C., Loewenstein would help guide a bold and brutal diplomatic initiative across the Western hemisphere.

"Militant Democracy" and U.S. Diplomacy in Latin America

As was the case for pro-democratic Protestants, Socialists, and Catholics, the rise of the Third Reich spelled the violent end of German liberals' political and intellectual activity. The Nazis had long disdained liberalism's belief in political rights, individualism, and the division of power. As the Nazi leader Dietrich Klagges blatantly declared, "liberals' vision of a brotherhood of man" led to "the corrosive influence of the Jewish people" in Germany and the "pollution" of the Aryan race.[26] The new regime quickly began harassing the weak and beaten liberal party, which meekly dissolved itself in June 1933. The Nazis then swiftly shut down or took over the intellectual circles, publishing houses, and universities that had fostered liberal culture. One after another, the luminaries of German liberal thought, such as Albrecht Mendelssohn-Bartholdy, Hans Kelsen, and Gerhard Anschütz, retreated from public life or went into exile. Among those purged by the new authorities were the University of Munich's liberal intellectuals, including Loewenstein, who were fired either for their political affiliations or because of their Jewish background. By 1934, little remained of the once vital political and intellectual movement that had helped shape Germany.[27]

But Loewenstein's quest for liberal reform did not die with the republic it sought to save. After fleeing to the United States in 1933, he quickly re-

---

[26] Dietrich Klagges, "Volk und Führer," in Anson Rabinbach and Sander L. Gilman (eds.), *The Third Reich Sourcebook* (Berkeley: University of California Press, 2013), 249.

[27] For the Nazi assault on liberalism, and the few liberals who sought to preserve liberal thought through secret meetings and reading groups during the Third Reich, see Eric Kurlander, *Living with Hitler: Liberal Democrats in the Third Reich* (New Haven: Yale University Press, 2009). On the Nazification of the University of Munich, see Elisabeth Kraus (ed.), *Die Universität München im dritten Reich* (Munich: Herbert Utz, 2006).

sumed his campaign to combat the radical enemies of representative regimes. This time, Loewenstein's ideological mission attracted the broader attention that he had failed to find in Germany. The publication of his writings in English coincided with a growing panic among American politicians that anti-democratic agents, especially Communists, were infiltrating the democratic system. His claim that a responsible elite could suspend the rights of extremists without harming democracy resonated with these anti-Communist activists and made Loewenstein a visible public intellectual. With the start of World War II, U.S. diplomats embraced these rigid visions and recruited him to help forge Washington's bold new diplomacy of mutual security in Latin America. As part of the war effort, Loewenstein and his American colleagues suspended the rights and ruined the lives of thousands they deemed "subversive" across the Western hemisphere. This violent campaign was the beginning of cooperation between the German liberal émigré and the U.S. military. After shaping policies in Latin America, its democratic zeal and obsessive fear of subversion would also set the intellectual and political contours of postwar Germany's reconstruction.

The Birth of "Militant Democracy" Theory

Loewenstein's mission to transform liberal democracy into an assertive and even aggressive regime began almost immediately after he fled to the United States. In 1934, with the help of Harold Laski and Harvard legal scholar (and future Supreme Court justice) Felix Frankfurter, Loewenstein secured teaching positions in law and politics, first at Yale and then at Amherst College.[28] In 1935 he resumed his analysis of political extremism and democratic liberties. Expanding on his earlier theory, Loewenstein called for all representative democracies to radically limit the liberties they provided and to crack down on their domestic enemies. He further called on the United States to abandon its respect for national sovereignty and to begin aggressive interventions against "radical" regimes abroad. Like Friedrich and Fraenkel, Loewenstein had little doubt that his conception of rights and their limits was self-evidently universal. Americans faced the same dangers as Weimar's liberals, and they had to embrace the measures that German democrats failed to adopt.[29]

If the crux of Loewenstein's theory remained largely unchanged, its ambitions grew exponentially. He exported his narrative of a Manichean ideo-

[28] Letter, Laski to Loewenstein (1 May 1933), Folder 8, Box 51, KLP; Letter, Felix Frankfurter to Karl Loewenstein (22 June 1935), Folder 85, Box 50, KLP. See also Lang, *Karl Loewenstein*, 172–191.

[29] The term appeared first in Karl Loewenstein, "Autocracy versus Democracy in Contemporary Europe," *American Political Science Review* 29:4 (August 1935): 571–593, and 29:5 (October 1935): 755–784.

logical struggle from the domestic sphere to the global arena. According to Loewenstein, the world was rapidly separating into two camps. On one side stood the liberal democracies, and on the other stood their mortal enemies, which Loewenstein now called "totalitarian," adopting language developed by émigrés such as Gurian."[30] In this narrative, the rise of Fascist Italy and Nazi Germany had accelerated radical endeavors to achieve a world revolution against representative democracy. A "Fascist International of the multi-colored shirts" was bringing together the world's revolutionaries, "transcending national borders and cutting deeply across historical diversities of traditionally disjointed nationalisms." This movement already encompassed Italy, Germany, Turkey, and Spain and was well on its way to consuming Austria, Bulgaria, Greece, Portugal, Romania, Hungary, and the rest of central and Eastern Europe. This international conspiracy sought to bring down all democratic regimes. The agents of totalitarianism were feverishly working to erect outposts in Britain, Holland, and the United States, preparing the ground for universal revolution.[31]

But totalitarianism was far more than a foreign threat. Like Friedrich, Fraenkel, and Gurian, Loewenstein asserted that the fundamental foe lay within the structures of liberal democracy itself; these radical revolutionaries exploited the freedoms that democracies offered all their citizens. The success of their revolution had been possible because of their "perfect adjustment to democracy." Unlike Fraenkel, however, who claimed that democracy was threatened by economic inequality and obsession with individual rights, or Friedrich's and Gurian's belief that democracy was damaged by secularization, Loewenstein argued that democracy's weakness stemmed from the freedoms it provided its enemies. Because liberal regimes adhere to the principle of universal liberties, the machine of radical subversion could be set in motion easily and legally. Just as in Weimar, "democratic fundamentalism and legalistic blindness were unwilling to realize that the mechanism of democracy is the Trojan horse by which the enemy enters the city."[32] This emphasis on internal threat—surprising when placed against the looming storm of World War II—would perpetuate an obsession with domestic subversion long into the Cold War.

All democratic regimes, including the United States, therefore had to recognize and respond to this existential threat. They had to "become mili-

---

[30] Karl Loewenstein, "Militant Democracy and Fundamental Rights I," *American Political Science Review* 31:3 (June 1937): 417–432, here 418. It is difficult to determine whether Loewenstein borrowed the term directly from Waldemar Gurian's writings, with which he was familiar (as evident from their correspondence), or from other sources.

[31] Ibid., 417–419.

[32] Ibid., 423–424. See also Karl Loewenstein, "Law in the Third Reich," *Yale Law Journal* 45:5 (March 1936): 779–815; "Dictatorship and the German Constitution," *Chicago Law Review* 4:4 (June 1937): 537–574.

tant" by radically and simultaneously transforming their domestic institutions and their international policy.[33] Domestically, liberal regimes should
suspend the constitutional rights of anti-democratic forces. The state should
preemptively deny basic freedoms to those who threaten democracy, before
they even take action. Although Loewenstein recognized that the Nazis utilized similar measures, he did not express concern about the potential
abuses of such actions against political minorities. In language that echoed
Friedrich, he asserted that democratic institutions depended on the guidance of capable elites, who held the vision and courage to remain committed to democratic rights even if they exercised the authority to suspend the
rights of their enemies.[34]

As a blueprint for these elites, Loewenstein provided a detailed list of
actions that liberal regimes had to adopt in order to become "militant." This
included curbing free speech and stifling anti-democratic movements by
censoring or shutting down all newspapers and radio stations that called
for an overthrow of the democratic regime. Furthermore, liberal regimes
had to restrict freedom of association and the movements of anti-democratic
sympathizers and deny their leaders parliamentary immunity. Officials
must disband all militias that challenged the democratic state's monopoly
on violence and outlaw paramilitary symbols and memorabilia. They
should likewise ban Fascists and Communists from holding positions in
public service, education, and law enforcement. Loewenstein called for the
establishment of a political police force "for the discovery, repression, supervision, and control" of anti-democratic activities and movements. "Fire," he
concluded in a phrase that would be quoted countless time in postwar Europe, "should be fought with fire."[35]

The ideas that failed to move German liberals in Weimar resonated
widely in the United States during the late 1930s. A key pretext to this popularity was the growing militancy of American labor. In 1936, in parallel with
similar actions in Europe, American Communists joined hands with Socialists and other labor activists in a "Popular Front," organizing massive
strikes in factories and at docks across the United States. In response, a
broad coalition formed between conservative activists, businessmen, and
politicians who were deeply concerned with the specter of Communist in-

[33] Loewenstein, "Militant Democracy and Fundamental Rights I," 423.

[34] It is unclear when Friedrich and Loewenstein began reading each other's works and
when they met for the first time. The earliest available correspondence between them, which
begins in 1935, reveals substantial mutual interest in each other's work. It is located in Folder
86, Box 50, KLP.

[35] Karl Loewenstein, "Militant Democracy and Fundamental Rights II," *American Political
Science Review* 31:4 (November 1937): 649–655, quotations from 655 and 643. See also "Legisla-
tive Control of Political Extremism in European Democracies," *Columbia Law Review* 38:4
(April 1938): 591–622, and 38:5 (May 1938): 725–774.

filtration and eager to discredit Franklin D. Roosevelt and the New Deal. Anti-Communist intellectuals and politicians vocally called for the government to vigilantly curtail Communist actions. In 1938 Martin Dies Jr., a Congressman from Texas, opened a highly public investigation against the alleged disloyalty and subversive activities of American Communists. The committee he chaired, which later became known as the House Un-American Activities Committee, launched attacks against labor activists and New Deal agencies such as the National Relations Board. In 1939 these fears of Communist subversion inspired federal laws such as the Hatch Act (named after Senator Carl Hatch of New Mexico), which banned members of "any political organization which advocates the overthrow of our constitutional form of government" from holding positions in the federal government. Members of the Communist Party were thus prohibited from federal positions. In 1940 the anti-Communist coalition won an even larger victory, when Congress required members of anti-democratic organizations to be imprisoned. The Smith Act (named after Virginia representative Howard Smith) unleashed a series of investigations and prosecution against militant labor activists in Detroit, Minneapolis, and other industrial centers. These acts marked the beginning of a new political approach to communism in the United States; indeed, the Smith Act would be used to prosecute the Communist Party after the war.[36]

In this atmosphere of expanding hysteria about domestic subversion, Loewenstein found a growing audience. For those anti-labor activists who sought to repress a perceived Communist threat, his ideas explained why the curbing of rights did not threaten but instead strengthened democratic institutions. As he asserted in a 1938 public lecture to legal scholars in Chicago, totalitarian agents operated in pro-Nazi clubs and through "Popular Front" labor unions, both of which equally threatened liberal democracy. From 1938 on, Loewenstein was a popular speaker across the United States. Businessmen and legal scholars invited him to Chicago, New Haven, New York, Saint Paul, and New Orleans to explain why the federal government had to ban "radicals" from participating in politics and from holding public positions. Largely ignored in Weimar, militant democracy gave voice to a momentous movement in U.S. politics.[37]

Militant democracy, however, could not be secured only through domestic repression. Of equal importance, yet almost universally ignored by his-

---

[36] Ellen Schrecker, *Many Are the Crimes: McCarthyism in America* (Boston: Little, Brown, 1998), 42–117; Landon R. Y. Storrs, *The Second Red Scare and the Unmaking of the New Deal Left* (Princeton: Princeton University Press, 2013).

[37] Lecture tours 1938, 1939, and 1940, Folder 12, Box 32; Lecture, "Civil Liberties and National Defense" (25 October 1940 and again on 28 January 1941), Folder 24, Box 58, both in KLP.

torians, Loewenstein called for a revolution in international affairs. According to Loewenstein, democratic states could not hope to confront the totalitarian revolution alone. They had to join forces to build a new "Democratic International" that would serve as a counterweight to the Communist and Fascist bodies. Loewenstein envisaged a permanent democratic federation that would provide its members with legal defense, democratic knowledge, and anti-totalitarian legislation. Its members would draft laws and advise governments on effective methods to defeat subversive agents. In a world of militant democracy, governments would forego state sovereignty and domestic autonomy, to be replaced by a mechanism of permanent mutual intervention. This would allow democracies to support and enhance one another's ability to overcome their global enemies. Just as democratic institutions were more important than the people's will, national sovereignty likewise had to be subordinated in the interest of preserving democracy.

As Loewenstein recognized, this vision had far-reaching implications for world politics. In articulating his ideas in a series of lectures at the Chicago School of Law, Loewenstein both drew from and expanded on Immanuel Kant's famous 1785 essay on war and peace. According to Kant, peace could only endure in a world of representative republics. When ordinary people, who are naturally inclined toward peace and stability, have a say in political decisions, they will avoid the upheaval and bloodshed of war. Loewenstein agreed that the state's domestic structures informed its behavior in the international sphere. Yet this was not an argument for state sovereignty but for democratic intervention instead. It was legitimate for representative regimes to intervene in other political regimes if such an action promoted peace. Since totalitarian regimes were inherently aggressive and threatened democracy, liberal regimes were entitled and even obliged to preemptively destroy them. Looking at recent history, Loewenstein maintained that the League of Nations had been unsuccessful in bringing about world peace because of its willingness to accept both liberal and totalitarian regimes into its ranks. Although Kant had never called on republicans to impose their regimes on other countries, Loewenstein argued that in the twentieth century such action was a matter of democratic survival. The "Democratic International" should coordinate international interventions and preemptive strikes against totalitarian states and transform them into representative democracies. As Loewenstein bluntly claimed, unless the citizens of totalitarian regimes "rise in a rebellion themselves, we have to impose constitutional order on their country."[38] Just as in the domestic sphere, the followers

---

[38] Lecture, "Reconstruction of Europe after the War," given six times to government officials and universities during January and February 1940, Folder 24, Box 58, KLP. See also Loewenstein, "Militant Democracy and Fundamental Rights II," 658.

of totalitarianism worldwide should enjoy no right to security and autonomy in the family of nations.[39]

Accordingly, Lowenstein called for the United States to intervene in Japan, the Soviet Union, Italy, and Germany. Throughout the late 1930s, as Nazi Germany and imperial Japan aggressively expanded their borders and their international influence, Loewenstein appealed to the United States to end its diplomatic disengagement with Asia and Europe and forge a Democratic International. Since the United States had always served as the lightning rod for representative democracy, he believed it was the most suitable power to lead an international democratic revolution. Traveling across the United States, Loewenstein lectured and distributed pamphlets to promote his ideas. "Germany, Italy, Japan, and Russia," he wrote in characteristic hyperbole, "cannot tolerate the existence of a free and democratic country like the United States in an otherwise totalitarian world. Survival of any *one* free and democratic nation would hold out a promise to the subjugated peoples to rise and shake off their chains, and this would constitute a permanent menace to totalitarian dictatorships."[40]

Before the Japanese attack on Pearl Harbor, this rhetoric had little practical impact. While many anti-Communists heartily embraced his domestic agenda, few supported the need to undertake foreign intervention. But once the United States entered the war, Loewenstein's ideas propelled him into the centers of American power. From positions in the Department of Justice and the State Department, he helped shape an entire set of new foreign policies that made militant democracy a reality.

"Militant Democracy" in Latin America

While Loewenstein had developed the concept of militant democracy with Europe in mind, it first became a guiding principle for diplomatic action in Latin America. After the United States entered World War II in December 1941, Loewenstein joined an ambitious, violent, and unprecedented diplomatic operation that unfolded across the Western Hemisphere. Initiated by U.S. diplomats and legal scholars, twenty-one countries in North, Central, and South America joined together to intern and deport thousands of Latin Americans, many of whom were incarcerated in the United States. At the same time that the United States notoriously arrested and interned countless Japanese American residents and citizens on the West Coast, it led an equally shameful internment campaign among its southern neighbors. In

[39] Lecture, "Militant Democracy and Fundamental Rights in Europe," Chicago Law School (30 December 1936), and "Address to the Peace Meeting" (22 April 1937), both in Folder 4, Box 57, KLP.

[40] Karl Loewenstein and Lawrence Packard, *America's Eleventh Hour* (Easthampton, MA: Easthampton News Company, 1940), 4.

the eyes of U.S. diplomats and lawyers who worked in this campaign, these measures were not hysterical but a proper, necessary, and thoughtful democratic response to its enemies' subversion. Through wartime institutions of power, Loewenstein's ideas helped inflict wide-scale misery.

This campaign was part of a broader reconfiguration of U.S. policy toward Central and South America. In the early 1930s, the U.S. government had avowed to end decades of military and political intervention in Latin America, inaugurating what Roosevelt called "The Good Neighbor" policy of disengagement.[41] In 1936, however, Washington's view of its southern neighbors again shifted sharply. As the president and his administration began to perceive Germany, Italy, and Japan's aggressive expansion as a threat, they came to regard Latin America as a crucial battleground in an imminent global conflict. They were convinced that German Nazis and Japanese imperialists were feverishly working to infiltrate Latin America, with the ultimate goal of invading the United States from the south. Viewed through this lens of growing anxiety, flourishing communities of Japanese and German immigrants in Peru, Brazil, Argentina, and other countries formed the vanguard in a plot to take over the entire hemisphere. The president repeatedly fueled these fears during the late 1930s and early 1940s, proclaiming that Axis agents had already built "bridgeheads in the New World." In a September 1941 radio speech Roosevelt warned that Axis agents had established an extensive web of secret military bases and militias and were preparing to annex Latin America to their global empires. So intense were fears of foreign subversion that in May 1940 FDR considered dispatching a hundred thousand U.S. troops to Brazil in a preemptive strike against what many believed was an imminent Nazi assault on Rio de Janeiro.[42]

This expansive view of U.S. security, which equated subversion in foreign countries with threats to the United States itself, drove U.S. policymakers to establish a comprehensive hemispheric alliance. Fearing that Latin American governments were too weak to suppress infiltration, they sought to mobilize the populations of Mexico, Venezuela, and the rest of Latin America behind U.S. leadership. In a burst of activity, State Department officials initiated academic exchange programs (the first such government-funded endeavors in American history), propaganda campaigns, and economic co-

---

[41] Historians have debated whether the policy of nonintervention was inaugurated by FDR or by his Republican predecessors. For an overview, see Fredrick B. Pike, *FDR's Good Neighbor Policy* (Austin: University of Texas Press, 1995); Irwin F. Gellman, *Good Neighbor Diplomacy* (Baltimore: Johns Hopkins University Press, 1979).

[42] On FDR's growing fears regarding Axis infiltration in Latin America, see Frank Nies, *A Hemisphere to Itself: A History of US-Latin American Relations* (London: Zed, 1990), 123–127. The quote and the information pertaining to the plan to occupy Brazil are from Paul Friedman, *Nazis and Good Neighbors: The United States Campaign against the Germans in Latin America in World War II* (New York: Cambridge University Press, 2003), 1.

operation among what they termed "the American Republics." These measures sought to convince the people of Latin America both of American benevolence and of the dangers posed by Axis activity. After entering World War II, the U.S. government dramatically expanded these efforts, especially as the majority of Latin American countries broke off ties with the Axis powers. Latin America thus became a site where U.S. diplomats experimented with new forms of diplomatic outreach, working to establish an international alliance against foreign aggression and local subversion. As would frequently be the case throughout the twentieth century, the United States' southern neighbors became the "workshop" for novel U.S. foreign policies.[43]

Within this broad effort, the leading initiative was the Emergency Advisory Committee for Political Defense (CPD), in which Loewenstein played a significant role. Created in January 1942 by the foreign ministers of all twenty-one American countries, from Canada in the north to Chile and Argentina in the south, the CPD was responsible for coordinating domestic measures against potential Axis enemies. Based in Montevideo and led by Uruguay's vice president, Alberto Guani, this team of diplomats sought to devise new political, diplomatic, and legal modes of operation. As the U.S. participants stated, its goal was to quash "acts of aggression of non-military character" such as espionage, sabotage, and anti-war propaganda. Moreover, the committee planned to lead an international public campaign against "doctrines tending to place in jeopardy the common inter-American democratic ideal or to threaten the security and neutrality of the American Republics."[44] Through frequent visits by committee delegations, the CPD would supervise each member's success and failure in implementing its recommendations. According to Carl B. Spaeth, the United States' chief delegate to the committee, this legal and political cooperation was "the most radical departure from past experience and tradition" of U.S. diplomacy.[45]

In the eyes of U.S. diplomats, Loewenstein's writings on democratic self-defense made him the ideal candidate to join the CPD. As one diplomat wrote to him, "[y]our knowledge of democratic response in times of crisis" and "your personal encounters" with its enemies in Germany were "invalu-

---

[43] Justin Hart, *Empire of Ideas: The Origins of Public Diplomacy and the Transformation of U.S. Foreign Policy* (New York: Oxford University Press, 2013), 15–40; Nies, *A Hemisphere to Itself*, 117–130; Emily Rosenberg, *Financial Missionaries to the World* (Durham: Duke University Press, 2003). On the role of Latin America as a "workshop" in the shaping of U.S. diplomacy and military operations in the twentieth century, see Greg Grandin, *Empire's Workshop* (New York: Metropolitan, 2006).

[44] List of tentative projects to be submitted by or supported by the U.S. Delegation, Box 1, Entry 291 [Resolutions of the CPD], RG 60 [General Records of the Department of Justice], National Archive II, College Park, Maryland [hereafter referred to as NARA].

[45] Carl B. Spaeth and William Sanders, "The Emergency Advisory Committee for Political Defense," *American Journal of International Law* 38:2 (April 1944): 281–241, here 219.

able" to the CPD's mission.[46] Moreover, Loewenstein had been a vocal proponent of U.S. action in Latin America well before Pearl Harbor. Like many diplomats in the FDR administration, he believed that it was a crucial front in the global struggle between totalitarianism and democracy and therefore a prime site for militant democracy. "The military machine of the Nazis," he wrote in a 1940 pamphlet, was plotting to take over "our vital Panama Canal and the very borders of this nation." Spaeth thus invited Loewenstein to join the Department of Justice shortly after the CPD's creation as "special assistant to the attorney general" on Latin American affairs. From this position, Loewenstein would coordinate research, draft legal measures against subversion, and provide U.S. diplomats with enforcement ideas to offer to their southern neighbors.[47]

The workings of the CPD, including Loewenstein's activities, were militant democracy incarnate. For two and a half years, Loewenstein utilized this new opportunity to implement his ideas. With fierce determination, he led the committee's Washington office and frequently joined diplomatic meetings in Montevideo. Working with a team of legal scholars, Justice Department officials, and State Department representatives, he prepared a stream of studies and draft resolutions and forcefully promoted them among the CPD's other members. Projects out of Loewenstein's office included a study of "totalitarian propaganda" in Latin America, which led Mexican and Brazilian officials to shut down radio stations and newspapers they perceived subversive.[48] It drafted laws that required the registration and surveillance of those deemed suspicious by the FBI and required them to report to local authorities prior to embarking on any trip. These measures were subsequently introduced as emergency decrees in several Latin American countries. The committee furthermore helped local governments identify small businesses that conducted trade with Germany, Italy, and Japan in order to ban them from all economic activity. The prime targets of these measures were generally immigrants and Latin American citizens of Japanese, Italian, and German descent, whom government officials viewed as inherently dangerous. They were preemptively put under surveillance for the duration of the war.[49]

---

[46] Letter, Laurence A. Knapp to Loewenstein (undated, 1942), Folder 22, Box 43, KLP.

[47] Loewenstein and Packard, *America's Eleventh Hour* (Easthampton, MA: Easthampton News, 1940), 7.

[48] Memo on totalitarian propaganda, Folder Resolution 5, Box 3, Entry 291, RG 60, NARA. The list of members of the CPD Washington office is in Department of Justice office diary, Folder 2, Box 43, KLP.

[49] This description is based on the reports submitted by CPD officials on their visits to individual countries throughout 1943 and 1944, which are located in Boxes 3 and 4, Entry 289 [Subject File of Miguel A. De Capriles], RG 60, NARA, as well as on testimony of Donald Perry,

Loewenstein also coordinated the political suppression of a variety of political groups operating in South and Central America. In a series of studies he composed for the CPD on Chile, Brazil, and Argentina, Loewenstein congratulated these governments for banning "totalitarian and anti-democratic organizations."[50] In Chile, for example, the authorities prohibited extreme nationalists and Communists from contesting elections in 1937. In Brazil, the government banned all foreigners from staging rallies, forming associations, or engaging in political propaganda in 1938. It also compelled all foreigners to regularly report to the police, which facilitated more effective supervision of potential Nazis and Communists. Loewenstein argued that these models had proved successful in crushing extreme anti-liberal subversion and should be replicated among all twenty-one members of the CPD. Upon receiving Loewenstein's reports, Carl Spaeth and other U.S. diplomats constantly urged other member states to emulate these measures, in some cases by reproducing another country's laws word for word. To Loewenstein's frustration, the United States did not itself follow this advice nor subject its own sovereignty to the supervision of its neighbors, but by 1944 the majority of Latin American countries had agreed to ban or restrict the operations of both potentially subversive individuals and entire political organizations. This was militant democracy in action.[51]

The CPD's most revolutionary operation, however, was the mass internment and deportation of civilian populations. In embarking on this effort, the CPD both replicated and expanded U.S. domestic measures. In February 1942 Roosevelt signed the notorious Executive Order 9066, ordering the evacuation and arrest of tens of thousands of Japanese Americans. A few weeks later, U.S. delegates to the CPD moved to coordinate the detention of thousands of Axis nationals living across Latin America.[52] Under the CPD's

---

Official Report of First Technical Session (29 July 1943), Box 1, Entry 286 [Reports on Sessions of Consultative Visits], RG 60, NARA; and on Remarks of Laurence Knapp, Liaison Officer to the US (27 July 1943), Box 1, Entry 286, RG 60, NARA.

[50] Karl Loewenstein, Report, Comparison of Latin American and U.S. Legislation for Control of Subversive Activities, Folder 67, Box 43, KLP.

[51] Karl Loewenstein, Report on Chile (May 1943), Folder Country Studies, Box 3; Report on Brazil (January 1943), Folder Country Studies, Box 4, both in Entry 289, RG 60, NARA. Further reports on Uruguay, Paraguay, Colombia, Ecuador, Bolivia, Peru, Mexico, and Cuba are held in Folders 78–92, Box 43, KLP. Many of these research projects were published during the war. See, for example, his "Legislation against Subversive Activities in Argentina," *Harvard Law Review* 56:8 (July 1943): 1261–1306; "Legislation in the Defense of the State in Chile," *Columbia Law Review* 44:3 (May 1944): 366–407; *Brazil under Vargas* (New York: Macmillan, 1942), esp. 133–234. The inclusion of Loewenstein's advice can be found in Alberto Guani, Annual Report 1944, Folder Annual Report July 1944, Box 1, Entry 289, RG 60, NARA.

[52] Given the intense scrutiny of the internment of Japanese Americans, it is striking how little attention scholars paid to this policy's expansion into a hemispheric internment campaign. The best work on the internment of Japanese Americans, and the long history of racial

guidance, police officials raided communities in Cuba, Paraguay, Chile, Brazil, and twelve other Latin American countries. They detained thousands of individuals whom government officials suspected of anti-war sentiments and then deported them to Asia or Europe. Throughout the war, CPD agents traveled across the region to assist Latin American officials with these arrests. Using research conducted by local U.S. embassies and by Loewenstein in Washington, the CPD compiled lists of "potentially dangerous" individuals and often participated in their interrogations. Beginning in 1943, the U.S. government also provided funding to recruit additional policemen and to transport the prisoners to camps. In several countries, such as Cuba, FBI agents even joined local policemen in conducting arrests and guarding detainee camps. No project sparked as much hemispheric cooperation as this large-scale internment.[53]

Unlike the better-known internment of Japanese Americans, the CPD-led international campaign was not based solely on race. Following the guidelines laid down by Loewenstein and the Washington office, the members of the CPD believed that the rights of all individuals and communities with ties to enemy countries should be preemptively suspended. Therefore, alongside individuals of Japanese origin, government officials also targeted Germans and Italians. In some cases, overly eager officials also arrested nationals from European Axis allies, such as Hungary, Romania, and Bulgaria, as well as individuals with no ties to émigré communities whatsoever. American diplomats were aware that not all these detainees could be classified as a risk to the security of the Western Hemisphere, even within Loewenstein's hysterical framework, and that the officials in charge of the arrests were often motivated by racism, greed, or prejudice. In both their correspondence and conversations, they routinely noted that officials in Peru were eager to get rid of hated Japanese neighbors, or that Costa Rican policemen arrested German immigrants whose property they hoped to confiscate. In fact, among the "dangerous aliens" arrested were German-Jewish refugees who had recently fled the Third Reich.[54] But in their eagerness to

---

discrimination that preceded it, is Greg Robinson, *The Tragedy of Democracy: Japanese Confinement in North America* (New York: Columbia University Press, 2009).

[53] Statement of Albert E. Clattenburg (State Department) on "Cooperation with Other American Republics on Detention Expulsion, and Repatriation of Dangerous Aliens" (30 July 1943), Box 1, Entry 286, RG 60, NARA; Statement of Edward Ennis, Alien Enemy Control Unit (30 July 1943), Box 1, Entry 286, RG 60, NARA.

[54] Statement of Nicholas Collear (Immigration and Naturalization Services); Official Report of the Second Technical Meeting (30 July 1943); both in Box 1, Entry 286, RG 60, NARA. On discrimination against Japanese in Peru, see C. Harvey Gardiner, *Pawns in a Triangle of Hate: The Peruvian Japanese and the United States* (Seattle: University of Washington Press, 1981); on the persecution of Germans, including German-Jewish refugees, see Max Paul Friedman, *Nazis and Good Neighbors: The United States Campaign against the Germans in Latin America in World War II* (New York: Cambridge University Press, 2003), esp. 102–166.

4.1. Karl Loewenstein wearing a U.S. military uniform. Loewenstein's vision of "militant democracy" helped justify a brutal campaign of incarceration and deportation across the Western Hemisphere during World War II. Amherst College Archives and Special Collections.

preempt infiltration, American policymakers were unmoved by this destruction. They accepted these problems as "collateral damage" and constantly sought to expand and enlarge the number of preemptive arrests. As Edward Ennis, director of the Alien Enemy Control Unit at the Department of Justice, dryly commented in July 1943, the arrests by Central and South American republics were "simply not enough and we should encourage more."[55]

Ultimately, U.S. diplomats' eagerness to broaden the scope of political suppression and arrests gave birth to an ambitious program of mutual defense: the erection of a hemispheric network of concentration camps (or as the officials' sterile language called them, both at home and abroad, internment camps). In their meetings, CPD officials maintained that the "democratic ideals" of the American republics (which they never outlined in detail) would be better secured if the interned individuals and their families were not kept in their countries but rather transferred abroad. As Loewenstein asserted, this would greatly reduce their chances of escape and interaction with other subversives. Since the United States had the most extensive experience with large-scale imprisonment, Loewenstein suggested that it

[55] Letter, Edward Ennis to James Kelley, Chief of Special Division in the State Department, and Mr. Duggan (State Department on Latin America) (4 September 1943), Folder CPD Alien Enemy Control Unit, Box 1, Entry 289, RG 60, NARA. The information on working with local police agents is from Memorandum on the Political Defense Situation in Cuba, Folder Cuba Follow-up Memoranda (24 April 1944), Box 4, Entry 288 [Reports on Visits], RG 60, NARA.

share its models for internment camps, which Latin American countries could then emulate. In July 1943 Nicholas Collaer, chief of the Detention and Deportation Office at the Department of Justice, embraced this idea, and showed the plans to the ambassadors of Brazil and Mexico, with the goal of reproducing them in South America "on a hemisphere basis." Both diplomats were enthusiastic about the idea and wrote to their governments suggesting the creation of a network of camps.[56] By the end of the summer, the CPD was recommending a specific plan involving the creation of several dozen camps across Latin America that would house "dangerous aliens," including those from the United States. This plan received approval at the highest echelons of the FDR administration, with U.S. Attorney General Francis Biddle asserting that it was "an excellent idea." In a letter to the secretary of state, he explained that "the resolution of the Committee for Political Defense in this respect is correct and should be effectuated," and would enhance democracy's resilience.[57]

While several Latin American governments objected to the CPD's hemispheric plan, this did not seem to be due to the violence and oppression it entailed. Largely unmoved by such concerns, diplomats from Honduras and Venezuela instead offered more complaints about the cost of shipping and feeding the detainees. Despite these concerns, Loewenstein and other members of the Washington office succeeded in convincing the United States to adopt its core recommendation: importing "subversive" detainees from the other American states. In the United States, they believed, U.S. agents could best supervise them and limit their actions. Twelve Central and South American countries—Bolivia, Columbia, Costa Rica, the Dominican Republic, Ecuador, El Salvador, Guatemala, Haiti, Honduras, Nicaragua, Panama, and Peru—deported some or all of their enemy alien detainees to the United States. Upon arrival, authorities distributed them in camps across Texas and Montana, where the U.S. military used them as cheap labor on local farms and in factories. In 1943 the United States received and imprisoned 4,656 aliens from Latin America, of whom about 3,000 were Germans and 1,400 were Japanese. This number had doubled by 1944 and included 4,058 Germans, 2,264 Japanese, and 288 Italians. At the war's end, the U.S. government deported most to Asia and Europe, never to see their homes again.[58]

[56] Official Report of the Second Technical Meeting (30 July 1943), Box 1, Entry 286, RG 60, NARA.

[57] Letter, Attorney General to Secretary of State (6 September 1943), Folder CPD Alien Enemy Control Unit, Box 1, Entry 289, RG 60, NARA.

[58] Numbers are taken from Statement of Albert E. Clattenburg (State Department) on "Cooperation with Other American Republics on Detention, Expulsion, and Repatriation of Dangerous Aliens" (30 July 1943), Box 1, Entry 286, RG 60, NARA. Information about the camps in the United States is from Official Report of First Technical Session (29 July 1943), Box

Loewenstein's aggressive concept of militant democracy also played a significant role in the dispute surrounding the detainees' right to citizenship. Throughout 1942 and early 1943, members of the CPD debated whether citizens who supported the Axis powers politically or ideologically could be stripped of their citizen status. While some, like the Mexican delegates, believed that citizenship was a fundamental right that could not be annulled, others maintained that revoking citizenship would be politically and ideologically beneficial to the Allies. During the committee's visit to the United States in July 1943, Loewenstein argued for an inviolable relationship between citizenship and an individual's loyalty to democratic values. "If they turned their back on the democratic order," he asserted, the liberal state was entitled to strip them of their citizenship and deprive them of civil and legal rights. In fact, to revoke a person's citizenship, it was sufficient to show that a person had "mental reservations or other fraudulent intent at the time of taking the oath of allegiance," regardless of the person's subsequent actions. As Loewenstein noted, the United States had preemptively suspended all applications for naturalization by Japanese residents, for fear they would exploit civil liberties for sabotage and subversion. He recommended that such measures be applied to Europeans as well and implemented across all of Latin America. At the end of the day, the committee's delegates voted to emulate the U.S. program and aggressively limit citizenship. This decision condemned Latin American detainees in U.S. camps to long periods spent in limbo without legal status, which extended well into the postwar era.[59]

Despite the CPD's repeated appeals to "the democratic values of the American Republics," Loewenstein and other U.S. officials were well aware that many of its member states were far from being adherents of liberal democracy. Leaders such as Getúlio Vargas in Brazil and Ramón Castillo in Argentina were authoritarian despots who utilized "defensive" measures as tools of domestic suppression. In several essays, Loewenstein repeatedly warned that to call such countries democracies would be "misleading and deceptive ... at best wishful thinking." Loewenstein in fact questioned whether any Latin American "subversive" movements were linked to Nazi Germany, Fascist Italy, or imperial Japan. "It may be doubted," he wrote in a lengthy report to his superiors, whether "indigenous totalitarian move-

1, Entry 286, RG 60, NARA. On the fate of the Japanese after 1945, see Joan Z. Bernstein et al., *Personal Justice Denied: Report of the Commission on Wartime Relocation and Internment of Civilians* (Seattle: University of Washington Press, 1997), 303–314. On the fate of the Germans, see Friedman, *Nazis and Good Neighbors*.

[59] Report, Karl Loewenstein to the CPD (4 August 1943), Box 1, Entry 286, RG 60, NARA. Drafts of this recommendation, which Loewenstein formulated together with Laurence Knapp, are in Folder 59, Box 43, KLP. For several examples of legal limbo, see Friedman, *Nazis and Good Neighbors*.

ments . . . if they should obtain control in the future, would invite Hitler or Mussolini or Japan to take over. On the contrary it seems more likely that [such movements] aim primarily at seizing power for themselves."[60]

Unlike some policymakers, however, Loewenstein did not view the CPD's main objective as regional stability through cooperation with dictators. In a continuation of a long-standing American approach to Latin American states, he claimed the CPD—including its work with authoritarian leaders— was to prepare the ground for genuine representative democracy in Latin America. In particular, Loewenstein believed that combating the agents of totalitarianism and cooperating with the United States showed local populations and political elites that democracy could triumph against its enemies. In this convoluted and repressive logic, by successfully suspending rights, the United States would ultimately teach other nations how to genuinely embrace them. As he wrote to the under secretary of state for Latin America, Sumner Welles, the committee's mission was to help build the foundations of democratic institutions in Cuba, Mexico, Panama, and the rest of Latin America. Welles, who shared Loewenstein's intellectual agenda, forwarded these reflections to the secretary of state and U.S. diplomats in Montevideo, Rio, Santiago, Lima, and other Latin American capitals.[61]

Thus, although U.S. diplomats joined the CPD out of strategic wartime considerations, Loewenstein regarded it as the first step toward establishing the permanent "Democratic International" he had envisioned before the war. The CPD put in place an initial framework of mutual democratic defense. In enabling other countries to suppress totalitarian activity, the members of the CPD recognized that acts of subversion, if directed against their neighbors, should be "punishable as if they were directed against their [own] state." Loewenstein believed that the CPD, as "the first promising germ of an incipient federation" of democracies, should be expanded and made permanent after the end of the war.[62] In a long memorandum to Laurence Knapp, the State Department's chief delegate to the CPD's office, Loewenstein explained that the United States must prepare to replicate the committee's mechanisms around the world. Whether U.S. diplomats recog-

[60] First quotation is from Karl Loewenstein, "South American Impressions of a Political Scientist," *Amherst Graduates' Quarterly* 31:2 (February 1942): 91–100, here 91–92. The second is from Memorandum, "Some Suggestions on the Organization of the Falange Material" (14 November 1942), Folder 10, Box 43, KLP.

[61] The scholarship on U.S. support of dictators in Latin America is vast. For a good overview of the 1920s and 1930s, see David F. Schmitz, *Thank God They're on Our Side: The United States and Right-Wing Dictatorships* (Chapel Hill: University of North Carolina Press, 1999), 46–84. Memorandum, Loewenstein to Welles, "Some Suggestions on the Organization of the Falange Material" (14 November 1942); Memorandum, Sumner Welles to the Secretary of State and U.S. Embassies in Latin America (8 February 1943); both in Folder 10, Box 43, KLP.

[62] Karl Loewenstein, "Pan Americanism in Action," *Current History* 5:27 (November 1943): 229–236.

nized it or not, the American states were forming the basis for a global confederation. As he explained, "the intrinsic importance of the CPD as an institution" lay in its imminent expansion.[63]

If this global vision seemed remote for many policymakers, its anti-Communist fervor enjoyed substantial resonance. Loewenstein's vision of the United States as the chief protagonist in democracy's century-old struggle against radicalism also rendered its clash with communism inevitable. As he never tired of repeating, militant democracy's struggle would not end with the defeat of the Axis powers. Just as in Weimar, representative democracy would also have to contend with radicalism's leftist incarnation, the Bolsheviks. Years before the start of the Cold War, Loewenstein warned his U.S. superiors that the United States must brace itself for a prolonged fight against the Soviet Union. In his mind, the CPD had laid the foundations for an international campaign against both domestic and international communism. In widely read reports from April 1943, Loewenstein urged the State Department to expand its preemptive restriction of rights to Communists. "Evidently," he wrote only weeks after the battle of Stalingrad, the Soviet Union's potential victory over the Nazis "is a political problem of the first magnitude . . . which might affect [our] internal security. It is to be expected that, with the Soviet Union occupying a prominent place among the victors, the missionary appeal of Bolshevism, at the present time subdued for tactical reasons, will emerge again. Internal legislation of the various [Western Hemisphere] states, if geared to the preservation of democratic processes," should be prepared in advance.[64]

This fierce anti-communism did not fall on deaf ears. Both U.S. and Latin American diplomats had little sympathy for communism and were willing to envision the extension of the CPD's frameworks to a future confrontation with the Bolsheviks. Indeed, following Loewenstein's comments, U.S. delegate Laurence Knapp and CPD chairman Alberto Guani called on their governments to begin drafting plans to confront postwar communism in the Western Hemisphere. While the Soviet Union was an ally in Europe, they claimed, global communism might well emerge as a destabilizing and subversive force in the future and seek inroads into Latin America. During World War II, these sentiments were merely simmering in the background. But they would soon become the central focus of militant democracy.[65]

[63] Memorandum, Loewenstein to Laurence Knapp (16 June 1943), Folder Annual Report July 1943, Box 1, Entry 289, RG 60, NARA.

[64] Memorandum, Loewenstein to Lawrence Smith and Laurence Knapp, "Future Activities of the Emergency Advisory Committee for Political Defense" (15 April 1943), Folder 52, Box 43, KLP.

[65] Alberto Guani, Annual Report 1943, Folder Annual Report July 1943, Box 1, Entry 289, RG 60, NARA.

Latin America thus became the site where Loewenstein's ideas from Weimar directly informed U.S. diplomacy. In the midst of wartime crisis, U.S. diplomats were deeply concerned about hostile subversion both at home and abroad. In Loewenstein's conviction that democratic institutions surpassed the "people" in importance, and that the limiting of democratic rights by a wise elite was necessary to defend democracy, they found the ideal language to explain their actions. The CPD, and its massive campaign of surveillance and incarceration, was thus not merely a product of U.S. geopolitical and security calculations. As with Fraenkel during the U.S. occupation of Korea, the committee also helped Loewenstein realize his old vision of combative democracy. For the thousands arrested and deported by the CPD, these ideas marked the abrupt disruption of peaceful lives. For Loewenstein, the experience gained by the CPD and the ties that it had forged were the beginning of a long and powerful cooperation with the U.S. government.

Yet this brutal campaign revealed the toxic potential embedded in Loewenstein's vision of democracy. Even more than Friedrich, Fraenkel, and Gurian, his dualistic vision, which divided the world between two antagonistic ideologies, called for harsh and violent policies. Egged on by American policymakers and wartime paranoia, Loewenstein and those who embraced his ideas fundamentally disregarded basic civil and political liberties, seemingly unaware they were destroying the very values they claimed to defend. For all his rejection of collectivist and radical political creeds in favor of individual liberties and elective institutions, Loewenstein seemed unable to grasp the tragic irony of his actions. If this vigilance ruined the lives of innocent civilians, it was not a sign of fundamental problems but a symbol of democratic assertiveness. The violation of liberties ultimately signified their endurance. With Germany's reconstruction and the rise of the Cold War, U.S. diplomats would again recruit Loewenstein and would make his political theories a crucial force in political reconstruction. Within a few years, this German-American collaboration would help turn militant democracy into one of the guiding principles of postwar German liberalism.

"MILITANT DEMOCRACY" IN THE COLD WAR: LIBERALISM AND ANTI-COMMUNISM IN WEST GERMANY

With the collapse of the Third Reich and end of the war in Europe, liberalism rapidly emerged as a crucial force in Germany's reconstruction. Many Weimar-era liberals returned from exile or forced silence to resume their political and intellectual campaigns for individual liberties by publishing, teaching, and drafting state constitutions. Veteran politicians such as Theodor Heuss reorganized liberalism under the new Free Democratic Party

(FDP), which quickly emerged as Germany's third largest party.[66] As part of this wave of returnees, Loewenstein landed in Germany in 1945 as a member of the U.S. occupation. He was tasked with reforming Germany's legal structures and political education as part of the U.S. program of "de-Nazification." Unsurprisingly, however, Loewenstein had larger goals in mind. Germany, he believed, would prove to be the decisive battleground between democracy and totalitarianism and had to be molded in a militant vein. Loewenstein therefore embarked on a campaign to transform German liberalism by mobilizing liberals in the service of anti-communism. In his eyes, the Cold War's anti-Communist crusade would not compromise liberal ideals but instead preserve and uphold them. This time, Loewenstein's ideas enjoyed tremendous success among German politicians and thinkers. By the mid-1950s, his aggressive conception of democracy had become the consensus, part of the fabric of West German politics, and one of the Cold War's guiding principles. It helped chart the contours of Germany's new democracy, both its possibilities and its harsh limits.

In July 1945, two months after the Third Reich's surrender, Loewenstein joined Solicitor General (and former New Deal lawyer) Charles Fahy and twenty other lawyers to build the Legal Division, the U.S. military organ that oversaw the reconstruction of Germany's entire legal system. For fifteen months, Loewenstein toured Germany, studied the Nazi legal system, and drafted laws to replace Nazi legislation on race, tax, criminality, agriculture, and family relations. He also helped identify German judges, lawyers, and law professors who should be banned from participating in Germany's legal life.[67] As one of the three returning German émigrés in the Legal Division, Loewenstein conducted countless interviews with the German legal elite, becoming "de facto one of the Division's chief intelligence officers."[68] When his service came to an end in the fall of 1946, Loewenstein had reformed the German bar association by making it independent of political oversight and had helped purge scores of former Nazi professors and lawyers, earning the title "the Pope of de-Nazification" from his colleagues. Like the CPD, the U.S. occupation was to inaugurate a long process of building

---

[66] Jürgen Hess, *Verfassungsarbeit: Theodor Heuss und der parlamentarische Rat* (Berlin: Liberale Verlag, 2008); Theo Rütten, *Die deutsche Liberalismus, 1945–1955* (Baden: Nomos, 1984); Lösche and Walter, *Die FDP*.

[67] Memoranda from Loewenstein to Fahy include recommendations on: "Denazification and Reform of Some Germans Laws" (28 September 1945); "Denazification Policy" (30 November 1945); "Reconstruction of German Agricultural Legislation" (15 August 1945); "On the Validity of the German Marriage Act" (8 January 1946), and many others, all in Folders 1 and 2, Box 28, KLP. For a detailed description of Loewenstein's work at the Legal Division, see R. W. Kostal, "The Alchemy of Occupation: Karl Loewenstein and the Legal Reconstruction of Nazi Germany," *Law and History Review* 29:1 (February 2011): 1–52. See also Lang, *Karl Loewenstein*, 247–262.

[68] Kostal, "Alchemy of Occupation," 21.

a vibrant liberal democracy in Germany by purging radical voices who had lost the right to operate in Germany's new postwar system.[69]

These early efforts propelled Loewenstein to the center of the broader effort by both Americans and Germans to resurrect German liberalism. After his appointment at the Legal Division came to an end in 1946, he quickly utilized his position as adviser for the U.S. military to mobilize other wings of the enormous U.S. occupation apparatus in order to help rebuild democratic culture in Germany. In the summer of that year, he elicited a favorable response in the educational and cultural divisions, where U.S. officials focused on building new educational programs, libraries, and cultural outreach. Officials in these divisions were enthralled by Loewenstein's combative liberalism and recruited him to build what he called "an intellectual crusade" for the German people. During the next four years, they sent him on dozens of lecture tours across the Western occupation zones, circulated his speeches among legal theorists, and provided him with unprecedented visibility in Germany. They set the stage for the reintroduction of his ideas about democracy and liberty.[70]

With the same intellectual zeal that guided his work in Latin America, Loewenstein used this platform to resurrect his older vision of a German liberalism based on individual liberties and representative institutions. After twelve years of devastation under Nazism, his lectures and writings sought to reintroduce a political vision based on the superiority of democratic institutions, like parliament and the political parties, over the people's will. Political authority, he explained in a lecture in Munich, did not stem from the organic nation, as German nationalists and the Nazis had argued, but from institutions that kept the separation of powers. The purpose of elections and parliaments was to ensure that power was diffused among different centers and actors, which would compel political leaders to compromise with their adversaries in a democratic, decentralized state. The mission of democracy, then, was to guarantee that "all members of the community, including minorities, would be part of the peaceful political process."[71]

These lectures quickly positioned Loewenstein as one of West Germany's most celebrated liberal intellectuals and a towering figure in molding the country's new political theory. Throughout the 1950s, his Weimar-era writings on democracy and politics were reissued by Germany's leading publishers, alongside his contemporary essays and books on party politics, parliamentarianism, and judicial review in the Anglo-Saxon world. Along-

[69] The quotation is from Karl Loewenstein, "Record of Written Word, 15 August," Folder 17, Box 28, KLP.

[70] Karl Loewenstein, Lecture, "Education in Germany" (19 March 1946), Folder 34, Box 45, KLP.

[71] Lecture, "Die Gesetzgebungsfunktion im modernen Staat" (10 August 1948), Folder 13, Box 61, KLP. List of lectures is in Folder 52, Box 47, KLP.

side Carl Friedrich and Ernst Fraenkel, he helped draft the curricula for the country's university departments of political science, and his books circulated among thousands of students. In 1959 this postwar work culminated in *Constitutional Theory*, one of West Germany's most comprehensive theories of political liberalism and individual liberties.[72] Many liberal theoreticians and politicians found in Loewenstein an articulate defender of individualist institutions. The most visible reflection of this prominent status was Theodor Heuss, the founder of the liberal FDP and West Germany's first president, who was deeply impressed by Loewenstein and considered him one of the country's most important political thinkers. As he noted in several personal letters, Loewenstein's lectures and writings deeply informed his own conviction that democracy's "political style" was dependent not on the people's will but on institutions and norms. Thus, although Loewenstein left Germany with the end of the U.S. occupation in 1949 and returned to Europe only for occasional lectures and seminars, his writings proved fundamental to German liberals' efforts to articulate their own political visions. Under the wing of the U.S. authorities, Loewenstein's Weimar-era theory contributed to articulating liberals' second attempt to establish a vibrant republican culture.[73]

Yet as in Latin America, the most powerful legacy of Loewenstein's work was ultimately the concept of militant democracy. And this time, unlike in the CPD, the central focus of Loewenstein's ire was first and foremost communism. As Cold War tensions began to rise in 1946 and 1947 and U.S. diplomacy became more explicitly anti-Communist, American officials in Germany recognized that Loewenstein's ideas could be helpful in their goal of anti-Communist mobilization. While they were often skeptical of Loewenstein's vision of a Democratic International, they did share his fear of Communist subversion. The occupation's educational and cultural affairs departments therefore sponsored Loewenstein's tours throughout German cities to recruit the local support for an anti-Communist campaign. Across the ruined country, Loewenstein called on Germans to combine the creation of democratic institutions with a vigilant suppression of Communist activities. These appearances drew massive crowds in Frankfurt, Koblenz,

---

[72] Karl Loewenstein, "Über die parlamentarische Parteidisziplin im Ausland," *Deutsche Rechtszeitschrift* 5 (1950): 241–245; "Verfassungsrecht und Verfassungsrealität: Beiträge zur Ontologie der Verfassung," *Archiv des öffentlichen Rechts* 77 (1952), 387–435; Karl Loewenstein, *Vom Wesen der amerikanischen Verfassung* (Frankfurt a.M.: Metzner, 1950); Karl Loewenstein, *Verfassungslehre* (Tübingen: Mohr Siebeck, 1959).

[73] Such sentiments appear in two letters from Theodor Heuss to Loewenstein (11 September 1954 and 7 January 1959), Folder 114, Box 50, KLP. The two men corresponded from 1953 until 1961 and developed a close friendship. For Heuss's writings on democratic "political style," see his "Freiheit als Aufgabe" (1946), in Peter Juling (ed.), *Was heisst heute liberal?* (Gerlingen: Bleicher, 1978), 31–34.

Nuremberg, Berlin, Bonn, Tübingen, Hamburg, and countless other venues. As enthusiastic U.S. officials reported, German politicians, students, and scholars were eager to hear about the United States' anti-Soviet campaign from a German who was so intimately familiar with the U.S. diplomatic establishment.[74]

Loewenstein's message articulated and reinforced the shifting sentiments among German democrats in the postwar era. With the memory of Hitler's abuse of democratic mechanisms to destroy the Weimar state still fresh, many abandoned their earlier belief in relativism and democracy's obligation to grant equal liberties to all. Instead, politicians, jurists, and political activists now embraced his continued insistence that militant democracy's mission entailed the restraining of liberties at home. As Loewenstein put it to an audience of 1,800 in the southern city of Schwäbisch Gmünd, Nazism proved that rights should be reserved for those who believed in the democratic system. Anyone who could potentially manipulate them, be they nationalists or Communists, had to be actively banned from free political competition. As American and German officials reported, German audiences time and again greeted these remarks with thunderous applause. From across the country, German mayors, local party leaders, and lawyers wrote enthusiastically that "Professor Loewenstein's lectures were amazing" and asked that his book be sent to their local libraries.[75]

The most important target group for Loewenstein's advocacy was the new political and legal elite in Germany. In his political theory, the formation of a responsible and wise elite, who would know when and how to curb rights of aggressive groups, was necessary for the preservation of representative democracy. Loewenstein therefore spent a good part of his lecture tours reintroducing his old theory and concepts to political leaders, law professors, and lawyers. These included the cabinet of the Bavarian state, the judges' association of Württemberg, the lawyers' union of Nuremberg, and the members of Bavaria's Supreme Court, who listened attentively to Loewenstein's address and received German translations of his essays prepared by the occupation authorities. Loewenstein reported to his American superiors that German politicians, judges, and legal scholars were now more receptive to the idea that democratic rights should be contingent on ideological commitment to its institutions. After liberalism's shattering defeat in Weimar and amid growing fears of Soviet dominance, they were far more comfortable with the notion of placing limits on civil liberties. With his long record of advocacy for such ideas and his unique experience imple-

---

[74] List of Lectures 1947–1948 (undated), Folder 27, Box 60, KLP.

[75] The lecture in Schwäbisch Gmünd is from transcript (13 September 1948), *Schwäbische Donau-Zeitung*, 1. Information on the other lectures is from Report (unsigned) by the Educational Division (15 September 1948), Folder 52, Box 47, KLP.

4.2. Karl Loewenstein giving a lecture to a German audience on democratic institutions and anti-communism in Coburg, 1948. Loewenstein's lectures and publications were instrumental in popularizing "militant democracy" as a crucial concept in postwar German politics and thought. Amherst College Archives and Special Collections.

menting them in Latin America and Germany, Loewenstein symbolized the liberating potential of curbing rights. For many of his listeners, he was the embodiment of the wise elite for which his theory called.[76]

The conviction that democracy was obliged to suspend the liberties of its enemies quickly began to circulate in German politics and legal thought. One after the other, German scholars embraced the term "militant" to describe the principles of postwar democracy. In 1949, at a gathering of Germany's leading liberal scholars of law and politics, the University of Cologne's Hermann Jahrreiß cited Loewenstein's ideas as being inherent to the democratic order. "In order to be democratic," he said, "must not the state shackle or exterminate (*vernichten*) the forces that opposed its democratic system, as soon as they pursue anti-democratic ... objectives? Whoever answers 'yes', thinks the theory of 'militant democracy.'" Richard Thoma, the foremost liberal constitutional scholar, agreed, appealing for a constitutional "defense against the right to [national] suicide." The constitutional

[76] Lecture, "Der Oberste Bundesgerichtshof—Supreme Court—und seine richterliche" (20 and 27 August 1947), Folder 15, Box 59, KLP; Report, Karl Loewenstein to Civil Affairs Administration (25 February 1949), Folder Democratization Branch, Box 6, Records of Civil Affairs Administration, RG 260, NARA.

legal scholar Friedrich August von der Heydte soon followed suit, asserting that anti-democratic parties should be banned. Only then, he argued, could the liberal state strike a balance between "the Scylla of too much freedom and the Charybdis of too little."[77] When sociologist Karl Mannheim's *Diagnosis of Our Time* was published in 1951 to general acclaim, Germans were well familiar with his call for militant democracy." What had been a controversial idea in Weimar now emerged as part of a postwar political consensus in German thought.[78]

The theory of militant democracy rapidly became one of the fundamental principles guiding Germany's emerging political and legal establishment. It became popular not only among liberals but also among Germany's two other major political camps, the conservative Christian Democrats and the Socialists. The constitutional scholars who began drafting West Germany's constitution in the summer of 1948 and the politicians who gathered in Bonn at the Parliamentary Council to complete it the following year both agreed that the new republic should be preemptively empowered to crush its enemies. Throughout the debates on the constitution's various articles, delegates from left and right alike devoted extensive energy to defining the list of rights that would be denied to anti-democratic subversives. Socialist Ludwig Bergsträsser, for example, who had attended Loewenstein's lecture in Heidelberg, suggested that academic freedom be denied to anti-democratic thinkers. Conservative Gustav Zimmermann, who had also met Loewenstein, evoked the concept of militant democracy to explain why the state should be permitted to abrogate the right to free speech and communication among anti-democratic parties. The new state, he maintained, had "to get at and eliminate the roots of evil" before they undermined it. Conservative delegate Hermann von Mangoldt further speculated that abolishing the free speech of extremists would not limit, but in fact expand, free speech by providing space for voices that might otherwise be overshadowed by anti-democratic propaganda. To many, curbing rights became synonymous with the democratic order.[79]

---

[77] Hermann Jahrreiß, "Demokratie: Selbstbewusstsein—Selbstgefährdung—Selbstschutz," *Festschrift für Richard Thoma* (Tübingen: Mohr Siebeck, 1950), 71–91, here 78. Richard Thoma, *Über Wesen und Erscheinungsformen der modernen Demokratie* (Bonn: Dümmler, 1948), 38; Von der Heydte is quoted in Markus Thiel, "Germany," in *The Militant Democracy Principle in Modern Democracies*, 109–146, here 11.

[78] Karl Mannheim published his book in Britain during his exile, in 1943, and it was published by returning émigrés in Germany in 1951. Some scholars have attributed the term's popularity to the publication of Mannheim's works; yet by then, the theory and the term "militant democracy" had circulated in Germany for several years. See, for example, Matthew Specter, *Habermas: An Intellectual Biography* (New York: Cambridge University Press, 2010), 77.

[79] For the debates about the essence and limits of "militant democracy" at the Parliamentary Council, see Hanshew, *Terror and Democracy in West Germany*, 18–67. The quotations by Zimmermann and Mangoldt are from 54–55.

As a result of this growing consensus, the constitution that emerged in 1949, the West German *Grundgesetz*, bore the marks of militant democracy throughout its many articles. Although it provided for freedom of faith, speech, and association, it preemptively denied these rights to the republic's domestic and foreign enemies. Article 21(2), for example, stated that "parties which, by reason of their aims or the behavior of their adherents, seek to impair or abolish the free democratic order … are unconstitutional." Article 9(2) extended this prohibition to less formal and more local associations, such as clubs, youth movements, and cultural institutions. Article 18 empowered the government to deny freedom of expression and communication to all individuals who "abuse" them "in order to combat the free democratic basic order." Article 5(3) declared that academic freedom "shall not absolve from loyalty to the constitution." Article 139 stipulated that former Nazis who had been punished under the de-Nazification processes could not regain civil rights. As many legal scholars have commented, these provisions placed West Germany at the vanguard of a new political and intellectual vision of liberalism. No other European country enshrined such robust clauses to limit political subversion in its founding legal document.[80]

During West Germany's first years, the state put these ideas into practice against both the right and the left. In 1951 the federal government under Konrad Adenauer, along with his liberal partners, petitioned the Supreme Court to outlaw the Sozialistische Reichspartei (Socialist Reich Party, or SRP), a neo-Nazi organization founded in 1949. The government argued that the SRP's extreme nationalism, violent rhetoric, and authoritarian structures rendered it an enemy of the liberal democratic order. In October 1952, after a year of deliberation, the Supreme Court ruled that the SRP's ideology made it an enemy of the democratic state and ordered its dissolution. The rights and liberties enshrined in the *Grundgesetz*, so the justices claimed, did not apply to democracy's opponents. As a result, the SRP's delegates in the parliament lost their seats, and the government confiscated the party's assets.[81]

While the SRP ruling was informed by fresh memories of Nazi violence, it was ultimately the Cold War–era sense that democracy was subject to a

---

[80] Quotations from the *Grundgesetz* are from "The Basic Law of the Federal Republic of Germany," in Elmar M. Hucko (ed.), *The Democratic Tradition: Four German Constitutions* (Oxford: Berg, 1987), 191–265. On the centrality of "militant democracy" to these clauses, see Jürgen Becker, "Die wehrhafte Demokratie des Grundgesetzes," in Josef Isensee and Paul Kirchhof (eds.), *Handbuch des Staatsrechts* (Heidelberg: Müller Juristischer Verlag, 1992), 4: 309–360; Donald P. Kommers, *The Constitutional Jurisprudence of the Federal Republic of Germany*, 2nd ed. (Durham: Duke University Press, 1997), 217–240; David P. Currie, *The Constitution of the Federal Republic of Germany* (Chicago: University of Chicago Press, 1994), 213–226.

[81] On the SRP and its role as precedent, see Markus Thiel, "Das Verbot verfassungswidriger Parteien," *Wehrhafte Demokratie* (Tübingen: Mohr Siebeck, 2003), 173–208.

permanent state of war that turned militant democracy into a fixture of West German political life. After the 1952 ruling, legal scholars continued to debate if this curbing of rights was an exceptional, one-time decision that held only for neo-Nazis or whether militant democracy applied to all anti-democratic forces. The subsequent initiation of similar proceedings against the German Communist Party (KPD) therefore marked "the birth of militant democracy" as a fundamental principle of West Germany.[82] In 1951, immediately after filing the lawsuit against the SRP, the West German government applied to the Supreme Court to ban the KPD on the grounds that it was unconstitutional. Even though the party enjoyed little political support, winning less than 5 percent of the votes in most state and federal elections, Adenauer's cabinet insisted that its "totalitarian essence" posed an existential threat to democracy. Aware of the importance of this ruling on a non-Nazi organization to the political culture of the West German state, the justices delayed their decision for five long years. To their minds, while banning Nazi parties was uncontroversial, the "KPD-case," as it became popularly known, would determine the boundary between legitimate opposition and political peril in a free yet combative democracy.[83]

The verdict, released in August 1956, crushed the Communists. In a 308-page opinion—the longest in the court's history—Chief Justice Josef Wintrich and his colleagues reviewed the history, ideology, leadership, and political structures of the KPD. According to the court, all these aspects showed that the party was a totalitarian and anti-democratic movement that sought to overthrow the republic by abusing its liberties. The court argued that the West German state was not obliged to wait until the KPD engaged in illegal activity or "concrete undertakings" in order to criminalize it. It was sufficient to demonstrate that the party, by dint of its ideological convictions, had the potential to execute its anti-democratic agenda at some point in the future. By preemptively suppressing potential future rebellions, the justices explained, "the free democratic state does not take out after parties with inimical aims on its own initiative. Rather, it behaves defensively; it merely wards off assaults upon its basic order." In their pivotal ruling, the justices took care to acknowledge the intellectual inspiration for their thinking about democracy, rights, and liberties. Banning the Communist Party, they wrote in the conclusion, "is an affirmation of 'militant democracy,' a constitutional value decision that is binding on the Federal Constitutional Court."[84]

---

[82] Kommers, *The Constitutional Jurisprudence*, 222. See also Tyulkina, *Militant Democracy*, 11–115.

[83] Kommers, *The Constitutional Jurisprudence*, 222–224.

[84] Quotations are from *Entscheidungen des Bundesverfassungsgerichts [BVerfGE]* 5 85 (Tübingen: Mohr, 1956), 139.

By invoking Loewenstein's theory and its conviction that the integrity of democratic institutions trumped the people's will, Wintrich and the other justices did not merely seek to explain their ruling. They were also signaling their expectation that the state would robustly enforce it. According to the court, the ruling on criminalization did not just apply to the KPD but extended to all current and future surrogate organizations that propounded a similar ideology. With this understanding in mind, the West German government unleashed a large campaign of political subjection. Government officials dissolved the Communist Party, stripped it of representation in state parliaments, and confiscated all its property. They swiftly moved to shut down its newspapers, youth movements, and all its cultural associations. Enthusiastically embracing the court's verdict, the West German government under Adenauer continued to exclude Communists from political life well after 1956. For years, the state unrelentingly invoked the court's ruling in order to prevent new Communist organizations from running for office. By 1964, no less than 328 associations had been banned. While these measures were never able to fully eradicate Communist activity in Germany, they radically confined the spheres in which oppositional forces could operate. With the onset of the Cold War, militant democracy became one of the central principles of postwar democratic life.[85]

There was, of course, a considerable irony in the urgent efforts to elevate such militant anti-communism as a source of democratic health. The burning hatred of communism, and the Soviet Union in particular, was fundamental to the Nazis' brutal suppression of democracy at home and key to their imperialist war. It is safe to assume that many Germans who so eagerly embraced Loewenstein's ideas did so at least in part because they echoed these familiar sentiments. Yet in channeling anti-Communist energies toward a new bond with democratic institutions, Loewenstein also reintroduced a political language that was radically different from Nazism. Forged decades earlier, it was independent of Nazi racist ideology and intellectually opposite to its authoritarianism. That democratic thought like Loewenstein's managed to appropriate Nazi anti-communism for its own purposes and at the same time perpetuated it is one of the great ironies of postwar German politics. While liberals during the Weimar era miserably failed in solidifying the authority of democratic institutions, after World War II they succeeded in doing so partially by embracing the anti-Communist obsession

<hr />

[85] On the anti-Communist campaign and its limitations, see Alexander von Brünneck, *Politische Justiz gegen Kommunisten in der Bundesrepublik Deutschland* (Frankfurt: Suhrkamp, 1978), esp. 117–195. The number of banned organizations is derived from Müller, "Militant Democracy," 1260. On the constitutional court's significance in making the mistrust of the people and the devaluation of popular sovereignty key to the protection of democracy in the postwar era, see Jan-Werner Müller, *Contesting Democracy* (New Haven: Yale University Press, 2011), 146–150.

of their worst enemies and gravediggers. Loewenstein and those who echoed his ideas seemed unaware of this irony, and never systematically reflected on it. It remained a glaring lacuna of postwar liberal political visions.

With its blend of democratic renewal and oppressive political irony, the mobilization of West German liberals in support of anti-Communist repression was not simply a response to the trauma of Nazism, as many scholars have argued. Intellectually, it was indebted to theories that had evolved decades earlier, when German liberals sought to craft a response to extremists' assaults on the Weimar Republic. The pressure of the early Cold War, and the forceful support of U.S. officials, allowed Loewenstein to revive this theoretical tradition. These international dynamics provided the stage for his lectures and writings, where he argued that the success of Germany's postwar democracy depended on the aggressive curtailment of its enemies. After long years in the service of the American state, Loewenstein's theory provided the language that merged American diplomacy with the triumph of representative and liberal democracy in Germany. It tied democracy to aggressive suppression and dramatically limited German political horizons. Militant democracy, then, both reflected and helped shape West Germany's participation in the Cold War.

The journey of "militant democracy" from Weimar's margins to the center of the postwar order did not end in West Germany. In 1957 the German Communist Party petitioned the European Court of Human Rights in hopes of recovering the right to participate in the political process. To their great disappointment, however, the justices in Brussels rejected their appeal, claiming that the ban followed the principles of militant democracy. Human rights, the justices explained, did not belong to those who denied them in their quest for political dictatorship. Nor did the term exhaust its value for jurists and political thinkers with the end of the Cold War. With the dawn of the "War on Terror" in the early twenty-first century, militant democracy provided an intellectual foundation for the call for democratic states to restrict the rights of their enemies. Both legal scholars and European courts frequently invoked it to justify preventive arrests and suspension of rights of radical Muslim preachers and activists. Long after the Cold War, Loewenstein's ideas have therefore continued to inform debates on the scope and nature of liberties in the condition of permanent war.[86]

As this longevity shows, the theory of militant democracy provided a powerful intellectual framework for those who believed that anti-democratic extremists abuse political liberties to overthrow the democratic

---

[86] On the European Court, see James A. Sweeney, *The European Court of Human Rights in the Post Cold War Era* (New York: Routledge, 2013), 192ff. The scholarship on "militant democracy" and radical Islamism in Europe is vast. For a good overview, see Müller, "Militant Democracy."

system. In their mind, the doctrine of militant democracy did not allow ruling elites to abuse power; rather, it enhanced the stability and health of democracy and liberalism. Because anti-democratic activists willfully excluded themselves from the sphere of human rights, suppressing their rights had no bearing on the freedom of other citizens. Loewenstein's theory positioned democratic institutions, and not the empowerment of the population, at the center of democratic legitimacy. If portions of the popular will conflicted with liberalism, the state's first responsibility was to defend liberal institutions, not to reflect the vast array of opinions held by the people.

While both Loewenstein and those who used his ideas believed that militant democracy was universally applicable, it emerged from the very concrete conditions of Weimar Germany. Many years before the rise of Nazism, the Cold War, or twenty-first-century terrorism, it responded to the vitriolic assaults on German liberals and their allies that marked Weimar's early years. Loewenstein's ideas stemmed from a combative liberal vision, which saw a need for democratic institutions and wise elites to manage the unruly masses and prevent dictatorship. In contrast to liberal claims of political relativism, Loewenstein called on German liberals to rethink their belief that the democratic order should remain neutral toward its Fascist and Communist enemies. During the 1920s, the claim that parliaments, elections, and parties reigned supreme over the universal liberties of all citizens was a bold claim even for the most liberal of German thinkers.

These ideas proved exceptionally appealing in the United States, where anxieties about "subversive" infiltration quickly spread from the late 1930s onward and informed politics through the Cold War. Loewenstein's arrival coincided with the growing conviction that Communists and foreign agents were plotting to overthrow the American government. His ideas provided the concepts and justification for those who advocated for aggressive action but sought assurance that repression was not destructive for democracy. He articulated an uncompromising and unhesitant course of action. During World War II, the most tragic consequence of this cooperation between Loewenstein and the U.S. diplomats who embraced his theory was the CPD's violent campaign of mass imprisonment. In Latin America, Loewenstein's writings helped policymakers speak perversely of "democratic ideals" while violating rights, arresting, and deporting thousands without trials. With their circular logic and glaring lacunae, Loewenstein's writings helped alleviate wartime and Cold War fears that the extreme measures required to protect democracy would sow the seeds of its destruction.

These Manichean ideas about democracy and rights proved equally powerful in postwar Germany. The trauma of Nazism and rising fears of Communist infiltration came together to fuel a shift in thinking about democracy and rights. German liberals and other supporters of democracy were deeply worried that West Germany's institutions might once more crumble from within. Loewenstein's ideas again provided the language for those who sought to limit rights. First during the drafting of the constitution, and then in the Supreme Court's anti-Communist ruling, militant democracy explained why the stability of democratic institutions should lead to active suppression of political freedoms. In the eyes of many, Loewenstein's theory solved the paradox of democratic self-defense. Through these ideas, German liberals found a path for anti-Communist mobilization without, in their minds, sacrificing their liberal principles.

Much like Friedrich, Fraenkel, and Gurian, Loewenstein's ideas from Weimar served as a crucial link between U.S. diplomacy and German participation in the Cold War. Even though U.S. diplomats and German liberals did not necessarily share his idiosyncratic vision of international politics, he powerfully articulated their mutual response to political "subversion." By carving his own space in the U.S. diplomatic establishment, Loewenstein helped disseminate his theory of "militant democracy" across the Western hemisphere. Embedded in this matrix of liberal thought, anti-Communist fears, and U.S. power, it would remain one of the most influential concepts of European politics and law for the rest of the twentieth century.

CHAPTER V

From the League of Nations to Vietnam

HANS J. MORGENTHAU AND REALIST REFORM OF INTERNATIONAL RELATIONS

In the summer of 1965, after months of growing pressure from Congress and young activists, the White House finally decided to confront the rising opposition to U.S. military involvement in Vietnam. On 21 June 1965 millions watched a televised debate between senior spokesmen for the conflicting views. On one side stood National Security Advisor McGeorge Bundy, one of the principal architects of U.S. intervention. On the other spoke the University of Chicago's Hans J. Morgenthau, a German émigré specialist on foreign relations and the foremost intellectual representative of the emerging opposition. Bundy warned that a decision to leave Vietnam would break America's promise to the Vietnamese people and abandon it to the horrors of a Communist dictatorship. Such a sign of weakness could precipitate a Communist takeover of the entire Asian continent. Morgenthau responded by attacking U.S. involvement in Vietnam as a diplomatic and moral catastrophe. Instead of bringing stability, he scoffed, the U.S. was pouring its resources into a strategically unimportant region and killing thousands of innocent civilians. The war in Vietnam was the product of a misguided leadership that saw all Communist movements and regimes as the incarnation of evil. The United States had to begin negotiations with Vietnamese Communists, end its intervention, and withdraw from Southeast Asia.[1]

Morgenthau's critique was particularly worrisome to policymakers, who circulated his writings and anxiously followed his public advocacy. In the years immediately after World War II, Morgenthau had emerged as the highest intellectual authority on international relations in the United States. His theory, which became known as "realism," explained why the United States had no choice but to oppose the Soviet Union and China and prevent them from expanding their power in Europe and East Asia. According to Morgenthau's provocative writings, the international sphere was inherently anarchic and violent. Nations had to compete for power and influence. Rather than seeking global peace or strengthening international law,

---

[1] "Vietnam Dialog," *Congressional Records: United States Senate* (Washington, D.C.: U.S. Government Printing Office, 1965), vol. 111 (89th Congress), part 11, 1st session, 15396–15401.

the United States had to protect its interests. Taming Soviet and Chinese power was a matter of survival. During the 1950s, these ideas strongly resonated with U.S. intellectuals and academics alike. Morgenthau served as adviser to key diplomats, such as George Kennan and Dean Acheson, and his books were read and taught in countless universities. Many regarded him as the most important German émigré in the United States and as the intellectual father of Cold War diplomacy. As one commentator hyperbolically proclaimed, "Morgenthau is to politics among states what Einstein is to mathematical physics."[2]

This paradoxical position, as a famous theoretician of the Cold War and an intellectual leader of the opposition to the U.S. campaign in Vietnam, has puzzled both contemporaries and scholars. Many were—and still are—especially confused by Morgenthau's contention that involvement in Vietnam was not only strategically misguided but also morally disastrous. In Morgenthau's eyes, the killing of innocent Vietnamese was corrupting the United States' moral fabric and destroying American democracy at home. Unlike other realist thinkers, who believed in a strict separation between domestic and international politics, Morgenthau claimed that the war in Vietnam was the direct result of growing civilian apathy toward democracy and the dangerous concentration of power in the hands of a small elite. Despite his reputation as a theorist of state power who cared little for democracy and morality, which persists to this day, Morgenthau claimed that international politics required robust democratic norms and attention to moral considerations. In his writings, he warned that the quest for power alone would lead to disaster.[3]

Despite this seeming transformation from warrior to Cold War dissenter, Morgenthau's initial support of the Cold War and his subsequent opposition to it both stemmed from the Weimar period. His ideas on international politics and diplomacy were shaped by the intense German debates over its

---

[2] Manfred Lachs, "Some Reflections on the Settlement of International Disputes," *American Society of International Law Proceedings* 68 (1974), 323–331, here 331. On his reputation as a leading German émigré and postwar thinker in general, see, for example, Joachim Radkau, *Die deutsche Emigration in den USA* (Düsseldorf: Bertelsmann Universitätsverlag, 1971).

[3] The scholarship on Morgenthau is vast and cannot be adequately summarized here. For works that present Morgenthau as a thinker of power politics, see, for example, Jürgen Habermas, *The Divided West* (Cambridge: Polity, 2006), 166–193; Seán Molloy, *The Hidden History of Realism: A Genealogy of Power Politics* (London: Palgrave, 2006), 75–98; Steven J. Bucklin, *Realism and American Foreign Policy* (Westpoint, CT: Praeger, 2001); Martin Griffiths, *Realism, Idealism and International Politics: A Reinterpretation* (London: Routledge, 1995); and others cited throughout the chapter. More recently, several scholars have begun to criticize this common conception of Morgenthau's writings. See, for example, Michael C. Williams, *The Realist Tradition and the Limits of International Relations* (New York: Cambridge University Press, 2005); and Richard Ned Lebow, *The Tragic Vision of Politics: Ethics, Interests and Orders* (New York: Cambridge University Press, 2003), 216–256.

place in the post–World War I global order. As a young thinker, Morgenthau maintained that countries must strike a balance between their necessary quest for power and their support for democracy at home and international collaboration abroad. They had to recognize that power politics was the "natural" order but at the same time strive toward a more equitable international system, in which all countries shared power and resources. Morgenthau maintained that Germany was well positioned to lead the way in building such a world order. Its diplomats could show the world that it was possible to simultaneously pursue national interests, democratic politics, and international cooperation. This was the vision that guided Morgenthau into the postwar era. The United States, he asserted, must continue the quest to build a new world order that would balance power politics with moral justice.[4]

Morgenthau's path from Weimar to the Cold War thus marked both the apex and the disintegration of the German-American symbiosis. Liked Friedrich, Fraenkel, Gurian, and Loewenstein, his ideas provided a crucial intellectual arsenal for Americans who sought to explain their country's role in the postwar era. His realist theory explained why mobilizing the American state against the Soviet Union and Communist China was the "natural" product of international relations, the result of universal and unchanging rules. In contrast to the other émigrés, however, his ideas eventually also helped inspire those who challenged Cold War diplomacy. They provided a new and younger generation with the terms to articulate their fears that anti-Communist mobilization was eroding the integrity of democratic institutions. Having supported Cold War mobilization for two decades, Morgenthau facilitated the beginning of its decline. Paradoxically, his intellectual authority in U.S. foreign policy lent legitimacy to those who began to challenge it.

INTERNATIONAL POLITICS, LAW, AND WAR

Germany's defeat in World War I not only initiated the country's first experiment with democracy but also marked the beginning of an even larger project: the establishment of a new world order guided by the principles of international law. In March 1918, in the midst of war, U.S. president Wood-

[4] Several works have explored the relationship between Morgenthau's Weimar-era writings and his postwar thought. The most important, which influenced my own interpretation, is William E. Scheuerman, *Hans Morgenthau: Realism and Beyond* (Malden: Polity Press, 2009). The other is Martti Koskenniemi's magisterial *The Gentle Civilizer of Nations: The Rise and Fall of International Law* (New York: Cambridge University Press, 2002), 436–494. Koskenniemi's interpretation of Morgenthau is somewhat one-sided, and focuses on his critique of international law, while ignoring much of his support for international collaboration.

row Wilson announced his plan to establish a new world organization, the League of Nations. Designed by Wilson and supporters of British imperialism, such as South African diplomat Jan Smuts, the League was intended to replace power politics and military alliances with international cooperation and open diplomacy. It was to function as a global legislative body in which all countries would take part as equals in resolving international conflicts (a goal that would always be undercut by its imperial roots). Alongside the League, a new Permanent Court of International Justice was to ensure that the rule of law guided international politics. The court would have the authority to rule on international disputes and, in Eastern and Central Europe, to defend minorities against potential abuse by their governments. In 1919, as part of the peace conference that convened in Paris, forty-four states joined the new organization and ratified the establishment of the court in the Hague. Together, as one American journalist put it, the two institutions were supposed to inaugurate "a new era in the history of the world."[5]

The Weimar Republic was initially excluded from the League, allowed to join only in 1926, after prolonged negotiations. This was part of the Treaty of Versailles's harsh punishment, which stripped Germany of its overseas colonies, ceded extensive German territories to Poland and France, and imposed enormous war reparations. Yet since the moment of its creation, Germans of all political convictions associated the Weimar Republic with the League and with international law. To many proponents of the republic, Germany's democratization had to proceed in parallel with its incorporation into a new community of nations. Hugo Preuss, the leading liberal scholar who drafted the Weimar Constitution, believed that both the republic and the League stemmed from the same vision of politics. Democracy depended on peaceful cooperation and the rule of law within a nation-state; it therefore required Germany to subject itself to international cooperation and international law. Many liberals and Socialists shared these sentiments and wrote them into the Weimar Constitution. Article 4, for example, proclaimed that the German Republic would abide by "the generally recognized rules of international law."[6]

---

[5] Thomas J. Kock, *To End All Wars: Woodrow Wilson and the Quest for a New World Order* (New York: Oxford University Press, 1992), 164; Zara Steiner, *The Lights That Failed: European International History, 1919–1933* (New York: Oxford University Press, 2005), 15–80; Mark Mazower, *No Enchanted Palace: The End of Empire and the Ideological Origins of the United Nations* (Princeton: Princeton University Press, 2009), 66–94.

[6] "The Constitution of the German Republic," in Elmar M. Hucko (ed.), *The Democratic Tradition: Four German Constitutions* (Oxford: Berg, 1987), 149; Hugo Preuss, *Reich und Länder: Bruchstücke eines Kommentars zur Verfassung des Deutschen Reiches* (Berlin: Carl Heymann, 1928), 84–98. For an excellent overview, see Peter Caldwell, "Sovereignty, Constitutionalism, and the Myth of the State: Article Four of the Weimar Constitution," in Rudy Koshar (ed.), *The Weimar Moment* (Lanham, MD: Rowman and Littlefield, 2012), 345–370. See also Frank

German nationalists and anti-democrats, too, equated the League with the new German democracy. The leading intellectuals and politicians of the German right considered both to be plots devised by Germany's enemies to weaken the nation and compromise its sovereignty. The conservative politician and former vice chancellor Clemens von Delbrück, for example, proclaimed that both democracy and international law were "fictions" and that authority stemmed solely from the German state. Other conservative leaders called the republic and Article 4 "a noose around the neck" of Germany. The most comprehensive critique was articulated by Carl Schmitt, Germany's leading right-wing legal scholar, who claimed that the republic and the League were the product of destructive liberal delusions. According to Schmitt, both sought to replace political conflict with legal mechanisms. They hoped to weaken the German state through the division of power at home and international law abroad. German democrats and the founders of the League refused to recognize that conflict and violence were part of human nature and could not be regulated by law. In Schmitt's eyes, these reformers were intent not on bringing global peace but on repressing German nationalism and sabotaging Germany's legitimate quest to become a world power. As he famously scoffed, "whoever invokes humanity, seeks to cheat." Throughout the 1920s, then, the relationship between the German Republic and the new international order inspired intense intellectual and political debate. Should Germany embrace international law or seek to dismantle it?[7]

These were the debates that shaped Hans Morgenthau's early thought. Born in 1904 into a Jewish family from Bavaria, Morgenthau began studying international law in Munich. In 1928 he completed a PhD on the League of Nations under the supervision of Karl Neumeyer, a renowned scholar of international law.[8] He later moved to Frankfurt to practice law under the guidance of the Socialist intellectual Hugo Sinzheimer and published several books and essays on international politics. As a supporter of Weimar democracy, Morgenthau sought to craft a new theory of interna-

---

Schorkopf, *Grundgesetz und Überstaatlichkeit: Konflikt und Harmonie in den auswärtigen Beziehungen Deutschlands* (Tübingen: Mohr Siebeck, 2007).

[7] The quotations are from Caldwell, "Sovereignty, Constitutionalism, and the Myth of the State," 348. Schmitt's statement, which he took from French anarchist Pierre-Joesph Proudhon, is from *The Concept of the Political* (Chicago: University of Chicago Press, 1996), 54. Schmitt's most important Weimar-era work on the topic of international politics and law is his *Die Kernfrage des Völkerbundes* (Berlin: Dümmlers, 1926).

[8] Hans J. Morgenthau, "Die internationale Rechtspflege, das Wesen ihrer Organe und die Grenzen ihrer Anwendung: insbesondere der Begriff des politischen im Völkerrecht" (1928), Folder 7, Box 115, Hans Morgenthau Papers, Library of Congress [hereafter referred to as MP, LoC]. Even though both Loewenstein and Morgenthau studied with Neumeyer and worked in Munich at the same time, it is unclear whether they ever met each other. The existing correspondence between them dates to their time in American exile in the late 1930s.

tional politics that would strengthen the republic. In a series of essays and lectures, he argued that Germany required a new vision for its diplomacy, one that would fuse the liberal search for international peace and justice with the nationalists' belief that conflicts were an unavoidable and inevitable part of international politics. This new theory would provide a blueprint for what Morgenthau called "dynamic" diplomacy in the new, post–World War I era. Weimar could lead the way in creating a new international system, in which international law and the national quest for power could coexist side by side.[9]

According to Morgenthau, the League of Nations, and the international system it created, presented a surprising conundrum. On the one hand, the strongest and most influential nations in the world, the United States, Great Britain, and France, had gone to great lengths to establish international institutions and complex legal mechanisms to resolve international conflicts. But despite their enormous power and unparalleled dominance, the League of Nations and the Permanent Court had miserably failed to reduce international tensions. They had been powerless, for example, to resolve violent clashes among the nations of the Balkans. They had likewise been unable to defuse tensions between Germany and France over the territories of Alsace-Lorraine, which, despite France's military victory in the war, both countries continued to claim. Despite the intense efforts that the great powers had invested in the League's creation, and even though dozens of countries participated in its institutions, it had turned out to be an incompetent organization that was unable to promote international peace and justice.[10]

Morgenthau argued that the League of Nations had failed to bring about peace and harmony because its founders misunderstood the nature of conflict. Reforming the international order depended on a fresh understanding of the essence of politics. To craft this new perspective, Morgenthau relied on Carl Schmitt's widely read essay, "The Concept of the Political." Schmitt argued that politics—or, as he wrote, "the political" (*das Politische*)—constituted a distinct and independent sphere of activity, different from other spheres of human life. While morality was based on the distinction between moral and immoral, and aesthetics was defined by the distinction between beauty and ugliness, politics was shaped by the distinction between friend and foe. To Schmitt, this definition proved that there could be no lasting peaceful relationships between nations. When coming together as a group, by definition, humans marked other groups as enemies. Conflict was thus inherent to human life, and the goal of politics was to prepare for it. The

[9] This biographical information is based on Christoph Frei, *Hans J. Morgenthau* (Baton Rouge: Louisiana State University, 2001).

[10] Hans J. Morgenthau, *Die internationale Rechtspflege, ihr Wesen und ihre Grenzen* (Leipzig: Universitätsverlag von Robert Noske, 1929), 56–57.

ultimate objective of the state was to mobilize the nation for victory in potential conflicts with other nations. Any institution that sought to eliminate or even regulate political tensions, such as the League of Nations, was fighting human nature, and it was therefore bound to fail.[11]

Morgenthau responded to Schmitt's argument by proposing his own definition of politics. He argued that Schmitt's definition falsely assumed that politics was a distinct sphere, separate from religion, art, or morality. In reality, however, *any* aspect of human life could become a source of tension and potential violence between collectives. Based on the subjective emotional values that people invested in them, morality, aesthetics, or the economy could thus all become political. "The concept of the political," Morgenthau maintained, "has no substance of its own ... it is rather a characteristic, quality, or coloration (*Färbung*) that any substance can acquire.... A question that today has a political character could tomorrow lose its political meaning, while an issue of minor importance could overnight become a political matter of the first degree." What defined political issues as such was therefore "the degree of intensity" to which they initiated conflict. Though any field of human activity *could* become political, it was only by becoming the focus of intense collective antagonism that conflicts acquired a political quality. Morgenthau admitted that it was difficult to define the precise point at which an issue crossed this line. But by defining the political as the most extreme form of conflict, one could better understand the difficulties that the League of Nations faced.[12]

Based on this definition of politics, Morgenthau distinguished between two kinds of international conflict. On the one hand were "disputes" (*Streitigkeiten*), which states could resolve through international legal institutions such as the League of Nations and the World Court. These were conflicts that nations did not consider to be existential matters, such as disagreements over trade policies. On the other hand were "tensions" (*Spannungen*), which unlike disputes were of an essentially political nature: these were conflicts that nations invested with extreme emotional intensity. They could not be resolved through legal mechanisms of the kind that the League

[11] Carl Schmitt, "Der Begriff des Politischen," *Archiv für Sozialwissenschaft und Sozialpolitik* 58 (1927): 1–33.

[12] Morgenthau, *Die internationale Rechtspflege*, 33, 68–69, 70. Schmitt and Morgenthau corresponded with each other and also met once. Some scholars in fact claim that Morgenthau's theory of politics led Schmitt to revise his own when he republished his essay in 1932. This interaction led several scholars to wrongfully characterize Morgenthau as a conservative or even Schmittian thinker. See, for example, Chris Brown, "'The Twilight of International Morality'? Hans J. Morgenthau and Carl Schmitt on the End of the *Jus Publicum Europeum*," in Michael C. Williams (ed.), *Realism Reconsidered: Hans J. Morgenthau in International Relations* (New York: Oxford University Press, 2007), 42–61; Jan Willem Honig, "Totalitarianism and Realism: Hans Morgenthau's German Years," in Benjamin Frankel (ed.), *Roots of Realism* (London: Frank Cass, 1996), 283–313.

sought to create. For example, even though France, Britain, the United States, and Germany had all signed the Treaty of Versailles in 1919 and were legally bound to it, the Germans continued to oppose it due to their intense anger over what they perceived as its injustice. German demands to revise or ignore parts of the treaty were not a legal dispute that could be decided by an international court. Germans hated the treaty with intensity, making their opposition to it political.

According to Morgenthau, the difference between disputes and tensions explained why both liberals such as Preuss and nationalists such as Schmitt had failed to produce a comprehensive and realistic theory of international law and politics. Each side believed that *all* international conflicts were either disputes or tensions. Therefore, they either viewed international law as panacea for solving all struggles, as Preuss did, or argued that international politics was an anarchic struggle that could never be regulated, as did Schmitt. Morgenthau maintained that both were wrong. In his writings, he sought to demonstrate the limitations of both visions of international politics.

Morgenthau directed his initial critique at liberals such as Preuss. In this telling, it was naïve to believe that political tensions could be settled by international law as disputes. In fact, attempts to transform political questions into legal ones were dangerous and could exacerbate violence rather than reduce it. Liberals expected legal institutions to adjudicate conflicts that they did not have the tools to resolve. "The legal and political," Morgenthau sneered, "are not at all an adequate pair of concepts.... The conceptual counterpart of the concept of the political is the concept of the nonpolitical, not the concept of the legal." There was no court, for example, that could find a legally acceptable solution to the toxic political tension between Germany and France over territories along the Rhine. The losing side in the dispute would always cast doubt on the objectivity of the international legal system and observe its decision as politically biased and unjust. This losing nation—which during the 1920s was Germany—would inevitably interpret its loss as a sign that it had not received a fair trial and would then grow even more angry and frustrated.[13]

Morgenthau therefore conceded that Schmitt was right to claim that the international order established by the League and its supporters was based on illusions. Thinkers such as Preuss failed to understand that settlements concluded through legal means did not establish the conditions for peace. International agreements only reflected the *political* will to end fighting. International peace relied "on the goodwill and the intentions of the interested state," and its survival could never be guaranteed through international law or organizations. "To this day," Morgenthau dryly commented,

[13] Morgenthau, *Die internationale Rechtspflege*, 62. See also 84–90.

"no international judicial organ ... has settled a conflict or achieved peace between two nations through its legal decision." The League of Nations could not eradicate politics. It could only resolve those legal disputes that nations did not regard as being particularly important.[14]

Morgenthau also based his argument on the psychology of human nature. He relied on Sigmund Freud's new theory of the human psyche, which was receiving much attention from German readers but had been largely overlooked by German scholars. According to Morgenthau's reading of Freud, as biological creatures, humans were driven by a primordial compulsion toward domination (*Herrschaft*). Since social norms prevented individuals from expressing this compulsion in everyday life, they projected their lust for domination onto the collective, and especially onto the nation. The aggressive nature of human psychology therefore generated a series of unavoidable collisions, within which humans were bound to "continuously struggle." While social institutions could channel these drives by peaceful means, they could never uproot them completely. For example, even if human society succeeded in eliminating one sphere of domination, such as the Soviet quest to abolish economic inequality, an alternative arena of conflict was bound to emerge. No human organization, however sophisticated it may be, could eliminate aggression and power plays altogether.[15]

To Morgenthau, the repercussions for international politics were clear: since individuals channeled their emotions to identify with their nations, they were bound to seek domination and power on the international level. Perhaps some conflicts could be resolved through human institutions, but the threat of violence was inevitable and ever present. According to this view, achieving permanent peace was not simply a matter of overcoming primitive nationalist selfishness, as many liberals argued. Rather, it went against the grain of human nature. Humans were locked in a tragic condition and could hope for nothing better than a fragile *modus vivendi*, one bound to be disrupted by international violence.[16]

Unlike Carl Schmitt, however, Morgenthau did not just single out the German supporters of the League for criticism. He also attacked the nationalists and conservatives who opposed it. In a series of scathing manuscripts

---

[14] Ibid., 97.

[15] Hans J. Morgenthau, Manuscript, "Über die Herkunft des Politischen aus dem Wesen des Menschen" (undated, probably 1930), p. 32, Folder 9, Box 199, MP, LoC. On the reception of Freud's theory in Weimar Germany, see Anthony D. Kauders, "The Mind of a Rationalist: German Reactions to Psychoanalysis in the Weimar Republic and Beyond," *History of Psychology* 8:3 (2005): 255–270. On Freud and Morgenthau, see Robert Schuett, "Freudian Roots of Political Realism: The Importance of Sigmund Freud to Hans J. Morgenthau's Theory of International Politics," *History of the Human Sciences* 20 (2007): 53–78

[16] Morgenthau, "Über die Herkunft des Politischen aus dem Wesen des Menschen"; Morgenthau, *Die internationale Rechtspflege*.

and lectures, Morgenthau asserted that German nationalists refused to recognize that *some* conflicts could become disputes; that they could, that is, be solved by legal means. Instead, they argued that all tensions must necessarily escalate into war, and even glorified combat and conflict. No one better symbolized this perverse sentiment than right-wing author Ernst Jünger, whose war novels and veneration of soldiers' experiences enjoyed enormous popularity among German nationalists. Morgenthau argued that Jünger's reverence of war failed to take into account the collective nature of political tensions. War was not an individual experience; rather, it was shaped by groups that collectively decided when conflict merited political action. Morgenthau mocked Jünger's and the German right's depiction of war as a liberating spiritual experience that fostered national steadfastness. Modern technology, such as the machine gun, artillery, and poisonous gas, had transformed war into a senseless slaughterhouse in which courage was meaningless. By hoping that Germany would one day again take up arms to abolish the League of Nations, nationalists were asking the nation to commit "suicide in good conscience." In Morgenthau's eyes, thinkers such as Jünger demonstrated that the German right had become nihilistic. Rather than seeking peace and security for Germany, it celebrated violence for its own sake.[17]

In subsequent lectures and addresses that remained unpublished, Morgenthau traced the "spiritual decay" of Germany's nationalists to the nineteenth century. Chronicling the history of moral philosophy from Immanuel Kant to Friedrich Nietzsche, he lamented what he described as German philosophy's growing tendency to renounce the concept of universal morality and replace it with an obsessive celebration of German greatness. According to this view, when thinkers such as Jünger and Schmitt rejected international law and urged Germany to leave the League, they did not soberly assess human reality. Their opposition to international law was instead a symptom of their inability to recognize any moral or legal norms. Lacking a moral compass, thinkers like Schmitt had produced "nothing more than aimless attacks on the parliamentary system and self-gratifying nationalist propaganda." In Morgenthau's telling, both domestic and international politics must be guided by moral codes. German nationalists' refusal to acknowledge a universal morality was leading the nation toward a bleak future of eternal chaos. Ultimately, they had nothing to offer beyond nihilism and eternal war.[18]

[17] Quotations are from Hans J. Morgenthau, Manuscript, "Der Selbstmord mit gutem Gewissen: Zur Kritik des Pazifismus und der neuen deutschen Kriegsphilosophie" (1931), Folder 1, Box 6, MP, LoC. Morgenthau further developed his critique of international sanctions in his *Habilitationsschrift* in Geneva, which was published as *La réalité des normes: En particulier des normes du droit international* (Paris: Alcan, 1934).

[18] Quoted in Hans J. Morgenthau, "Der Kampf der deutschen Staatslehre um die Wirklich-

Morgenthau's intellectual project was therefore not, as many scholars have argued, part of the nationalist campaign against the interwar international order. On the contrary, Morgenthau clearly detested thinkers like Jünger and Schmitt, who claimed that national sovereignty overrode all law and thus rejected the attempt to reform the international system. Indeed, Morgenthau attributed Germany's misguided entry into World War I to power politics. Ever since the days of Otto von Bismarck, he maintained, the leaders of Germany had mistakenly believed that aggressive expansion would strengthen the nation, but it ultimately led the country to defeat and humiliation. Power politics of the kind that Schmitt celebrated were therefore not only morally bankrupt. They were also disastrous for Germany and self-defeating.[19]

If both liberals such as Preuss and nationalists such as Schmitt failed to provide comprehensive guidelines for diplomacy, how was the Weimar Republic to relate to the League and to international law? Should German diplomats embrace international law or reject it? In order to answer these questions, Morgenthau turned for inspiration to the work of one of his mentors, a Socialist legal scholar from Frankfurt, Hugo Sinzheimer (who had also mentored Ernst Fraenkel).[20] According to Sinzheimer, the Weimar Republic suffered from a partial democratization. Formally, the republic granted full legal equality and freedom to all its citizens; they were equal under the law and had the same political rights. Socially, however, the republic remained deeply unequal. Because Weimar maintained a capitalist economy, Germany suffered from what Sinzheimer saw as unjust and immoral inequality between the poor working class and the middle classes. According to Sinzheimer, in order to achieve a more egalitarian and democratic society, Germany's legal establishment, and especially its judges, had to consider social inequalities in their rulings. Rather than simply interpret the law, they should be obliged to use the legal system to empower workers and facilitate social equality. For example, in legal disputes between workers and employers, judges had to recognize that workers were economically and socially dependent on their employers and were thus not on an equal footing with them. In Weimar, Sinzheimer's call to preserve the rule of law

---

keit des Staates" (1933), Folder 1, Box 110, MP, LoC. The summary of his critique is based on Hans J. Morgenthau, Manuscript, "Kann in unserer Zeit eine objektive Moralordnung aufgestellt werden? Und wenn ja, worauf kann sie gegründet werden?" (1934), Folder 2, Box 112, MP, LoC; Hans J. Morgenthau, Manuscript, "Die Entstehung der Normentheorie aus dem Zusammenbruch der Ethik" (undated, 1935?), Folder 3, Box 199, MP, LoC; Hans J. Morgenthau, Manuscript, "Die Krise der Metaphysischen Ethik von Kant bis Nietzsche" (1935), Folder 2, Box 112, MP, LoC.

[19] Hans J. Morgenthau, "Genfer Antrittsvorlesung" (1932), Folder 2, Box 110, MP, LoC.
[20] The following relies substantially on Scheuerman, *Morgenthau*, 12–32, as well as his "Realism and the Left: The Case of Hans J. Morgenthau," *Review of International Studies* 34 (2008): 29–51.

while taking nonlegal and social factors into consideration when making judgments was highly original. It sought to enhance social equality through legal measures.[21]

Morgenthau applied this social-democratic legal theory to the international sphere, maintaining that it could both clarify the issues and point to solutions for the post–World War I international order. Like the republic, the League of Nations and international law officially granted equal rights and power to all states. They were all represented at the League and were formally equal before the World Court. However, as Schmitt correctly argued, international law ignored the substantial social, political, and economic inequalities between nations. For example, the League had created a "mandate system" that stipulated numerous legal responsibilities on the part of the British and French empires toward their overseas colonies. But by doing so, it merely provided a legal mask for what in reality was a system of crude exploitation and inequality. Just as the formal equality of the Weimar Republic served to maintain marked social stratification in the country, the League and the World Court had done nothing to temper the harsh and unjust social and economic inequalities between nations. Like the German courts, these international organizations served as tools of the powerful. As Morgenthau put it, "the development of international law stopped" after World War I. It thus "froze" the inequalities between victors and losers by law.[22]

A just and credible international order required a balance between respect for international law and the recognition that some inequalities had to be solved through political means. Echoing Sinzheimer's call for judges to preserve the rule of law but consider social realities in their adjudication, Morgenthau maintained that diplomats should embrace and strengthen international law but at the same time seek political solutions to international tensions. Unlike Sinzheimer and his students, Morgenthau did not regard economic inequalities as the most fundamental source of injustice. Following from his definition of politics, he believed that all spheres of life could become potential sources of tension and inequality between nations. There was therefore no single legal or political mechanism that could achieve a greater degree of international equality. Diplomats had to constantly negotiate with one another and craft diplomatic agreements that diffused political tensions. Morgenthau argued that an international system could never guarantee a just and harmonious peace; due to human nature, the potential for violent conflict remained ever present. But by seeking to

---

[21] This description is based on Hugo Sinzheimer, *Arbeitsrecht und Rechtssoziologie* (Frankfurt: Europäische Verlagsanstalt, 1976). For more on Sinzheimer and the context of his ideas, see chapter II.

[22] Morgenthau, *Die internationale Rechtspflege*, 75.

strengthen international law while recognizing its limits, countries could build a system that would be "relatively just and accepted by all sides." Contrary to the "static" League of Nations, such a system would be "dynamic" and the best humans could hope for.[23]

According to Morgenthau, the creation of a "dynamic" international system depended on capable leadership. Talented diplomats, who sought international peace but at the same time understood that violence was inherent to human nature, could determine whether conflicts were legal disputes or political tensions. In Morgenthau's eyes, German diplomats could lead the way in the creation of such a dynamic system. As those who had suffered from injustice the most under the Treaty of Versailles but had subsequently become members of the League, Germans had a unique sensibility to both the injustice and the liberating potential of the international order.

In particular, Morgenthau celebrated the achievements of Gustav Stresemann, Germany's eminently capable minister of foreign affairs from 1923 to 1929. A German nationalist who had at first opposed both the Weimar Republic and international law, Stresemann ultimately changed his mind. In 1926 he led Germany into the League of Nations, helped end its diplomatic isolation, and resolved territorial disputes between Germany and France. Morgenthau argued that Stresemann had demonstrated precisely the kind of dynamism that international politics required. He used the League both as a tool to further international peace *and* as a venue at which to pursue Germany's political, economic, and social interests. Stresemann demonstrated that with the right leadership, the League could function as an organ of "dynamic" law: namely, as a legal system that would acknowledge and address inequalities and political tensions. Morgenthau remained vague about how Stresemann's diplomacy could serve as a model for more general mechanisms. It was unclear how future diplomats could continue his legacy. In Morgenthau's eyes, however, Stresemann had demonstrated that embracing international law and pursuing national power were not mutually exclusive and could potentially go hand in hand. German diplomats had shown to the entire globe that a "dynamic" international law— one detached from utopian dreams and attuned to the realities of political life—was possible.[24]

Amid Weimar's furious debates about the nature of international politics and the country's place in a new global order, Morgenthau's theory sought to offer a new vision of diplomacy, which fused left and right in the

[23] Ibid., 150.
[24] Hans J. Morgenthau, "Stresemann als Schöpfer der deutschen Völkerrechtspolitik" (1929), 169–176, here 176. In an otherwise attentive reading of Morgenthau's Weimar-era writings, Kosenniemi interprets this text as a sign of Morgenthau's opposition to the League, while the article's argument is actually far more complex and not nearly as one-sided. Koskenniemi, *The Gentle Civilizer of Nations*, 445.

service of the republic and international cooperation. Morgenthau called on Germany to lead reforms of global proportions, which would further the quest for international peace and justice. At the same time, such a system had to accept that certain political tensions could not be diffused by legal mechanisms. In such cases, it was tragically inevitable and even justifiable that nations would occasionally resort to violence. It would be futile to seek a priori definitions that stipulated when legal tensions became political: the leaders of the world would have to decide each case on merit. They should rather adopt dynamic principles and eschew both utopian visions of everlasting harmonious relations based on international law and right-wing imperialist dreams devoid of morality. In Weimar's final years, many regarded Morgenthau as a rising star of international thought. In both Germany and other European countries, leading scholars of international law such as Paul Guggenheim and Hersch Lauterpacht found in his writings a blueprint for international politics that strove for peace but recognized the League of Nations' weaknesses.[25]

When the Nazis came to power in 1933, they swiftly quashed any attempt to balance power politics with international cooperation. Like Schmitt and other nationalists, the Nazis believed that democracy and international cooperation both stemmed from the mistaken belief in the equality of people and therefore had to be crushed. As Hitler proclaimed in a speech, "internationalism and democracy are inseparable conceptions ... [which would] lead to the destruction of a people's values." To the Nazis, global politics were an arena of eternal struggle between races over scarce resources and territory that precluded respect for international law. One of Hitler's actions upon assuming power was therefore withdrawing from the League of Nations, which was followed by the suppression of any voices calling for international cooperation.[26] But for Morgenthau, the search for a dynamic foreign policy did not end. After leaving Germany for Switzerland and continuing on to Spain, in 1937 he arrived in the United States. In 1940, with the support of Carl J. Friedrich, he became a professor at the University of Chicago. From there, he would resume his intellectual project. With the reshaping of the world following World War II and the beginning

---

[25] Those who reviewed Morgenthau's works found them to be a major original contribution to international law. See, for example, Paul Guggenheim, "Review," *Juristische Wochenzeitschrift* 35/36 (1929): 3469; Hersch Lauterpacht, "Review," *British Yearbook of International Law* 30 (1931): 229; Hersch Lauterpacht, "Review," *Zeitschrift für Sozialforschung* 3 (1934): 461. On the reception of Morgenthau's writings, see Oliver Jütersonke, *Morgenthau, Law and Realism* (New York: Cambridge University Press, 2010), 51–64.

[26] Adolf Hitler, "Speech to the Industry Club in Düsseldorf," in Roderick Stackelberg and Sally A. Winkle (eds.), *The Nazi Germany Sourcebook* (London: Routledge, 2002), 103–107, here 104. On the Third Reich and the League, see Mark Mazower, *Hitler's Empire: How the Nazis Ruled Europe* (New York: Penguin, 2008), 31–45.

of the Cold War, his theory would contribute to the articulation of a new diplomatic project of global proportions.[27]

MORGENTHAU AND THE COLD WAR ESTABLISHMENT

Morgenthau's appearance as a major theorist of international politics in the United States coincided with a dramatic shift in U.S. foreign policy. As World War II drew to an end, a wave of support for global reform washed over the United States. Many believed that the American government would take the lead in establishing a new global system that would secure international peace and stability. Underpinning these hopes was President Franklin Roosevelt's 1941 "Atlantic Charter," which advocated global cooperation, international law, and collective disarmament. Countless intellectuals, journalists, and politicians believed that the United States would create a new global organization that would put an end to international conflict. Within just a few years, however, this optimism gave way to a pervasive anxiety. Rather than global cooperation, the world observed the growing Cold War tensions between the United States and the Soviet Union. In their attempt to curb what it perceived to be an imminent Communist threat, the American state and its diplomats abandoned Roosevelt's previous call for disarmament. Instead, they created a massive military apparatus and anti-Communist alliances. Relegating international law to the sidelines, they focused on expanding the power of the state. The visions of global cooperation had now morphed into hostility.

Morgenthau played a central role in this transformation. He quickly emerged as the most important intellectual opposed to global collaboration, believing that the United States should concentrate on containing Soviet power. Morgenthau drew on his Weimar-era theory to lambast global cooperation as a delusional and dangerous project that was bound to fail. In a series of blistering attacks on those who called for global collaboration, he formulated what he called a "realist" theory of international relations, claiming that global cooperation went against the grain of human nature and the essence of politics. With the rise of the Cold War, these ideas were readily adopted by American policymakers and intellectuals. Morgenthau became a close adviser to Cold War diplomats, who often referred to his writings and ideas when formulating policies. But his ascendancy as a Cold War intellectual was not free of tensions and misunderstandings. Echoing the position he had articulated in the days of Weimar, he did not call on the United States to embrace power politics at the expense of morality but to engage in

[27] For a more detailed description of Morgenthau's exile, see Frei, *Hans J. Morgenthau*, 44–73.

a "dynamic" form of diplomacy that balanced ethics and power. Many of his readers, however, did not fully understand or embrace this aspect of Morgenthau's ideas. As the 1950s progressed, Morgenthau became increasingly frustrated with diplomats who espoused his realist theory to justify policies he opposed. While such tension remained largely latent during this period, it presaged his subsequent vocal opposition to Cold War policies. During the 1960s, his theories would play a central role in challenging the same diplomats he had earlier supported.

The devastation brought about by World War II sparked a surge of intellectual, political, and popular calls for global reform in the United States. Across the country, a variety of politicians, intellectuals, and journalists offered competing visions of a new world order while arguing for the creation of novel institutions of global cooperation. Alfred Zimmern, the British intellectual who helped build the League of Nations, asserted that the United States had to build a global commonwealth. Like the British Empire before it, the United States had a unique mission to bring law and justice to the entire world. Wendell Willkie, former Republican presidential candidate and consultant to President Roosevelt, proposed the notion of "collective security." In a book entitled *One World*—which by 1945 had sold two million copies—he contended that "there can be no peace for any part of the world unless the foundations of peace are made secure throughout all parts of the world." Some journalists, intellectuals, and political activists went so far as to maintain that the time had come to impose a world republic. The United States, they claimed, could abolish national sovereignty, eradicate international violence, and usher in an era of global peace.[28] When the victorious nations began to design the United Nations (UN), many believed that a new international era was about to commence. Unlike the failed League of Nations, the UN would inaugurate robust cooperation, strong commitment to international law, and lasting stability.[29]

Morgenthau soon emerged as one of the leading voices that opposed the UN and global cooperation. In a series of widely read books and essays that appeared from 1946 onward, he warned that, like the League before it, the UN was the product of misguided liberal political theory. Thinkers such as

[28] Alfred E. Zimmern, "Athens and America," *Classical Journal* 43:1 (1947): 3–11; Alfred E. Zimmern, *The American Road to World Peace* (New York: Dutton, 1953); Wendell Willkie, *One World* (New York: Simon & Schuster, 1943), 12. On the movement toward the establishment of a world state, see Lawrence S. Wittner, *One World or None* (Stanford: Stanford University Press, 1993), 44–45; and Joseph Preston Baratta, "The International History of the World Federalist Movement," *Peace and Change* 14:4 (1989): 372–403.

[29] On the role of U.S. diplomacy and thought in the establishment of the UN, see Stephen C. Schlesinger, *Act of Creation: The Founding of the United Nations* (Oxford: Westview Press, 2003); Elizabeth Borgwardt, *A New Deal for the World: America's Vision for Human Rights* (Cambridge, MA: Belknap Press of Harvard University Press, 2005). On the role of British imperial and racist thought in the establishment of the UN, see Mazower, *No Enchanted Palace*.

Zimmern, he claimed, sought to repress politics through international law. Like Woodrow Wilson, they sought to resolve political conflicts by treating them as legal disputes. Translating sections of his unpublished Weimar-era manuscripts, Morgenthau asserted that the nature of the human psyche and politics stood in stark contrast to the liberal hope of eliminating conflict. As Freud had shown, Morgenthau wrote, "dark and evil forces . . . as manifestations of the unconscious, determine the fate of man." Human collectives were guided by the urge to dominate, to compete for the world's limited resources and achieve superiority. Every aspect of human life could serve as the source of this quest for power. There was therefore no mechanism that could completely eradicate political tensions. Failing to recognize that "the lust for power . . . is common to all men," internationalists sought to eliminate the force that dominated human action in collective life.[30]

To Morgenthau, the UN, like the League of Nations before it, sought to diffuse political conflicts through legal means. Its founders hoped to circumvent the political issues at the heart of international conflicts. Pointing to the first conflicts that the UN sought to solve, Morgenthau wrote,

> [w]hat was true for the League of Nations has already proved to be true of the United Nations. In its approach to the Greek, Syrian, Indonesian, Iranian, and Spanish situations, the Security Council has remained faithful to the legalistic tradition established by the Council of the League of Nations. These cases have provided opportunities for an exercise in parliamentary procedure, but on no occasion has even an attempt been made at facing the political issues of which these situations are the surface manifestations.

By granting the right of veto to the world's greatest powers, the UN had perhaps gone a step further than the League in acknowledging the existence of real power relations. However, it remained a "legalistic" project that operated in "a social vacuum," heir to the dream of replacing international politics with international law.[31]

Proposing an alternative vision, Morgenthau maintained that the United States must abandon its attempts to build a global order of permanent peace. Instead, he advocated a form of "realist" diplomacy, which would focus on the United States' "national interest." According to Morgenthau, the interests of a nation could vary in kind and could change over time. A country's interests could be economic, military, social, and cultural. What

---

[30] Hans J. Morgenthau, *Scientific Man vs. Power Politics* (Chicago: University of Chicago Press, 1946), 205.

[31] Morgenthau, *Scientific Man*, 117. Oliver Jütersonke, "The Image of Law in *Politics among Nations*," in *Realism Reconsidered*, 93–117. For more on Morgenthau's writing on international law in the immediate aftermath of World War II, see Oliver Jütersonke, "Hans J. Morgenthau on the Limits of Justiciability in International Law," *Journal of the History of International Law* 8:2 (2006): 181–211.

was crucial was that diplomats should direct all their policies and actions at identifying and securing these interests. "The idea of interest," Morgenthau explained, "is indeed of the essence of politics." According to this realist view—as opposed to what Morgenthau disparagingly termed "idealist" illusions—diplomats had to ignore any issue that was peripheral to their country's interests. For example, they must refrain from "humanitarian interventions" in foreign conflicts and stay away from parts of the world that were not crucial to their country's prosperity. Morgenthau did not advocate national unilateralism or isolationism: the best diplomacy identified interests that overlapped with those of other nations and led to cooperation with these nations to secure shared interests. He stressed, however, that diplomats should shy away from global aspirations, such as the promotion of human rights or international law. The ultimate objective of diplomacy was to secure interests, nothing more. As he polemically wrote, the dilemmas of international politics "cannot be answered by lawyers but by the statesman. The choice is not between legality and illegality but between political wisdom and political stupidity."[32]

U.S. diplomats had no business seeking world peace and global disarmament, as Roosevelt had envisioned in the Atlantic Charter. Rather, the United States had one core interest in world politics, namely to maintain a balance of power in Europe and East Asia. In Morgenthau's eyes, World War II had shown that the stability and prosperity of these regions was crucial to the United States' own security. If Europe and East Asia were to fall into the hands of the United States' enemies, these foes could weaken American trade and use these regions as springboards to attack it. According to Morgenthau, the interests of the Soviet Union stood in stark contrast to those of the United States. The Soviet Union's key interest was to dominate Europe and expand its power in Asia in order to strengthen its economy and military power. Morgenthau asserted that the clash between these interests could not be resolved. No international law or global organization could reconcile the incompatibility of the two superpowers' goals. The United States therefore had to decisively curb Soviet power in Europe and Asia. In particular, it had to ensure that the industrial powerhouses of these two continents, Germany and Japan, would not fall into Soviet hands. This was

[32] The first quotation is from Hans J. Morgenthau, "Another 'Great Debate': The National Interest of the United States," *American Political Science Review* 46:3 (1952): 961–988, here 970. The second is from his *Scientific Man*, 120. Morgenthau recognized that his definition of "interests" was vague at best and could not provide guidelines for diplomats who sought to define them. In some of his works he emphasized economic and military interests as the most important, while in others he claimed that cultural interests were just as important. See his "Commitments of a Theory of International Politics" (1959), in *The Decline of Democratic Politics* (Chicago: University of Chicago Press, 1962), 55–61; and "What Is the National Interest of the United States?" *Annals of the American Academy of Political and Social Science* 282 (1952): 1–7.

the only kind of diplomacy that could protect the nation's interests. Only by tying Germany and Japan through alliances to the United States and defending them from the Soviets could American diplomats secure international stability.[33]

In 1948 Morgenthau published the most comprehensive articulation of his theory, which became a foundational text for an entire school of "realism." In a mammoth book entitled *Politics among Nations: The Struggle for Power and Peace*, he claimed to have uncovered the universal rules of international politics. According to Morgenthau, all international relations revolved around states' fight for domination. "The struggle for power," he mused, "is universal in time and space and is an undeniable fact of experience." All countries, whether their leaders admitted it or not, sought to increase their own power. Their diplomatic, economic, and cultural interactions with other nations fueled their quest for domination. Power, like "politics" or "interests," was manifested not only in the military or economic spheres. A country's power was the product of many elements, including the solidarity among its members and its prestige in the eyes of other nations. To Morgenthau, the most important insight of "realism" was that the path to peace and stability did not come through universal cooperation but rather through a balance between powerful states. By strengthening their own countries instead of seeking international peace, diplomats would not exacerbate violence but would in fact help temper it. States that pursued their own power rather than universal justice and peace would avoid involving themselves in unnecessary conflicts. Their wars would be confined to necessary struggles over essential interests, rather than becoming universal crusades to save humanity. By recognizing that their ultimate goal was to secure power, diplomats would resist the delusions of permanent peace. They would not eradicate violence completely, but it would be reduced to a minimum.[34]

To the many scholars, journalists, and diplomats who feared the rising power of the Soviet Union in the immediate postwar years, Morgenthau's ideas provided a powerful theoretical framework for understanding the world. Many were convinced by Morgenthau's explanation of why the United States had to abandon the dream of building a demilitarized global order and instead mobilize its resources against the Soviet Union. His ideas

[33] The most articulate expression of these ideas appeared in Hans J. Morgenthau, *In Defense of the National Interest: A Critical Examination of American Foreign Policy* (New York: Knopf, 1951), quotation from 108. Morgenthau had, however, presented these ideas in articles and lectures a few years earlier. See, for example, "National Interest and Moral Principles in Foreign Policy."

[34] Hans J. Morgenthau, *Politics among Nations: The Struggle for Power and Peace* (New York: Knopf, 1948), 2. On the reception of the book and its status as the foundational text of realism, see the special issue of *International Studies Notes* 24:1 (1999).

elucidated why seeking to block the Soviet Union and expand American power in Europe and East Asia was not a paranoid reaction to imaginary threats, and why this course of action constituted the best and possibly only path to securing international stability. Indeed, Morgenthau's writings proclaimed that American opposition to the Soviet Union was in line with human nature and followed the universal rules of international politics. U.S. suspicion toward the Soviet Union was "realist" and "natural," in contrast to the naïve and "idealist" visions that guided the supporters of the UN. Morgenthau's ideas therefore enjoyed enormous popularity and circulated among countless thinkers, diplomats, and readers. *Politics among Nations* became an immediate blockbuster, and by 1949 it had been adopted as a textbook for classes on international politics at Yale, Princeton, Harvard, Columbia, and ninety other American institutions of higher education. Over the following decade, U.S. universities assigned Morgenthau's theoretical work more than all other texts of international relations combined. It was by far the most influential text in the field of international relations in the early Cold War.[35]

The most important of the diplomats who read and embraced Morgenthau's ideas was George Kennan. After serving at the U.S. embassy in Moscow during World War II, in 1946 Kennan gained enormous attention as the first American diplomat to describe the Soviet Union as an expansionist entity that posed an imminent threat to the United States' security. In the famous "Long Telegram" that he sent from Moscow and later published in *Foreign Affairs*, he recommended that U.S. national security should "contain" the Soviets by psychological, economic, and diplomatic means. In 1947 Kennan returned to Washington, D.C., where Secretary of State George Marshall appointed him director of the Policy Planning Staff, the department's new internal think tank. After reading Morgenthau's texts in late 1946, Kennan believed he had found the most astute theoretician of international relations, whose ideas matched his own. Morgenthau and Kennan shared a bleak view of international politics as an arena of inevitable conflicts as well as a belief in the superiority of dynamic leadership over global institutions. They both believed that the Soviet Union sought control over central Europe and Japan and that the security of the United States depended on preventing Soviet control of these crucial industrial centers. Most important, Kennan believed that Morgenthau's realist theory revealed the universal rules of international politics. It provided practical guidelines for action in a dangerous and unfamiliar international environment.[36]

[35] Frei, *Hans Morgenthau*, 73.

[36] Letter, George F. Kennan to Morgenthau (17 May 1948), Folder 7, Box 33, MP, LoC; Letter and Memorandum, Morgenthau to Kennan (26 June 1949), Folder 7, Box 33, MP, LoC. The literature on Kennan and his conceptualization of the Soviet Union is vast. For especially helpful works, see John Lewis Gaddis, *George F. Kennan, An American Life* (New York: Penguin

Kennan therefore invited Morgenthau to join discussions on U.S. policies regarding Europe and East Asia. Morgenthau's conception of "interest," Kennan believed, would help U.S. diplomats decide where to invest their energies and resources. In a series of long meetings and consultations in 1949, for example, Morgenthau helped Kennan and his staff decide that the newly founded West Germany had to become a member of the Western alliance. Despite its Nazi past, Morgenthau argued, it was a powerful country with strategic value, which the United States should militarize and integrate into the North Atlantic Treaty Organization (NATO).[37] Kennan and his associates were persuaded that these were the clearheaded calculations that should guide American diplomacy, and that moral considerations must remain secondary to international interests. In an emotional letter, Kennan would later write to Morgenthau, "[y]ours is one of the few clear and sober voices speaking on these subjects [of international politics] . . . and the need [for it] is tremendous." In a different letter, he claimed that he had always accepted Morgenthau's advice "with warm approval and great admiration."[38]

Morgenthau's growing reputation and his strong relationship with Kennan launched him into the highest echelons of the emerging Cold War establishment. Morgenthau became a sought-after member in the network of economic, academic, diplomatic, and military elites that joined forces to block the Soviet threat. In June 1949, for example, the State Department invited Morgenthau to join a series of discussions on the then still vague idea of forming a European union that could counter Soviet expansion. Alongside the German émigré, Kennan invited also the theologian Reinhold Niebuhr, who had advised the State Department during World War II; John J. McCloy, the newly appointed U.S. high commissioner to Germany; Walter Bedell Smith, former ambassador to Moscow and incoming director of the CIA; philanthropist Frank Altschul, who later founded Radio Free

Press, 2011); Nicholas Thompson, *The Hawk and the Dove: Paul Nitze, George Kennan, and the History of the Cold War* (New York: Henry Holt, 2009); John Lewis Gaddis, *Strategies of Containment: A Critical Appraisal of American National Security Policy during the Cold War* (New York: Oxford University Press, 2005), esp. 24–86; Wilson D. Miscamble, *George F. Kennan and the Making of American Foreign Policy, 1947–1950* (Princeton: Princeton University Press, 1992).

[37] Policy Meeting Staff 93 meeting (6 June 1949); Policy Meeting Staff 97 meeting (7 June 1949); PPS meeting (8 June 1949); all in Folder Policy Planning Staff Minutes of Meetings 1949, Box 32, RG 59, General Records of the Department of State, Records of the Policy Planning Staff 1947–1953, Minutes of Meetings, National Archives II, College Park [hereafter referred to as NARA].

[38] Letter, Kennan to Morgenthau (21 March 1951); Letter, Kennan to Morgenthau (25 January 1955); both in Folder 3, Box 32, George F. Kennan Papers, Mudd Manuscript Library, Princeton. Morgenthau and Kennan's friendship and intellectual cooperation continued well into the 1950s and 1960s. Kennan's most important book on foreign policy originated in talks he gave in Chicago in 1950 at Morgenthau's invitation: George F. Kennan, *American Diplomacy* (Chicago: University of Chicago Press, 1951).

Europe; and Coca-Cola chairman Robert W. Woodruff. According to one historian, these meetings launched "the State Department's first full-blown effort to hammer out a policy on European unification." Morgenthau was invited to similar meetings at which potential U.S. responses to the rift between Stalin and Yugoslav leader Josip Tito and the Communists' victory in the civil war in China were discussed. In all these meetings, Morgenthau reiterated his call for U.S. diplomats to direct their energies toward containing Soviet and Chinese power. To his mind, only through such "dynamic" alliance building with other nations against the Soviet Union and China, along with continual expansion of its military power, could the United States defend its crucial interests.[39]

The beginning of the Korean War in 1950 and the continuation of the Cold War in Europe merely served to solidify Morgenthau's status as an intellectual pillar of the Cold War. Diplomats and scholars alike sought his advice in planning U.S. foreign policy and circulated his texts. Dean Acheson, for example, who in 1949 replaced George Marshall as secretary of state, often referred to Morgenthau's advice and writing in his own thinking about Europe.[40] The most influential of the diplomatic forums that sought Morgenthau's advice was the Council on Foreign Relations. First as a consultant and then as a member, Morgenthau took part in the council's long series of confidential meetings, at which the highest-ranking military, diplomatic, and academic personnel discussed U.S. nuclear policies and debated how the diplomacy of "containment" could be updated. William Bundy, a senior CIA official, reported on his estimation of Soviet diplomacy. Military strategist Herman Kahn, who gained notoriety by virtue of his claim that the United States should not shy away from a "limited" nuclear war, presented calculations of the potential death toll in such a war. Henry Kissinger—at the time a promising political theorist from Harvard—offered his ideas about stronger transatlantic cooperation to block Soviet expansion. Dean Rusk, Paul Nitze, media mogul Henry Luce, and Admiral William Miller all proposed plans for effective policies to confront Soviet expansion. By the late 1950s, therefore, Morgenthau's realist ideas had en-

[39] Michael J. Hogan, *The Marshall Plan* (New York: Cambridge University Press, 1987), 258. On the policy staff, see Miscamble, *George F. Kennan and the Making of American Foreign Policy*, 283–300. On the Truman administration's turn to national security, see Michel Hogan, *A Cross of Iron: Harry S. Truman and the Origins of the National Security State* (New York: Cambridge University Press, 1998); and Melvyn P. Leffler, *For the Soul of Mankind: The United States, the Soviet Union, and the Cold War* (New York: Hill and Wang, 2007), 37–83.

[40] This point is mentioned in Hans J. Morgenthau, "Germany: The Political Problem," in *Germany and the Future of Europe* (Chicago: University of Chicago Press, 1951), 76–88. The book emerged from a conference that Morgenthau organized at Acheson's request to discuss potential policies in central Europe.

tered the mainstream of the Cold War establishment. His writings helped articulate and justify U.S. efforts to contain Soviet power.[41]

Morgenthau's rising prestige as a Cold War thinker, however, masked growing tension. As the 1950s progressed, he became concerned that the Cold War establishment misunderstood his realist theory. This frustration was not unfounded. Despite their polemical rhetoric and mocking of internationalist "delusions," Morgenthau's writings were more nuanced than many readers had noticed. As he had done during the Weimar era, Morgenthau advised that diplomats should not be guided by power calculations alone. They should rather strive toward "dynamic" leadership, which also incorporated moral and ethical considerations in pursuing the national interest. During the early Cold War, Morgenthau correctly discerned a tendency among many of his readers to ignore this part of his theory. Numerous scholars and diplomats saw in "realism" a theory that asserted that morality had no role to play in international politics. During the early 1950s, Morgenthau's desire to take part in shaping U.S. foreign policy and curtail the power of the Soviet Union and China left him hesitant to speak about this tension. However, with time, his frustration would lead him to articulate a devastating critique of U.S. diplomacy.

In his postwar writings, Morgenthau expanded on his Weimar-era work to reflect on the role of morality in politics. According to him, the "lust for power" and urge toward domination were not the only forces that shaped human life. Equally important, humans were also inherently moral. They were possessed by an urge to limit their own power and to respect the happiness of their fellow humans. Even though they desired power for themselves, they also had a natural aspiration to support and empower others. As he put it, "[m]orality is not just another branch of human activity, coordinate to the substantive branches, such as politics and economics. Quite to the contrary, it is superimposed upon them ... delineating the legitimate sphere of a particular branch of action altogether." In Morgenthau's eyes, the human condition was essentially a tragic one, locked in contradiction. Individuals were both political and moral and therefore sought both to expand their power and to limit it. He believed that it behooved all individuals to accept this tension and to strike a delicate balance between their conflicting urges. "In the combination of political wisdom, moral courage, and moral judgment," he wrote, "man reconciles his political nature with his moral destiny."[42]

---

[41] Bundy's report is in Discussion Meeting Report (27 October 1958); Herman Kahn's report is in Discussion Meeting Report (24 April 1959); Henry Kissinger's report is in Discussion Meeting Report (19 May 1959); all in Folder 1, Box 14, MP, LoC. The information on Morgenthau's participation in the council's work is from Letter, Philip Mosley, Director of Research, to Morgenthau (25 November 1957), Folder 10, Box 13, MP, LoC.

[42] The first quotation is from Hans J. Morgenthau, "The Moral Dilemmas of Political Ac-

While Morgenthau was not a moral philosopher and did not elaborate on his ideas in this field, his view of human nature led him to maintain that no international order could survive on power calculations alone. In his eyes, regimes that sought only power and ignored morality were not well prepared for the harsh realities of international politics, as many realists believed. Such regimes not only transformed human beings into power-hungry "beasts" but also suppressed the fundamental human urge to build a just and ethical world order. Fascist Italy and Nazi Germany, for example, sought to strip diplomacy of moral considerations. These evil regimes therefore worked against the natural impulses of their citizens. In Morgenthau's eyes, this contradiction had weakened the Axis powers from within and led to their own demise. Their collapse was not solely brought about by their opponents' military superiority but was also a symptom of their misguided attempts to suppress human nature. Morgenthau therefore claimed that those who pursued a diplomacy of crude power were ultimately similar to their opponents, the internationalists who believed in global law. Both sought to build a world order that ignored human nature and were preoccupied with only one of its elements: either the lust for power *or* the urge for justice. "[W]hether they swear by Wilson or follow Machiavelli," Morgenthau sneered, "they are always Utopians pursuing either nothing but power or nothing but justice, yet never pausing to search for the rules of the political art."[43]

Morgenthau therefore insisted that diplomats had to balance their political quest for power with moral considerations. Like the Weimar-era German diplomat Gustav Stresemann, they should strive toward "dynamic" diplomacy, to enhance their own country's power *and* at the same time minimize the damage that this would inflict on others. A great leader must "choose among several expedient actions the least evil one."[44] Even in his *Politics among Nations*, which many read as a call for power politics, Morgenthau warned that diplomacy that focused on power alone was dangerous.

> Superior power gives no right, either moral or legal, to do with that power all that it is physically capable of doing. Power is subject to limitations, in the interest of society as a whole and in the interests of its individual members, which are not the result of the mechanics of the struggle for power but are superimposed

---

tion" (1950), in *The Decline of Democratic Politics*, 318–327, 326. The second is from his *Scientific Man*, 203.

[43] Hans J. Morgenthau, "Diplomacy," *Yale Law Review* 55 (1946): 1067–1080, here 1080. Morgenthau expressed similar ideas in countless other essays written during this period. See, for example, his "National Socialist Doctrine of World Organization" (1941), in *The Decline of Democratic Politics*, 241–246; "The Machiavellian Utopia," *Ethics* 55:2 (1945): 145–147; and "The Political Philosophy of Prussianism" (1945), in *The Decline of Democratic Politics*, 220–226.

[44] Morgenthau, *Scientific Man*, 203.

upon that struggle in the form of norms or rules of conduct by the will of the members of society themselves.

Successful and realist diplomacy therefore recognized the harsh facts of power politics but strove toward justice notwithstanding. Diplomats could not be concerned exclusively with the well-being of their own state while ignoring the rest of the world; they had to promote justice abroad. This balance required constant reflection and calculation, and there were no simple guidelines for action when power and morality clashed. But the search for this balance was the only way to avoid disastrous diplomacy.[45]

During the early 1950s, Morgenthau became increasingly concerned that U.S. leaders and diplomats failed to recognize the need for this balance. Like German liberals and nationalists before them, Americans viewed the Cold War either as a moral quest for universal justice or as a Machiavellian competition for crude power. Some, Morgenthau believed, like Truman and later Eisenhower, believed that the United States was the champion of universal justice and should seek to disseminate it to all corners of the earth. Like Wilson before them, they believed that the United States embodied universal justice and that its enemies were evil nations that would not negotiate. Others, Morgenthau argued, cynically viewed the Cold War as a competition between the West and the Communist bloc for resources and prestige. Thinkers such as E. H. Carr, the British scholar who emerged alongside Morgenthau as a leading realist, asserted that diplomats had to ignore morality completely when seeking to expand the West's power. To Morgenthau's mind, both these camps were seeking to override human nature. They emphasized either the lust for power or the impulse for moral behavior, while ignoring the other dimension of human motivation.[46]

In its pursuit of dynamic diplomacy, the United States had to abandon its view of the Cold War as a moral crusade against global communism. According to Morgenthau, American diplomats must recognize that their competition with the Soviet Union was not an ideological battle for the hearts and minds of all humanity, but merely a struggle over interests. The United States had to engage in negotiations with Moscow and seek a peaceful international equilibrium. While the two superpowers indeed had contradictory interests, it might be possible to work out compromises that would prevent the two sides from perpetually observing the other as an existential threat. Moreover, Morgenthau urged American leaders to abandon

---

[45] Morgenthau, *Politics among Nations*, 206.

[46] Hans J. Morgenthau, "The Political Science of E. H. Carr," *World Politics* 1 (1948): 127–134, here 128. See also Morgenthau, "The Twilight of International Morality," *Ethics* 58 (1948): 79–99. On the differences between the two thinkers' ethical views, see Seán Molloy, "Hans J. Morgenthau vs. E. H. Carr: Conflicting Conceptions of Ethics in Realism," in *Political Thought and International Relations*, 83–104.

their view that all Communist movements and regimes were identical. The Communist movements in Asia and Africa, he maintained, pursued different interests from those of the Soviet or Chinese regimes. There was therefore no reason why the United States could not collaborate with Communist movements in Vietnam or in the Congo. If American leaders abandoned their obsession with fighting communism everywhere, the United States could make the world a more peaceful and stable place.[47]

On the other hand, the United States had to persist in the quest to build a just international order by limiting the pursuit of its own power. American diplomats should thus energetically pursue international cooperation and understanding. Despite his harsh critique of its "idealist" flaws, Morgenthau in fact asserted that the UN could be an avenue for such reform. In essays and chapters that scholars often ignored, he called on the United States to reform the UN and to fashion it into a more robust and powerful organ of international cooperation. The UN had a taming effect on the great powers. Since the United States and the Soviet Union had to seek allies and gain support in order to pass resolutions in the General Assembly, they could not act unilaterally according to their own selfish interests. They had to present their policy "in terms transcending the national interest of a particular nation" and were obliged to craft policies that appealed to other countries. Morgenthau therefore called on the United States to empower the UN and enhance international cooperation. For example, it should agree to an increase in the number of permanent members of the Security Council so as to allow more countries to take part in shaping international policies. He firmly believed that such measures would constitute a "dynamic" diplomacy. Just as Stresemann had simultaneously strengthened Germany and the League of Nations in the days of Weimar, U.S. diplomats could do likewise through the UN in the early Cold War.[48]

Unlike Friedrich, Fraenkel, Gurian, and Loewenstein, therefore, Morgenthau's support for the Cold War was not fueled by intense anti-communism. Rather, his ideas about U.S. diplomacy stemmed from his belief that the United States could continue the project begun in Weimar of forming a dynamic world order that would balance power politics with international peace and collaboration. To many in the Cold War establishment, Morgenthau's ideas best expressed the country's priorities in the Cold War. His real-

[47] See for example Hans J. Morgenthau, "American Diplomacy: The Dangers of Righteousness," *New Republic* (22 October 1951): 117–119; "Should We Negotiate Now?" (1958), in *The Impasse Of American Foreign Policy* (Chicago: University of Chicago Press, 1962), 168–180.

[48] The quotation is from Hans J. Morgenthau "What Can the United States Do to Strengthen the United Nations?" (1954), in *The Purpose of American Politics* (New York: Knopf, 1960), 275. The suggestions for reforms of the UN are from *Politics among Nations*, 2nd ed. (New York: Knopf, 1954), 463ff.; as well as from his "The New United Nations and the Revision of the Charter," *Review of Politics* 16 (1954): 3–21.

ist attack on the UN, together with his anti-utopian concept of "the national interest," helped articulate their belief that the United States had no choice but to combat the Soviet Union for its own survival. But at the same time, the Cold War establishment overlooked substantial parts of Morgenthau's thought. Many of his readers saw the Cold War as a global and ideological conflict that could not be limited, and most ignored his call to negotiate with the Soviet Union and reform the UN. Within a few years, and especially in light of the growing American involvement in Vietnam, this tension between embrace and disregard would become unmanageable. Morgenthau, one of the leading intellectuals of the Cold War establishment, would come to symbolize the protest against it.

POWER AND MORALITY: OPPOSITION TO THE INTERVENTION IN VIETNAM

Nothing challenged the American belief in Cold War diplomacy as much as the United States' involvement in Vietnam. Since Vietnam's division in 1954 between a Communist state in the North and an anti-Communist regime in the South, the United States increased its involvement in the country's unstable politics. Throughout the latter half of the 1950s and early 1960s, a plethora of U.S. academics, diplomats, and philanthropists traveled to Southeast Asia, seeking to strengthen the South Vietnamese state in the face of Communist attempts to overthrow it. To their mind, Vietnam served as a prime model for the United States' ability to modernize and democratize "backward" countries around the world. Preventing South Vietnam from falling into Communist hands was a crucial diplomatic priority. Yet this growing involvement also provoked a national protest of unparalleled intensity and magnitude. In the mid-1960s, after long years of gathering momentum, opposition to U.S. involvement in Vietnam culminated in massive demonstrations, riots, and protest. An unlikely coalition of politicians, scholars, and activists came together to oppose the U.S. commitment to Vietnam and its involvement in fighting Vietnamese Communists. Cold War diplomats, elected politicians, and young radical activists joined forces in unleashing an unprecedented wave of hostility toward the U.S. government's diplomacy.[49]

[49] The literature on U.S. intervention in Vietnam is of course enormous. Scholars have debated the different motivations for U.S. interest and involvement there. For an emphasis on anti-communism, see George Herring, *America's Longest War: The United States and Vietnam, 1950–1975* (Boston: McGraw-Hill, 2003); for a focus on economic factors, see Marilyn Young, *The Vietnam Wars* (New York: HarperCollins, 1991); and Andrew Rotter, *The Path to Vietnam* (Ithaca: Cornell University Press, 1989). On the role of religion and racialist thought, see Seth Jacobs, *America's Miracle Man in Vietnam* (Durham: Duke University Press, 2004). For a focus on visions of modernization and development, see Edward Miller, *Misalliance: Ngo Dinh Diem*

Morgenthau stood at the center of this unlikely coalition. His ideas about power and morality helped inspire the two principal but distinct groups that joined the protests. In 1955 he became the first member of the Cold War elite to criticize U.S. involvement in Vietnam in public. The U.S. presence in Southeast Asia, he claimed, was the product of internationalists' delusions. Like the founders of the League of Nations and the UN, those who advocated U.S. involvement ignored reality and the national interests of the United States. Morgenthau's critique helped articulate the fear that many politicians and diplomats came to feel regarding U.S. policy. It presented opposition to Vietnam in terms that were familiar to members of the Cold War establishment. At the same time, Morgenthau also articulated a more radical critique. Evoking his Weimar-era attacks on German nationalists, he maintained that the intervention in Vietnam was also a *moral* catastrophe, a symptom of American democracy's decline into political nihilism. These ideas resonated widely among the radical students who led the protest against Vietnam across U.S. university campuses. In their view, the intervention in Vietnam demonstrated the need for far-reaching reforms that would rebuild American democracy. Morgenthau's attempt to formulate a "dynamic" diplomacy, which considered aspects of power politics as well as morality, thus forged a rare link between the two groups that opposed involvement in Vietnam. Together, they would deeply shake American diplomacy.[50]

Realism and Opposition in the Cold War Establishment

Morgenthau's opposition to U.S. policies in Vietnam began almost immediately after South Vietnam's independence. In 1955, following an international conference in Geneva, the former French colony was divided between a Communist regime in the North and an anti-Communist state in the South. The new leader of South Vietnam, Ngô Đình Diệm, sought to ally his country with the United States, where he had spent a few years in exile. A group of American academics and diplomats saw in Diệm and the new state an opportunity to demonstrate American commitment to democracy,

---

and Nation Building in South Vietnam (Cambridge, MA: Harvard University Press, 2013). Miller also provides an excellent overview of the scholarship on 8–18. On the United States' involvement in Vietnam before 1955, see Kathryn Statler, *Replacing France: The Origins of American Intervention in Vietnam* (Lexington: University Press of Kentucky, 2007).

[50] Two studies have described some of Morgenthau's role in the protest against Vietnam. Both, however, did not connect it to the long evolution of his ideas and describe only parts of his multifaceted influence. See Louis B. Zimmer, *The Vietnam Debate: Hans J. Morgenthau and the Attempt to Halt the Drift into Disaster* (Lanham, MD: Lexington Books, 2011); and Ellen Glaser Rafshoon, "A Realist's Moral Opposition to the War: Hans J. Morgenthau and Vietnam," *Peace & Change* 26 (2001): 55–77.

development, and anti-communism in East Asia. To their mind, Vietnam could become a model for the universality of American values, democratic politics, and science. Wesley Fishel, who studied with Morgenthau in Chicago and who specialized in international politics at Michigan State University, was the leading light of this group. A personal friend of Diệm since 1950, Fishel headed Michigan's "Vietnam Advisory Group," a team of professors who were committed to "modernizing" Vietnam. From 1954 he served as Diệm's personal adviser and the main advocate of U.S. investment in his country. In 1955 Fishel organized an extended trip to South Vietnam for Morgenthau and himself. After touring Saigon and meeting with Diệm, so Fishel hoped, Morgenthau would lend his considerable reputation to the creation of solid American-Vietnamese ties.[51]

The visit, however, had the opposite effect. Morgenthau returned from Saigon a fierce and vocal opponent of any American commitment in Southeast Asia. Over the next decade, Morgenthau expressed his hostility toward this trend with growing urgency. In a series of essays and short books, he sought to exploit his status as a renowned Cold War thinker to end U.S. involvement in Vietnam. This hostility toward U.S. involvement in Vietnam rested on four key claims. First, Morgenthau maintained that the regime that President Diệm had established in South Vietnam under U.S. auspices was tyrannical, and its chances of surviving for longer than a few years were slim. The Vietnamese president was without doubt an impressive and dynamic individual, but his energies were clearly focused on solidifying his own rule, and his regime could contribute nothing to the creation of a democratic order in Asia. "Here is a man," Morgenthau wrote upon his return to the United States,

> who a year ago was hardly more than a name pulled out of a hat by some desperate American officials, and who possesses today an independent basis of power. Here is a man whose genuine moral fervor is beyond question, yet who acts with a craftiness and ruthlessness worthy of an Oriental despot. Here is a man who as a statesman lives by his opposition to Communism, but who is building, down to small details, a replica of the totalitarian regime which he opposes.

According to Morgenthau, Diệm's regime was maintained by an aggressive propaganda machine and brutal repression. "Freedom of the press does not exist . . . [w]hen one tries to engage private persons in political conversation, one meets a furtive glance and silence." Morgenthau warned that under

---

[51] Letter, Wesley Fishel to Morgenthau (7 October 1955), Folder 7, Box 21, MP, LoC. Correspondence and itineraries of the trip are in Folder 1, Box 90, MP, LoC. On Fishel's and Michigan State University's role in shaping U.S. policies in Vietnam, see John Ernst, *Forging a Fateful Alliance* (East Lansing: Michigan State University Press, 1998); and Miller, *Misalliance*, 37–41, 77–78, 148–157.

such conditions Diệm could not claim to represent the Vietnamese call for liberation. Alienating his own people, his regime was bound to collapse soon.[52]

Second, the effort in Vietnam was a distraction from the real objectives of the United States in the region, the most important of which was the containment of Chinese might. Following his realist conviction that states always sought power, Morgenthau argued that China was motivated not by Communist ideology but by its long-standing desire to increase its dominance in Asia. The Chinese hoped not to spread communism but to "expand its influence and power westward and southward." Vietnam had no value in this strategic mission. Unlike Japan or central Europe, it was a small, poor country, lacking valuable resources and geopolitical advantages. Morgenthau claimed that Chinese leaders had shown they were uninterested in Vietnam. Even though they had the military capabilities to invade the country and hand it to the Communist Vietnamese in the North, they had decided not to do so. "It would certainly be absurd to suggest that it was its magnanimity which induced the Communists to make these concessions," Morgenthau wrote. From a geopolitical point of view, Vietnam was clearly too marginal to play a part in the competition over dominance in Asia. The United States should therefore ignore those who, like Fishel, called for growing investment in Vietnam. The country had no strategic, economic, or political value.[53]

The third reason for Morgenthau's opposition to intervention in Vietnam was his claim that U.S. politicians were obsessed with military power and sought to solve every conflict by force. Like his friend Kennan, Morgenthau contended that the Korean War had given rise to "a broad interpretation of the Asian problem in military terms."[54] The strength of Communist forces in Vietnam, however, was the result of widespread political discontent in the country. Morgenthau asserted that no single framework—be it military, legal, or economic—could repress the Vietnamese quest for independence. If the United States wished to bring about stability in Vietnam, it had to abandon its military strategy and provide far more ambitious and multilayered economic, political, and institutional support. Rather than supporting Diệm, it must establish a "decent and stable political regime" in Vietnam. "We have identified ourselves with a regime that suppresses the

[52] Hans J. Morgenthau, "Building New Totalitarianism: Vietnam Chief a Multi-Paradox," *Washington Post* (26 February 1956): 7–9.

[53] The first quotation is from Hans J. Morgenthau, "The Political and Military Strategy of the United States," *Bulletin of the Atomic Scientists* 90 (October 1954): 325. The second is from his "Vietnam—Another Korea?" *Commentary* (May 1962): 372–375, 374. See also his "The 1954 Geneva Conference: An Assessment," in *A Symposium on America's Stake in Vietnam* (New York: American Friends of Vietnam, 1956), 64–70.

[54] Hans J. Morgenthau, "Military Illusions," *New Republic* (19 March 1956): 14–16.

opposition and equates it with communism. In consequence, the popular aspirations for change tend to flow into Communist channels."[55] Only a new regime that remained receptive to its people's political desires could secure stability in the region. And it was only "our willingness and ability to support effectively the national and social aspirations of the peoples of Asia," rather than military might, that could safeguard the U.S. national interest.[56]

Finally, and most crucial, Morgenthau attacked U.S. involvement in Vietnam as a symptom of the nation's dangerous ideological and moral crusade against communism. In his view, instead of recognizing that the powers were engaging in geopolitical competition for influence and the promotion of national interests, U.S. leaders observed every challenge as the manifestation of a global Communist conspiracy. They therefore failed to recognize that Ho Chi Minh and the Communist forces he led were not servants of Chinese or Soviet expansionism; first and foremost, rather, they constituted a national liberation movement with which the United States could potentially cooperate. Bolshevik theory was marginal to Ho Chi Minh's goals of national liberation. Nowhere in Vietnam was "the conflict between Communism and democracy relevant or even intelligible." The triumph of Communist ideology in Vietnam was in fact a "victory of anticolonialism for which Communism supplied effective leadership and organization." By seeking to repress Vietnamese liberation forces, the United States was not containing communism but acting like an imperialist power. U.S. leaders treated every conflict as part of the global struggle to eradicate evil. They thus failed to understand that some conflicts had complex origins and a history that had nothing to do with global communism.[57]

Both Presidents John F. Kennedy, in the early 1960s, and later Lyndon Johnson escalated the United States' involvement in Vietnam, steadily increasing military and economic assistance. Morgenthau's opposition, in response, became ever more vocal and urgent. He became convinced that the entire diplomatic elite of the United States was possessed by an idealistic blindness that was leading the country to war. There was no doubt, he wrote in 1964, that "our national interest, as presently defined, requires the containment of Russian and Chinese power." Western Europe and Japan re-

---

[55] Hans J. Morgenthau, "Asia: The American Algeria," *Commentary* (July 1961): 43–45. The same argument appeared earlier in Hans J. Morgenthau, "The Revolution We Are Living Through" (1955), in *The Impasse of American Foreign Policy*, 247–250.

[56] Hans J. Morgenthau, "The Unfinished Business of American Foreign Policy" (1953), in *The Impasse of American Foreign Policy*, 8–15.

[57] The first quotation is from Hans J. Morgenthau, "The Immaturity of Our Asian Policy: Ideological Windmills," *New Republic* (12 March 1956): 20–22, 22. The second is from his "The Dangers of Doing Too Much," *New Republic* (16 April 1956): 14–16, 15.

mained important industrial centers that the United States had to protect from other strong nations. However,

> [a] Communist government may or may not be subservient to the Soviet Union or China—and so may a non-Communist government. It is ideologically consistent, but politically and militarily foolish, to oppose a Communist government for no other reason than that it is Communist. . . . Rumania, though Communist, is less dangerous to our interests than is the United Arab Republic, even though it is ideologically opposed to Communism.

By seeking to eliminate communism everywhere, U.S. diplomats had transformed diplomacy into a moral mission and lost touch with the realities of politics. U.S. policies in Vietnam not only ignored the laws of national interest but flew in their face, and were thus leading to "a national catastrophe," an "American Algeria."[58]

To counter this perceived blindness in Vietnam, Morgenthau offered an alternative along the lines of "dynamic" diplomacy. The United States should, he maintained, initiate and lead broad regional negotiations, which would include China, South Vietnam, North Vietnam, and the Communist underground operating in the South, the National Liberation Front (NLF). These negotiations should seek the country's peaceful unification, and the United States should offer generous political and economic support. Morgenthau had no doubt that the failure of the South Vietnamese regime and the popularity of the NLF would eventually lead to Communist control over Vietnam. Yet with the right sort of engagement, this could become "a Titoist state," an independent entity that would help stabilize the region. Only by turning toward such diplomacy could the United States achieve its goals in the region. If it continued to pour its resources into South Vietnam, it would face a colossal quagmire.[59]

Throughout the first half of the 1960s, Morgenthau's remained a lone voice within the Cold War establishment. As long as Vietnam remained on the periphery of public attention, the small number of diplomats and politicians who sought to limit or end U.S. intervention expressed their views only in private circles, in secret memos to the White House, and in confidential conversations. Under Secretary of State George Ball, for example, while deeply worried about U.S. intervention, limited his critique to closed-door discussions. The same was true of George Kennan and Senator Mike Mansfield, who both opposed the war but voiced their concerns only in private communications and conversations. But as discontent began to stir

---

[58] The first quotation is from Hans J. Morgenthau, "The Realities of Containment," *New Leader* (8 June 1964): 3–6, 4. The second is from his "Asia: The American Algeria," 44–45.

[59] Hans J. Morgenthau, "The Case against Further Involvement," *Washington Post* (15 March 1964): 88; Hans J. Morgenthau, "War with China?" *New Republic* (3 April 1965): 12–14.

from 1964 onward, those who advocated an alternative diplomacy began to focus attention on Morgenthau. They believed that opposition on the part of a Cold War realist to anti-Communist diplomacy would carry a special weight in shaping the United States' diplomatic priorities.[60]

In the summer of 1964, the first national petition on Vietnam, signed by five thousand professors and journalists, adopted Morgenthau's call to engage with the Ho Chi Minh regime and support the country's unification under American guidance. In a widely covered press conference, Morgenthau served as the group's spokesperson and declared, "if Ho Chi Minh were willing to become the Tito of Southeast Asia," and Vietnam were "to remain Communist but not Chinese," then the United States should welcome his victory and support him.[61] A few months later, Democratic senator Frank Church, a member of the Senate Foreign Relations Committee, began to doubt U.S. policy in Vietnam and sought an authoritative analysis of its sources and alternative solutions. Church consulted Senator Wayne Morse, who had known Morgenthau since 1955 and was among the few early opponents of involvement in Vietnam. Morse recommended Morgenthau's work to Church, who was suitably impressed and subsequently invited Morgenthau to present his ideas to his fellow senators. In early 1965 Morgenthau held a long discussion with a group that included Senators William Fulbright, chairman of the Senate Foreign Affairs Committee, and Jacob Javits. It also included reporters David Broder, Charles Roberts, Max Frankel, and Richard Strout as well as President Johnson's personal adviser and lawyer, Harry McPherson. As McPherson reported to President Johnson, the group was impressed by Morgenthau's forceful assertion that the United States had to withdraw from Vietnam. The senators, McPherson reported, saw much potential in this "Titoist" solution.[62]

The encounter with Morgenthau helped Church articulate and crystallize his growing opposition. In a confidential letter to the president, he complained that the war was the consequence of a misguided and "intensely ideological view of the cold war." "We have come," he wrote, "to treat 'communism,' regardless of what form it may take in any given country, as the enemy ... [and] seek to immunize this world against further Communist infection through massive injection of American aid." It was time, he concluded, to replace this view with a more pragmatic diplomacy of engagement.[63] Fulbright, too, read Morgenthau's books and essays and became

[60] Logevall, *Choosing War* (Berkeley: University of California Press, 1999), 134–153.

[61] "Professor Morgenthau Signs Petition in New York," *New York Times* (11 July 1964): 11. On the petition's coverage in the media, see Logevall, *Choosing War*, 167.

[62] Letter, Church to Morgenthau (28 December 1964); Letter, Morgenthau to Church (31 December 1964); Letter, Church to Morgenthau (15 January 1965); Letter, Morgenthau to Church (31 January, 1965); all in Folder 7, Box 12, MP, LoC.

[63] David F. Schmitz, "Congress Must Draw the Line: Senator Frank Church and Opposition

5.1. Hans Morgenthau giving a lecture on U.S. foreign relations, early 1960s. Despite his complaint that his ideas were only partially understood, Morgenthau's theory of "realism" had tremendous influence in shaping U.S. efforts to combat Communist states in the early Cold War. Associated Press.

convinced that Vietnam presented a potential disaster. After consulting Morgenthau, he declared his support for a "Titoist" solution to Vietnam.[64] Later, in 1965, Fulbright initiated the first public hearings on the war, ignoring Johnson's angry protest. He wrote that, according to his estimation, "a clear majority of the Committee agrees ... [with] Morgenthau." The hearings, which were broadcast on national television, became a central stage for U.S. diplomats and politicians who opposed their administration's policies in Vietnam. George Kennan, for example, who had gone public with his opposition, explained that he, like Fulbright, agreed with Morgenthau. Morgenthau's ideas thus provided a powerful framework for those who opposed the war in Vietnam. A growing section among the American political

to the Vietnam War and the Imperial Presidency," in Randall B. Woods (ed.), *Vietnam and the American Political Tradition* (New York: Cambridge University Press, 2003), 121–148, 129.

[64] The correspondence between Fulbright and Morgenthau, which began in 1963 and continued until 1965, is in Folder 12, Box 22, MP, LoC. On Fulbright's reading of Morgenthau's work and his support for a "Titoist" solution, see William C. Berman, *William Fulbright and the Vietnam War: The Dissent of a Political Realist* (Kent, OH: Kent State University Press, 1988), 35–36, 42.

elite had come to regard his ideas as the most succinct articulation of their own misgivings.[65]

In the winter of 1965, the White House itself identified Morgenthau as one of the main voices of opposition. Aids to the administration circulated his writings among their colleagues, and National Security Advisor Mc-George Bundy remarked in writing to Johnson that people "like Morgenthau, [and] Fulbright ... do great damage" to the efforts in Vietnam.[66] After hundreds of academics demanded that Bundy confront Morgenthau, on 21 June 1965 the two men met at Georgetown University for a debate broadcast on CBS to millions of viewers. Reiterating Johnson's words, Bundy justified U.S. intervention in Asia. The United States, he claimed, had made "a national pledge" to help South Vietnam defend itself from Communist subversion. To dishonor this pledge would be both morally wrong and would weaken the United States' prestige around the world. "We are also there," Bundy continued, "to strengthen world order. Around the globe from Berlin to Thailand are people whose well-being rests in part on the belief they can count on us if they are attacked. To leave Vietnam to its fate would shake the confidence of all these people in the value of American commitment." Should the United States retreat, the battle would be renewed in one country after another. Morgenthau responded by saying that "it was we who installed the first government in Saigon ... the state of South Vietnam is in a sense our own creation.... So when we say we must keep a promise, we have really made a promise to our own agents." He then went on to restate the main principles of his perception: the United States had no geopolitical interest in Vietnam, nor was the country of value for the containment of Chinese power. The United States had to end its military intervention, which entirely lacked "moral, military, political, and general intellectual grounds."[67]

The televised debate exposed the rift within the Cold War establishment to the public. Johnson was in fact so furious at the damage that he believed Morgenthau's critique had done that he immediately fired Bundy. The White House believed that Morgenthau's stature as a pillar of the Cold War

---

[65] Fulbright is quoted in William Conrad Gibbons (ed.), *The U.S. Government and the Vietnam War: Executive and Legislative Roles and Relationships*, Prepared for the Committee on Foreign Relations, United States Senate, vol. 3 (Washington, D.C.: Congressional Research Service, Library of Congress, 1988), 210. On the hearings, see Julian E. Zelizer, "Congress and the Politics of Troop Withdrawal," *Diplomatic History* 34:3 (2010): 529–541; and Gary Stone, *Elites for Peace: The Senate and the Vietnam War* (Knoxville: University of Tennessee Press, 2007).

[66] Quoted in DeBendetti, *An American Ordeal*, 105. On the circulation of Morgenthau's writings, see Logevall, *Choosing War*, 140.

[67] "Vietnam Dialog," 15397, 15398. Kai Bird, *The Color of Truth: McGeorge Bundy and William Bundy, Brothers in Arms* (New York: Simon & Schuster, 1998), 318–319.

rendered him an especially dangerous critic. His access to prominent politicians, and his ability to articulate opposition in terminology familiar to them, was deeply disturbing to those who sought to maintain or enhance involvement in Vietnam. As one of the intellectuals who had formulated central concepts that justified the struggle against the Soviet Union for two decades, Morgenthau's assertions about the futility of American efforts in Vietnam appeared particularly threatening; indeed, the White House never felt the need to confront any other intellectual. Morgenthau's own frustration with U.S. diplomats had been simmering for years. But now, his ideas gave voice to a growing opposition.[68]

Opposition and Morality: Participatory Democracy and Student Protest

Morgenthau's opposition to the Vietnam War resonated not only among politicians and others who believed in "realism" and tough-minded foreign policy. Equally important, Morgenthau articulated a broad critique which claimed that the intervention in Vietnam threatened the fabric of American democracy. During the Cold War's first decade, the issue of democracy had been peripheral to Morgenthau's writings. While he remained a left-leaning liberal and an active member of several progressive organizations, his writings made only passing comments on the origins of democratic thought and the need for domestic reform. However, in a series of publications from 1958 onward, he began to argue that U.S. failures abroad stemmed directly from the weakening of its democratic norms. Returning to the Weimar roots of his theory, he claimed that democracy and foreign policy were not separate spheres but were in fact closely linked. This critique helped inspire a radical protest movement, which began to emerge on U.S. university campuses in the mid-1960s. Morgenthau's ideas were among those that led angry students to attribute U.S. military action in Vietnam to what they saw as the weakening of American democracy. To this generation, Vietnam was a symptom of moral decline at home. Morgenthau's ideas helped inspire their call for a more robust democracy.[69]

---

[68] Gordon M. Goldstein, *Lessons in Disaster: McGeorge Bundy and the Path to War in Vietnam* (New York: Henry Holt, 2008), 196–198. Johnson changed his mind after a few days, but Bundy later maintained that the debate was a breaking point in their relationship and that his influence on policymaking waned substantially thereafter.

[69] See, for example, Morgenthau, *In Defense of the National Interest*, 80–81. Morgenthau was a member of Americans for Democratic Action, the largest and strongest progressive organization, founded in 1947, which included the leaders of the liberal wing of the Democratic Party, national union leaders, and intellectuals. Among other activities, Morgenthau served as the organization's consultant on foreign affairs. See, for example, Letter, John Hoving to Morgenthau (26 February 1952); Letter, Robert Nathan to Morgenthau (25 March 1958); Letter, David Williams to Morgenthau (2 December 1959); all in Folder 3, Box 5, MP, LoC.

In 1960 Morgenthau published *The Purpose of American Politics*. Largely ignored by later scholars, the book sought to clarify his concept of "national interest" and to elucidate the crucial moral aspects that it encompassed. It was Morgenthau's most explicit call to readers to recognize that "realism" was not equivalent to power politics but was deeply linked to ethical considerations. According to Morgenthau, diplomacy could not rest upon strategic and power calculations alone. To be worthy of the efforts and commitment of its citizens, government policy must also have ethical and spiritual substance.

> In order to be worthy of our lasting sympathy, a nation must pursue its interests for the sake of a transcendent purpose that gives meaning to the day-by-day operations of its foreign policy. The empires of the Huns and Mongols, eminently successful in political and military terms, mean nothing to us, but ancient Greece, Rome, and Israel do. We remember Greece, Rome, and Israel ... because they were not just political organizations whose purpose was limited to their survival and physical growth but civilizations, unique realizations of human potentialities that we have in common with them.

A nation's normative principles, Morgenthau explained, were generated by the collective action of its citizens. Each important civilization drew its strength from a consensus among its citizens around one fundamental principle. The citizens of the Roman Empire, for example, shared a belief in the rule of law. The ancient Hebrews were united in their devotion to monotheism. These spiritual concepts emerged from "a continuum of actions that reveal a common and unique pattern," whereby citizens create and define this interest. "[A]wareness of the national purpose ... followed upon its achievement in action."[70]

According to Morgenthau, the United States had originally encompassed such spiritual content. It had introduced to the world the ambitious experiment of "equality in freedom," which conceived these two principles as linked. Morgenthau argued that the United States was the first nation to implement a pluralist democracy, a system based on the belief that no single group could claim a monopoly over transcendental values. The key ethos of its democracy lay in allowing citizens to respect one another's moral views, to join in public discussion, and to form joint policies based on compromise. All participants in public debate shared certain basic moral principles, such as a fundamental belief in the individual's right to develop and pursue happiness. The United States had thus created a political system based on a unique moral balance, in which all actors "remain within this relativistic ethos of democracy [in which no actor possesses monopoly over truth],

---

[70] Hans J. Morgenthau, *The Purpose of American Politics* (New York: Knopf, 1960), 8, 10.

while at the same time respecting those absolute, objective principles that are beyond the ken of that relativism."[71]

In this telling, the United States, with all its flaws, had realized the principles of pluralism more fully than any other nation. As such, "it always carried within itself a meaning that transcends the national boundaries of America and addresses itself to all other nations of the world." The power of the United States lay not only in its military and economic might but also— and more importantly—in its search for equality amid freedom. The ideals of participatory democracy and self-government were part of its appeal to people beyond its boundaries. The diplomacy of the United States was therefore not independent of its domestic politics. The strength of its democracy was the motor for its engagement with the world.[72]

Morgenthau warned, however, that this unique experiment was quickly disintegrating. Special interests had taken over the country's institutions of administration and had replaced the direct relationship between the public and its government. "State legislatures," he wrote, "have been controlled by mining companies, public utilities, and railroads, and many individual members of Congress represent specific economic interests." Legislators and administrators

> tend to transform themselves into ambassadors of economic forces, defending and promoting the interests of their mandatories [sic] in dealing with each other on behalf of them. The result is a new feudalism which, like that of the Middle Ages, diminishes the authority of the civil government and threatens it with extinction.... In the end, the constitutionally established government tends to become ... a "solemn mockery," glossing over the loss of political vitality.

With the break between citizens and government, political action was being replaced by apathy. The public sphere was undergoing a transformation from an arena of discussion to a mindless consumerism. Morgenthau warned that the United States was forgetting its intellectual origins and failing to reform its system to adapt to the new social conditions. Special interests were taking over the institutions of democracy and threatened the free exchange of ideas.[73]

---

[71] Hans J. Morgenthau, "The Right to Dissent," inn *Truth and Power: Essays of a Decade* (New York: Praeger, 1970), 40–44, 44. See also Morgenthau, *The Purpose of American Politics*. These ideas echoed Hans Kelsen's claim that democracy stemmed from ethical pluralism; see the beginning of chapter IV.

[72] Morgenthau, *The Purpose of American Politics*, 34.

[73] Hans J. Morgenthau, "The New Despotism and the New Feudalism," in Committee for Economic Development, *Problems of United States Economic Development*, vol. 1 (New York: Committee for Economic Development, 1958), 281–286, quotations from 284. See also Hans J. Morgenthau, "The Decline of the Democratic Process" (1956), in *The Decline of Democratic Politics* (Chicago: University of Chicago Press, 1962), 380–389.

The disintegration of these democratic norms, Morgenthau warned, was not merely reprehensible. Since American power relied on the vitality of democracy, the weakening of democracy also diminished U.S. prestige abroad and harmed its national interest. "The United States," he wrote, "is not judged in view of its domestic situation as other countries are. We are not judged as British are judged with regard to, say, the race problem, or as the French with regard to Algeria. We are judged in a rather peculiar sense, which is a reflection of the particular moral virtue which we have represented to the rest of the world." In order to secure its international position, the United States had to lead by example, to restore people's faith in "equality in freedom." Morgenthau therefore called on the U.S. leadership and public to confront special interests and reclaim the power to shape public policy. The American public had to regain its authority and democratic rights through active participation in state institutions. According to Morgenthau, the United States should invest its energies in correcting the morally shameful treatment of its African American population, its poor, and its undereducated. The U.S. government must invest its energy in empowering its least fortunate citizens by investing in public education, inaugurating public works, and expanding welfare programs. In Morgenthau's eyes, such programs, rather than military might, were paramount to the national interest. By pouring its resources into violent conflict in Vietnam instead of empowering its own citizens, the United States was exacerbating its own domestic weakness and undermining democracy.[74]

Morgenthau therefore saw the growing U.S. intervention in Vietnam not only as a strategic miscalculation. Equating morality with democratic norms, Morgenthau claimed that U.S. intervention was also an anti-democratic morass that generated nihilism. "We have embarked upon a scorched-earth policy by destroying villages and forests," he wrote. "[W]e have killed combatants and non-combatants without discrimination.... We must go on torturing, killing, and burning, and the more deeply we become involved in Vietnam, the more there will be of it."[75] This brutalization was causing the United States to lose "its moral attractiveness" and to seek only expansion and oppression. Indeed, the war not only epitomized the destruction of democratic norms but was also contributing to this process, as U.S. leaders sought to suppress public protest and muzzle all opposition. American citizens had to rise up against the degeneration of their polity. They had to resist the destruction of their country's "intellectual, moral, and political constitution."[76]

[74] Hans J. Morgenthau, "The Present Tragedy of America," *Worldview* (12 September 1969): 4–5; Morgenthau, *A New Foreign Policy for the United States*, 138–139.

[75] Morgenthau, "We Are Deluding Ourselves in Vietnam," 88.

[76] Hans J. Morgenthau, *A New Foreign Policy for the United States* (New York: Published for the Council on Foreign Relations by F. A. Praeger, 1969), 139–140.

The line that Morgenthau drew between foreign policy and domestic politics, between the violence in Vietnam and social injustice at home, was soon echoed in the emerging protests that spread across U.S. college campuses. Among growing numbers of students, military involvement in Vietnam became a symbol of what they saw as anti-democratic and tyrannical leaders who dominated national politics and educational institutions. It was a symptom of a plethora of social, racial, economic, and gendered forms of oppression, which made a mockery of the United States' claim to be a country of democratic quality. In 1965 the introduction of a national draft contributed increasing urgency to such convictions. Students began to embrace Morgenthau's call for protest against foreign policy in Vietnam as the key to radical domestic reforms. Across the United States, students sought various channels through which to engage in what they called "direct action." To their mind, the Vietnam entanglement demonstrated an urgent need to reclaim the country from corrupt elites and to establish a radical and vibrant "participatory democracy."

The first student protest erupted in March 1965 at the University of Michigan in the form of a "teach-in," a joint forum of faculty and students. Screening films, listening to dozens of lectures, and freely discussing "the new American arrogance" through the night, participants in the event sought to inform the public of the horrors of the war and mobilize further protest. While Morgenthau himself did not attend the event, students wrote to thank him for his inspiration and sought his advice with regard to further action. The teach-in protests rapidly spread across academic campuses. A week after the protest at Michigan, students and faculty at the University of California–Berkeley gathered for a series of similar discussions, establishing the Vietnam Day Committee. In April, teach-ins took place at New York University, the University of Chicago, the University of Wisconsin–Madison, Harvard University, and Marist College in New York; in May and June dozens of other institutions joined in, inviting Morgenthau as one of the main speakers. By year's end, the teach-ins had reached Paris and London.[77]

Across the country, hundreds of young students who had heard Morgenthau's speeches at these events, read his articles, and heard him in radio interviews wrote to ask for assistance. "We are deeply depressed by the actions of the State Department," wrote two students from Maine, "and your voice is one of the few sober ones." Others asked, "How can we protest this insan-

[77] On the beginning of protest against Vietnam, see James Miller, *Democracy Is in the Streets: From Port Huron to the Siege of Chicago* (New York: Simon & Schuster, 1987), 229; W. J. Rorabaugh, *Berkeley at War* (New York: Oxford University Press, 1989); Jeremi Suri, *Power and Protest* (Cambridge, MA: Harvard University Press, 2003), 166–172. The information on Morgenthau is from Letter, Irene Murphy to Morgenthau (4 October 1965); Letter, Former Student from Michigan (unsigned) to Morgenthau (11 March 1965); both in Folder 1, Box 95, MP, LoC.

5.2. Hans Morgenthau leading the opposition to U.S. intervention in Vietnam in a public debate in Washington, D.C., May 1965. The debate was broadcast to more than 120 college campuses across the country. Sitting next to Morgenthau is historian and former Kennedy administration adviser Arthur Schlesinger Jr., who supported the intervention. Associated Press.

ity? Please advise." It is only "your great intellectual courage" that has provided a solution to the moral catastrophe in Vietnam, wrote another student from Pennsylvania. Framing opposition to the war as part of a wider struggle for a just society, this growing crowd viewed Morgenthau as a rare voice of reason from within the Cold War establishment. Military veterans, political activists, and journalists turned to him with petitions, requests for access to policymakers, and detailed proposals for the president. As the protest movement expanded beyond the borders of the United States, letters of support and requests for advice began to arrive from students in Australia, Britain, and France. From Chicago, a lengthy manifesto for the transformation of society was entitled "God Bless You Professor Morgenthau!"[78]

When the protests reached the nation's capital, Morgenthau stood at its center. In May 1965 an ad-hoc group called the Inter-University Committee

[78] Donald I. Bender and Daniel Mirsky to Morgenthau (16 March 1965), Folder 1; J. T. Howes to Morgenthau (20 September 1965), Folder 2; Floyd Mulky to Morgenthau (16 March 1965), Folder 1; Letter, George Liberman to Morgenthau (25 March 1966), Folder 1; Letter, S. Dell Scott to Morgenthau (26 May 1965), Folder 4; Major General Julius Klein to Morgenthau (29 November 1965), Folder 2; Letter, George T. Tideman to Morgenthau (18 July 1965), Folder 2; R. M. Cann to Morgenthau (April 1965), Folder 4; Letter, Margaret Smelser to Morgenthau (19 November 1965), Folder 2; all in Box 95, MP, LoC.

for a Public Hearing on Vietnam sponsored the first national teach-in at Sheraton Park. Lasting for more than three hours, it was broadcast to one hundred thousand people at over a hundred colleges and universities. The U.S. government's point of view was presented by Arthur Schlesinger Jr., deputy to National Security Advisor Walt Rostow, and political scientist Zbigniew Brzezinski (who a decade earlier had helped Carl J. Friedrich write anti-Soviet books). Historian William Appleman Williams and political theorist Seymour Melman spoke for the opposition. The organizers invited Morgenthau to deliver the opening address, entitled "Political Folklore in Vietnam." Speaking to the enormous crowd, the German émigré not only repeated his by-then famous critique of U.S. diplomatic miscalculations but also reiterated his warning about the state of U.S. democracy. The government, he claimed, was seeking to silence its opposition by engaging in a campaign of lies and deceit. In this atmosphere, direct student action was the only force keeping alive the promise of U.S. democracy. In their protest and political mobilization, these students were protecting the fundamental morality that defined the nation's historical core.[79]

As the conflict in Vietnam intensified and the protest grew louder and more violent, the opposition adopted many of Morgenthau's arguments. Boston University's Howard Zinn, who surfaced as one of the opposition's central figures, sent drafts of his writings to Morgenthau. He proclaimed that Morgenthau had inspired his own realization that the intervention in Vietnam represented the United States' moral bankruptcy as a society. Noam Chomsky, the renowned linguist from MIT, forcefully argued that Vietnam was a symptom of the destruction of U.S. democracy by special interests. Citing Morgenthau, students radicalized their protest, channeling their anger into violence against state institutions and government installations.[80] Morgenthau himself continued to join marches, deliver speeches and radio broadcasts, contribute to radical publications, and encourage resistance to the war. By the 1970s, intellectuals often referred to him as the single most important thinker in the debate on Vietnam. His ideas, they believed, exposed the structural and domestic origins of the United States' diplomatic catastrophe.[81]

[79] On the national teach-in, see DeBendetti, *An American Ordeal*, 115–116. Hans J. Morgenthau, "Political Folklore in Vietnam," in Louis Menashe and Ronald Radosh (eds.), *Teach-ins USA: Reports, Opinions, Documents* (New York: Praeger, 1967), 158–164.

[80] Howard Zinn, Manuscript, "Vietnam: The Logic of Withdrawal" (1967), Folder 4, Box 190, MP, LoC. These essays were collected in Noam Chomsky, *American Power and the New Mandarins* (New York: Pantheon Books, 1969). On the radicalization of protest, see Jeremy Varon, *Bringing the War Home* (Berkeley: University of California Press, 2004); Todd Gitlin, *The Sixties: Years of Hope, Days of Rage* (New York: Bantam Books, 1987).

[81] On Morgenthau's support for war resistance, see his "Freedom, Freedom House and Vietnam," *New Leader* (2 January 1967), 18. On his participation in rallies in New York, see Nancy L. Zaroulis and Gerald Sullivan, *Who Spoke Up: American Protest against the War in Vietnam*,

The student protest against U.S. intervention in Vietnam drew on many intellectual sources. Searching for channels for their growing discontent, students were inspired by earlier activist traditions, interwar pacifism, and neo-Marxist philosophy, among others. Morgenthau remained uninterested in most of these intellectual traditions. Unlike the students who led the protests, he was deeply suspicious of Marxist ideology. Yet despite these differences, Morgenthau's theory of power and morality, and his insistence on the interdependency of a just foreign policy and radical domestic reform, helped students articulate their anger. He provided the vocabulary necessary to articulate their demand for a more participatory democracy as part of a greater and more equitable national mission. In Morgenthau, protesters found a rare voice from within the Cold War establishment that supported their cause.

Morgenthau's theory thus provided a rare link between the two different groups that gathered in resistance to the war in Vietnam. His ideas inspired and gave voice to the concerns of established politicians of the Cold War elite as well as the anger of young protesters who sought to overthrow the Cold War establishment altogether. Each group found in Morgenthau's ideas the language to articulate its own frustration. Each also utilized his prestige as a pillar of Cold War thought as a powerful tool to promote its own agenda. Paradoxically, the source of Morgenthau's early influence among diplomats became also the source of his hostility to their policies in Southeast Asia. As one of the towering figures of the opposition to Vietnam, he helped facilitate the greatest challenge to Cold War diplomacy in U.S. history.

The rise of "realism" as a driving force in American diplomacy and thinking about international relations was closely tied to the beginning of the Cold War. The growing tension with the Soviet Union provided fertile ground for the tremendous popularity and influence that Morgenthau's provocative writing gained among diplomats and scholars. By portraying the international system as an inherently anarchic one, in which states were locked in existential competition over resources and power, Morgenthau helped present the struggle with the Soviet Union and later China as tragically natural and unavoidable. Instead of investing its energies in futile projects of global collective security and international law, the United States had no choice but to secure its own interests by containing these foreign powers. It had to ensure that the industrial and economic power centers of the world

---

1963–1975 (New York: Holt, Rinehart and Winston, 1985), 44. In a poll taken among academics and journalists, Morgenthau was ranked second in importance for his contribution to the public discourse on Vietnam. See Charles Kadushin, *The American Intellectual Elite* (Boston: Little, Brown, 1974), 187.

remained beyond the control of these Communist states. This was the only way to prevent another world war. For Morgenthau's vast readership in academia and the Cold War establishment, his realist theory laid a crucial intellectual foundation for the United States' new global mission to combat communism. His writings and recommendations explained new fears and actions in terms of the unchanging and eternal truths of international politics.

Morgenthau's realism, however, also became an intellectual motor in challenging Cold War diplomacy. As the United States became drawn into Vietnam, Morgenthau stood out as a key voice articulating growing opposition to the war, both within the political establishment and among the student movement. This critique did not signal an intellectual transformation. Rather, it reflected Morgenthau's increasing concern throughout the 1950s that the United States was adhering to a dangerous and contradictory logic. American diplomacy was locked in an alarmingly moralistic "crusade" against communism, which seriously jeopardized the crucial need to contain Chinese power and precluded the option of dynamic cooperation with local forces in Asia. At the same time, the degradation of American democratic norms was leading the United States to embrace an immoral form of power politics that sanctioned the indiscriminate use of violence and reeked of genocide. While few had noticed the two disparate facets of this critique during the 1950s, as discontent over involvement in Vietnam grew in the 1960s, Morgenthau's dissenting voice began to reach a wide and varied audience. His close ties within the Cold War establishment and his emphasis on power had won him considerable influence among senators and diplomats, while his call for radical domestic reforms and a return to just diplomacy inspired many on college campuses and provided the conceptual arsenal for their protest. Indeed, Morgenthau's theory positioned him as a unique link between the two opposing camps, a rare channel of protest that the White House itself felt compelled to confront.

The roots of both these conflicting roles lay in the ambitious theory of international relations that Morgenthau had developed in the Weimar era. As part of the intense debates about the relationship between democracy, the League of Nations, international law, and power politics, Morgenthau had sought to offer a new blueprint for Germany's diplomacy. In this view, the Weimar Republic had to strike a delicate balance. It had to abandon the liberal hope that the League of Nations and international law would uproot violence and conflict but, at the same time, combat the nationalist quest to dismantle international organizations in the pursuit of national sovereignty and power. The Weimar Republic had to lead the world in constructing a new international system in which dynamic and capable diplomats would balance morality and the quest for power. For Morgenthau, this balance was the core of realism.

Morgenthau's dual position as a member of the Cold War establishment and an active voice of protest against U.S. intervention in Vietnam thus marked both the high point of the German-American symbiosis and the moment of its crisis. His writings reflected the confluence of U.S. diplomacy and German intellectual theories that began during World War II and reached its zenith in the early Cold War. More than the works of Friedrich, Fraenkel, Gurian, and Loewenstein, Morgenthau's theory resonated and gained enormous prestige among American readers. As the United States became ever more deeply involved in Vietnam, however, his ideas just as forcefully inspired those who challenged the Cold War establishment, its members' obsessive fears of global communism, and their conceptions of democracy. Morgenthau's harsh critique of its policy undermined the U.S. government's attempts to rally citizens at home and abroad against the Communist enemy. With this massive protest, the self-mobilization that other German émigrés helped initiate began to unravel. For many, the visions that fueled their work had now lost much of their appeal.

Conclusion

THE 1960s WERE NOT KIND to the German émigrés. In both West Germany and the United States, a new generation of students and activists emerged that did not share their values and ideas. To these young men and women, who were born after the war and had grown up in an era of stability and prosperity, the Cold War order made little sense. Fear of communism and support for strong, "responsible" elites seemed to them like antiquated relics of bygone eras, irrelevant to the challenges of contemporary life. Moreover, this generation's image of the United States was shaped by the disastrous military intervention in Vietnam. Students in West Berlin and Frankfurt, Berkeley and Madison, came to see the United States and its allies—including West Germany—not as benevolent defenders of democracy but as aggressive and oppressive neocolonialists. Portraying Communist regimes as "totalitarian" no longer spurred people into urgent action; instead, these assertions read like a hollow attempt to justify horrifying violence.[1]

The generation of the 1960s thus fostered a new vision of democracy. Unlike the architects of the postwar order, left-wing students challenged, rather than celebrated, the legitimacy of elected institutions and party politics. Parliaments were merely stages for oligarchies, tools for self-perpetuating elites. As German student leader Rudi Dutschke asserted, the postwar order was made of empty, "formal democracies." West Germany and the United States were failing to promote civic equality and evoked nothing but "existential disgust." Dutschke and others propagated a "direct democracy," in which political decisions evolved from mass meetings, demonstrations, and citizen actions. Perhaps most crucial, this new generation did not see the state as a tool for collective improvement. In both West Germany and the United States, students claimed that state institutions inevitably reinforced rigid hierarchies and oppressive norms. A "true" democracy could not be built by state agencies. Rather, it would emerge from "autonomy," from small organizations, student movements, NGOs, and, later, human rights organizations.[2]

---

[1] Jeremi Suri, *Power and Protest* (Cambridge, MA: Harvard University Press, 2003), 164–212; Martin Klimke, *The Other Alliance: Student Protest in West Germany and the United States in the Global Sixties* (Princeton: Princeton University Press, 2010); Quinn Slobodian, *Foreign Front: Third World Politics in Sixties West Germany* (Durham: Duke University Press, 2012).

[2] The Dutschke quotation is from Jan-Werner Müller, *Contesting Democracy* (New Haven: Yale University Press, 2011), 177. On the student movement's conception of democracy, see 171–201.

When the frustration and anger of this new generation exploded in protest in the late 1960s, German émigrés were therefore among its main targets. With the exception of Morgenthau, who joined the opposition movement against Vietnam, student journals and pamphlets frequently attacked and ridiculed the leading thinkers of the older generation. Such criticism was especially ferocious in West Germany, where returning émigrés came to represent Cold War ties with an amoral and depraved United States. Students staged demonstrations against the institutions that symbolized collaboration with American culture, such as the DAAD and America Houses. They hurled Molotov cocktails at Fraenkel's institute for American studies in West Berlin. After the height of their influence in the 1950s, German émigrés found their ideas and institutions under intense attack. Their earlier success had ironically turned them into symbols of a disgraced order.[3]

The passion of this protest in Europe and the United States has eclipsed the intellectual and political legacies of these German émigrés. While this new generation failed in its attempt to create "direct democracy," it did challenge and undermine the intellectual stature of its predecessors. The theories and writings of Friedrich, Fraenkel, Gurian, Loewenstein, and, to a lesser extent, Morgenthau gradually disappeared from academic curricula and from debates on political theory. Many of the programs and institutions they helped establish, such as the Center for American Studies in Berlin or the School for Public Policy at Harvard, continued to exist but lost much of their prestige. Their theories and policies no longer constituted the pillars of the postwar order. It became easy to forget how fresh and powerful their ideas had once seemed.

The harsh critiques aimed at German émigrés were not unfounded. Their obdurate espousal of the superiority of democratic states and the Western alliance appeared hollow in light of military atrocities in Vietnam, support for authoritarian dictatorships, and the persistence of racial, economic, gender, and other inequalities at home. But the generation of the 1960s often mischaracterized the émigrés' goals. The theories that Friedrich, Fraenkel, Gurian, Loewenstein, and Morgenthau first crafted in Weimar, and continued to promote during the Cold War, addressed challenges that were fundamentally foreign to the prosperity of the 1960s. The trauma of World War I and the explosive upheavals of the Weimar era led the future architects of postwar democracy to prioritize stability. Democracy, they believed, would channel Germans' anger and frustration at a humiliating defeat and Weimar's chronic instability into peaceful competition. It would allow citizens to transcend their own religious and political communities and bring them together in new coalitions. Reducing polariza-

---

[3] Jeremy Varon, *Bringing the War Home* (Berkeley: University of California Press, 2004).

tion and violence required a strong and stable state that could overcome political volatility; no university, religious community, or labor union could alone foster political collaboration and consensus. Most important, to the generation that matured in Weimar, elected institutions and party politics were revolutionary endeavors. The republic's hold on the German population was frail, and it continually had to fend off Communist and extreme nationalist challenges. Thus in the émigrés' eyes, democracy's main challenge was to mobilize citizens in support of the republic's institutions. The health of democracy was to be measured by citizens' devotion to constitutions and parliaments, not by their eagerness to challenge social and cultural hierarchies.

For all the revolutionary rigor and the new horizons they opened in Weimar, these visions of democracy were rife with blind spots and oppressive consequences. While they came from different schools of thought and distinct cultural, political, and religious milieus, these émigrés shared an obsession with political consensus and a paranoid fear of Communist subversion. In their intellectual universe, the boundary between legitimate critique and subversion was murky and often ceased to exist. This dualistic worldview, which starkly divided the world between democracy and its mortal enemies, contained the seeds of brutal coercion. It could easily lend legitimacy to the vigilant limitation of liberties, to political coercion, and to brutal violence.

This fusion of bold innovation and oppressive rigidity resurfaced as a crucial force in the formation of the postwar world. On both sides of the Atlantic and across the political spectrum, Weimar political visions both enabled new possibilities and fundamentally limited the political imagination. West German and American politicians, scholars, and philanthropists articulated their own support of the émigrés' ideas by investing enormous resources in resurrecting their former projects. West Germans found in their ideas a coherent and comprehensive democratic language. Returning émigrés provided ready-made models for democratic education, constitutions, and languages. Their focus on peaceful political competition and vigorous state institutions resonated widely following the destruction and dislocation of war. Their hierarchical conception of politics and fixation on stability appealed to an exhausted and population, Protestants and Socialists, Catholics and liberals. Equally important, by tying democratic vibrancy to combative anti-communism, their theories resonated with widespread German animosities. Their dichotomous worldviews helped channel existing anti-Communist sentiments into the service of new political institutions. Therefore, as they rebuilt academic centers in Heidelberg, reached out to labor unions in Berlin, or lectured to Catholics in the Rhineland, they encountered a receptive audience. They provided a crucial intellectual arsenal to many Germans who sought to forge a new political identity based on commitment to democratic institutions and international cooperation. By the end of the 1950s, their ideas became the mainstream of German thought and political culture. Their theories and writings provided strong foundations for the architecture of the West German republic.

Americans, too, found much to draw upon from the German émigrés in the postwar years. Their knowledge of foreign cultures and visions of democracy provided powerful tools in conducting Cold War diplomacy. The émigrés' Weimar-era belief that democracy required constant mobilization and state-sponsored consensus against its mortal enemies merged closely with the sensibilities of the Cold War. They could spearhead the massive coalition of individuals and institutions that came together to defeat global communism. Moreover, and in no small part due to the writings of German émigrés, many in the United States came to regard the struggle with the Communist regimes as a continuation of the titanic battle against Nazism. The insights of those who had observed the demise of the Weimar Republic and the rise of the Third Reich seemed crucial to preventing a recurrence of the German catastrophe under a Communist guise. U.S. diplomats thus not only read their works but also vested considerable political authority in them. They appointed them to lead cultural outreach, conduct educational overhauls, and conduct crucial elements of Cold War diplomacy. In their ideas and actions, German émigrés helped chart the contours of American sensibilities. As in Germany, they both broadened and constrained the American Cold War imagination.

While working under U.S. diplomats, however, German émigrés did not merely promote American power and interests. U.S. institutions and diplomats opened spaces for these Germans to advance their own ideas. When founding area studies in U.S. universities, drafting constitutions in South Korea, or arresting perceived "subversive" agents in Latin America, German émigrés implemented ideas they had brought with them from Weimar. In fact, they believed that the United States was preserving and defending an admirable project that they themselves had begun in the Weimar Republic. To each of them in turn, the United States was the agent of a Calvinist covenant, Socialist collective democracy, Catholic personalism, militant democracy, or dynamic diplomacy. The high hopes that émigrés pinned on the United States were not simply a product of their gratitude toward the country that had rescued them from Nazism. They were not, as one scholar has claimed, the outcome of "pathetic . . . over-identification with America."[4] Rather, the United States fulfilled the promises of Weimar democracy. It was a bastion of democratic visions that were born in other times and other cultures.

[4] Alfons Söllner, "German Conservatism in America: Morgenthau's Political Realism," *Telos* 72 (Summer 1987): 161–172, here 170.

This symbiosis between Germans and Americans, in both its liberating and dark manifestations, rested on a shared belief in the superiority of the European and North American nations. Both Americans and Germans were convinced that democracy as they understood it was universal and could be duplicated across the globe. Despite Germany's horrific crimes during World War II, and France's and Britain's brutal imperial projects, to many in the United States, Europe remained the most "advanced" and "civilized" region in the world. U.S. diplomats and intellectuals therefore did not hesitate to co-opt German émigrés into their institutions of knowledge and power. Ironically, while many of these émigrés found their way to the United States because of racial and political persecution in Germany, it was their ethnic background as Europeans that enabled them to attain positions that were inaccessible to members of other religious, political, or ethnic minorities. Existing—and exclusionary—social structures and cultural beliefs in the United States enabled this specific group of white, male, European émigrés to become integrated into the institutional, intellectual, and political circles that formed the Cold War establishment.

German émigrés, for their part, carried from Weimar a strong faith in the relevance of their ideas beyond Germany's borders, one that undergirded and dovetailed with American confidence in its own capabilities of international transformation. They had no hesitation about exporting their projects to new countries and societies in East Asia, Latin America, the United States, and Europe. Having grown up in a Eurocentric environment, they considered their concepts, theories, and models to be self-evidently relevant in interpreting and organizing not only Germany but diverse societies around the world. They found little reason to reconsider their ideas of social justice, defense of democratic institutions, or power politics as they moved between radically different cultures and societies. As many of the 1960s generation recognized, these paternalistic visions that bonded Americans and German émigrés often had tragic consequences. In Korea and Latin America, German émigrés helped devise policies that inflicted enormous destruction and destroyed the lives of many.

The French philosopher and political theorist Raymond Aron famously remarked that the twentieth century should have been "Germany's century." In his view, had Germans resisted the temptation of Nazism and shunned the Third Reich's racist and imperialist adventures, the combination of Germany's intellectual acumen, formidable economic production, and political power would have made it the most influential country in the world.[5]

---

[5] Quoted in John P. McCormick, "Democracy and Technology in the Intellectual Life of the Ill-Fated 'German Century,'" in *Confronting Mass Democracy and Industrial Technology: Political and Social Theory from Nietzsche to Habermas* (Durham: Duke University Press, 2002), 1–14, here 1.

Yet the ultimate triumph of the United States in the war with Germany, and the subsequent rise of the "American century," did not negate postwar German influence. The diverse avenues through which ideas from Weimar Germany resurfaced inside American Cold War discourses and institutions illustrate the hidden yet lasting effects of German networks, theories, and individuals beyond the borders of Germany. When the United States decisively intervened in other nations' politics, culture, and economies as part of its Cold War policy of containing Communist influence, it empowered former German agents and disseminated their ideas throughout the globe. These concepts and people helped chart both the revolutionary possibilities and harsh limits of postwar politics. As the examples of Friedrich, Fraenkel, Gurian, Loewenstein, and Morgenthau demonstrate, the "American century" was made of domestic and foreign, old and new forces. Under the American umbrella, ideas from Weimar's margins made their way to the center of thought and action in West Germany, the United States, and around the world.

Abbreviations

BAK	Bundesarchiv Koblenz
ED 163, IfZG	Karl Thieme Papers, Institut für Zeitgeschichte
EVP, HIA	Erich Voegelin Papers, Hoover Institution Archives, Stanford University
GS	Ernst Fraenkel, *Gesammelte Schriften*
HStAD	Hauptstaatsarchiv Düsseldorf
HUE	Harvard School of Overseas Administration Collection I, Harvard University Archive
HUGFP	Carl J. Friedrich Papers, Harvard University Archive
KLP	Karl Loewenstein Papers, Archives and Special Collections, Amherst College
LBINY	Leo Baeck Institute, New York City
LoC	Library of Congress, Washington, D.C.
MP	Hans Morgenthau Papers, Library of Congress
MssCol 922, NYPL	Emergency Committee in Aid of Displaced Scholars, Special Collections and Manuscripts, New York Public Library
NARA	National Archives II, College Park, Maryland
NL Fraenkel	Ernst Fraenkel Papers, Bundesarchiv Koblenz
OKFC, LSEA	Otto Kahn-Freund Collection, London School of Economics Archive
RAC, RFA	Rockefeller Foundation Archive at the Rockefeller Archive Center, Tarrytown, New York
UAH	Universitätsarchiv der Ruprecht-Karls-Universität, Heidelberg
UAV	Harvard School of Overseas Administration Collection II, Harvard University Archive
UFU	Universitätsarchiv der Freie Universität, Berlin
WGP	Waldemar Gurian Papers, Library of Congress

Archives

Library of Congress, Washington, D.C.
Hannah Arendt Papers
Waldemar Gurian Papers
Hans Morgenthau Papers

National Archives II, College Park, MD
Records of the Department of State [RG 59]
Records of the Department of Justice [RG 60]
Records of the U.S. Military Occupation of Germany [RG 260]
Records of the U.S. Military Occupation of Korea [RG 554]

Rockefeller Archive Center, Tarrytown, NY
Rockefeller Foundation Archive

Seeley G. Mudd Manuscript Library, Princeton University, Princeton, NJ
George Kennan Papers

Special Collections and Manuscripts, New York Public Library, New York, NY
Emergency Committee in Aid of Displaced Scholars

University of Notre Dame Archives, South Bend, IN
Waldemar Gurian Papers
Jacques Maritain Papers

Index